But Is It Garbage?

But Is It

The University of Georgia Press

Athens and London

Steven L. Hamelman

Garbage?

ON ROCK AND TRASH

© 2004 by the University of Georgia Press

Athens, Georgia 30602

All rights reserved

Set in 10/13.5 Minion by Bookcomp, Inc.

Printed and bound by Thomson-Shore

The paper in this book meets the guidelines for
permanence and durability of the Committee on
Production Guidelines for Book Longevity of the
Council on Library Resources.

Printed in the United States of America

08   07   06   05   04   C   5   4   3   2   1

08   07   06   05   04   P   5   4   3   2   1

Library of Congress Cataloging-in-Publication Data

Hamelman, Steven L., 1952–

But is it garbage? : on rock and trash / Steven L. Hamelman.

p. cm.

Includes bibliographical references (p.) and index.

ISBN 0-8203-2536-8 (alk. paper) — ISBN 0-8203-2587-2
(pbk. : alk. paper)

1. Rock music—Analysis, appreciation.

2. Rock music—History and criticism.   I. Title.

MT146.H36 2004

781.66—dc22

2003019203

British Library Cataloging-in-Publication Data available

CONTENTS

PREFACE   Start Me Up

In 1812, Samuel Taylor Coleridge delivered his eighth lecture in a series on William Shakespeare. This lecture included a passage defining the romantic philosophy of form:

> The form is mechanic when on any given material we impress a predetermined form, not necessarily arising out of the properties of the material—as when to a mass of wet clay we give whatever shape we wish it to retain when hardened—The organic form on the other hand is innate, it shapes as it developes itself from within, and the fullness of its development is one & the same with the perfection of its outward Form. Such is the Life, such the form—Nature, the prime Genial Artist, inexhaustible in diverse powers is equally inexhaustible in forms—each Exterior is the physiognomy of the Being within, its true Image reflected & thrown out from the concave mirror.[1]

In *But Is It Garbage?*, the Coleridge of this quotation has been my inspiration, along with Ralph Waldo Emerson, a poet and essayist who preferred organic to mechanic form. Another inspiration has been an object: the rock 'n' roll record album, a vinyl canvas conforming to certain technological parameters (duration of side, for instance, and dynamic range) but otherwise designed to preserve any number and type of musical impressions. This medium invites visual creativity too. The best LPs boast cover art that scripts an identity in tune with the music within. The sleeve contributes to a synergistic package the consumer relishes aurally, visually, and textually. The LP even smells good.

But Is It Garbage? grew organically out of long years browsing, buying, listening to, looking at, reading the sleeve notes to, and savoring the aroma of rock 'n' roll record albums; then, with less looking and smelling, beginning in 1990, buying and listening to compact discs, which as a rule sound either much better than LPs or much worse, this depending on many factors, primarily whether the CD was mastered from a quality analog source, whether it was recorded digitally in 1985 or thereabouts, or whether it was cut on better, "warmer," machinery circa 1995 to the present. My admiration of CDs notwithstanding, the LP is my formal model because it and its sleeve are comparable to the paper products making up this book, and its "tracks" are reflected in my sections. Granted, the analogy can hold up only so well. A book can't have "sides," of course, and if read aloud it wouldn't be mistaken for a rock 'n' roll album. It can, however, have parts and sections written and arranged to play off each other tonally, thematically, and dynamically, as long as coherence and unity aren't sacrificed in the name of innovation; and it can have forward momentum, as did all the classic record albums of the sixties. While each tune was a pleasure to hear, the next one had you humming *it* and not the one just ended: "Lucy in the Sky with Diamonds" giving way to "Getting Better" giving way to "Fixing a Hole"; "Tombstone Blues" giving way to "It Takes a Lot to Laugh, It Takes a Train to Cry" giving way to "From a Buick 6"; "Purple Haze" giving way to "Manic Depression" giving way to "Hey Joe." Pulled in this way toward the LP's last cut, you found yourself back at the beginning, not a bad place to be. With the same idea in mind, I hope to pull my readers to the end of *But Is It Garbage?* Each section is meant to be a satisfying read unto itself while contributing to the larger argument about rock 'n' roll music and garbage. Whether or not I have achieved this goal the reader will decide.

Two notes on form:

1. *But Is It Garbage?* is divided into three parts—"Trashed," "Wasted," and "Saved"—which are further divided into thirty-four sections varying widely in length. The first three sections of "Trashed" are introductory—they define my terms, spell out the thesis, set tone—and in a conventional format would probably be rounded up under the label "introduction." But because of the book's organic form, an introduction would be wrong altogether. To combine and then call these initial sections an introduction would be like calling the first few months of a baby's life an introduction to real life. Are the first minutes, days, and weeks of a person's life, no matter what its duration, any less part of his existence than the last? No. Is there a moment other than the first breath when the business of living commences? No. Just so, this book must begin somewhere, but it begins in earnest, and this beginning is at one with its middle, end, and every stage in between. Therefore, it has no official introduction.

2. Each section is named after a rock song that the majority of readers will recognize. Choosing obscure titles, easily done, would have benefited no one. The song title echoes an idea, not always the main idea, of its section. A discography of these titles is provided in the appendix.

Two notes on style and usage:

1. I use the third-person masculine pronoun in reference to indefinite antecedents, not because I don't believe in gender equity but because it makes sense for males to use masculine forms and females to use feminine forms. All writers should feel free to switch gender or to employ the "his or her" method if doing so will improve logic, flow, or conscience. On the other

hand, writers shouldn't feel obligated to employ awkward "he or she" or "s/he" constructions in the name of gender equity. They should never, in the name of the same cause, dispense with numerical logic and use the plural "they," "them," or "their" to represent a singular indefinite antecedent.

2. Whether a band takes a singular or a plural verb and/or pronoun depends on the context and sound of the sentence. The hobgoblin of a foolish consistency won't haunt this book. I might write, "Wilco *is* a band," adding that "*their* second album is highly recommended."

ACKNOWLEDGMENTS

At Coastal Carolina University, I am indebted to Bill Edmonds, Allison Faix, Jack Flanders, Charles Gidney, Peter Lecouras, Treelee MacAnn, Paul Peterson, Joan Piroch, Michael Ruse, Jose Sanjines, Bonnie Senser, and Philip Whalen. Department Chair Jill Sessoms supported me professionally and personally from the day I conceived this project, and Dean Lynn Franken funded my participation at conferences where I tested many aspects of my thesis. With a smile and a snap of the fingers, librarian Margaret Fain solved every bibliographic problem I put on her desk. Without the amazing efforts of interlibrary loan specialist Sharon Tully, this book would not have evolved beyond its start as a ten-page conference paper. After hearing that paper, Professor Dan Ennis shook my hand and said one word: "Book!" In the ensuing months, he backed up this command with encouragement and helpful materials.

I thank these off-campus colleagues and friends: Barbara Beauregard, Gary Burns, Brett Cox, Nate Evans, Michael Gilmore, Chiho Kaneka, Tom Kitts, Alexander Lian, Eduardo Mendieta, Allen Michie, Doug Noverr, Heather Steere, Malory Hope Tarses, Larry Ziewacz, and the late Anne Cheney. David Schulz provided tapes, compact discs, titles, and Web addresses that took me deep into the indie underground. Without his guidance, I would have stumbled during the vertiginous descent. Thanks to Bo Bacot, Seth Funderburk, Mike Graham, and manager/owner Jeff Roberts—friends at Sounds Familiar, my local independent music store. I can't begin to gauge the positive impact of their discounts and conversations on the composition of this book.

I thank Derek Krissoff, acquisitions editor at the University of Georgia Press, for exemplifying the kind of transcendent editorial comradeship that most authors merely dream about. He also led me to several bands that enriched my reflections on rock trash. Jon Davies, project editor, was unstinting and exact in his advice, and Courtney Denney, copy editor, scrutinized the manuscript with exemplary precision. From me to these three editors, who were all instantly responsive to my phone calls and E-mails: my admiration and gratitude.

Finally, family. Not once during my adolescence did my mother, Carol, or late father, Robert, cry, "Turn it down!" In fact, they often asked me to turn it up. I thank my brother Jeff for decades of inspiration on many fronts—also for letting me have that rare first Buffalo Springfield LP. My brother Pete gave me food and shelter, time and time again, when I needed to use libraries in Washington, D.C., and my sister, Susan, long ago aroused my interest in morbid rock 'n' roll. My radiant daughters, Phoebe Sue and Hannah Jean, give me plenty of reasons to rock forever.

I dedicate this book to Gillian Frasier Farquhar—mother of my daughter and eternal friend, not to mention purchaser of my first compact-disc player. From such gifts are books like this made. A much greater gift has been her unwavering belief that I possessed the ability and vision to write what had to be written about the music that, like her, saved me.

I thank these music publishers for permission to quote lyrics from these songs:

"Cold Irons Bound," "Highlands," "Love Sick," "Million Miles," "Not Dark Yet." Words and music by Bob Dylan. Copyright © 1997 Special Rider Music. All rights reserved. International copyright secured. Reprinted by permission.

"5 D (Fifth Dimension)." Words and music by Roger McGuinn. Copyright © 1966; renewed 1994 Songs of DreamWorks (BMI) and Sixteen Stars Music (BMI). Worldwide rights for Songs of DreamWorks administered by Cherry River Music Co. International copyright secured. All rights reserved.

"Frontwards." Words and music by Stephen Malkmus. Copyright © 1992 DBA Treble Kicker Publishing. All rights reserved. Used by permission.

"Garbage In, Garbage Out." Words and music by Jim MacLean.

"Place to Be." Words and music by Nick Drake. Copyright © 1972 Warlock Music Ltd. (PRS). All rights controlled and administered by Pubco (BMI). All rights reserved. Used by permission.

"Rock 'n' Roll/Ega." Written by Daniel Johnston. Copyright © 1994 ETERNAL YIP EYE MUSIC (BMI)/Administered by BUG. All rights reserved. Used by permission.

"The Summer of My Wasted Youth." Written by Amy Rigby. Copyright © 1998 Songs of Welk (administered by Yak Yak Music). All rights reserved. Used by permission.

"Texas Never Whispers." Words and music by Stephen Malkmus. Copyright © 1992 DBA Treble Kicker Publishing. All rights reserved. Used by permission.

"Twenty Questions." Written by Amy Rigby. Copyright © 1996 Songs of Welk (administered by Yak Yak Music). All rights reserved. Used by permission.

"Wasted." Words and music by Hope Sandoval and David Roback. Copyright © 1993 SAND DEVIL MUSIC and SALLEY GARDENS. All rights controlled and administered by EMI BLACKWOOD MUSIC INC. All rights reserved. International copyright secured. Used by permission.

I thank the editors, publishers, and/or authors for permission to quote excerpts or reprint material from these texts:

If we talk about art like polite little ladies and gentlemen, one approved baby step at a time, we not only DEMEAN art—by treating it like a bowl of cereal—but waste our allotted breath and time and fluids.

—Richard Meltzer

Part 1 Trashed

1. It's Now or Never

American culture is trash culture.

This is a cliché no one has analyzed at length in relation to one of America's main entertainment-cum-art forms—rock 'n' roll music. Surprisingly, the theme of trash in rock 'n' roll has escaped the attention (more often than not, the drubbing) that academicians have given to other big media: television shows, commercials, mass-market paperbacks, big budget disaster movies, the Internet. Meanwhile, nonacademic writers on rock 'n' roll don't seem to care much about the implications of trash in their music of choice. In this book I try to correct these oversights, in the process blending the academic impulse to theorize, formalize, and annotate, with the nonacademic impulse to indulge in personal reflection, play with form, and avoid jargon. The analysis of rock as trash is needed because it reveals a fundamental yet complex interrelationship between trash, both literal and figurative trash, and rock music and culture. In other words, that the cliché about America's trashiness is supportable, perhaps indisputable, doesn't mean we should accept it at face value if we wish, as I do, to increase our understanding and enjoyment of rock 'n' roll music, which appears to be this trash culture's main form of musical expression.

Like most clichés, the one about America's trashiness is dangerous if we're too intellectually lazy to question its origins and to test its accuracy. After all, it might be wrong. Many clichés are wrong—for instance, the one that says white men and women can't play the blues or the one that says to make the most of a Grateful Dead concert, a fan should get good and stoned and stay that way for the next four hours. Likewise, the "America is trash" cliché misleads us as long as we take it for granted without deciding its truth or falsehood for ourselves. We need to base our harsh opinion of America on facts rather than on our impressions or the impressions of others. And there's never been a better time to examine the cliché vis-à-vis rock 'n' roll music.

Quickly approaching is the period when the first generation of fans for whom rock was from their birth a prevalent cultural force, an inescapable fact of existence, a billion-dollar business—that is, baby boomers, my generation—will have passed away.[1] Federal and state politicians are already worried about how the nation will marshal the financial and medical resources to support this generation during its retirement. Little time, thirty years at most, remains for the people who have been there since the beginning—one beginning, anyway—

and who have had decades to reflect on and to study rock's evolution, to bear witness to the glory of rock music before it became a different music in the hands of their children and their children's children.[2] Just as each succeeding generation dilutes or otherwise alters the values, styles, and art forms of its predecessors, each succeeding history rewrites the original eyewitness accounts that soon turn into reductive textual or visual abstractions that can't do justice to the original. Think of three-credit college courses on the history of rock 'n' roll; think of VH1 specials. These treatments are just that, treatments that never can and never will get it right. As such, my generation has a duty to testify now.

To illustrate the urgency of this point, let me draw an analogy (which at first glance may seem far-fetched) between two historic men, one sacred, one profane, each legendary. The two men are Jesus of Nazareth, a town in Galilee, and James Marshal Hendrix of Seattle, a city in the state of Washington. Few human beings were privileged to see, hear, or touch these two men. The rest of us, like the billions still to be born, will never be able to experience the drama when each man performed feats that made him appear larger than life, even divine, to ordinary people. Because we will never again behold either Jesus Christ or Jimi Hendrix in the flesh, we must decide whether or not to put faith in each man's triumphant feats, faith dependent on the quantity and quality of the verbal and physical evidence of their actions and accomplishments, faith contingent on the time that has elapsed since these two geniuses last drew breath. Time is a key variable both in determining the credibility of their feats and in sustaining the faith that depends on that credibility. The passage of time is as likely to erode faith as it is to enhance legend.

Given his chronological precedence and his incomparable influence on world history and culture, it makes sense to begin with the Savior, beside whom Jimi Hendrix will seem insignificant. In the manner of a charismatic prophet, Jesus Christ attracted a large number of followers for whom the advent of the Messiah had long been predicted. These followers thrived on his parables, sermons, and miracles, on his very presence as he passed through cities and patches of wilderness. The time given Jesus to preach and to attract believers was brief, a few years at most. Perceived by his disciples and confirmed by himself to be the Savior, Jesus didn't have long before he was rounded up by authorities worried by his impact on the rabble. To maintain order these authorities deemed it necessary to crucify the man of God. But execution of the Prince of Peace prompted the faithful to establish a religion based on his teachings. Over succeeding years the Gospels were written, collected, translated, and bound with other books of the New Testament. Wars would be waged in dispersing or defending the second half of the Bible. Christians were persecuted, tortured, and slain; martyrs gladly entered the lion's mouth.

An obvious problem for second- and third-generation Christians who trusted that the authors of the New Testament had chronicled Jesus' life accurately and quoted Jesus verbatim was that they couldn't rely, as had the chosen few of the first generation of his disciples, on direct evidence of the Savior's power. His authenticity couldn't be tested by people who believed in a messiah who had died decades before they were born, thus robbing them of the opportunity to meet him, to have their deformities cured by him, or to hear a parable flow from his lips. Here arises a problem related to the entanglement of faith and text. According to Thomas Jefferson's rationalist reading of Scripture, "the committing to writing [of Jesus'] life & doctrines fell on the most unlettered & ignorant men; who wrote, too, from memory, & not till long after the transactions had passed." Far from being impressed by what was recorded in the Gospels, the Sage of Monticello believed the evangelists laid "a groundwork of vulgar ignorance, of things impossible, of superstitions, fanaticisms and fabrications."[3] The evidence needed to substantiate the Messiah's existence had been corrupted from the start. This fact didn't discourage each new generation of Christians from reading their Bibles, clutching and kissing their crosses, attending services, paying tithes, praying to Jesus, living by the principles set down by him, and essentially worshipping a deity—a man, Jefferson would have said—without the help of sensory proof or direct revelation.

Now let's turn to the rock 'n' roll prophet Jimi Hendrix. In terms of years on earth, twenty-seven, this man (demigod to many music lovers) came and went even faster than did Jesus Christ, although Jimi's three or four years of temporal acclaim did match the Messiah's. Materializing in the midsixties, Hendrix outexploded everyone on an already explosive scene; he shattered conventional ideas about rock guitar-playing on stage and in the studio; he dazzled audiences at Monterey, then everywhere else he flew his freak flag, including at Woodstock; he recorded and approved the release of just four albums (all revolutionary) in less than five years; and he ingested excessive pharmaceutical and alcoholic substances that eventually caused him to die by choking on his own vomit, his musical peak still not reached, on 18 September 1970. Far from possessing the historical or spiritual force of Jesus Christ, Jimi Hendrix nonetheless performed for millions of people in his blip of a career. In the rock 'n' roll cosmos, Hendrix rapidly became a secular god whose blues-based psychedelic visions and compositions pioneered for millions of fans a trek into personal revelation and freedom. His recordings were instantly canonized as rock 'n' roll holy writ, to such an extent that in the seventies Hendrix watchers were upset by a bunch of posthumous albums whose previously unreleased tracks were ruined by over-dubs foisted on them by a misguided producer and studio musicians (who, let's face it, were probably tickled to jam with Jimi Hendrix even though he was dead).

Now let's suppose that one day in 2003 a teenager born after Jimi's death dis-covers his records and is astonished by them. In time this person, who let's also assume has evolved into a rock journalist or scholar, decides to write a biography of this musical genius. Playing with chronology and perhaps strict logic too, let's suppose again that in A.D. 60 a citizen of Jerusalem with a religious bent, but with no personal knowledge of the Son of God whose crucifixion and resurrec-tion continued to generate much whispered gossip, wished to write a chronicle of the man reverenced as the Savior by more and more inhabitants of the region. Both researchers, separated by centuries and yet sharing the same ambition, would have to rely on whatever scraps of evidence relative to their project they could recover and study—eyewitness testimony based on interviews ("I heard Jesus preach the Sermon on the Mount on the outskirts of the Sea of Galilee!" "I heard Jimi perform 'The Star Spangled Banner' at Woodstock!"), scrolls, books, anecdotes, film clips, vignettes, rumors, photographs, record albums. No mat-ter how imaginative, energetic, dedicated, exacting, resourceful, studious, and comprehensive the authors of these two biographies could hope to be, they and their readers would have to face the fact that there would have to be, and always would be, something—indeed, much—missing in the final reckoning.

In terms of rock 'n' roll, this fact of "something—indeed, much—missing" explains why many rock 'n' roll fans care more about the bands they haven't seen than about the ones they have. Not to have seen the Beatles, Elvis Pres-ley, Bob Dylan, Janis Joplin, or Little Richard—or contemporary acts such as Guided by Voices, Sleater-Kinney, Dave Matthews, or Yo La Tengo—in person is to have missed a chance to verify a hunch regarding an artist's power to trans-form by testing it for yourself at a concert. There it can be tested, assuming the artist performs well that night, despite the crush of spectators jostling you for their own peek at the celebrity on stage. I know more about the Beach Boys having seen them in concert in Rochester, New York, in 1972, than by having read fifty articles, reviews, and books about them and by having grown up on their hot-rod and surf-theme albums. By 1972, I didn't even like the Beach Boys (by then they were well out of fashion) and expected little more than to hear the canned strains of a golden-oldies act. But I bought the tickets, did the long drive, found a place to park, waited in line, got inside the arena, and took my hard seat. And then, mirabile dictu, a two-hour epiphany occurred. "Califor-nia Girls" thumped along salaciously—it was no longer a clean paean to blond babes that boys like me could only dream about—and "I Get Around" raced full throttle away from teen innocence. The Beach Boys rocked the bricks, rattled the plumbing, and harmonized like proverbial birds. Following the encore, "Student Demonstration Time," all wailing sirens and blasting band, I walked away blinking and shaking, having taken it right between the eyes, staggered by the rock 'n' roll prowess and vocal splendor of the Beach Boys. Because other bands can do to others what the Beach Boys did to me that night, and because it's only by seeing bands live that fans can get that final "something" about them, many people will go to their graves regretting they didn't attend a given concert because they had been too busy with work or otherwise unwilling to trouble themselves with the nuisance of purchasing tickets, driving, parking, waiting in line, and then mingling in what's often a rambunctious crowd leaning on the limits of license, or because they were unaware that a band they would someday love was playing nearby, or because they were too young at the time, or out of town, and so on and so forth.

Maureen Tucker, drummer for the Velvet Underground, understood the twin sense of regret and deficiency to which I refer. Years after her band broke up, she was interviewed by Philip Milstein, who was curious about the consistency of the Velvet Underground on stage. Tucker told him "[t]here were nights when I would get chills, we were so good. We were good. We were never rotten." Then she asked Milstein what seems to have been a rhetorical question: "You ever hear us live?" To which Milstein replied, "No." In this monosyllable lies a world of regret. Brought up short, Tucker said, "You're kidding. Oh, that's a shame. All this devotion is based on records? That's sad."[4] It's sad because the chance to see the Velvet Underground live would never come again and because Philip Milstein, a fan's fan, would forever lack access to a key insight into the identity of the Velvet Underground, no matter how many bootlegs he owned or how many former members of this seminal band he interviewed or might see in a solo show. For the rest of us, too, the Velvet Underground passed long ago into a legend we'll never be able to measure against anything but their recorded legacy, albeit a marvelous one, and against the experience of seeing other great bands live.[5] The various live recordings, even the recently released *The Quine Tapes* (2001), three seventy-minute compact discs, won't console Milstein for having missed the vu boat.

Not counting the respective acquaintances and intimates of our two representative men, what human beings knew something, anything, unmediated by time or text, about Jesus Christ and Jimi Hendrix? Spectators, of course. For the Savior there were traders, merchants, shepherds, pickpockets, laborers, priests, officials, travelers, beggars, servants, children, soldiers, tax collectors, and peasants in town on the day of Crucifixion. In the weeks, months, and years before the Crucifixion there were back-desert seekers, recent converts, nomads, farmers, and townspeople, all those curious souls who gathered in village squares to hear him preach. On the other hand, Jimi Hendrix drew millions of spectators in the form of ticket holders to his club dates and concerts. The guitarist regaled audiences in places such as Atlanta, St. Louis, Chicago, Boston, London, and the Isle of Wight; centuries earlier, the prophet regaled peasants in present-day Palestine. Now, no matter what my religious leanings may be in regard to Christianity, this much is certain: I'll never "have" the real Jesus, never have a chance to judge or worship him (or Him) firsthand because I never saw him preach and I wasn't there the day he was nailed to the cross. I missed the most historic "concert" of all—think of the voyeurs jostling each other for a view of the main execution that day—and like everyone else alive I must film the scene for myself in the theater of imagination. No testament, exegesis, personal revelation, or Passion scene on a stain-glassed window will supply the lack.

I do, however, "have a piece" of the real Jimi Hendrix (and it should be clear by now that this extended comparison between Godhead for a billion-plus believers and Rock Star is one of kind, not degree). In fact, I have a big piece because I saw him, Mitch Mitchell, and Noel Redding "do their thing" in the full meaning of this sixties catchphrase. The Jimi Hendrix Experience, headliners, were preceded by the Soft Machine, the Chambers Brothers, and Janis Joplin, respectively, at the Singer Bowl in Corona, Queens, New York City, 23 August 1968. My first rock concert. Three dollars and fifty cents (!) to gaze on Mitch Mitchell thrashing the skins of his Gretsch drums, Noel Redding fibrillating the strings of his Fender bass, and Jimi Hendrix flaunting full psychedelic regalia, a radiant semidivine Strat-wielding wizard who, incredibly, reproduced his parts on one of rock 'n' roll's touchstones of virtuosity, *Are You Experienced?* Hendrix's charisma touched thousands of spectators who had come to witness and participate in a rock show that savored of ritual and nearly crossed over into riot. He drew ear-wrenching feedback from an embankment of speakers; he jabbed his Stratocaster into his stage amplifier; he reenacted a moment from a biblical battle, dozens of policemen shoring up the stage like soldiers beset by a phalanx of philistines and infidels. Hendrix biographer David Henderson attended the same show:

A few skirmishes start up near the stage and the momentum spreads back into the crowd. . . . People begin to smell riot. . . . Some move toward the revolving stage area, some recoil in fear. A gang of cops quickly hustles [a] kid out through the musicians' entrance, and as the music continues the crowd settles back into a jagged groove.

Jimi ends his set by charging the amps like a knight, with his guitar as the lance. He skims the fret board against the felt covers of the amps, achieving a frenzied bottleneck effect. Then he squats over his white Stratocaster and swirls it around and around under him while still playing.[6]

Gaping at these events with the eyes of a nice little sheltered middle-class kid from out on Long Island, I believed in Jimi Hendrix. I don't see how any spectator in the Singer Bowl that night could have failed to believe in him. Then, snap, two years later this supernatural musician was dead. Rock 'n' roll music might well lend itself to individual salvation—indeed, I argue later that it does, which is one reason for the religious figuration in this section—but the music's masters aren't literally gods. Jimi Hendrix became a legend, an abstraction, as quickly as did Jesus Christ, and with the making of a legend come corruptions of history in step with whisperings of divinity. But rock stars are human beings through and through. They do stupid things. They take drugs. They chase these drugs with alcohol. They overdo it. They choke on their own vomit. They stop breathing. They turn blue and die.

In Ralph Waldo Emerson's opinion, Jesus Christ was first a man, second a moral and spiritual figure of vast significance. This is what his followers forgot in their haste to deify him, to enshroud him in mystery, and to relegate his teachings to a series of ever more formal and thus, in Emerson's view, lifeless sacraments and rites. In "The Divinity School Address," Emerson declared to an audience of future Unitarian ministers, "[W]hat a distortion did [Christ's] doctrine and memory suffer in the same, in the next, and the following ages!"[7] Emerson goaded the new-minted ministers not to facilitate Jesus worship through hollow ritual but to advance the Savior's ethics in the quest for spiritual rebirth by dispensing with forms for the sake of forms. Mindless ritual causes the True Church to decline. It enervates faith even while the masses congratulate themselves for conforming to a superficial Word: all's well, world without end, amen to each and all. Worship is the easiest thing in the world when worshippers aren't engaged in the struggle to question or analyze rituals that are to sincere prayer what a Muzak cover in a supermarket is to the original version of a pop or rock masterpiece.

In the secular sphere of rock music, this same kind of decline marked by the deadness of formula and formalization has alarmed more than one faithful follower. Notwithstanding a stream of exceptions—yes, plenty of fine new releases can be downloaded or purchased in 2004—rock 'n' roll has been and is being trivialized, dumbed down, and misrepresented by second- and third-generation simplification, corruption, and mangling of it in both prose and performance. This process began at least twenty years ago and, again, many exceptions aside, gets worse each year. It *must* get worse, which is why I insist that one of the last duties facing baby boomers before we depart this vale of media overload and cyber saturation is to write the truth about rock music, write it copiously, write it now, because before we know it, it will be too late to find a person who forty to fifty years ago was blessed with an unmediated vision of Little Richard, Elvis Presley, Buddy Holly, the Beatles, the Rolling Stones, Cream, the Beach Boys, or Jimi Hendrix, not to mention scads of earlier rock 'n' rollers such as Wynonie Harris, Wanda Jackson, Hank Ballard, and the young Big Joe Turner—actual men and women plying their art on an actual stage in an actual club or arena. It will soon be too late, in short, to call on a reliable first-person witness to relate to posterity the real rock 'n' roll events made legendary by the distortions of time.

2. It's Still Rock and Roll to Me

The terms *rock 'n' roll* and *rock* are used interchangeably in this book. Here's why.

Record reviewers, pop music scholars, and serious fans can point out differences between rock 'n' roll and rock, just as they know what defines the subgenres of each term—rockabilly's twang, pop's sheen, hard-core's volume, disco's thump, grunge's distortion, and so on. In *Rhythm and Noise: An Aesthetics of Rock,* Theodore Gracyk dissects the differences between rock 'n' roll and rock, arguing that rock 'n' roll is a *"performance"* style. "If rock and roll is the performing style most closely associated with rock," he writes, "the more inclusive category of rock was not clearly differentiated until around 1965." The second half of this sentence states the conventional view, open to question to be sure, but destined to remain the official, because most sensible, version. Gracyk argues that even though borders between the two genres are fuzzy, rock incorporates more performance styles, thus making it a broader category than rock 'n' roll. "[T]he rock aesthetic," he concludes, "invites stylistic flexibility and innovation that supersedes rock and roll." From this conclusion it follows that *Rubber Soul* (1965) is the first *"rock"* album by the Beatles.[1]

Gracyk's point is convincing. But his choice of *Rubber Soul* to support his thesis calls attention to the fluidity of the labels, including their subgenres (which may not be that "sub" after all), that he and other experts try to define. Apparently this was Gracyk's idea. *Rubber Soul*'s very fluidity proves it's a work of rock, not rock 'n' roll. But is either term satisfactory? Fourteen songs comprise the "rock" album *Rubber Soul,* including "Girl" (a folk rock lament), "What Goes On" (a rockabilly shuffle), "Michelle" (a pop ballad), "In My Life" (another ballad, this one embellished with producer George Martin's Bach-like piano solo), and "Norwegian Wood" (a third ballad, this one in 12/8 time, well known for George Harrison's pioneering use of the sitar, an Indian instrument).

Built around a fifties Elvis lyric, the album's closing number "Run for Your Life" regresses to the rock 'n' roll genre. Agreed, *Rubber Soul* is galaxies removed from the performance style of fifties rock 'n' roll, but does that mean it's *rock* simply because it's "innovative" and "flexible"? So are jazz, classical, opera, and pop music, all full of new ideas and new directions. If one eliminates the songs with the sitar, the rockabilly, the balladry, and the period-piece touches, the only rock songs left on *Rubber Soul* are "Drive My Car" and "The Word," maybe "You Won't See Me" and "Think for Yourself" too.

All of this suggests not that Gracyk is "wrong"—in fact, this overview of *Rubber Soul*'s diverse program might seem to prove his case—but that a simple definition of rock is suddenly quite complicated. I think *Rhythm and Noise* is one of the best academic books on rock music, and I half-agree that *Rubber Soul* is a rock album (not, however, the Fab Four's first rock album) but not for the reasons Gracyk has stated. Questions begin to mount. What happened to *Help!*, an "innovative," "flexible" album preceding *Rubber Soul*? How many performance styles does rock include, and which ones? What exactly counts for innovation? Is *Rubber Soul* comparable to rock albums by Bad Company, Heart, Aerosmith, Pearl Jam, and Motörhead? Then there's the possibility that one person's rock might very well be another person's folk rock, the label usually affixed to *Rubber Soul*. Or in the case of other records, one person's rock 'n' roll might very well be another person's pop, pap, rap, hip-hop, or trip-hop. In the ocean of popular music, there are hundreds of big and little genres swimming around feeding on each other, and it's not clear that rock music is the great white shark swallowing the tuna fish of rock 'n' roll.

The rock 'n' roll/rock/subgenre question is an important subject on which I won't dwell. To succumb to the temptation would be to digress pointlessly because as I sift through the garbage and trash, the two genres are both inclusive and similar enough to be understood by anyone reading these pages. None of my arguments or examples hinge on the connotations of two closely related musical terms that, frankly, are daunting enough to define in the first place. Experts have been trying in vain for decades. As Johan Fornäs wrote in 1995, "There are innumerable possible ways to define rock, but not all of them are meaningful in a given context. On the other hand, there is no consensus around one single definition." He views "pop/rock as one single, continuous genre field rather than as distinct categories. . . . A continuous definitional struggle is going on among the interpretive communities of listeners and musicians."[2]

To worry about their differences would be to treat rock 'n' roll and rock music too pedantically and to be restricted by arbitrary definitions that would not serve the present thesis. (The spelling of *rock 'n' roll* confuses the semantic problem further. If we can't agree on an orthodox spelling of the word, how can we agree on its meaning? I chose "rock 'n' roll" for this book. Variations include rock and roll, rock & roll, rock 'n roll, rock n' roll, rock'n'roll, rock-n-roll, RocknRoll, and others.) It should be noted that in 1999 the editors of *Rolling Stone* published an anthology called *Raves: What Your Rock and Roll Favorites Favor,* and that the majority of "rock and rollers" quoted in this book—for example, Fred Schneider, Trey Anastasio, Paula Cole, Bootsy Collins, D'Arcy, Emmylou Harris, Marilyn Manson, and John Tesh—don't make a living doing Elvis covers.

John Tesh! As Patsy Cline once sang, *imagine that.* Rock 'n' roll is a term of such elasticity that it's wise to give it lots of space to breathe in interviews, glossaries, silly anthologies, and serious monographs. It doesn't thrive when formalized, pigeonholed, fenced in, tweaked to fit a rigid category, or dressed up to gain admittance to a rock club whose management wouldn't dream of booking John Tesh, a name that doesn't belong in a book about either rock 'n' roll or rock. Intuitively we know what rock 'n' roll is and isn't. Those who don't never will.

I hear someone objecting that since 1990 or thereabouts, the editors of *Rolling Stone* haven't known what they're talking about anyway, not if the subject is rock 'n' roll or rock, and that their *Raves* anthology was a marketing, not musical, venture, thus a bad example all around. To which I would reply, assuming the knock against *Rolling Stone* is true, that most reputable magazines and 'zines use the labels rock 'n' roll and rock synonymously, treating them generically rather than technically. (If I ask a person to look at the beautiful *night sky* instead of the *firmament* or for that matter the *heavens,* he will know that I'm referring to a broad expanse of stars overhead. What a person calls it doesn't matter very much.) Advertisers having a stake in this issue don't seem concerned about the distinctions between rock 'n' roll and rock music. In the spring 2002 issue of the *Big Takeover,* Bomp Records advertises "4 releases of maximum *rock and roll* on America's greatest *rock and roll* labels" (italics added). The four bands and their labels are the Warlocks (Bomp), the Brian Jonestown Massacre (Bomp), Thee Michelle Gun Elephant (Alive), and the Richmond Sluts (Disaster). The music of these bands represents a number of diverse post–rock 'n' roll sounds. In other words, Gracyk would call them rock bands. To be exact, they're postpunk. In the same issue, the Bombardier label crows that it produces and distributes "the highest quality rock-and-roll for music fans around the world," its roster including Sugarsmack (alt-country), Baby Carrot (postpunk), Junkie (power pop, new wave pop), and other groups.[3]

If my approach to genre strikes some readers as nonchalant and lacking in rigor, I encourage them to buy Neil Young's *Live Rust.* Before he and Crazy Horse dig into the tune "Sedan Delivery," Young shouts, "Let's play some rock 'n' roll!"[4] This isn't Young's way of telling his audience to expect a song bearing a style predating 1965 or so—that is, a white "rock 'n' roll" number with primitive instrumentation, trebly guitars, echo-drenched production, straight and narrow drums, lo-fi acoustics, and words about a hot rod, surfing, high school, or puppy love. Nor, to be historically accurate, should his audience expect to hear a black "race" record (a.k.a. rhythm and blues) with a pumping sax, a gritty guitar, thrusting drums, a hoarse lead vocal or perhaps a velvet one cushioned among three-part harmonies, and words full of erotic puns. All the screaming audience knows, and all Neil Young wants it to know by virtue of his rallying cry, is that a passionate, loud, four-man performance of another self-penned classic is about to roar forth from the Marshall stacks. Having listened to scores of tracks—innovative, stylistically flexible tracks, impossible to label—by Neil Young solo artist and Neil Young group player, I know he knows what rock 'n' roll is and what it isn't. What suffices for him as he faces ten thousand delirious ticket holders will suffice for us in the present essay.

3. Do It Again

My "bearing witness" (see section 1) to the miracles of rock 'n' roll from the midfifties to this day will take the form of an analysis of how this musical genre, being a reflection of contemporary Western (with an emphasis on North American) culture, is permeated with the concept of trash. I'll ask and answer three main questions:

1. What guises does the "trash trope"—that is, the metaphor or figurative rendering of trash—assume in rock 'n' roll music?
2. What meaning does this trash trope convey?
3. To what extent does the idea of garbage, especially in its rhetorical usage, encode or define a rock aesthetic—a systematic or formal mode of evaluation applied to a specific art form—one complicated by the fact that, depending on the rock 'n' roll product and the person writing or speaking about it, the trash trope can be used in one of two contradictory ways, either as praise or disparagement?

The short answers are:

1. The trash trope assumes the guises of trash, garbage, rubbish, waste, debris, junk, and other synonyms that describe the disposed-of products of a throwaway society. The trope can be applied both literally to products of rock music and figuratively to the six categories listed in the next answer.

2. The meaning conveyed by the trash trope depends on each specific case, where a writer's or speaker's tone—sarcastic, bitter, cutting, exuberant, approving, and so on—must be taken into account. The six main categories in which signs of the trash trope appear and then invite interpretation are musical, visual, rhetorical, biographical, ideological, and lyrical. Within each of these categories, various contradictions and double or multiple readings occur. For instance, in the lyrical realm, one encounters dozens of themes based on the trash trope, and in the realm of biography, while a deceased rock star's "wasted" lifestyle may well be romanticized by a young fan who proceeds to emulate the unsavory habits of the dead hero or heroine, this same wasted lifestyle (and wasted life) would be condemned by this fan's guidance counselor, Sunday school teacher, and parents.

3. To a great extent. The persuasiveness of the trash aesthetic depends, as do all theories of aesthetics, on the introduction and analysis of a sufficient number of specific examples to substantiate the whole.

These three questions presuppose one overarching question, which is: How does trash as a literal and figurative signifier shape and inform one of our culture's main art forms? Or in plain language: Is it—rock 'n' roll music generally and its products specifically—garbage? Assuming as I do that rock 'n' roll music *is* garbage, what (defaulting for the moment to an easy dichotomy) good or bad thing does this assumption of garbage suggest about rock 'n' roll? Why? In pursuing answers to these and related questions, I'll identify and explain the forms that garbage and trash assume in rock music and the significance behind these forms. More precisely, in part 1 ("Trashed") and part 2 ("Wasted"), I'll approach the trash trope from four main directions, in this order:

- Rock music as disposable object (the throwaway nature of vinyl albums, compact discs, and packaging analyzed in the context of American society's trash crisis)
- Rock criticism (the tendency of rock critics and rock artists to describe the music they love and hate by employing variants of the trash trope)
- Rock lyrics (the role played by the trash trope in forty tunes dating from 1958 to 2000)
- Rock morbidity (the sickness and death of rock artists and characters in their songs taken as a tragic dimension of the trash trope; the ultimate form of waste—men and women dying well before reaching middle age, often as a result of embracing the rock musician's stereotypical "wasted" lifestyle— interpreted from a "morbid-romantic" perspective)

Rock 'n' roll music reeks of trash. Thousands of unsold songs and albums could be melted down without upsetting one record buyer and the trashy tracks of many rock stars could be stamped as disposable plastic. Although I'll often refer to this sort of product, I'll also reverse pejorative assumptions about rock-trash. I'll exhibit beauty in the midst of the garbage heap, just as do Melanie Molesworth and A. R. Ammons, two writers who dwell on the literal loveliness inherent in junk and garbage. Molesworth, an interior decorator, does "new, unexpected, and stylish things with objects . . . too good to be consigned to dumpsters. . . . Each source [of junk] is unpredictable and offers its own secrets: What you end up with depends on where you look, when you get there, and what your tastes are."[1] Ammons, a poet, would have us believe that the greasiest bag in the town dump could very well hold castoffs worthy of recovery or contemplation, and that, observed from certain vantage points, and understood to be the dumping ground of lots of things that shouldn't have ended up there in the first place, the landfill—swarming with bickering birds, clanking with heavy machinery, and stinking of a civilization rotting from the inside out—inspires affection and even reverence because it underpins transcendence:

> here, the [garbage truck] driver knows,
>
> where the consummations gather, where the disposal
> flows out of form, where the last translations
>
> cast away their immutable bits and scraps,
> flits of steel, shivers of bottle and tumbler,
>
> here is the gateway to beginning, here the portal
> of renewing change.[2]

With rock 'n' roll music in mind, I'll take this idea another step further into the realm of spirit. As I wade through the rock 'n' roll landfill and explain its layout and its contents, readers of *But Is It Garbage?* will understand what I was too young to understand as a preteen plunking down three dollars for his first record album (*Walk, Don't Run '64*, the Ventures), understand what I've learned to articulate to myself as a fan listening to a fresh cache of compact discs list-priced at eighteen dollars each: that rock 'n' roll is equal parts trash and salvation. As a preteen I only understood the second half of the equation. Inherent in this quintessentially trashy and paradoxical art form is its beautiful plenitude. (Discoursing on rock 'n' roll, one is sometimes reduced to the hyperbole of cosmic terminology.) My conviction that rock music's trashy essence isn't necessarily at odds with its unique beauty will be examined in part 3 ("Saved"). Rock 'n' roll has the power to save its fans—not just to make them "feel good" (although it does that too)—as surely as any art form has saved, replenished, inspired, gladdened, nurtured, purged, transformed, rejuvenated, and enlightened boys and girls and men and women over the centuries. To drink once again at the Emersonian fount, adapting his claim about capital-*P* Poets in "The Poet" to capital-*A* rock 'n' roll Artists, I suggest at the risk of persecution by postmodern reviewers (see section 34) that a select corps of rock musicians fulfills Emerson's conditions for acknowledgment as "liberating gods."[3] And sometimes, oddly enough, so do the least select rock artists. Out of garbage and rubbish come songs by both never-to-be-forgotten geniuses and blink-and-they're-gone hacks who emancipate souls yearning for a three-minute dose of higher as well as lower truth. Although much rock music contains all the melody and emotion heard in the din of a hundred thousand cars doing the morning commute on a Los Angeles freeway, some rock music makes you shiver and all but levitate, spreading through your nervous system with the swiftness of the black plague. Sometimes you find yourself swaying to the sound, sometimes you halt and laugh, sometimes you lie down and weep. Then the song or album ends and you play it again—now for the mere pleasure of repetition and reassurance—or instead, satisfied, wait until another time, place, and mood are in tune; and then, perhaps with a different record cued up, you might reenact that same ineffable feeling of music emanating from a mysterious source within you and at the same time coming from a material source without, a feeling that can only be termed a spasm of grace.

But treatment of this cosmic theme must wait. In what remains of part 1, I'll share mundane thoughts about the rock 'n' roll artifact. This concrete object is recorded, manufactured, packaged, marketed, sold, and then discarded as a medium of exchange in a global industry motivated by profit margins. I'll then turn from plastic object to plastic language, specifically to rock 'n' roll rhetoric. Regarding the trash trope, what do professionals in the field say and write about the music that pays their rent? The discussion traces the connotations of the trash trope as it mutates into garbage, rubbish, crap, junk, and so on. My examples of how the trash trope is used rhetorically will be limited to illustrations of the trashing of rock from the inside of the medium, that is, by critics and musicians, not the outside by disapproving ministers, disgusted teachers, nervous parents, and antirockers in general. Some of rock's harshest critics function within the rock press and some of rock's most insightful thinkers are the musicians themselves. None of them hesitate to use the trash trope, which of course foregrounds all my examples. Rhetorical analysis will take into account the fact that the metaphor of trash is volatile and multivalent. Contrary to logic, in the domain of rock 'n' roll criticism, sightings of garbage, trash, and waste often designate not low but high quality.

The trope of trash, expressed commonly in metaphors of waste, also circulates throughout rock lyrics. Thrown-away love, trashed environments, wasted time, and wasted people—these subjects appear again and again in records dating from the Fabulous Fifties to the Preening Present. A survey of forty rock songs will constitute section 27. As their titles indicate, many of these songs underscore the theme of waste, for instance Metallica's "Disposable Heroes," Mazzy Star's "Wasted," Napalm Death's "Throwaway," and Phish's "Waste." Most of the time, however, a tune's lyric, as opposed to a self-reflexive title, refers in passing to some aspect of waste, such as the time a person wastes in the effort to win someone else's heart. Passing references to the trash trope don't necessarily lessen its importance in a song.

Consistent with references to disposability in lyrics is the subject of death, which is the ultimate form of waste when it involves men and women dying on the altar of rock 'n' roll. The usual culprits, heroin and alcohol, are supplemented by sundry airplane and motorcycle crashes, which have been known to do the trick. What a waste! In rock music, youth is wasted and lives discarded as a matter of course. But physical death receives little attention in "Wasted." Instead, waste understood as a morbid sensibility engrained in bleak but beautiful rock albums—wasted mental states, broken-down personae, and unstable composers; the trash trope transmuted into a musical art depicting sickness, despair, and death: these are my concerns. The morbid-romantic nature of much rock 'n' roll music is defined, discussed, and then analyzed in a classic example, Lou Reed's album *Berlin*. Morbidity and waste run together here, there, and everywhere in the vast field of rock 'n' roll, tied and bound to each other until the bitter end like McTeague handcuffed to Marcus in the last scene of Frank Norris's *McTeague* or like two pit bulls snapping and snarling at each other in a pirouette of death down Desolation Row. Morbidity saturates many rock masterpieces, exemplars of how the trash trope can be construed in the broadest terms of a performer's or band's wasted emotional or psychological state, this state determining the subject, lyrics, melody, arrangement, and production of a given record album. Faced with evidence that such a recording can be a major work of art, we must acknowledge the contradiction that waste understood in terms of sickness and extinction is good for the artist and consequently good for his audience. The melancholy that dominates the tone in morbid recordings reflects the emotional and psychological state of artists who were depressed, unstable, and in several cases mere weeks from death when they recorded them. My reading of *Berlin* will illustrate the thesis that waste is the Carrara marble out of which a select number of rock classics have been painstakingly carved and polished for future generations to cry over and enjoy.

4. Give the People What They Want

I wish to return to a word mentioned in the "overarching question" posed a moment ago: "How does trash as a literal and figurative signifier shape and inform one of our culture's main art forms? Or in plain language: Is it—rock 'n' roll music generally and its products specifically—garbage?"

The phrase "main art forms" raises a question that must be answered before we decide if rock 'n' roll is garbage. This question should have been laid to rest long ago but continues to incite debate. Is rock art? Is it art in the prepostmodern Western meaning of the term as passed down and understood over the ages? Or is rock 'n' roll music little more than mindless entertainment? This is what many of my colleagues think.

So much for the postmodern "valorization" of popular discourse and the reapportionment of the traditional, time honored, and elite! "Do you mean art as in uppercase Art? As in classical music and canonical novels?" one junior professor shot back after I asked her if she ranked rock music alongside other art forms. There was uncertainty in her eyes, a touch of chagrin. Training in graduate school doesn't always eradicate a person's disposition toward common sense. She couldn't quite say that rock 'n' roll was *art*. "It depends on how you define art," she hedged; "maybe some of rock, the Beatles maybe, Dylan's lyrics, of course, Paul Simon's too, possibly Elton John, Sting, Patti Smith, and people like that" was as far as she would go, frowning.[1] Oh yes, she liked rock music and named some of her favorite acts—buying time—but in the end this was a question of theory not practice and thus had triggered a conflict that lay in her multicultural and historicist education (context in, aesthetics out), which had constrained her to believe, even though it remained difficult to accept this belief on some personal, intuitive, or logical level, that rock artists had to be accepted into the same club boasting Shakespeare, Eliot, Woolf, Cather, Millay, and Faulkner . . . on condition, naturally, that most of us in the Academy had tacitly agreed (sometime after 1975) that *art* had more or less been dismissed, rightly dismissed, along with quaint concepts such as aesthetics, univocality, the intentional fallacy—anything, in short, to do with well-wrought urns. Over the course of two or three decades *art* had become another anachronistic term whose meaning (or perhaps nonmeaning) had at long last been exposed—Whose art? Whose criteria? What author? Whose authority?—as a divisible phallocentric transcendental sign and archaic shibboleth standing buck naked and defenseless under the glare of the searchlights of deconstruction, revisionism, and canon correction.

It had been just a simple question.

So . . . art? Entertainment? A little of each? Just garbage? Stupid questions? Irrelevant? Who cares anyway? Perhaps. But because one of my main concerns in this essay is aesthetics—the terms garbage and trash, when applied to rock music, are invested with connotations of value and quality, beauty and ugliness—I can't shrug these questions off as rhetorical. Nor do I wish to belabor them. Studies of rock 'n' roll that do belabor aesthetics (a term as amorphous as rock 'n' roll) tend to be as tedious and unrewarding as—shall we say John Tesh's music?[2] My discussion of art, though necessary, will be brief.

Rock stars have been referred to as recording and performing artists for so many years that I presume most people who grew up with rock music see no reason to question a rock musician's claim to that title or to rock's portrayal in the media and rock's reception by the public as a type of art. Everyone versed in the criticism of rock 'n' roll knows that the label *artist* is applied across the board, even in cases where *entertainer* would more accurately define a performer. This democratization of art and artistry, hand in hand with the postmodern razing of canons populated by false idols and their artificially propped-up "masterpieces," means that Britney Spears is no less an artist than Patti Smith, that Justin Timberlake shares the stage of art with Van Morrison, and that Paula Cole is as fully vested with the artist's mantle and mystique as Sir Paul McCartney. While we might hesitate (as did my colleague) to acknowledge the artist in all rock musicians—an insupportable idea, after all—it would be difficult to refute the contention that genuine rock artists stand above their less competent or less visionary peers.

Most people simply enjoy the music and don't trouble with the semantics of art (or with the distinctions between rock and rock 'n' roll) or with the need to study these questions. "Shut up and play yer guitar," they would say. "Why split hairs? It's only rock 'n' roll. What's there not to like about it?" Some listeners, however, do ponder these questions, do split hairs, and have nothing good to say about rock 'n' roll. The critique of high art and low entertainment is fraught, so these listeners contend, with moral, intellectual, ideological, and political repercussions. The critique of rock 'n' roll must be undertaken for the good of a society depraved by its appetite for substandard forms of fun and for empty entertainment misconstrued by philistines as art.

A discriminating listener par excellence, and something of a straw man in defenses of rock, is Theodor Adorno. Adorno's disdain for popular music (a much broader field than rock or pop rock) could well puzzle people who value rock 'n' roll from the sixties (Bob Dylan, the Beatles, the Doors) to the twenty-zeroes (Spiritualized, Flaming Lips, Built to Spill). "For Adorno," Theodore Gracyk explains, jazz and other forms of popular music are "the exemplar[s] of music debased as commercial commodity, and of music *that fails utterly as art"* (italics added). And the opposite of art? Enter my first example of the trash trope in the rhetoric of rock 'n' roll criticism. "Presumably," Gracyk says in reference to Adorno, "anyone who gives in to the barbarism of popular music lacks the requisite qualitative insight to discern the true ideological effect of such vulgar trash."[3]

A pillar of the Frankfurt school, Theodor Adorno published numerous diatribes (first appearing in the 1930s) against popular music, at that time the products of Tin Pan Alley. These attacks originated in Adorno's conviction that jazz and pop are fetishes dear to bourgeois consumers mechanized by the processes of capitalism so intensely materialistic that it has all but leveled refined culture and alienated the most innovative artists. "On Popular Music" (1941) argues that "the fundamental characteristic of popular music" setting it apart from "serious" music is its "standardization" of details and form. This standardization is integral to Adorno's contention that popular music dehumanizes the masses and enriches the few industrialists who regulate the discourse. In pop, "[t]he whole is pre-given and pre-accepted, even before the actual experience of the music starts. . . . No stress is ever placed upon the whole as a musical event, nor does the structure of the whole ever depend upon the details. . . . A musical detail which is not permitted to develop becomes a caricature of its own potentialities." In other words, pop goes nowhere; it's intellectually and emotionally bankrupt. Pop exists only because "[a] fully concentrated and conscious experience of art is possible only to those whose lives do not put such a strain on them [as it does on the masses] that in their spare time they want relief from both boredom and effort simultaneously. . . . [C]heap commercial entertainment [pop and jazz] . . . induces relaxation because it is patterned and pre-digested." The audience's hunger for "fun" is at best pathetic. The jaded masses have degenerated into automatons satisfied with clichés of debased and debasing music.

Ironically, consumers flatter themselves that their choice of entertainment is determined autonomously. Contrary to this fallacy, insists Adorno, consumers are led to their indulgence in superficial delights and to their false sense of freedom by the machinations of exploitative capitalists: "Listening to popular music is manipulated not only by its promoters, but as it were, by the inherent nature of this music itself, into a system of response-mechanisms wholly antagonistic to the ideal of individuality in a free, liberal society." Corruption in taste is linked to the economic principle that moneyed interests reap profits from the standardization of pop. Standards "have been taken over by cartelized agencies, the final results of a competitive process, and rigidly enforced upon material to be promoted. Noncompliance with the rules of the game [becomes] the basis for exclusion." Since the masses are themselves turned into objects by capitalistic systems that thrive on standardization and pseudoindividualization, and since the tedium of meaningless work renders these masses incapable of seeking true novelty or substantial intellectual fare in their leisure time, they accept the stimulant offered by popular music, where low quality is further vitiated by the endless and empty cycle of production and consumption. New stimulants, all predigested, are constantly needed to beguile boredom, and these stimulants, to be effective, must conform to homogenous, interchangeable systems while the uniformity of product is disguised by substitutable surface details. Choice is never more than an illusion, as is novelty. But in the short and long run, this doesn't matter, Adorno contends, because "people clamor for what they are going to get anyhow."[4] There can't be anything new and groundbreaking if units are to be shifted and benumbed consumers are to lap up their manufactured pleasures, all fleeting and aesthetically nil.

Adorno's critique might appear to rock fans unfamiliar with the cerebral achievements of Adorno's hero, the composer Arnold Schoenberg, like the ravings of a close-minded ideologue or disgruntled Marxist whose economic theories are about as relevant as the cold war—basically, the opinions of a man who should spend, if he were alive, a month woodshedding with midsixties Dylan albums, with Frank Zappa's songbook, or with the recordings of like-minded anticorporate rockers such as Steve Albini and the boys from the Minutemen and Wire, not to mention thousands of other indie-hard-core bands.[5]

But Adorno was far from close minded and disgruntled, and more than once his shafts struck the target dead-on. It would be a sign of insecurity at best and perverseness at worst for defenders of pop music to ignore his analysis of how the system works. His gripe against standardization and interchangeability of details is a good place to start. Bernard Gendron first assumes that Adorno's critique can be applied to rock 'n' roll and then concedes the existence of some standardization in rock music, both in diachronic and synchronic terms. "[P]unk," for example, "has standardized the musical sneer," Gendron writes, and "[t]here is also some standardization between rock 'n' roll genres."[6] Gendron focuses on doo-wop and its chord progressions. Let me apply his reasoning to the punk rock he mentions. A typical punk tune, in addition to sporting a sneer, is characterized by a throbbing bass line competing with a wailing or barking singer and a drummer punishing his four-piece kit, everyone rushing through verse, chorus, verse, chorus, bridge (maybe), solo (maybe), verse, chorus, out. Synchronically, from song to song and album to album in any given year after 1977, the parts, roles, and sounds of punk tunes are largely interchangeable. Diachronically, the majority of punks sow the same black seeds and rain the same black rage on the same rocky ground year after year. Moreover, punk form is closely related to, say, surf music. In lieu of a sneer appears the insouciant grin of a beach-bound youth, and in the typical surf rock tune a keep-it-simple-stupid bass line supports either a lead guitar twanging out the melody line or a singer without much vocal training carrying it while a drummer breaks up the elementary backbeat/ride cymbal pattern with five-stroke rolls on snare, small rack tom-tom, and floor tom-tom. Like the punk song, the surf song is over long before anyone has any reason to complain of being bored by it. Musical hooks (the main sign of pseudoindividualization) change, but not much else.

Standardization is just another word for formula. A person who has listened to a country music single, seen a music video, or bought a mainstream rock album lately is deafened by a cacophony of duplicates, copies, mindless (or mindful) imitations, mercenaries, frauds, careerists, and clones. Clichés and veneer abound. Moreover, if one hates the predictability of "classic rock" radio, then it's almost impossible to experience a rock 'n' roll buzz beyond the wattage of a college radio station. But all this is nothing new. Adorno's conviction that successful pop is determined first and foremost by "[t]he promoters of commercialized entertainment" has been conventional wisdom for the better part of five decades.[7] It's easy to disillusion anyone who thinks artistic integrity and quality are prerequisites for airplay, fame, photo-ops, and platinum sales. Exceptions don't disprove the rule. Record executives prefer the same-old to the brand-new unless the brand-new succeeds in cracking open a lucrative market untapped until then. Remember Nirvana, grunge, and the ensuing gold rush whose epicenter was Seattle? Dollar-fisted executives and talent scouts converged on the low-living, hard-living, true-blue rock 'n' roll bands who were taken aback by the press's (and market's) infatuation with Nirvana.

Nevertheless, we must not surrender the field to Adorno too hastily; we must insist that his misconceptions are legion and even baffling to anyone with the most rudimentary understanding of and affection for jazz, pop, and rock 'n' roll. Gendron cites several such misconceptions. For one, Adorno falsely transfers Marxist notions about mass-produced "functional artifacts" (such as automobiles) to "textual artifacts" (such as compact discs): "The processes used to produce [the textual] are quite different from those used to produce [the functional]." Furthermore, the "periphery" of the functional artifact clearly has little to no bearing on the same artifact's "core"—that is, the motor makes the car move whereas custom stripes or custom hubcaps do nothing functionally. In a textual artifact of popular music, however, "there is no clearly defined function that enables us to distinguish between core and periphery."[8] What this means is that countless details differentiate—let's focus on major acts—the Beatles, Bob Dylan, Jimi Hendrix, and the Velvet Underground, not to mention the details, synchronic and diachronic, within each act's respective oeuvre. In Adorno's scheme of predigested form, the Velvet Underground's epic death-march "Sister Ray" would appear to resemble their languid hate-ballad "Candy Says." But this is nonsense. The live versions of "Sister Ray" alone sound like different songs, each clocking in at between twenty-five and thirty-five minutes. In Adorno's scheme, the Beatles' "Penny Lane" would be a dead ringer for "Helter Skelter" and the same sameness would obtain between Hendrix's "Little Wing" (delicate ballad) and "Machine Gun" (antiwar feedback fest). Dylan's "Subterranean Homesick Blues" (paranoid postfolk rap) would be indistinguishable from "Lay Lady Lay" (quasi-country come-on ditty). Now think of the music of jazz artists on the order of Charlie Parker, John Coltrane, Bill Evans, and Sonny Rollins. The structural and stylistic differences—the cores and peripheries— of the work of these musicians are immediately apparent to aficionados, and with a little training lay people can identify them as well. Whatever might be standardized, pseudo, or corporately regulated in their music is insignificant compared to what's innovative and vital.

But to bring my argument back to the trash trope, let me quote Gracyk on Adorno one more time: "For Adorno, the assumption that there are qualitative differences within popular music, so that the audience for jazz has something over heavy-metal fans, or that Van Halen is better than Motorhead, is an allowable but ultimately pointless differentiation among levels of junk."[9] *Junk.* Ironically, when an antirocker employs junk and trash as modifiers and synonyms for rock 'n' roll, he isn't aware that rock's disposability is an attribute to embrace and appreciate, not something to deprecate and defend. Rock's partisans know junk when they see it and know when it's redeemable, magnetic, and beautiful, just as they know when it's irredeemable, repellent, and ugly.

Quite apart from how valid or untenable Theodor Adorno's theories seem to us today, his comments at the very least stimulate his opponents to think of ways to defend rock 'n' roll from him and other imposing detractors, for he doesn't stand alone. Even after acknowledging the limitations in Adorno's dismissal of pop and jazz, Roger Scruton in the brilliant study *The Aesthetics of Music* states, "Much modern pop [that is, rock 'n' roll] is cheerless, and meant to be cheerless. But much of it is also a kind of *negation* of music, a dehumanizing of the spirit of song." These comments were published in 1997. Scruton is an antipop moralist armed with an encyclopedic knowledge of musical theory and practice. "What I have described," he remarks in a passage that proves the gist of Victorian moral aestheticism hasn't been bleached out by thirty years of poststructuralist discourse, "is not the *decadence* of popular music, but its final *freedom*—its breaking-loose from the channel of taste, into the great ocean of equality, where the writ of taste no longer runs." Having earlier challenged postmodernists for placing "inverted commas" around the verities of Art, Truth, and Morality, and for taking a "sophisticated way of avoiding the question of modern life—the question of what we are to affirm in it, and what deny"—Scruton concludes that the "postmodern world denatures music only because it denatures everything, in order that each individual might have his chance to buy and sell." In this denatured world, the sad premise perpetuated by pop music is "that we live *outside* society, that we too, in granting equality to every human type, have become monsters, and that a monster is an OK thing to be."[10] Monsters, need it be said, don't create art for moral uplift. Moreover, rock 'n' roll, or rock, isn't art, and art matters very much to Roger Scruton. (One of the few rock bands that Scruton lambastes for its dissemination of "anomie" is R.E.M., who released in 1994, to bad reviews, an album named *Monster*. "Monster" is also musician's slang for a virtuoso.)

Despite his own sour opinions, Scruton chides Adorno for having failed to notice quality in pop and jazz where it does exist. Scruton likes George Gershwin and Louis Armstrong and within the rock canon he welcomes evidence of "[t]he long tradition of musical utterance" in the music of the Beatles, citing "She Loves You." He pans Nirvana, however, for "melodic deficiency," "loss of harmonic texture," and "the soup of amplified overtones" bubbling from Kurt Cobain's guitar, citing "Dive."[11]

Vague criticisms for sure, but I think I understand what Scruton objects to. Personally, I don't object to it at all—"it" being Nirvana's manic-depressive urgency cohering around a lethal hook; a fleet yet thundering bass line; the fire-emergency clang of slash-and-burn cymbal flurries and the roar of deep-snare backbeats that pin the word RAGE at the back of one's quaking heart; guitar solos like the shriek of fans in rows one through five undergoing root canals by dentists wielding chisels; and a vocal screech like an F-15 skidding along a runway coated with gunpowder, Al Qaeda land mines, gravel, broken glass, and thumbtacks. Cobain's fix-death-ulcer lyrics leave an after-burn of napalm in one's intellect. In Nirvana I hear not deficiency but excess, not loss but gain, and nothing resembling the first course of a formal dinner or some cheap high-sodium gunk scooped out of a tin can (Scruton's "soup"). I hear calamity. I hear blacker-than-black humor. I hear amplified double-strokes of sin and redemption and the symbiosis of death and rebirth. I hear masochistic rites of passage as well as squeals of penitence from young men compelled to batter and vandalize. I hear prayers croaked by a self-hater with his finger on the trigger as he begs his wife and no-name god for forgiveness. I hear the so-called Voice of a Generation shipped platinum for medicated minions unable to speak a syllable in their own defense in the tribunal of teen convention—the platinum Voice strangling in the speaker's haste to fulfill his own suicidal pact in the collective catharsis. I hear a young father craving the day's third injection of heroin as he coos into his baby girl's ear. I hear the hatred of pettiness, stupidity, and hypocrisy. I hear rock 'n' roll that rattles the ossified bones of the timid, the jaded, and the forlorn. Scruton's appraisal of Nirvana doesn't begin to convince me that Kurt Cobain wasn't an artist with all that *artist* connotes about devotion to craft, original vision, suffering, and sacrifice, one of the greatest new, and one of the last great, rock artists of the last twenty years. And one can't have an artist without an art.

On the other hand, Scruton and Adorno are right about one thing regarding rock 'n' roll music in general. It *is* trash. In their flight from its amplified overtones they overlook an odd orthographic coincidence. The first three letters in *trash* spell *art*. Art is encoded in this particular form of trash.

To analyze rock 'n' roll as trash is to discover not reasons to abominate it but to learn wherein lies much of its force and beauty. For as ingenuous as this thesis might seem in an epoch defined for better or worse by postmodern pastiche, deconstructed subjectivity, and irrelevant aestheticism, the best rock 'n' roll artists create well-crafted objects that impervious to trends in theory and changes in social norms stimulate and/or satisfy the sensory, emotional, moral, and spiritual needs of audiences attracted to that art form, for whatever reason. Motti Regev, writing in 1994, argued that "the producers of rock meanings [i.e., critics, reviewers, and scholars] have formulated an interpretation of the music which applies the traditional parameters of art to the specificity of rock and popular music." The aesthetics of rock has developed around a repertoire of great songs and albums, a gallery of outstanding musicians, a canon of criticism (magazines and books) by well-known critics, and "a repertory of musical codes, sounds patterns and specific works." In addition, lyrics, subgenres, amplification, recording practices and technology, and autonomous creative entities (the composers and musicians themselves) have constructed over decades "a hierarchy of 'authenticity' [that] should be understood . . . as a type of meaning production which was aimed at raising the artistic prestige and cultural status of popular music." Regev reads the autonomous forces behind rock masterpieces (no "death of the author" nonsense for him), reviews the major epochs in relation to major products and performers, and contemplates the aesthetic conditions of electric sound, studio work, and lyrical "grain." Rock 'n' roll music has penetrated the "dominant cultural capital," which thus "has enabled [its] recognition as art."[12]

Which isn't to say all rock is art. Even the best rock isn't all, or only, art. Consistent with the culture in which it is produced, the vast majority of individual pieces of rock music *are* disposable. Yet the disposability factor of a rock record has the potential to increase, not diminish, its appeal. Rock songs and albums are capable of soothing a listener's craving for the Beautiful, the Moral, and the True despite, if not because of, the music's inherent trashiness. As a collector scarfs up records, tapes, and compact discs searching for aesthetic fulfillment, he wastes money and time seeking the Beautiful Sound amid recordings that after a spin or two he sells, trades, tosses into the closet, or throws away.

5. Isn't It a Pity

The discussion must now turn from transcendent art to material garbage as preparation for the analysis of trash as representation (the trash trope), not referent. In rock 'n' roll music as in all industries, simulacra (substitutions drenched in image, repetition, and hype) are manufactured so relentlessly that the authenticity of "the art object" is displaced by videos, compact discs, and other modes of representation. Mary Poovey uses the decentered Bruce Springsteen as her model. The "real" Springsteen on stage is both dwarfed and upstaged by massive screens that "even in the moment of supreme presence, the moment of performance itself" denaturalize him and render his distant figure exactly that: a figure, a repetition, a postmodern sham, a not-original substitution, "an effect of multiple representations, which allude to and quote each other, while the original recedes into a haze of nostalgia, a fantasy of what rock 'used' to be."[1] Barred from touching a rock simulacrum, a fan instead purchases concert tickets and throws away the stubs, expends fossil fuels driving an automobile to the show, buys concessions and discards the wrappers and cups, and buys compact discs at the merchandise booth: commodities all, all destined for the city dump.

In her history of the production and removal of waste products, Susan Strasser identifies the core of the problem of disposability in the United States:

> The new [post–World War II] consumer culture changed ideas about throwing things away, creating a way of life that incorporated technological advances, organizational changes, and new perspectives, a lifestyle that linked products made for one-time use, municipal trash collection, and the association of traditional reuse and recycling with poverty and backwardness. Packaging taught people the throwaway habit, and new ideals of cleanliness emphasized swift and complete disposal. Paper cups, towels, and straws in public places, and Kleenex and commercial toilet paper at home, reinforced that habit. Nor could the new throwaways serve as fuel in houses with radiators and gas furnaces; they went in the trash, along with the lightbulbs.[2]

Since the 1950s the one-way flow described by Strasser has been perpetuated by a consumer ideology in which disposability has been packaged and sold as a virtue. Nature wastes nothing; however, a civilization predicated on rampant materialism wastes much. This irreversible flow means that waste products are returned to landfills, toxic dumps, and other treatment centers without nourishing the ecosystem from which the raw materials that led to this waste were extracted in the first place. As we swim in consumer goods, we drown in the trash that the consumption of these goods necessitates. Strasser:

> In an industrial system, the flow is one-way: materials and energy are extracted from the earth and converted by labor and capital into industrial products and byproducts, which are sold, and into waste, which is returned to the ecosystem but does not nourish it. Thus, the late-twentieth-century household procures goods from factories, mends little, bags the detritus in plastic, and places it at the curb to be conveyed to the transfer station or the incinerator. The late-twentieth-century city takes in most of what it uses by truck and train and airplane, and flushes its waste into landfills, sewage treatment plants, and toxic dumps.[3]

A few statistics (some conservative since they date from the 1990s) will put Strasser's points into perspective. Annually, Americans (hereafter, "we") generate well over 300 million scrap tires; another three billion languish in tire dumps and millions more end up in landfills or stockpiles.[4] Annually, at least ten million motor vehicles are dismantled and shredded.[5] Every year about half a billion fluorescent bulbs are discarded, 450 million improperly.[6] Publishers of American magazines distribute more than twice as many issues as retailers can sell, the unsold copies adding up to forty million tons of paper wasted monthly (these totals for 1990 are surely much higher today).[7] Annually, the average home in 1993 generated one hundred pounds of hazardous waste; this waste added up to a national total of 1.6 million tons.[8] Annually, we improperly discard 200 million gallons of used motor oil and our manufacturers generate 7.6 billion tons of nonhazardous industrial waste.[9] By 2005, hundreds of millions of computers and their toxic components will have been discarded in our landfills.[10] Every twelve months a billion or two used syringes enter "the municipal solid waste stream instead of the medical waste stream."[11] Yard waste weighs in at thirty-one million tons (1992 figures).[12] In 2001, offices used an estimated 1.1 trillion sheets of copier paper and 1.2 trillion sheets of printer paper.[13] Daily, our businesses generate enough paper to circle the earth twenty times.[14]

It goes on. Annually, we receive four million tons of junk mail; we don't open 44 percent of this junk. Annually, we discard twenty-five billion nonrecyclable Styrofoam cups. Daily, our newspapers produce six million tons of waste that mulches forty-one thousand trees.[15] Annually, our babies require sixteen billion disposable diapers, which, weighing 1.9 ounces dry and 5.6 ounces soiled, generate 2.8 million tons of municipal solid waste, or 1.76 percent of the total.[16] Hourly, we discard 2.5 million plastic bottles.[17] In 1999, ninety-seven billion beverage containers were trashed.[18] Annually, we dispose of at least fifty-seven million tons of packaging, 32 percent of the national total of municipal solid waste.[19] Our consumer and food service sources wasted an estimated ninety-one billion pounds of food in 1995 (eighteen billion pounds of fruits and vegetables, fourteen billion pounds of grain products); another five billion pounds was lost in various stages of food marketing.[20] Daily, according to some experts, the per capita average weight of discarded garbage surpasses five pounds, adding up to more than 200 million tons of solid waste a year; residential, business, and industrial waste combined tipped the scale at twelve billion tons in 2001.[21] Between 1960 and 1999, the production of municipal solid waste in the United States increased by 161 percent (88 million to 230 million tons), outpacing the 52 percent increase in population (180 million to 273 million people).[22]

William Rathje and Cullen Murphy pinpoint how the system of one-way consumption is reflected in the rubbish heaped in mammoth landfills:

> Each of us throws away dozens of items every day. All of these items are relics of specific human activities. . . . Taken as a whole the garbage of the United States . . . is a mirror of American society. Of course, the problem with the mirror garbage offers is that, when encountered in a garbage can, dump, or landfill, it is a broken one: our civilization is reflected in billions of fragments that may reveal little in and of themselves.

Rathje and Murphy worry that "[t]he profligate habits of our own country and our own time—the sheer volume of the garbage that we create and must dispose of—will make our society an open book."[23] Not one that will make good reading. As we all contribute to the authorship of this open book, most of us are whistling along to some form of rock 'n' roll music, unaware that it too is grounded in garbage.

Apt metaphors—the broken mirror, the open book—are like the seals of a notary on the cover of a thick report. They authenticate the report's contents and authorize the introduction of the report into other debates. In the present instance, they shift the light in which we view rock 'n' roll music—the musical counterpart of society's one-way flow of rubbish—by repositioning the discussion of it in the harsh glare of waste and wastefulness. But apt metaphors must be fine tuned, adapted, developed, and unpacked in order for them to function as more than self-evident generalizations. That rock 'n' roll music mirrors American trash culture as literal trash mirrors American excess, and that consequently rock must assume or reflect many features of trash or waste, is a thesis that fifty years after Elvis Presley entered Sun Studios has elicited no attention from journalists, critics, rock historians, or rock musicologists. It's a thesis that to my knowledge has neither been identified as a feature mirrored in the nation's narcissistic gaze nor expressed in one of its open rock 'n' roll books. To correct the oversight, this book.

6. Reflections

As a qualifier or as a medium, *trash* or one of its variants has been used by states-persons, novelists, filmmakers, photographers, scholars, and poets—for example, José Saragamo, T. S. Eliot, William Kennedy, Nathaniel Hawthorne, Jane Austen, Howard Nemerov, Alexandra Martini, Bern Porter, James Twitchell, Andy Warhol, William Friedkin, Thomas Jefferson, Alfred Kazin, Janice Radway, Al Hansen—who have assessed the value of a derogatory word or concept. That said, it should surprise no one that castigations involving trash appear much more frequently in critiques of rock 'n' roll music, which had to work for years to gain mass acceptance and respect. While it may hard to imagine an opera, jazz, or classical music critic stooping to the epithet *trash*, even in the harshest review, it's harder to imagine a rock critic not using it at the first opportunity. The critical vocabulary is well suited to the mass medium it de-scribes, but with this twist. Because of rock's paradoxical nature, applications of the qualifier *trash* can be, in fact often are, meant not as the ultimate insult but as the ultimate compliment. Because of its need to serve double duty at the drop of a hat, *trash* is one of the most slippery signifiers in the rhetoric of rock criticism.[1]

A musical form and a cultural phenomenon that blurs lines between the prin-ciples of longevity (as in canons and high art) and evanescence (as in trends and pop culture), rock music not only pivots on paradox and inconsistency, but it's mired in trash. Greil Marcus makes it one object of an overloaded prepositional phrase: "Rock 'n' roll is a combination of good ideas dried up by fads, terri-ble junk, hideous failings in taste and judgment, gullibility and manipulation, moments of unbelievable clarity and invention, pleasure, fun, vulgarity, excess, novelty and utter enervation."[2] The only problem with this list is that "terrible junk" is seen as antithetical to "good ideas." At the very least, "terrible junk" should be given pride of place at the head of the other negative objects. "Terrible junk" often—not always by a long shot, which is one reason rock criticism is so much fun to read and write (basically, the critic's job is to explain why a disc is fabulous trash, terrible junk, or mediocre rubbish)—enlivens those good ideas and often can't be distinguished from them. When that happens, the result is no longer terrible but terrific.

Many standouts of rock endure because their disposability impresses everyone. "Ninety-six Tears" (? and the Mysterians) and "Louie Louie" (the Kingsmen) are two classic examples. At the same time, the worst rock music vanishes without a trace because it stinks. But what about masterworks celebrated for flawless design, smooth execution, and rich content? Commentary about rock 'n' roll must account for the finished beauty of albums such as Beck's *Odelay*, Pink Floyd's *Dark Side of the Moon*, Love's *Forever Changes*, and Bruce Springsteen's *Born to Run* and singles such as Richard Harris's "MacArthur Park" and the Beach Boys' "Good Vibrations," all highly produced recordings. Commentary must also explain the appeal of rough-hewn albums such as Beat Happening's *You Turn Me On*, Bikini Kill's *Pussy Whipped*, Neil Young's *Tonight's the Night*, and the Stooges' *Fun House* and songs such as the Velvet Underground's "Sister Ray" and Fairport Convention's "A Sailor's Life," all one-off productions by performers who clouded distinctions between neophyte and master. Bridging the two extremes of the polished and the raw, the professional and the amateur, the slick and the sloppy, the fabulous and the terrible, is the trope of trash.

Between these extremes lies the clue to why rock critics and fans can't do without the trash trope. The figure is often the only thing that makes sense when there's nothing else to say about a group or a recording. The music doesn't even have to be recorded. Trashing can occur without bothering to take intermediate steps of securing good sound representation. Legions of trashy garage bands have proved that instantly forgettable yet sometimes fantastic music can be cranked out by kids rehearsing next to garbage cans in suburban garages all across the land. No wonder the qualifier *trash* has long pervaded rock 'n' roll criticism. The metaphor and the music are interchangeable.

An informal syllogism has emerged. *Major premise:* Above and beyond all nation-states in documented history, modern America wastes, trashes, and disposes. *Minor premise:* Modern America produces rock 'n' roll in quantities so vast as to frustrate any consumer who tries to keep pace with new releases in any one of rock's hundreds of subgenres. *Conclusion:* Because waste imbues our culture, it also imbues rock 'n' roll music, which is the soundtrack of the unfettered consumerism responsible for this waste. Therefore, rock 'n' roll is the art of waste. It would be unusual if tropes, conceptualizations, and images of trash didn't pervade the discourse of this art of waste. To understand what gives rock music much of its vitality and meaning, we must rummage through these tropes and images of trash, pick out some in relation to the artifact, and scrutinize trope and artifact in terms of the consumer's acceptance or rejection of the artifact or the critic's estimation of it.

To put it another way: Insofar as rock 'n' roll reflects American values, it's interwoven with, first, the vices of acquisitiveness and extravagance that produce mind-numbing amounts of waste, garbage, trash, and rubbish, and with, second, the virtues of individualism, rebellion, self-expression, youthfulness, and simple fun. Time and time again, in book after book, in museums and movies, in television specials and tribute albums, rock's virtues have been showcased, documented, disseminated, and celebrated. A study of rock-trash, a virtue concealed as a vice (and vice versa), is, however, long overdue. The results of the effort will show a compelling reason to analyze the correlation between trash as a literal fact pervading life in America and trash as a multivalent metaphor finding a haven in rock 'n' roll music.

7. Big Yellow Taxi

It should have been obvious to fans from the moment the first compact disc showed up in the corner record store—obvious enough to cause earth-friendly citizens to denounce and boycott the medium right away—that this flat circular thing is stored in a case that *much more than is necessary* exceeds in weight and size the magic disc itself. (The same disproportion isn't true of long-play albums, 45s, and cassettes.) When all is said and done, to buy units of rock music is to buy excess plastic and thus to contribute to the waste disposal problem.[1] Strasser's model of one-way flow applies to rock because this music is essentially sold through the medium of compact discs packaged in "jewel boxes." Rock is more than just the soundtrack of modern life played back on boom boxes, stereo speakers, mall sound systems, automotive rigs, and television sets. It's more than just an abstraction or pleasant diversion. It's more than entertainment, more than art. Or perhaps it's less than all these things combined. Because before it can be cued up on a carousel, accessed on a radio, or downloaded off a Web site, popular music must be recorded on plastic discs duplicated and distributed by the millions. How many millions? In the year 2000, global sales of full-length music compact discs surpassed 800 million units; singles totaled about forty million units.[2] During the past twenty years, billions of compact music discs have been manufactured, and untold millions of these have been discarded. Annually, more than a billion jewel boxes are manufactured to house the two-ounce discs.[3] Presumably, the pleasure derived from rock 'n' roll music is so great that its fans don't stop to gauge its materiality, thus its disposability, thus its impact on the environment.

It's easy to grumble about the waste produced by compact discs, but to be fair it should be stressed that in their heyday vinyl LPs generated their fair share of dead weight. By 1979, just on the cusp of the digital coup, record companies habitually flooded the market with vinyl, hoping that saturation would pay off in a higher yield of platinum certifications, creating an impression of an album's success and increasing sales. Even though many titles shipped platinum, they didn't sell platinum, and unsold units came back by the hundreds of thousands. It was noted at the time that "[a]verage returns rates in the industry were given at about 25% of shipments, with as many as 200 million units in the returns system at any one time."[4] The big companies soon stopped accepting returns, which in turn meant stores started to stock fewer titles—the financial risk was all theirs now—which to this day makes it hard for the vinyl collector to find the album he wants in a store packed to the ceiling with compact discs.

If only the problem were limited to solid waste. Carbon emissions are involved too. A bulletin released late in 2001 by Global Environmental Change calculates the emission of 2.2 pounds of CO_2 in the manufacture and sale of every compact disc. Annually, take one billion discs, multiply by 2.2 . . . the math is easy. The GEC bulletin cites *Echoes: The Best of Pink Floyd* (2001, projected sales: a minimum of four million units) as an example of rock's effect on global warming:

> The full lifecycle of CD production is taken into account when figuring CO_2 emissions, from the energy used by the band in the recording studio to the shipping of the master to the manufacturing plant, the manufacturing process itself, packaging, and distribution to record stores. Even the lighting of the retail stores is accounted for, as is the distance an average fan travels to the store to purchase the CD (seven miles) and the electricity used by that fan listening to the product for five years.[5]

Celestial Harmonies, a New Age label based in Tucson, Arizona, has instituted an earth-friendly approach to minimize waste. Printed on the program guides of its compact discs, the company's policy "demonstrates . . . unwavering support of responsible environmental behavior" in regard to its artists and patrons: "Our environmental mission [is] to engage in innovative, environmentally-conscious practices in all elements of our production, packaging, distribution, and other operations, and"—this stipulation shows much courage and commitment—"to record artists whose environmental views are in accord with responsible environmental behavior." The label uses recyclable plastic; duo-boxes for two-fers, which reduces volume by 60 percent and weight by 25 percent; "slim-line" boxes for singles, which saves 34 percent in weight; recyclable paper in all corporate matters; and nontoxic vegetable inks—illustrious examples of "safer, less wasteful means of packaging."[6] Other record companies don't follow suit for two reasons: cost and efficiency.

In the digital dawn, the mideighties, the connection between trash and digital recording was more overt than it is today. Ostensibly for security and protective purposes, most compact discs came wrapped up in one of two modes, either a thick transparent plastic sheath that to open required a utility knife or pair of scissors, or a cardboard "long box" remarkable for doing nothing else but doubling the size of the merchandise within it. Long boxes were also defended as functional insofar as they helped record stores display compact discs in the same racks that had held albums. Two long boxes equaled an LP's height and width. In any event, the discs were compact while their packages were hard-to-open bulk. Brave new worlds have trade-offs with old ones. Excess trash was one trade-off. Another was sound quality. When compact discs hit the shelves, they impressed music lovers fed up with the warp, wow, flutter, and distortion of skipping and popping long-play records revolving on temperamental turntables. Aside from audiophiles who huffed that digital sound waves were dry, harsh, sterile, and chilly—"Many [such recordings] were a disgrace," wrote David Denby, "steely, cold, unresonant, lacking warmth and naturalness"—the vast majority embraced compact discs.[7] Digital discs staged their coup against analog platters and seized power within what now seems like a few weeks back when Ronald Reagan presided over the land.

Despite digital infatuation, a bloc of consumers soon became vocal about bad packaging, and a controversy was born. In 1989, 200 million compact discs were sold in America. That same year the long boxes in which they were packaged became, according to Michael Goldberg, twenty million pounds of nonrecyclable garbage.[8] In 1990, the number of compact discs sold domestically jumped to 286 million, resulting in a proportionate amount of cardboard waste.[9] The Ban the Box movement that peaked in the early 1990s saved all that trash—that is, the reforms saved the 157,276 trees (Goldberg's statistic) harvested annually for the cosmetic and antishoplift design inhering in the long box.[10] But during the phase-out period of long boxes, efforts to recycle them weren't a priority for most big chains if we can judge by a report published in *Billboard* as late as 1993. It stated that an employee at Tower Records in New York City "indicated [that] the bags full of cardboard waste sitting on the floor . . . were going straight to the garbage."[11]

It should be stressed that long boxes may be in disfavor but they're not extinct. In the fall of 2001, I purchased the Johnny Mathis Christmas album (for $6.49) at a Sam's Club superstore. Like every other compact disc on display, this one was packaged in a long box (as they continue to be and presumably always have been). As if consumers have learned nothing from the long box debacle, millions of digital video discs are sold in long boxes. Worse, the plastic case surrounding a DVD far exceeds the content of a compact disc's jewel box. Six or seven DVDs could be molded from the case in which, say, *The French Connection*'s two discs are stored.

Despite making improvements in packaging, the recording industry still faces at least two unhappy truths ten years after settling on a more streamlined unit of sale. First, jewel boxes, which are nearly as hateful to open and as wasteful as long boxes were, remain the packaging norm. In 1996, Dave Stein, Reprise's vice president of stateside sales, said he was opposed to paper packaging "probably for the same reason other execs are—it's just a pain in the ass." It's a pain in the ass because paper/cardboard containers are harder to fit into racks, require more specialization in design, tear or bend at the edges, and, bottom line, are more expensive to manufacture—thirty to sixty cents more for a paper case than a plastic one.[12] Second, not all compact discs that reach wholesale warehouses and retail store shelves are sold. Wolfgang Spahr discovered that a full 10 percent of PolyGram's "entire production of its CD plant [in 1993 was] expected to come back as rejects or returns." Because "the level of environmental consciousness in Germany is very high, and all industries are under government pressure to minimize waste and pollution," PolyGram recycled the material in new packaging, hoping to reduce waste by 50 percent.[13]

An anonymous Heloise sensitive to digital waste offers tips to consumers burdened with unwanted CDs. String them together to make a digital version of a bead curtain. Hang them in the garden to frighten birds. Place them under furniture legs. Shape them into Frisbees by centering a disc in a cereal bowl, stacking six more bowls above the disc, and heating everything in an oven for twenty minutes. Home improvement nuts can notch the edges of undesired discs and use the altered unit as a circular blade for cutting balsa wood and Styrofoam.[14] Now, while creative consumers can do what they like with hated discs, record manufacturers don't have that luxury. They must eat the costs, of course, and then dispose of the millions of units that are annually returned to their distributors. In 1991, *Billboard* reported that unsold, unpackaged compact discs destined for landfills would amount to 600 million units (twenty million pounds) by the year 2000.[15] Two years later *Billboard* reported that only a fraction of these unsold discs ended up at a recycling processor in Atlanta, Georgia, which was taking in one hundred thousand pounds of scrap compact discs per month. The industry was busy pursuing "methods of reducing landfill waste from rejected or returned discs and jewel boxes . . . at a number of manufacturing facilities" in Europe and the United States.[16] Typically, recycled remains are put into circular service, fueling the production of more disc cases and disc trays. Ground-up discs and trays are also used to produce an item unrelated to music: asphalt.

A strange state of affairs! At considerable expense—on average, fifty to one hundred dollars per hour—musicians record seventy-five minutes of original material in their local studio (conservative estimate, twenty hours), then add vocal overdubs (another several hours), mix everything (five to ten hours), and master the finished work, which is transferred digitally from the master tape to a bright silver disc, which is then reproduced in increments of one thousand, packaged, and sold (or at least offered for sale) in a plastic case that breaks (or comes already broken) at the hinge or in the splayed center ring.[17] If this merchandise doesn't appeal to the demographic base targeted by the band and its management, then the unsold inventory is *sometimes* sold in bulk, for pennies a pound, along with crates full of other rejects, as scrap to an industrial processor belching out toxic smoke in Georgia, North Carolina, Indiana, or Germany. At these plants huge machines crush and grind truckloads of compact discs and their cases, after which the pulverized plastic is refashioned into asphalt. It's hauled away and steamrolled into place. At any given moment our motor vehicles might be cruising or parked on top of the remnants of an artistic endeavor rendered digital.

Long live rock!

8. Over and Over

When one listens to rock music, two questions invariably arise: Is it garbage—disposable, not worth a second more of my time, bad? Or is it art—durable, worth "burning" or buying, good? What I'd like to explore now are the implications of the paradox that the answer to each of these questions—garbage? art?—can be and much of the time is yes. Whereas logicians might insist on the mutual exclusiveness of such a proposition, students of rock 'n' roll see no fallacy at all.

Let's begin at the bottom/top to illustrate the arbitrariness of the garbage/art dichotomy. Frank Zappa reportedly said that the Shaggs are greater than the Beatles. (Zappa, incidentally, has toyed with the trope of trash to describe his own forays into avant-art rock. A promotional poster for *Absolutely Free* boosts an album that is "Hateful, Repugnant & A Waste of Money."[1]) Many other rockers and rock fans have been content simply to applaud the uniqueness of the Shaggs.[2] The *who?* That few people have heard, or heard of, the Shaggs, or that the Shaggs couldn't sing in tune, couldn't play in tune (or play at all), couldn't write a melody, and couldn't begin to construct records such as *Rubber Soul* or *A Hard Day's Night*—in sum, that the Shaggs were an incompetent rock outfit doesn't necessarily render Zappa's assertion, that the Shaggs are greater than the Beatles, untenable or perverse. An expert on "outsider music," Irwin Chuswid suggests that the Shaggs were marvelous despite and because of the "[h]acked-at chords, missed downbeats, out-of-socket transitions, blown accents, and accidental convergences" on 1969's *Philosophy of the World*.[3] The sisters Shagg—Dorothy, Helen, and Betty Higgins—were fantastically good at being spellbindingly bad and their one album placed them apart, far apart, not from their peers (for they're peerless) but from every other rock 'n' roll combo that ever taped a track or played a dance in a town hall on a Saturday night. Like the Beatles, the Shaggs are incomparable, a category unto themselves. What makes the Beatles/Shaggs comparison possible if not inevitable is that rock 'n' roll, vacillating as it does between silliness and gravity, ribaldry and innocence, and anguish and effervescence, is marked by a sensibility and suffused with a soul that in tandem pivot on the push-pull forces of disposability and durability. The best rock simultaneously achieves a synthesis of evanescent junk and lasting beauty and sets up a conflict between them. The worst rock is just garbage.

Garbage? Art? Robert Christgau implies that to fans listening to lyrics the answer doesn't matter. Then he yanks the trash trope out of his hat to say something profound about rock's transformative power. "People just identify; they don't analyze," he writes, adding,

> But what happens when someone finds that the banal song situation is *his life*? He listens to every word. Suddenly all that waste verbiage becomes immensely powerful, almost by accident, and the power is real, only it resides in the perceiver rather than in what is perceived. And is that Art? The perceiver doesn't much care.[4]

That Jimmy Guterman and Owen O'Donnell rate Billy Joel the worst rock 'n' roller of all time doesn't alter the fact that Joel's multiplatinum sales have secured him a spot in the stratosphere of rock 'n' roll superstars and that many of his songs are irresistibly hummable and thought provoking, notwithstanding some "soporific ready-mades," some "dense pop pastiches," and the "facile dissection of . . . early sixties pop styles."[5] In other words, that the ditties of Billy Joel, a piano virtuoso and a master songwriter with three greatest-hits albums under his belt, strike some listeners as garbage may partially explain why *The Stranger* and Joel's other albums are addictive to the millions of other people who think he's an Artist and gobble up his records and concert tickets. One could argue the not original idea that this over-the-top performer inspires such immense popularity precisely because he's so good at being bad in some critical but unfathomable way different from the way the Shaggs are bad, and that the masses can't now and never have been able to tell the difference between quality and crap—or, as Edgar Allan Poe puts it, "The dogma . . . is absurdly false, that the popularity of a work is *primâ facie* evidence of its excellence in some respects; that is to say, the dogma is false if we confine the meaning of excellence . . . to excellence in an [artistic] sense" because the masses are

guided "by uneducated thought, by uncultivated taste, by unrefined and un-
guided passion."[6]

Rather than belaboring this platitude and the related point that aesthetic ab-
solutes don't and never did exist, I want to focus on the trash trope. To understand the role of trash in the art that enriched Billy Joel and the Beatles (but
not the Shaggs) is to understand that as a figure of speech it's equally capable of
undermining and reaffirming conventional ideas of excellence and inferiority.
For this reason I will at no point offer a list, a flourishing industry these days,
of the one hundred best rock albums or singles of the year, the decade, or the
millennium. Such lists make plenty of marketing sense and have the secondary
benefit of offering quick history lessons to viewers or readers unfamiliar with
"the classics." Meanwhile, people familiar with most or all of the records on a
survey enjoy disagreeing with the compiler's bad choices and agreeing with the
good ones. At worst a list's rankings flatter a reader's taste and at best compel
him to establish it by inviting him to challenge the judgment of a self-appointed
authority. In the process of identifying a canon of must-hear discs, lists and critics' polls beg the question of prioritization. To contend, as VH1 has done, that
the greatest rock long-play ever made is *Revolver* doesn't explain why the top
disc isn't rather *With the Beatles* or the soundtrack to *Yellow Submarine*, not
to mention another disc by another band.[7] *Revolver* is indeed magnificent; but
how can a listener who hasn't heard anything else, or anything at all, by the
Beatles judge it against those other two records or for that matter against every
other record on the poll by, and not by, the Fab Four? To those who believe
there's no such thing as Best-Ever, best-of surveys will always seem amusing but
naive, entertaining but trivial, at best expedient and at worst insidious.

It would seem that superlatives such as best, worst, great, and awful, as well
as other qualifiers, demand a definition or rubric—either that or we risk dilut-
ing the argument with subjectivity and hyperbole. But even after centuries of
literary criticism commencing with Plato's *Republic,* no absolute rubric exists
or is universally accepted for any art form and thus won't be found in the these
pages. Although they may seem to indicate an unassailable opinion (for example, "That Sex Pistols song is trash and should be banned!" screams an outraged
father in 1977), the qualifiers *garbage* and *trash* are neither signs existing in a
pre-Derridean utopia of linguistic transcendence, nor concepts dwelling in a
Platonic cosmos of stable aesthetic forms, nor terms petrified in the amber of an
Aristotelian handbook of criticism. Granted, standards of good and bad are either implied or expressed throughout *But Is It Garbage?* At the same time, however, these standards are irrelevant except to the extent that the reader's judgments either clash or conform with my own or with those of the sources I cite,
and that they have been contextualized sufficiently in relation to the reader's

own system for determining value. Happily for all concerned, no one is right, no one is wrong, and a splendid time is guaranteed for all.

9. Bad Boy

One rock 'n' roll writer for whom *trash, garbage, junk,* and other signifiers of waste are indispensable tools of the "rockwrite" trade is Richard Meltzer. "[W]hat's better/worse than utter trash?" he asks in what I deem the most profound rhetorical question in rock 'n' roll history because it paralyzes logic and forces us to take a leap of faith into the embrace of contradiction.[1] It's also the most unnerving question because it begs all other questions that can possibly be answered as one assesses the value of rock 'n' roll music. Savvy readers and record collectors can intuit the answer to Meltzer's question; beyond that, it eludes verbal expression. Nothing? Everything? Each? All? The Beatles? The Shaggs? Rock is dead? *Their Satanic Majesties Request? Self Portrait? Wild Life? Having Fun with Elvis on Stage?*[2] Meltzer's question is a koan presented to those of us who care about rock but who don't care to justify their judgments of records they hate or love, which is to say that those who care about rock can answer it best by inserting a compact disc and asking the questioner to leave the room. The answer is crystal clear, so clear that it can't be represented in language. Richard Meltzer's appeal lies in the fact that he nevertheless tries to do just that—to decode the crux of the koan—in idiosyncratic essays that sometimes make about as much sense as an electric guitar placed in front of an amplifier whose volume knob has been turned to ten. In other words, perfect sense. He has written hundreds of thousands of words in response to a question the inquirer doesn't try to settle to the satisfaction of literal-minded readers who wish the man would just call a record good or bad and give clear reasons why. Usually Meltzer's wild words can be contradicted by whatever serious or flippant answer someone else chooses as rebuttal. In rock music there are no absolute terms other than the words *garbage, trash,* and the like—and they *seem* absolute but aren't because when bandied about without much discrimination they distil all critical discourse into one warm hum, the rock 'n' roll counterpart of the sacred utterance "Om." Ineluctably, Meltzer's entanglements with his own koan require that a stream of trash flow through his profiles, memoirs, character killings, rantings, and reviews.

For example, in an early essay entitled "A Very Important Person" Meltzer trashes the album *Inside Bert Sommer* by Bert Sommer. This little-known musician performed on opening day—"pass-the-trash day," Meltzer sneers—at the Woodstock Festival made legendary by the appearance of so many superstars.

Going for the kill, Meltzer asks, "What's the worst thing on the disc? They're *all* the worst!" With one exception: "Tied for 6th worst is 'It's a Beautiful Day' and 'We're All in the Same Band.' There is no 7th worst because the tie eliminates that."[3] Sometimes Meltzer's sarcasm is a little less direct—pass-the-trash day!—and sometimes his syntax stumbles along like a drunken man with broken ankles being jostled by a crowd in a subway station at rush hour. Meltzer leads off a piece on John Lennon, dated 1973, with waste and garbage flying:

> John Lennon continues to waste his time being a waste of time in N.Y.C. . . . [He and Yoko] stunk up the city with their beef & kidney pies for far (far far far) too long. . . . Like at the Xmas party Mercury threw in '72. . . . Nothing was edible on account of proximity to the limey fish (smells like stuff a dying cat wouldn't eat out of a garbage can) but now we can breathe easier with the Lennon-Onos headed back to the United Kingdom where they belong.

Their departure, Meltzer happily reports, will leave local talent the chance to put out some "good shit."[4] Presumably, the Lennons put out bad shit.

Ten years later, eyeing rock videos in a piece called "Merde . . . Turd . . . Vomit," Meltzer again figures rock in terms of bodily excretion. He ponders Music Television's impact on the youngsters who would eventually be labeled the deadbeats of Generation X. Garbage is added to the vomit and shit: "Could be a lie but so far MTV's apparently getting sizable nos. of asskids to again start purchasing vinyl garbage in nos. commensurate with what radio used t' be able t' generate." Meltzer is irritated that the music being peddled through videos is worthless, "it no longer MATTERING that same [MTV's programming] sucks scrotum poop off a dead rat's mother. (I.e., make a rock vid of scrotum poop pop POO and asskids will consume it f'r breakfast.)"[5] The scatological imagery interests me less than does the allusion to "vinyl garbage" and not because it's less offensive. *Garbage* in this context is offensive enough. Most of the time Meltzer trashes, not shits or vomits on, rock music and musicians, and the MTV eighties served up plenty of easy targets.

Even his enemies would have trouble accusing Meltzer of false pride. As a handler of trash and garbage, he's willing when necessary to soil himself with the trope, sometimes humorously, as when he divulges that Robert Christgau, his editor at the *Village Voice,* considered him "anti-intellectual trash! scum!—and a college graduate yet—akin to being a Commie or a junkie (or a rock and roller) in those dark, dark (oooh) Eisenhower '50s." Meltzer deploys self-deprecation as a weapon to mock the enemies of True Rock. In 1985 he fretted about the pressure from record companies that force "writefolk trash" to "abdicate our Responsibility, that of *being* rock & roll, and accede toot sweet to our first official 'duty,' that of SHILLING for the bastards by keeping the urgency down."

Meltzer's probity caused him to characterize most rock 'n' roll music after 1970 as trash. Record congloms and trade magazines don't thrive on bad reviews by soothsayers such as Meltzer. Good rock reviews abet the profits that underwrite the in-crowd's high life. Marketers and publicists don't need some wise guy with a sixties grudge telling impressionable readers how much the latest batch of releases by corporate stooges stinks. "The bulk of current sonic fodder is (dare it be said) more ephemeral than ever": an attitude like this doesn't help to shift units.[6] If it's ephemeral, it's disposable, it's trash.

In "Vinyl Reckoning," a "valedictory address" and "deathbed blather" concerning the author's disposal of long-play albums despite his conviction that "pre-digital rock ALWAYS sounds superior" to compact discs, Meltzer plays the trash motif like an aging violin virtuoso knocking off variations by Paganini. Early in the piece, he lays down an essential truth about rock 'n' roll and the album collections that many people have amassed over the years:

> At the absolute height of my collectional zeal, bloated by too many years on the promo-album dole, my LP stash numbered in the THOUSANDS. . . . But even among those eminently playable, there isn't that much turntable action. (I also have, oh, at least a thousand CDs—so what's new? My acquisitiveness appears undiminished.)
>
> Thousands down to hundreds—for all the fine and stupid reasons I or you or anyone periodically tosses stuff. Every time it seems like I've hit rock-bottom, nothing left to toss, it turns out there's another item or five to weed out. In any case, it feels *mandatory* to regularly check the stack, and rarely if ever is playability, alone, a criterion.[7]

Record albums must be thrown away. (And compact discs, manufactured to last "a lifetime" under normal use, also need weeding out occasionally.)[8] It's their nature. And yet we resist the urge to throw them away, to give them away, to barter them, or to sell them. Why? Aside from the familiar reasons—*I might fix or replace that broken turntable someday; my albums will always remind me of my youth; I can't get a decent price for them; there's at least one good song and one good guitar solo even on the dullest record; the covers are great; digital stinks; I actually play them sometimes*—it's because there exists "even in their DISPOSABILITY, a residuum of sonic potential: records as Frisbees—the adventitious sounds of flight and smackup."[9]

Meltzer's valedictory address imparts the flavor of a cynical sage summing up his outlandish creed before he departs a world preferring not to hear truths that must be uttered, that can hardly be denied, and that send a Billy Joel fan into denial. What person building a compact disc library intended to last forever wants to hear that what he has been collecting at eighteen bucks a pop isn't worth keeping? And what record company executive wouldn't want to muzzle Meltzer lest he make some teenagers in a mall think twice before spending money on tunes to which they won't be listening in six months? Rock 'n' roll, whether digital or analog, compact disc (whose vaunted lifespan Meltzer belittles as a "ridiculous metaphor/illusion of indestructibility") or vinyl long-play, is designed and destined to go down the drain, to give up the ghost, to go out with the trash every five years or so. This Meltzer knows: "All culture, certainly all of it built around the sequential offering of product—TV, movies, mags and books, cars, sports, clothing—is about turnover—a truism—but only rock foregrounds and RITU-ALIZES it in extremis. (Roll over, Beethoven . . . roll over, Plastic Bertrand.)"[10] Rock ritualizes turnover. "There is a built-in expendability both of materials and artist," wrote Stuart Hall and Paddy Whannel in the midsixties, long before Meltzer's valediction. "They are designed, one feels, to be here today and gone tomorrow."[11] Rock thrives on throwaways. I would add that it pivots on trash. But it can hardly be easy to come to terms with the thought that the collection one has lovingly and laboriously amassed over the years is disposable matter. Bravely, Meltzer fesses up. A person awakes, he writes, as from the end of a twenty-year dream to find that his stacks of records, cassettes, and now compact discs have become "[t]he disposable, too long undisposed of. All dust in the wind." Neither technological progress nor one's receding hairline (that is, changes in taste) is necessarily the root cause. Being trash, their fate is to be expected.

To finish with Richard Meltzer, the shaman and wild man, the gadfly and seeker, the literary embodiment of this amazing music that came roaring out of Dixie fifty years ago; Meltzer, the self-proclaimed "Curator and Propmaster, Vinyl Division. RECORDS," caught in a rare maudlin mood: "The printed page as recycle bin: pass it on, reassign responsibility for babysitting hotstuff with no ongoing use even as ballast—I'm already topheavy—yet too valuable to treat as mere trash, to relegate to some nameless ideative landfill. . . . Cut me some slack, okay?"[12]

On this day of vinyl reckoning, Meltzer refers not to sackcloth, ashes, and dust but to the junk he wrote about the junk to which he listened and in which he sought pleasure and meaning for forty years. Perhaps too he intimates a standard by which to fashion an honorable life. He asks for some kind of absolution, some "slack," in the face of obsolescent prose about obsolescent rock albums that, though worthless, are somehow, taken together, not "mere trash" after all. "What's better/worse than utter trash?" indeed! There's some garbage a person can't bring himself to discard. Meltzer doesn't want his reflection on trash to be reduced to trash too. At the same time, he knows that everything related to rock 'n' roll ends up either recycled or buried in a landfill, "ideative" or otherwise, the site of a trashy immortality. It's where he's headed too, along with his discarded albums as well as the ones he intends to keep, but not where he wants to be.

10. It's All Too Much

One of Richard Meltzer's comrades was Lester Bangs, who died, his constitution weakened by years of alcohol and substance abuse, at the age of thirty-three in 1982. Despite being, or more likely because he was, the paradigm of "human waste" peculiar to many rock 'n' roll celebrities, Bangs could see and smell rock trash a mile away. Bangs could sniff out the subtle differences between great and gross garbage, and he didn't hesitate to back up his nose's conclusion. By turns obnoxious and oracular, Bangs drove his prose the way a good rhythm guitarist whips his band into a groove, the way a good lead guitarist fractures the universe in a fleet-fingered solo, the way a good drummer pounds the right pulse through the infinite permutations of time: relentlessly, with no backward glance at a measure, verse, chord, or critic, and with an eye focused on consummating the rock 'n' roll moment. Beyond being unconventional expressions of unconventional opinion, Lester's strongest essays resemble rare rock 'n' roll performances where the listener cares less about clarity or high fidelity or about what's "said" than about what's played and how it's played, a holistic impact that momentarily stifles analysis and is never forgotten. I remember Dylan, King Street Theater, Charleston, South Carolina, 1997. Springsteen, Lewiston Armory, Maine, late seventies. MK Ultra (a bar band with a great name and brilliant rhythm section), Benjamin's, Orono, Maine, winter of 1985 . . . stupefying shows. And there was that foursome in Kelly's, a packed college bar in downtown Missoula on a Saturday night in April 2000. Never got their name. The drummer lashed his cymbals and bashed his kit, making the clatter of a train tumbling into a canyon, passengers screaming for priests, freight cars sparking shrieks in broken boulders. The singer added chapters to a black-bile Bible, his lips lapping sweat like drug-drops of sin. Distant in a bardo of funk, the bassist plucked the bottom of the universe while the guitarist ripped notes out of his Les Paul as if performing cesareans. From his fret board came the keen of women, their babies screeching for teat and air. Someone couldn't take it, swung a chair.

I remember each band's moving wall of sound, the form-fitted impact of instruments and voices, the paralysis of motor reflex and the blur of sensory pleasure as the spectator's ego was submerged yet not drowned under waves of ferocious but life-affirming rock 'n' roll music. My analogy may be a little farfetched, but Lester Bangs does this kind of thing in his rock-writing. If you can't quite dance to Bangs, and if it's true that he won't make you go deaf, you can nonetheless groove mentally to the rhythms of his syntax and the dynamics of his point of view. You don't take notes on his essays any more than you would take notes on a band whose performance stimulates you from the neck down and dumbfounds you from the chin up. Nor do you care much about Bangs's verdicts, many of which are unclear anyway, which, of course, might be expected in essays written by a person under the influence of some deadly dose of beverage or pill. If it's often hard to decide whether Lester's parodies are paeans or his paeans parodies, this too is to be expected of a writer who lists *The Sounds of the Junkyard* as one of his favorite albums because of its high "wretched squawl" quotient.[1]

In the discourse of the trash trope, Bangs came up with some classic tips. Because he was possessed by rock music, he was deep into its trash, a fact seen implicitly in an essay he wrote about the Count Five of midsixties "Psychotic Reaction" fame. In this piece, written in 1971, Bangs stakes his ground in rock's junkyard: "It wasn't until much later, drowning in the kitschvats of Elton John and James Taylor, that I finally came to realize that grossness was the truest criterion for rock 'n' roll, the cruder the clang and grind the more fun and longer listened-to the album'd be." No wonder Bangs worshipped a pack of snarling midwestern mongrels dubbed the Stooges to whom artists such as Elton John and Taylor (whose recording careers, to do them justice, had just commenced) could only be compared invidiously. This menacing gang of malcontents, Bangs pronounced in 1970, as if conferring a mark of distinction on them for being coarse and obscure, were "not for the ages—nothing created now is."[2]

Note the paradox. Before the decade had fairly begun, Bangs wrapped up the throwaway seventies as personified by the Stooges and Iggy Pop (the band's demented front man): it was precisely because they merchandized disposability that these same four sloppy musicians had succeeded (without selling many records) as masters of the rock idiom. Bangs remarks that "Ig writes some of the best throwaway lines in rock, meaning some of the best *lines* in rock, which is basically a music meant to be tossed over the shoulder and off the wall."[3] In other words, throw away your rock music if you want it to last, and then maybe, just maybe against a thousand nonmusical odds, it will. Proof of Lester's dictum of desirable disposability lies in the scarifying second Stooges album, *Fun House*, a recording every bit as savage, untutored, desperate, and naked as anything to emerge during punk rock's imminent heyday. *Fun House* has lasted. Available since 2000 as a six-disc box set are the complete sessions from which was plucked the running order of the original seven-song forty-minute album. One hundred and forty-two tracks, nearly eight hours in duration, all but seven thrown away for thirty years! *Fun House* proves that the throwaway line, song, and session should be kept because they may come back as a deluxe box set.

Meanwhile, the dark side of disposability and garbage bothered Bangs. In 1970 he predicted, "I believe that real rock 'n' roll may be on the way out, just like adolescence as a relatively innocent transitional period is on the way out. What we will have instead is a small island of new free music surrounded . . . by a vast sargasso sea of absolute garbage."[4] With the rock 'n' roll universe about to expand in 1970 at an unprecedented rate, Bangs's prediction could be taken as vaticinal failure. The seventies, usually seen as unable to contend with the sixties, would produce many "canonical" bands. Black Sabbath, the Eagles, and the Buckingham-Nicks version of Fleetwood Mac spring to mind, and from the Rolling Stones would come *Sticky Fingers, Exile on Main Street,* and *Some Girls.* In 1970, Bruce Springsteen and Michael Jackson were just around the corner. So were the punks. Then aged thirteen to eighteen, they were learning the chord patterns and lyrics of the Stooges, the Velvet Underground, and the MC5 and getting ready to save the world from the pretensions of art rock, the self-absorption of singer-songwriter rock, the bombast of arena rock, and the stupidity of disco. They would soon perfect what one musicologist, echoing Lester's use of the trash trope ten years earlier, called "the strident, nasal, throw-away lines that [were] both a scream of aggression and a scream for help."[5] Clearly, Bangs's "real rock 'n' roll" was primed for a resurgence—albeit a brief one, followed by another fallow period in the eighties, then another fertile one in the nineties—and yet his prophecy was vague enough to allow for plenty of "real" rock before the prophecy came to pass. (His "small island of new free music surrounded" corresponds to what is presently an archipelago of cross-continental indie bands.) There's no more solid evidence that rock was "on the way out" in 1970 than that punk would soon be biting at the heels of the hacks with guitars and at the throats of the big bad corporations bloating themselves on the profits of *not* real rock 'n' roll. But we must remember that the golden age of punk rock (c. 1977–80) passed about as quickly as did the golden age of rock 'n' roll (c. 1955–59) and that most of that punk music was dumped straight into Bangs's polluted Sargasso Sea, where it sank straight to the bottom undetected and unmourned. Most punk rockers at their best played at a level far beneath that of the so-called "dinosaur bands" of the seventies (the Who, the Kinks, Pink Floyd, Led Zeppelin, the Rolling Stones) at their worst. In the discussion of trash and waste, the subject of rock 'n' roll's death is crucial. It will be reviewed in the second part. For now it's enough to emphasize Lester's portrayal of the transience of rock music in terms of a vast sea of garbage, surely one of the most powerful metaphors in rock criticism.

Nearing the end of his short life, Bangs, his standard still held high like Tashtego's flag over the sinking *Pequod,* harnessed the trash trope again, lamenting "all the wretched excess that's being marketed disguised as its diametrical opposite" and the "worthless swill" to which entertainment had been reduced.[6] By "swill" he meant product made by the obvious candidates, Chicago, Linda Ronstadt, Boston, REO Speedwagon, Styx, and so forth. Although no one is constrained to insist on the correctness of the opinions of Lester Bangs, it's safe to assume the disappointment caused by the failure of postfifties rock 'n' roll to live up to its initial promise and glorious past drove him, along with Richard Meltzer, to extreme applications of rhetorical trash. Few writers have smeared the music these two critics loved and hated better than they themselves did as the most effective way of putting what rock had become where it belonged: into a rhetorical Dumpster heaped and reeking with vinyl, digital, and celluloid garbage.

We've only reached Lester Bangs but have already amassed ample evidence that the aesthetics of trash is anything but one-dimensional. Without question, for Bangs *garbage* was a fluid signifier. Iggy and the Stooges are good garbage; Elton John and James Taylor are bad garbage. When pondering Lou Reed, the rock star he loved more than any other to hate, Bangs doesn't make it clear if it's Reed's great or Reed's terrible garbage (no in-between with Reed) that makes him a great rocker or for that matter an exasperating one. (It's a huge loss to music criticism that Bangs missed out on everything Reed recorded after 1982. Lester's reviews of Reed might have been more entertaining than Reed's eighties recordings.) Because Bangs's compadre Meltzer understands rock 'n' roll, this latter gadfly understands the contradiction voiced so well by the former. Meltzer is self-confident enough to concede that his articles in the *Village Voice* are "claptrap," "shit," "garbage," and "crap," but this doesn't mean they're bad: "Hey, I'm not saying this junk isn't 'good'—it's veryveryverygood."[7] It's good because it's innovative, provocative, obscene, obnoxious, shocking, smart, and sui generis, reflecting the uncorrupted yet trashy soul of the music itself.

Cultivating a trashy soul and sound may be a smart artistic goal. The Litter, remembered for their midsixties prepunk ditty "Action Woman," figured out this paradox and so developed a strategy to express it. They selected "a name to reflect their dirty, trashy image" and then sought to become the "loudest, meanest band in the area."[8] In his introduction to the four-disc *Nuggets* compilation, which includes "Action Woman," Greg Shaw touches on the polarities of greatness and garbage: "What we have here is the quintessence of what could, with justification (and a brief disclaimer or two), be called the coolest period in rock 'n' roll's long history." Rounded up on *Nuggets* are waxings by the Brogues, the Chocolate Watch Band, the Night Crawlers, the Hombres, the Leaves, the Barbarians, the Brigands, the Standells, the Remains, and a hundred more nonhousehold names, all-American bands who, though for the most part hustling their repertoire in regional obscurity, added at least one, sometimes three or four trash classics to the rock canon. "But for every work of genius," Shaw advises, "there were a hundred cases of misguided, pompous, overwrought malarkey, which eventually brought garage punk to a grinding halt."[9] The connoisseur of rock 'n' roll is, like an enologist sipping two goblets of French vintage, able to tell why "Run, Run, Run" by the Third Rail deserves a place on *Nuggets* while "She's Gone" by the Dovers doesn't (their "What Am I Going to Do" makes the cut instead). The metaphor of discrimination that best works for rock, however, isn't something aromatic and tasteful like French burgundy selected from the cellars of the Four Seasons to please the finest palette, but something seamy and disposable like American "malarkey" or garbage recorded at a local studio in one take by four teenagers in Minnesota or Oregon in 1966.

The rock biographer Philip Norman (his subjects include Buddy Holly, the Beatles, and the Rolling Stones) also understands the difference between good and bad garbage: "Teenagers [during the 1950s] bought records to dance to, not listen to, which explains why so many primal rock 'n' roll classics, if not pure gibberish, were simple declarations of how mind-explodingly wonderful the music itself was." "Mind-explodingly wonderful"—this phrase from a writer not known for purple prose or hyperbole. Sticking with the "gibberish" motif, Norman writes, "For hardcore rock 'n' roll fans, the highlight [of the film *The Girl Can't Help It*] was [Gene] Vincent performing a piece of sublime gibberish called 'Be-Bop-A-Lula.'"[10] The "sublime" denotes the awe, grandeur, elevation of soul, and romantic effusion a person feels when beholding nature's magnificence. Even allowing for some modification over time—it's an eighteenth century concept that hasn't aged well in our virtual society—*sublime* is meant to describe natural sites such as the Grand Canyon and Niagara Falls, mind-bending man-made edifices such as the Pyramids of Egypt and the (ever-missed) Twin Towers of the World Trade Center, or towering works of art such as Bach's *St. Matthew Passion*, Beethoven's ninth symphony, and Michelangelo's *David*—not a pop tune. Norman co-opts the word and concept to elevate a vulgar art form because he knows that rock 'n' roll music untouched by sublime nonsense, and just as often by sublime ineptitude on instruments, is unimaginable. Needless to say, Norman, a fan's fan, will not apologize for rock's vulgarity or rein in the big modifiers when overstatement is one's last resort. The music is too much for words, especially tame ones.

Norman isn't alone. Vivid images of trash and waste circulate throughout rock criticism. Writing about a cornerstone of sublime gibberish in the rock repertoire, Mike Stax finds the "timeless appeal" of the Kingsmen's "Louie Louie" to lie "in the sloppy spontaneity of the performance. . . . [It] exemplifies the perfection of imperfection: a simple, almost retarded three-note riff; slamming, lead-foot drumbeat; and lyrics so slurred and nonsensical that some lines were interpreted as pornographic."[11] The human rock encyclopedia Ira Robbins takes the scatological route when he congratulates the band Weezer for perfecting "the art of pissing on itself, both embodying and renouncing the ethos of pop in one sly strum." Their eponymous album "is something of a '90s marker, a deliciously entertaining piece of crap that floats in the punchbowl like a rare jewel."[12] Drummer Butch Trucks confided to journalist Mikal Gilmore that it was Duane Allman, not Eric Clapton, who contrived the signature phrase that announces the tour de force "Layla." Gilmore translates the significance of this achievement: "The most revelatory riff of Eric Clapton's career was actually one of Duane Allman's inspired throwaway lines."[13] Regarding the 1954 smash hit "Sh-Boom" by the Chords, historian James Miller remarks that it "sounded like gibberish, but the song had a crazy bounce and it felt *great*." Then the gibberish degenerated. Their next release, moans Miller, was "a contrived piece of junk called 'Zippity Zum,'" which "flopped."[14] In rock 'n' roll music, throwaways are likely to be inspired, imperfection can be perfect, crap can resemble a jewel, and gibberish can ensure a song's immortality or sink it instantly into oblivion. Theodore Gracyk validates what I felt as a preteen grimacing to the screech of skidding motorcycle wheels and mangled metal in "The Leader of the Pack" by the Shangri-Las—that this two-minute tearjerker was, is, and will forever be "gloriously trashy." On the other hand, Gracyk writes off Linda Ronstadt's *Mad Love* album as "a piece of junk."[15] That is, the record is ungloriously trashy. Tom Carson thinks the Rolling Stones, declining in the midseventies with their designer-drug jet-set funk, got it back together on the album *Some Girls* because "[t]hey had remembered trash."[16] Robert Christgau valorizes trash in his remarks on the Dave Clark Five's British Invasion hit "Bits and Pieces." This stomping number is "a wonderfully serviceable rock throwaway, raucous and meaningless, perfect for shouting into the night."[17] Another two minutes of sublime gibberish and glorious trash, rock as garbage and garbage as art.

11. Graceland

Whereas Philip Norman and Lester Bangs bend the literal meaning of *trash* and its variants, other critics are more consistent in their use of *garbage* as a term of contempt. For such writers "good garbage" is exactly the kind of flummery you might expect from the pens of deviant mavericks and overwrought romantics like Bangs and Norman. Garbage is garbage, period.

Contributors to the *The Rolling Stone Record Guide* (1979) often throw garbage into the faces of recording artists. A Donny Osmond long-play is deep-sixed for being "well-crafted garbage—trash is too elevated a description," an example of how metaphors of garbage can be fine tuned and hierarchized. "Garbage redeemed only slightly by success" is the verdict, which History has sealed, on Tony Orlando's oeuvre (his records used to sell by the zillions).

A long-forgotten band named Ozo released an album of "[p]ost-psychedelic garbage," while a Jim Stafford disc included his sole hit "along with gallons of other garbage." "Gallons" connotes fluid, meaning that garbage comes in both solid and liquid form, another example of the term's multivalence. David Cassidy's *Home Is Where the Heart Is* provokes this jibe: "As a teenage TV rage, Cassidy spewed out mewly crap. This solo LP (his second) attempts to float above that image, but it's strictly a lead zeppelin."[1] Trashy epithets such as these are meant not only to alert readers to the dangers inherent in buying David Cassidy albums but also to amuse those readers who had never given thought to such a purchase in the first place.

An irony in regard to these attacks is that some were written by Dave Marsh, who coedited the *Guide*. Years later in his book-length study of "Louie Louie," Marsh demonstrated that garbage and trash don't always connote garbage dumps and trash cans filled with bad records. "Louie Louie," he asserts, is primitive, half-baked, unhip, unchic, and nonsensical, yet nonetheless it remains timeless, "a genuinely transcendent object." Sure, he admits, it's a "ridiculous, damnable piece of trash." Still, Marsh thinks this worthless three-chord artifact demands a book to explicate its brilliance. Transcendent trash has a way of wreaking havoc with conventional aesthetic codes.

Marsh is the only source cited in these pages who theorizes about the distinction between good and bad trash. Marsh's binaries, to whose analysis he devotes little more than one page, are assigned allegorical names. "Termite Trash" is good because it affirms the Real as it burrows and breathes life into culture, while "Elephant Trash" is bad because it denies the Real as it tramples everything unlike itself. Marsh decides that "rock is now inhabited by [these] two species of trash. . . . At this point, sorting one from the other could be a fulltime job."[2] This sorting is what I do in these pages, using aesthetic terms based on the trash trope rather than Marsh's animal symbolism or pop-psych model (affirmation/denial).

Another collection of rock reviews, these targeting "alternative" bands, is edited and penned (compare Marsh's double role above) largely by Ira Robbins. Aside from being beautifully written, the volumes of *The Trouser Press Record Guide* are encyclopedic and consequently rank among the best sources of information on the underside of rock music that mainstream magazines generally ignore. Garbage pickers will treasure their editions of the *TPRG* as indispensable aids in their search for good and bad throwaways. *Beat Torture* by the Times, a sixties-psychedelic retread band, includes some "notable" cuts, but "too much of the record is halfbaked and disposable." *Gang War*, recorded by Johnny Thunders and Wayne Kramer, two of punk's hoariest hack legends, is marred by such "[t]otally crap sound" and insignificant tunes that it's "a total waste." Robert

Palmer's "Simply Irresistible" is simply a "trashy (and awful) pop hit"—note the writer's care to clarify the type of trash. Adam Ant's *Friend or Foe* is dismissed in eight words: "This may be junk, but it's classy junk."[3] Again, the type of junk—classy now, not awful—must be clarified. J. Mascis of Dinosaur Jr. is charged with creating all kinds of bad sounds summed up in the phrase "slack rubbish," and yet Robbins expresses ambivalence about such rubbishy rock in this passage: "Strumming badly with a wavering sense of rhythm, picking fills like a three-lesson amateur who forgot to practice and generally showing less than no care or concern, Mascis could just as well be any no-talent singing these songs—but he's not." Echoing Marsh's concern that sorting the termites from the elephants is a full-time job, Robbins suspects "[t]here's a lesson about fame and flimsiness in here someplace but it would be too much work to try and think what it might be."[4] This is the Shaggs conundrum continued, that's all.

Which is also to say, it's a lesson pervading decades of commentary on the King of Rock 'n' Roll. Writing in the tradition of literal trashing, the best Roy Carr and Mick Farren can say about Elvis Presley's single "Clean Up Your Own Backyard" from the soundtrack *The Trouble with Girls* is that it "may have been somewhat superior to the sheer rubbish Elvis had crooned in recent movies, but it was still a pale shadow of most of the material this man was now laying down in the studios."[5] Albert Goldman offers a reason for the pale shadows and sheer rubbish. Elvis "would allow the musicians to record the entire soundtrack [of a movie]; then, he'd go into the studio alone, put on the earphones and pour his voice like molasses over the trash that came pouring out of the 'cans.'"[6] These recordings were done by rote, no interaction between singer and session men. Quality control was sacrificed to formula.

Pairing Elvis and trash is natural, like pairing Elvis and Cadillacs. So connected are Elvis and trash that for the cover illustration of her book *The Trash Phenomenon* (2003), Stacey Olster selected Joni Mabe's lithograph *The Official Elvis Prayer Rug* (six identical portraits of the King) even though Olster neither touches rock 'n' roll nor mentions Elvis's name once in a study of trash and popular culture in the "American Century." The King himself sealed the connection between him and trash long before he told an audience in Las Vegas in the early seventies that what the gossip tabloids wrote about him was "pure junk" (lies). Elvis inadvertently links tabloid rumors and dope, strengthening the rumors connecting him to "junk" (drugs). Junked from every direction, Elvis protests his innocence too much:

> So I don't pay any attention to rumors. I don't pay any attention to movie magazines. I don't read them. JUNK. . . . In my case, they make it up. I hear rumors flying around—I got sick in the hospital. In this day and time you can't even get sick. You are [dramatic

pause] *strung out*. By God, I'll tell you something, friend, I have never been—*strung out* in my life, except on music.[7]

Liar.

Because Elvis is the King of Rock and thus the King of America, he's also the King of the Wasteland. Goldman, one trash master feeding off another, jumped on the theme early in his bruising biography of the King. (Nick Tosches on Goldman: "a miserable little wad of failed manhood, gnawing in abject rancor at the crotch of a dead hero [and] driven by self-loathing and greed."[8]) Goldman's description of Colonel Tom Parker's typical breakfast during a Las Vegas engagement doubles as a lecture on the ethics of gluttony and waste. A "prodigious meal" is served to Parker, "the finest fruits . . . costly rib-eye steaks topped with fried eggs; imported cheeses; country ham and bacon; hot biscuits and coffee cake." He takes his pick. He sates himself. He rules the world because he rules Elvis Presley. While the Colonel gorges himself, the fat, drug-deadened King slumbers in his suite, cocooned in fame, heavily guarded, surrounded by books of mysticism. Goldman writes, "When the meal has concluded, at least half the expensive food will be carted back to the kitchen as garbage. The Colonel, like Elvis, is a heroic consumer, a great waster and squanderer, an exemplar of that age now past when every successful, self-made American felt a deep and satisfying compulsion to piss it all away." As with food, so with souvenirs for the fans. Goldman works the trash trope with a mean determination, making of it a tool to lance through blubbery layers of hero worship:

> Originally the scarves [he tossed to the crowd] were authentic items of wardrobe. Then, Elvis realized that it was foolish to throw away anything of value to the fans. So he ordered a load of gaudy rags from a little tailor in Vegas, which he distributes now with princely gestures. . . . He buys a lot of cheap junk, such as Tiger's Eyes, that flash in the stage lights like real gems. The fans assume that the rings must be valuable because Elvis is wearing them. Actually, they're just the tawdry pieces that come with this particular box of Cracker Jack.[9]

Goldman is hardly the last word on the King, not just because his meanness invalidates any claim to objectivity and cancels any sign of humanity. But Goldman got something right, something Elvis's idolaters are in no hurry to see. Because no one threw away more than Elvis did (and to say this isn't to say he didn't give away, in actual gifts to hundreds of acquaintances and in music to billions of human beings, a much greater amount), matching him with trash feels unforced; and it is this, ironically, that makes us more likely to keep him up there on rock 'n' roll's tallest pedestal. Elvis's sublime prodigality makes him less distant, less regal, more recognizable, more human; it brings us closer to him and to the spirit of America he was born to embody. Trashiness humanizes this fantastic caricature flouncing his cape on the stages of Las Vegas or immuring himself in a pharmacy-cum-armory-cum-bedroom in Graceland. The pathos of rock's greatest tragedy lies in the discrepancy between promise and abdication, fulfillment and self-destruction, epic acquisition and prodigious disposability. Greil Marcus traces the inevitable trajectory in Elvis's career and life from fame to drugs to waste. There was "dope, Herculean quantities of it; then sex, orgies, and homemade pornographic videos piled upon fetishes, phobias, and neurotic dysfunction; then violence, a much thinner theme, but including accounts of cruelty, gunfever, and gunplay; then fat, then waste." More than anything else, there was for years just Elvis, always the King, and his squandered genius, his squandered life.

Marcus often defaults to the trope of trash in describing the King's persona, his brilliance as an artist, and his tragic decline. Reacting to Peter Guralnick's praise of performers who can relate to, and therefore reach, their audiences, Marcus argues, "The values that power such a social fact are honesty, sincerity, refusal of ambiguity, loyalty between performer and audience, stoicism, endurance, and dignity—the antithesis of pop trash, sensationalism, irony, persona, frivolousness, or outrage." Marcus implies that few artists in the pop or rock realm have been able to rise above the genre's inherent trashiness. I believe none can. Elvis Presley certainly didn't.

Trash—the word haunts all histories of Elvis Presley. All commentators have had to grapple with it, Marcus included. He tries to defend Elvis's heritage as well as his domestic style. He concedes that tourists to Graceland "have returned with one word to describe what they saw: 'Tacky.' Tacky, garish, tasteless—words others translate as white trash." Nonetheless, Marcus insists "[t]here is not a hint of this in [William] Eggleston's photographs" of the mansion. Marcus's inconsistencies reveal that he toils gamely but in vain to keep Elvis clean, as if Elvis had ever been clean or were better off clean. This effort is found in a sentence of extraordinary defensiveness: "Elvis as white trash . . . will only take you so far into the mystery of why it has been so easy to deflect Elvis's music away from the realm where the music of Bob Dylan, Billie Holiday, Prince, or even Jim Morrison takes on the aura of art, and thus invites thought."[10] This is a prolix way of saying that Elvis's roots have given snobs reason to patronize or tolerate his mysterious appeal.

Regarding the "white trash" reference, I would submit contra Marcus's claim that we should honor Elvis's inherent trashiness if indeed it's this quality above all others that makes it difficult for us to honor his oeuvre with the word *art* or to applaud his ability to make us think. An aura of "white trash" surrounds Elvis because he's at the top of the pile, he rules the heap. Trash is neither a coincidence nor a sign of failure, neither an accident nor a badge of shame. Quite the opposite: in this court of opinion, it signifies royalty. Accusations of trash don't signify cheap shots at the King's heritage or his permanent reign. Or if they do, they fall flat before reaching their target. Arguably, it's Marcus the hagiographer who for once in his outstanding body of rock 'n' roll criticism sounds defensive; he's the one uncomfortable with Elvis's trashiness. My interest in Greil Marcus, however, lies not in the validity or the tenuousness of his judgments but in his struggle with the image of waste and trash in his chronicle of a dead king.

Before Elvis, by dying, forced Marcus to write *Dead Elvis,* Marcus ended the main portion of *Mystery Train* with a fantasy of Elvis reaching the pinnacle of rock artistry, throwing away just about everything—reputation, genius, the American Dream—and then reclaiming it all with a laugh of health and joy, not of contempt for fans or mockery of their adoration. In this fantasy two rock geniuses converge, supercharging history with the same mythic resonance of Thomas Jefferson visiting Ben Franklin's deathbed and taking the manuscript of the *Autobiography* from the dying man's hands. "Elvis would take the stage . . . the roar of the audience would surround him, as it always will. After a time, he would begin a song by Bob Dylan. Singing slowly, Elvis would give it everything he has. 'I must have been mad,' he would cry, 'I didn't know what I had—Until I threw it all away.' And then, with love in his heart, he would laugh." [11]

He would laugh, a sentimentalist might say, because his heart was as big as the state of Tennessee, big and kind and flooded with love. And his talent, as everyone else would say, was even bigger than his heart. And he would laugh as the only way to forgive himself the tragic fool he had become. He would laugh because the madness had passed, the painful lesson had been learned, and sanity had prevailed. He would laugh because he had also been forgiven by millions of people who reciprocated his love and who every single day for twenty years had needed to hear him sing a song, and because this need wouldn't diminish for the rest of their lonely lives. He would laugh because somehow his love had redeemed his self-destructiveness and prodigality, and because he knew that he alone among entertainers and artists, or he most of all, possessed the power to throw it all away, throw away more than any of us can imagine ever having in the first place, and then get it back at will, by singing a country song by Bob Dylan with conviction, reclaiming everything wasted with a belly laugh enjoyed at no one's expense but his own.

Until one day in Graceland, two years after Marcus published his fantasy, Elvis Presley didn't get it back. Nothing was delivered. He was finally gone. His departure was no dream or tabloid lie. And no one in the King's loyal audience laughed at the thought of His Majesty's wasted frame or at the moral of this rock 'n' roll tragedy.

12. Tell It Like It Is

The Bob Dylan song that Greil Marcus heard Elvis singing is "I Threw It All Away." The trash trope is like a broad muddy river swollen by a hundred tributaries running through Elvis country and saturating it: food, money, souvenirs, material possessions, people, music, future, self—all wasted, thrown away, trashed. Other metaphors work. Rock icons, the more visible the better, are sitting ducks for applications of the trash trope. Bob Dylan is one such duck that critics have occasionally tried to blow out of the water.

Jimmy Guterman and Owen O'Donnell take aim at postsixties Dylan. (The cover of their *The Worst Rock n' Roll Records of All Time* shows a metal trash can brimming with 45s and compact discs.) They cite *Self Portrait* as the first of "twenty ideas that Dylan should have thrown into the garbage."[1] Nineteen other such ideas suggest that Dylan's fame doesn't preclude trash from marring his career in other ways. Guterman and O'Donnell argue that the criteria needed to gauge trash involve, first, an artist's stature (he must be "great") and, second, his approval of the release being trashed: "a miserable record by a great performer (say, Bob Dylan) is far more interesting than the latest garbage installment from a hack (say, Neil Diamond)."[2] The twist here lies in the idea that some listeners are anything but indifferent to the worst records by the best artists. It might not be a waste of money to buy records such as, to stick with Dylan, *Hard Rain, Down in the Groove, Self Portrait,* and *Dylan.* If the product is bad enough, say Guterman and O'Donnell, garbage can be "interesting," the bad album good. Lester Bangs said as much in a review of Black Oak Arkansas: "There is a point where some things can become so obnoxious that they stop being mere dreck and become interesting, even enjoyable, and *maybe because they are so obnoxious.*"[3] The vague adjective "interesting" is used by Guterman and O'Donnell and Bangs to pinpoint an interesting rock paradox. A record can be so unlistenable that it's enjoyable ("interesting") to listen to. Some trash exerts such a fascination that the consumer feels compelled to go through the garbage pail (the contents of a given record album or compact disc) again and again, looking for some reason why the artifact is worth keeping or worth tossing. As a kind of perverse bonus, one can triple the waste (one, the artifact itself; two, the money thrown away on it) by wasting time searching for a sign of quality or listing signs of inferiority.

Evidence of such compulsion on the part of consumers doesn't prove that as a rule artists intentionally release bad product in the hope that enough cognoscenti of trash will get the joke and buy the record because it's so bad it's irresistible. An artist can't expect to sustain a career on such gambles. As Guterman and O'Donnell indicate, trashy product is enjoyable usually when an artist has previously created music judged magnificent by normal standards. At the end of the day, only Lou Reed can tell the world why he recorded and released *Metal Machine Music* about which the best one can say is its audacity has no equal in rock 'n' roll, and only John Lennon and Yoko Ono can tell why they recorded and released *Wedding Album* about which the best one can say is its title is splendid. The reason/s for these three artists may be arrogance, complacency, provocation, insult, boredom, self-fulfillment, vanity, temporary insanity, contempt for either self or audience, contempt for record company, desire to break a contract, excessive drug use, inspiration, or perverseness.

Perverseness works both ways. According to one Dylanologist, Dylan on occasion threw away not the right but the wrong songs. In his analysis of *Down in the Groove*, Clinton Heylin nags that Dylan tinkered with an earlier version superior to the final release. Heylin invokes trash: "Seemingly determined to convince fans that all he could now muster was a series of stopgap releases, Dylan for the second time in a year abandoned an album held together for one permed [*sic*] from trash cans." Specifically, at the last minute Dylan scrapped the running order of an album that was already weak, replacing and arranging some of the tunes with ones that made *Down in the Groove*, along with *Knocked Out Loaded*, one of Dylan's worst two albums. Heylin targets two songs, "Silvio" and "Ugliest Girl in the World," as being "in need of . . . a trash can."[4] These comments were made by a man who has devoted years to the study of Bob Dylan's music. Loving and trashing the love object aren't mutually exclusive acts.

Guterman and O'Donnell had nineteen other reasons to belittle Dylan. One of these was a live album. Carping that "even a garbage dump full of A. J. Webermans couldn't explain away the hatred that absorbs Dylan on *Live at Budokan*," the duo alludes to rock's premier (perhaps sole) garbologist.[5] Acting on his creed that "you are what you throw away," Weberman inspected the Dylan family's disposable diapers, fast-food containers, and whatnot for clues to the personal habits of the reclusive rock star.[6] Weberman invented "garbology" in his quest to decipher Dylan's symbolism.

"Use every man after his desert, and who should 'scape whipping?" Prince Hamlet asks Polonius, who thinks "players" (the Elizabethan equivalent of touring rock musicians) deserve less than royal treatment. I interpret this as Shakespeare's way of saying that if Bob Dylan can be trashed, no one's safe in Guterman and O'Donnell's book. They rip the wings off Iron Butterfly's *Live*, sniveling about its endless solos at the expense of ensemble playing. "All this garbage on an Atlantic record," they grumble, adding with a modicum of relief that "at least Otis wasn't around to hear it." The Beatles' conquest of America in 1964 brought great music but "like a ship docking in a harbor, they also dragged along with them every bit of garbage that got caught in their wake" such as the Herman's Hermits single "I'm Henry VIII, I Am." The Knack "left us hip-deep in garbage" with 1979's "Good Girls Don't," and (the trash trope shifts from an artist's product to her wasted efforts) "a truly great vocal stylist [Aretha Franklin] has no business wasting her time" on records such as her 1979 disco-drivel *La Diva*. The two critics smear Sammy Hagar, a "bottom-of-the-barrel rock lyricist." "[C]osmic sludge," referring to Anderson, Bruford, Wakeman, and Howe's eponymous album in 1989, trashes rock musicians who dump trash into their audience's lap and try to pass it off as profound.[7]

Bradley Smith, author of *The Billboard Guide to Progressive Music,* is partial to art-rock bands of the ABWH variety. He rates such bands high above the rock rabble spitting out superficial love songs. Pop/rock tunes are disposable (and contemptible) while the musical banquets of progressive bands are lasting (and praiseworthy). In the late sixties and early seventies, Smith writes,

[t]he composer/instrumentalist became a new kind of pop star, personified by emerging artists like John McLaughlin, Keith Emerson, Mike Oldfield, and Klaus Schulze, who had a glorious—even heroic—instrumental proficiency and who brought the musical values of classical and jazz spheres into the popular realm. It was precisely at this point that segments of popular music left behind trendiness and disposability, moving instead toward the complex creation of personal and lasting art.[8]

Smith's book attempts to skirt the trash trap by sticking to the advanced work coming from virtuosity, studio wizardry, and orchestral sweep. He prefers complexity and sophistication to directness and simplicity. He'll take mystical soundscapes and multitracked profundity over hard-headed punk rock or dumb rockabilly any day. Smith's elitism parallels his inability to understand the double nature of disposability in rock music. Disposability is rock's secret weapon, secret ingredient, and secret to success . . . as well as its not-secret to failure. In the suspense conveyed by one little ellipsis lies the paradox of each rock 'n' roll album's being expected to sound impermanent as a precondition of its having any chance of enduring beyond a week or two on the charts. Many of the "heroic" seventies albums raised by Smith to a level of High Art sound today like curios from a bloated, self-indulgent, post-Beatles, prepunk epoch. They weren't made to be disposable, so that's what most of them turned out to be. Reviewing Supertramp's *Even in the Quietest Moments . . .* back in 1977, Robert Christgau rebutted Smith's thesis of art rock twenty years before it was articulated: "Most 'progressive' rock is pretentious background schlock that's all too hard to ignore." Adding bulge to Christgau's art-rock garbage bag is Supertramp's best-seller *Breakfast in America:* "the lyrics turned out to be glib variations on the usual *Star Romances* trash. . . . I'll wait until this material is covered by artists of emotional substance—Tavares, say, or the Doobie Brothers."[9] Albums by Emerson, Lake & Palmer are graded C and D. Mike Oldfield's *Tubular Bells* earns a C+. Bradley Smith considers these artists and their platinum achievements among the best in rock history.

Two more collaborators, Julie Burchill and Tony Parsons, sling garbage as if no other term or verbal gesture could begin to convey their disgust with the punk scene of the midseventies. *"The Boy Looked at Johnny": The Obituary of Rock 'n' Roll* (1978) is splattered with trash drenched in venom. Their text debunks legend, deflates hero/ine worship, forestalls revisionists in the early 2000s busy revamping punk's golden age, and prepares us for the predictability of punk during the past thirty years. Punk rockers and their troops of pack-mentality fans were knee-deep in garbage, dreck, debris, waste, and junk. Burchill and Parsons laid them further to waste.

The year is 1977. The band is the Clash, soon to be hailed as the "only band that matters," cheered as saviors of English rock 'n' roll, soon to devise *London Calling,* a stunning mélange of styles, the punk epoch's White Album, one of rock's Desert Island double-discs.

None of this adulation is reflected in Burchill and Parsons's trash talk. They disdain the band's fans, possessing "the passion of persecuted religious dissidents—posing at the bar with obsessive dedication, pogoing like epileptic dervishes to the onstage acts pumping out endless three-chord wastelands." Mayhem ruled the Roxy, so that only "when a handful of human dregs lingered, kicking at the lager can scrap-heap, did the workshy bouncers make their presence felt." Fans became interchangeable with the trash accumulating around them. Ultraviolence, personal mutilation, "amphetamine psychosis," shitty music, and perhaps worst of all, marketing savvy produced a wasted scene that only in retrospect seems revolutionary or spontaneous. The Clash, forming around Joe Strummer (whose earlier band, the 101-ers, "were garbage"), are accused of being "the first band to use social disorder as a marketing technique to shift product[;] [t]he band had been manufactured" and weren't the real thing after all.[10] They embodied a scene that was mercenary from the start.

One aspect of punk culture slammed by Burchill and Parsons was heroin. Peter York writes that because Julie and Tony were "anti-drug, save for speed," they "came on a like moral scourge."[11] Did they ever. "It takes a conscious, continuous decision to become a junkie . . . and, therefore, those who choose this route cannot be pitied or excused. The junkie is driven down by . . . self-hatred, puritanism and a failing to come to terms with the fact that he is a human animal."[12] Junk is the chemical equivalent of musical garbage that leaves the ears a bleeding mess craving another hit. Punk music played without the additive of junk and the junkie's complacent (conspiratorial?) attitude about addiction is inconceivable. Sid Vicious, Topper Headon, Keith Levene, Iggy Pop, Johnny Thunders, Jerry Nolan, Lou Reed, and Nancy Spungen—a long roster is as integral to classic punk culture as it is to classic jazz. Junk is a metaphor of a metaphor of a metaphor: to wit, white-powder garbage that trashes the user. While addiction may seem glamorous when related to jazz titans such as Sonny Rollins and Charlie Parker, it's a sloppy romantic craving nurtured by self-hatred when related to punk rockers such as Sid Vicious who couldn't tune a guitar and who OD'd at the age of twenty-one. Junk powders the pages of *"The Boy Looked at Johnny"* because the book is about punk.

After disposing of junk-punks the Heartbreakers, assembled "from the debris of the New York Dolls," Burchill and Parsons turn to the Ramones.[13] It's important to note that a poll in the May 2001 issue of *Spin* elected the Ramones' debut album as the greatest punk album of all time.[14] Burchill and Parsons demeaned the creators of the greatest punk title in a passage that distils the craft of critical trashing, at once savage, funny, and illuminating:

> The stage-brother's [*sic*] roll-call was spot-blitzed shaded short-ass Tommy "Pox Chops" Ramone on drums and Valderma; moon-featured round-shouldered Quasi-modo-hunchbacked Johnny "Guitar" Ramone; one of Mother Nature's most tragic mistakes on vocals Joey "Who's A Pretty Boy Then?" Ramone, a decrepit inferno crippled with infirmities; and blank bassist Dee Dee "Stands For Dead and Dumb" Ramone, pig-eyed, pea-brained and fitting in perfectly with his brothers.[15]

In our nostalgic era, these four caricatures wear the punk crown. Burchill and Parsons would have put them where Polonius wanted to put the players—out where the chamber pots are emptied and the boar carcasses tossed. Whether rock royalty or punk trash, one thing about the Ramones is sure: "Basically, wherever rock 'n' roll trash might be found," asserts Robert Duncan, "there is likely to be found . . . something of the substance and something more of the spirit of the Ramones."[16] Tom Carson, writing concurrently with Burchill and Parsons, develops this motif:

> One of the chief delights of rock 'n' roll is that it's trash music for a trash culture. . . . This is obvious enough, but it's something rock 'n' roll is trying to forget. . . . The Ramones, however, never needed to be reminded [of this]. The Edenic, antimaterialist sentimentality of an event like Woodstock would have been utterly alien to them, as

alien as the glossy emptiness that followed it; they were living out Nabokov's dictum that nothing is more exhilarating than philistine vulgarity. . . . Their reveling in the trashy vitality of such an overwrought atmosphere [of big city violence and brutality] was a life-affirming manifesto.[17]

A photograph of these life-affirmers appears in the February 2002 issue of *Time Out New York*. Emblazoned across the cover are three words, the last one printed seventies punk style: "Why Music Sucks." The text explaining why music sucks is another one of those get-it-over-quick overviews of rock music that non-music magazines occasionally publish—here, lots of pix, thin text, three pages or so, taking readers from the late fifties to the early zeroes—not enough data to convince *me* why music sucks. A photograph of the Beatles, acid-droppers and potheads, 1967 psychedelic, is set beside the photograph of the Ramones, glue-sniffers and junkies, 1976 black-and-white. Art Rock versus Punk. The Beatles are resplendent and gorgeous. The Ramones aren't—they sit and slouch on an industrial Dumpster, a huge rectangular bin in which a small family (or inner-city rock band) could live. Monochrome, ugly.[18] A not insignificant anecdote about these garbage-squatters from Queens graces Dee Dee Ramone's autobiography (1997). At the age of twelve, he "found a whole bunch of . . . morphine tubes hidden in a garbage dump."[19] A lifetime pact sealed: garbage, junk, Ramone. Gabba gabba hey! Let's affirm life!

Also contrary to the Burchill and Parsons critique of the Ramones is what two members of the Clash said about them in 1976. In the fourth issue (October 1976) of the fanzine *Sniffin' Glue,* Joe Strummer and Mick Jones slagged the musical garbage flooding London. Joe bitched, "[M]ost people in London are going out every night to see groups or something and . . . it's not immediately apparent that it's rubbish. People are prepard [sic] to except [sic] rubbish, anything that's going. I mean, every single LP anybody plays me in any flat . . . it's rubbish." With one exception: "The only good one is that Ramones one . . . the Ramones record is good."[20] Since punks talk about the Ramones' first album the way boomers talk about *Meet the Beatles,* did Burchill and Parsons unfairly trash the Ramones?

Burchill and Parsons deserve the space I'm giving them not merely because they excoriate rock characters better than anyone else; not because they see that rock 'n' roll is immersed in trash and poisoned by junk (they hate heroin); and not because they write about rock 'n' roll with a conviction that justifies their high standards. It's because Burchill and Parsons grasp the full sociological picture of rock and express *that* in a nutshell that makes the pair's study of punk so vital. In a startling apothegm, they boil down the difference between English and American punk music—"English punk bands want to be the best—

American punk bands want to be the richest"—and follow up this provocation with an equally stunning insight that uses the trash trope in a new way. A reference to dietary disposability triggers an exposé of the symbiosis of rock music and American trash culture:

American kids get everything on a plate, especially their recreation. After a decade of munching trash-food from foil plates while staring at their interminable Technicolor television brain-candy, pre-teen kids at Aerosmith, Kiss and Queen concerts are equipped for nothing more strenuous . . . than being able to *focus on the stage*. . . . [T]hey're there purely to be bludgeoned into the merciful cosmic oblivion of misplaced and mushy mysticism.[21]

Punk and hard rock is the musical counterpart of TV dinners served up on aluminum trays, efficient, non-nutritious, tasteless, and eminently disposable. Maybe all rock is. Allan Bloom thinks so. Rock 'n' roll music is "a leveling influence; the children have as their heroes banal, drug- and sex-ridden guttersnipes who foment rebellion not only against parents but against all noble sentiments. This is the emotional nourishment they ingest in these precious years. It is the real junk food."[22] Elsewhere, Bloom calls rock music "junk food for the soul," a judgment consistent with a more general idea that "[l]ack of education simply results in students' seeking for enlightenment wherever it is readily available, without being able to distinguish between the sublime and trash, insight and propaganda."[23] Bloom's opponents might have to concede this much when thinking of the rock poseurs who have ripped them off. To concede this much, however, isn't to convert to his creed. (We know, thanks to Philip Norman, that in rock 'n' roll music *sublime* and *trash* aren't mutually exclusive terms.) As long as Professor Bloom is offended by rock music, no fan of the Clash or the Ramones need care that Julie Burchill and Tony Parsons trash an entire scene and mythology. Their anger feeds off a passionate love of rock 'n' roll. Bloom just loathes it.

(Bloom's talk about junk food demands mention of X-Ray Spex, one of the best Spirit of '77 punk groups. They recorded "Junk Food Junkie" in 1995, a cute midtempo tune profiling three food junkies undone by "sticky trashy fast food." Punk wailer Poly Styrene grew up only to share Bloom's disgust for the junk food he equates with rock 'n' roll songs such as "Junk Food Junkie," which satirizes that same food.)

Onward Burchill and Parsons tramp, machetes swooping, through the jungle of cliché, homily, cant, lie, and myth that has thickened around rock music and obstructed an approach to it. One junkie was Debbie Harry (idolized, historicized in the 2000s), founder of "garbage band The Stilettoes" and lead singer of Blondie, who ended up "pawn[ing] pride for pounds and pence." They pan

Patti Smith, who before declining into a "silly old biddy" made "the best debut album of all time" and they denounce trends such as fake reggae, pouncing with bared fangs on the rock press: "[B]y mid '77, the fanzines were wallowing in the mire of a golden age long gone; duplicated, sated drivel written by obnoxious whiners for over-grown wimps." The rampage continues with an analysis of how governments tolerate and capitalism tames rock music: "The chart-rigging scandal of early 1978, in which it was revealed that dreck vinyl could be bought into the Bottom Twenty of the Top Fifty, totally overlooked the fact that payola is a way of life in the music business." They finish with an anecdote about a "loser *Sounds* writer who was also a junkie." To support his habit, the doper sold boxes of discs that he picked up daily for free from distributors. From all angles, rock is junk, it can be sold for junk, and punk is trash: its critics, the addictions it engenders, the food that nourishes it, its "artists" (half of whom are junkies or drunks), and its albums, mostly the dreck, drivel, and debris of the wasted Western world.[24]

13. Total Trash

That's one theory, anyway. *Please Kill Me*, Legs McNeil and Gillian McCain's oral history of seventies punk rock, presents another one.

Focusing on the punk scene in New York City, *Please Kill Me* is told in the form of interviews with everyone who was anyone. Having the advantage of narrative immediacy, which allows it to communicate titillating scenes of violence and decadence involving the book's eyewitnesses and participants, this oral history surpasses Burchill and Parsons's English counterpart. This approach means, however, that the McNeil and McCain version lacks the scathing point of view—arguably, any point of view—that Burchill and Parsons cultivate. Naturally, *Please Kill Me* is an exercise in paradox. Exhilarating and exhausting, flippant and somber, titillating and tragic, and authoritative and anecdotal, *Please Kill Me* spills the beans on a network of suicidal, wasted, talentless, besotted, depraved, selfish, manic, and drug-depressed performers, managers, groupies, and assorted hangers-on. Punk, trashiest of rock genres, gave them a reason to live. Punk also crippled or killed them by the score (literally, the number twenty; figuratively, the deal gone down).

References to garbage are plentiful for two reasons. First, punk rock celebrates trash and derives much of its power from a "trash this" attitude. Punk is an aggressive form of rock 'n' roll that self-consciously trashes itself in a statement of style. Speaking with Ari Up of the Slits in 2000, Bryan Swirsky recalled that early punk fanatics would "empty garbage bins on their heads, make clothes out of the liner, and accessorize the contents." Ari agreed: "Absolutely!"[1] Trash fashion was punk ideology dressed to caper down a runway strewn with debris and corpses. Joe Strummer explained the trash aesthetic in the *Sniffin' Glue* interview quoted previously: "We deal in junk, you know, I just realized that the other day. We deal in junk. We deal in . . . the rubbish bin. What we've got is what other people have put in the rubbish bin. Like Mick's shirt was gonna be put in the bin until he paid 10p for it." Mick Jones added, "I think the way we do it is much more accesible [*sic*] to kids cos' anyone, at very little price and it encourages 'em to do something for themselves. It's to do with personal freedom."[2] Trash denoted an ideology that according to Roger Wallis and Krister Malm "embodied such things as second-hand clothing and cheap ways of living. Instruments and amplifiers could well have been salvaged from a garbage dump—the music did not require sophisticated gadgets and gear."[3] This ideology explains why its followers dressed up, in Peter Wicke's marvelous phrase, like "rubbish sculptures." Punk rock took "its materials from the suppressed waste products of bourgeois everyday life . . . the rubbish mountains of a questionable civilisation." It was (is) made by young people who "experience the world as a heap of worthless junk."[4] (Extreme postpunks prefer lip piercings, tattoos, and natty clothes; for everyone else, filthy sneakers, grubby jeans or shin-length shorts, and an old black DK T-shirt will do. As for axes and amps, I've seen unknown bands in hole-in-the-wall clubs create their din on Fenders, Gibsons, Marshalls, Tama Starclassics, K Zildjians, Shures, and Korgs. Not unsophisticated, not cheap.) So that when the punk band the Damned is described as "high-energy rubbish," it's to be understood that this is partly why "the group are great."[5]

The second reason for plentiful references to garbage in *Please Kill Me* is this: since punk rockers and fans of punk have been known, believe it or not, to be discriminating about the *real thing* (they hate sellouts), the trope of trash serves them better than any other trope when they assess their music. To them punk rock shouldn't be spit on for being a subsubgenre of chaos and dissonance, sloppy three-chord early Stones/Kinks rip-offs, pogo-inciting pandemonium, and junk- or beer-slurred vocals. Within this realm of belligerent and feral amateurism, a standard of excellence reigns. Punk lovers can explain why the early Ramones are superior to the late Ramones, where the Dead Kennedys go astray, why Green Day and the Offspring are frauds, how hard-core differs from straight edge, which differs from emo, how 1988 improved on or declined from 1977, why Team Dresch matters and why Aerosmith doesn't, why Iggy is king, godfather, and savior, why the Fumes (who?) had a future, and why many punk lyrics should be taken seriously because they're as "poetic" as the best mainstream lyric. The monologues of *Please*

Kill Me portray trash in all its diversity, laying it out before the reader in its relation to the personalities, behavior, sensibility, and recordings of a five-year epoch.

On the subject of punk politics, Kathy Asheton nails down John Sinclair's ruinous impact on the MC5: "He really took over the MC5 as far as instilling them with his political garbage." The staff of *Punk Planet* might beg to differ, but for first-generation purists, politics and punk didn't mix. Legs McNeil backs Asheton. Pure punk, no matter how sensationally the media presented the movement and music to the appalled public as the ranting of unemployed ruffians, violent junkies, and the occasional anarchist, endorsed no specific political stance: "[I]t had no political agenda. It was about real freedom, personal freedom."

Shifting gears from politics to charisma, Leee Childers observed that trash fascinated his most famous client, David Bowie, driven to collaborate with Iggy Pop, punk's shaman of excess. Bowie was more sham than shaman. To manipulate image was as important as to make good music, which, of course, he did for ten years or more. During one of his masquerades, Bowie (born David Jones) became infatuated with Iggy (born James Osterberg) because this maniacal performer, satyr, and drug gobbler was basically "a Detroit trash bag," the real McCoy, while Bowie was "a wimpy little South London art student [who could never] achieve the reality that Iggy was born into." The Pop/Bowie comparison implies a chain of synonyms: trash = reality = punk = great music. The diverse applications of trash are matched by the trash's nominal plasticity. Before it resolves itself into a positive or a negative term, the metaphor of trash keeps the reader or listener guessing. The trope and the music it modifies are forever in flux.

Speaking specifically about Arthur Kane (bassist of the New York Dolls) and his manic girlfriend (she had stabbed him in a jealous fit), Malcolm McLaren stated a general thesis about New York punk rock: "much of their behavior was wasted energy—I didn't think it even had any philosophical purpose. It was a trashy energy, easily disposable energy, an energy that didn't really bear any genuine point-of-view, except jealousy, which is so time wasting." It was beneath him. Yet we must look past McLaren's hauteur and acknowledge his acumen regarding the trendy, somewhat despicable allure that trash held for the art/punk crowd colonizing the Lower East Side. "I just loved fucking with that kind of pop-trash culture of Warhol," he bragged, "which was so goddamn Catholic, and so boring, and so pretentiously American, where everything had to be a product, everything had to be disposable."

Yes, it had to be. But at street level, for a spell, pop-trash culture wasn't watered down, cut with baking soda, or mass-produced. At its trashiest, punk rock, McNeil recalls,

was about doing anything that's gonna offend a grown-up. Just being as offensive as possible. Which seemed delightful, just euphoric. Be the real people we are. You know? I just loved it.

I remember my favorite nights were just getting drunk and walking around the East Village kicking over garbage cans. . . . It just seemed so glorious. And you'd be humming these great songs and anything could happen, and it was usually pretty good.[6]

Looking back in 1990, Greil Marcus assessed the discrepancy between punk's disposability and "its desire to change the world." This sounds very serious and in marked contrast to Legs McNeil's avowal of punk as the taking of delight in offending grown-ups and sending garbage-can lids into the gutter. In 1990, the Ramones, the Sex Pistols, the Buzzcocks, and other bands hadn't yet been canonized (that is, remarketed) for a new generation of consumers (both clueless Xers and jaded, or deaf, boomers): "[L]istening to this relatively small body of work, now exiled to cut-out bins, bargain racks, collectors' sales, or flea markets—I feel a sense of awe at how fine the music was: how irreducible it remains. What remains irreducible about this music is its desire to change the world."[7] Punk's "irreducible desire" can also be taken to mean that a person could now, literally at any time today, purchase a punk record (rather, punk compact disc) that had been cast off (in its LP form) in one of the four places mentioned by Marcus and that this same title could make itself heard above the din and babble of Top Forty and change this person's world, the rest of the world be damned. To change one person's world is cause enough for celebration.

Anticipating the observation that today a punk-seeking person could much more easily and efficiently buy a given punk record online from the band itself or from a big company (such as Amazon) that provides categories and best-of lists to expedite a consumer's purchase of the top twenty of this or that subcategory of rock, I would add that the aura of permanence rendered seemingly absolute by cyber technology underscores the pathos of Marcus's litany of flea markets, bargain racks, exile, and awe. In April 2002, while browsing used compact discs at my local record store, I came across a punk compilation that included X-Ray Spex performing their famous battle-cry "Oh Bondage, Up Yours!" at the Roxy. Four bucks. A giveaway. Per my request, the salesman played this track over the store's loudspeakers, then handed the disc to me. Well—? I put this object of irreducible desire back in the rack where I had come across it. In effect, I threw it away.

14. Vicious

The documentation of garbage, dregs, scrap heaps, rubbish, and wastelands doesn't say much for rock 'n' roll . . . does it? Look at other discourses. Do reviewers spit out "Garbage!" when critiquing a monograph published by a university press? Rarely, if ever. Do reviewers scream "Rubbish!" when panning productions in opera, theater, photography, poetry, and art? Rarely, if ever. The 5 March 2001 cover of the *New Yorker* pokes fun at this code of civility. Illustrated is the marquee of a Broadway theater emblazoned with one- and two-word antiblurbs of the play inside: "Gratuitously Prurient!" "Lurid!" "Unabsolvably Sleazy!" "Sordid!" At the bottom of one panel are "Trash" and "Junk," the only two aspersions unmarked by exclamations.[1] (The joke lies in the fact that such reproofs are selling points. Even the Upper Crust loves trash.) Certainly there's an excess of ephemera and bad work done in the elite disciplines patronized by the *New Yorker*'s more affluent subscribers. Disparaging the poems at a poetry recital or the arias at the Met's season opening as garbage or trash, however, might come off as a bit déclassé.

The trash talk pervading rock criticism was coincident with its inception in the early 1950s. Attacks on rock 'n' roll have found ample expression in print and broadcast media since the days Elvis was doing fifteen-minute shows at country fairs in Tennessee, and the trash trope has often been the ammunition in these attacks. This new music, packaged for middle-class teenagers with a little disposable income and a lot of repressed libido, was subjected to revilement from the expected sources—ministers, politicians, parents, teachers, promoters, even entertainers (such as jazz musicians or Tin Pan Alley songsmiths) who felt threatened by electrified beat music. Although rock had become mainstream by the early seventies, it continued to arouse resistance and to elicit reproach—continues, indeed, to this day. Yes, even in the jaded, aesthetically spent present, it can evoke snarls from the nicest people. A reproof from 1999 could have been penned on any day between 1954 and 2004: "We reap what we sow, and if we're filling our kids' heads with this garbage . . . what comes out is what you put in."[2] This intelligent sentence is a parent's reaction to the demonic image, lyrics, and music of Mr. Marilyn Manson. But my grandfather said very much the same thing about the likeable, lyrical Beatles. As the family sat spellbound in front of the television set watching the four beautiful invaders shake their mop heads on the *Ed Sullivan Show,* Gramp hissed at the screen: "Garbage! Noise! Depravity! Trash!" Now, if a millennial dude such as Manson or Eminem is able to outrage parents and preachers in an age of mass cynicism, imagine the threat to civic decency posed by giants such as Elvis Presley, Jerry Lee Lewis, Little Richard, and—gulp, a girl!—Wanda Jackson. Their Dionysian license appalled and terrified censors in every corner of the republic. The first rock 'n' rollers had their stiff little fingers on the sex button of a nation's teenage population, and that fact alone polarized many a daddy, mommy, guidance counselor, principal, and minister.

America's disapproval of rock music is such a well-documented story that we need only touch on it here as a prelude to the next section. Indeed, Linda Martin and Kerry Segrave have documented the antirock literature so well that it would be redundant to repeat their task. *Anti-Rock: The Opposition to Rock 'n' Roll* reviews the barbs shot at rock from 1953 to 1986. The rock bashers cited by Martin and Segrave are partial to rhetorical garbage and trash and to the practice of throwing away perfectly good 45s and LPs. Some samples: in 1955, *Variety* editorialized against rock's "leer-ic garbage." Also in 1955, a radio station in Alabama trashed 50 percent of the records sent to them: straight into the garbage bin went records whose value today would make collectors weak in the knees. In 1958, the British Musicians' Union wrote off rock 'n' roll as "rubbish," and in the same year *Melody Maker* announced that rock music was "trash" and called for its censorship. Ronald Butt, on behalf of the London *Times,* griped in 1976 that punk was "rubbish," and in 1965 a fundamentalist preacher named David Noebel directed his flock to "[t]hrow your Beatle and rock and roll records in the city dump." Hundreds complied. One notorious attack on rock 'n' roll cited by Martin and Segrave, as well as by other historians of the genre, spewed from the mouth of Frank Sinatra in 1957. The Entertainer of the Century had seen the rapid ascension of a possible usurper, a white trash southern punk named Elvis *(Elvis?)* Presley. Tripping over nasty adjectives, Sinatra sneered, "[R]ock 'n' roll smells phony and false. It is sung, played and written for the most part by *cretinous* goons and by means of its almost *imbecilic* reiteration, and sly, lewd, in plain fact, dirty lyrics" (italics added). Since rock was the music of "every sideburned delinquent on the face of the earth" (girls didn't listen to it?), Ol' Blue Eyes decided it was "the most brutal, ugly, desperate, vicious form of expression it has been my misfortune to hear."[3] Naturally, the momentous changes occurring between 1954 and 1957 brought out the worst in entertainers who had to protect their careers while living through cultural revolution. But fifties kids already knew what Sinatra didn't understand and what Lester Bangs would someday memorialize as rock's cardinal virtues.

Careful though Martin and Segrave were in trolling through thirty-three years of journals and newspapers, some juicy little quotations squirmed clear, no matter how fine their net and broad their sweep. Of two keepers I personally snagged and kept—small, yes, but too delicious to throw back—one was spied lurking in the shadows of a sidebar in *Time* in 1956. The editors were pleased to reprint "[t]he major sociological comment of the week" on rock music, that of a letter writer to the *Denver Post* who crabbed, "This hooby doopy, oop-shoop, ootie ootie, boom boom de-addy boom, scoobledy goobledy dump—is trash."[4] The same year a reporter for *Scholastic* magazine tried to trash rock 'n' roll by suggesting that compared to jazz it's "a more violent, sound-shattering, solid-beating type of music. It is frequently accompanied by a 'nonsense phrase' or a *moronic* lyric sung in hillbilly style" (italics added).[5]

Behold the adjectives: cretinous, imbecilic, and moronic—implying music made by cretins, imbeciles, and morons. As it turned out, the cretins, imbeciles, and morons, as well as Sinatra's sideburned delinquents, of rock 'n' roll ignored their critics, swept past the censors and scrooges, and proceeded to create over the next half-century a trove of beautiful music. And yet, good news, rock 'n' roll's critics have always been right to some degree, not realizing (too taken with their own condescension and righteousness) that the more "moronic" it sounds to their unrefined ears, the better it sounds to the lucky ones who hear it for what it is. In fact, "[p]andemic moronity . . . has always informed the best rock 'n' roll," write Scott Isler and Ira Robbins in their profile of—guess who?—the Ramones, the ultimate trash rockers.[6] In time, rock's cretins, imbeciles, morons, and other retards, many savants and Mensas among them, would have much to say about the presence of trash in this "brutal, ugly, desperate, vicious form of expression."

15. Fame and Fortune

The *Scholastic* reporter *tried* to trash rock music, not aware that it can't be trashed by accusing it of imbecility because it's always already pandemically moronic and that's the whole point. In fact, smart rock critics trash the music *because* they love it for being trash and for reflecting the handiwork, sometimes subtle, sometimes heavy-handed, of pandemic morons. One suspects, however, that rock's foremost critics intend less to expose what's trashy than to mimic it on typewriters. Lester, Richard, Julie, and Tony didn't don elbow-length gloves as they penetrated the rubbish, groping for a record worth praising and scorning the rest. They leaped at the task with sleeves rolled up, taking off their shoes and jumping into the heap, getting good and covered with rock's noise, performance attitudes, and culture. Their prose became one with it, just as the garbageman becomes indistinguishable from the raucous truck and the stinky bins he heaves to and fro. Rock 'n' roll trash permeates the syntactic pores of numberless rock critics, filtering down into the foundation and filigree of style. It would be unusual if rock 'n' roll rhetoric didn't absorb the flavorful filth of rock 'n' roll music because no rock 'n' roll music is finally "clean," not—take the "cleanest" names—Buddy Holly's, not Marshall Crenshaw's, not XTC's, not even Steely Dan's music. The thesis that rock is imbued with trashy attitudes, sounds, values, and personalities presupposes that it can't be trashed further, at least not by anyone who understands it, including rock 'n' rollers themselves. Simultaneously, this thesis presupposes the antithesis, that rock can be trashed only by someone who understands it, including rock 'n' rollers themselves.

Some of rock's "morons" have contemplated the allegations against their craft. Luminaries from Elvis Costello to Elton John, from Mick Jagger to Bob Dylan, and from Pete Townsend to Lou Reed have deprecated some of their own recordings, in essence contradicting the article of faith among fans that rock 'n' roll, in the worn-out phrase, "is here to stay" or that it's Great Art. The bulk of its repertoire is *not* here to stay because it manages at best to beguile a fleeting moment. As if aware of this, some bands seeking fame and fortune (a phrase immortalized in song by Elvis Presley, rock's chief avatar of trash) are able at the same time to mock or deflate their own ambitions. There are solo artists and groups such as Garbage (whose 2001 release is named *Beautiful Garbage*), White Trash, the Trashmen, Soul Junk, the Trash Can Sinatras, Waysted, Junkyard Jane, Junkyard, the Garbage Gurus (strictly for grades K through 4), and the Lords of the Wasteland. There are albums such as *Sorry Ma, Forgot to Take Out the Trash* by the Replacements (self-anointed "power trashers"), *Wasted . . . Again* by Black Flag (leading off with the cut "Wasted"), *Garbage Can* by the Nights and Days, *Big Trash* by the Thompson Twins, *One's Man's Trash Is Another Man's Treasure* by the Jody Grind, *Trashed* by Lagwagon, *Elegantly Wasted* by INXS, *Throwaway Generation* by the Zillionaires, and *God Don't Make No Junk* by the Halo Benders. There are songs such as "Junkyard" by Treat Her Right, "Wasting Away" by Girls against Boys, "Wastin' Time" by Ron Sexsmith, "White Trash Heroes" by Archers of Loaf, "Waste" by Skrape, "Are You the Trash" by Mark Eitzel, "Wasted and Ready" by Ben Kweller, the forty songs reviewed in section 27, and scores more. There are fanzines proud of the fact that their writers are rank amateurs and that the ink on their pages smudges your fingers even before you pick it up—'zines such as *Stomp and Stammer* out of Atlanta, Georgia, whose masthead reads: "news • music • noise • opinion • garbage." There are "trash or smash" radio programs and Trash-O-Rama rock tours.[1] There are indie stores such as Junk Records in Cypress, California, and indie labels such as Trash, founded by Maureen Tucker, whose hallowed name will be soiled by garbage many times in these pages: that's what she gets for having been one of rock 'n' roll's greatest drummers. Some or all of these less-than-famous artists and groups seem content to live with the prospects of obscurity, musical amateurism, poor sales, and low expectations of ever being inducted into the Rock 'n' Roll Museum Hall of Fame.

On the other hand, many stars who can't count the number of their platinum discs have been known to be less than pompous about their achievements. An album review penned by none other than Pete Townsend included the revelation that "My Generation" was written "as a throwaway, naturally," and that "Magic Bus," loved by the composer for the sound's "mystical quality," had "garbage" for words.[2] Interviewing Mick Jagger in 1968, Jonathan Cott praised the lyrics to "Get off of My Cloud," thinking they made a "nice poem." Jagger responded, "Oh, they're not, they're crap. It's nothing. Thank you for the compliment, but I don't think they're great at all. If a person is that hung up on lyrics he can go and buy the sheet music because it's all there, wrong, of course."[3] Of course, the song is a stone classic. But the trash trope (stretched a bit here to include "crap") can't be pinned down. Talking many years after the initial response to *Exile on Main Street,* Jagger is defensive rather than dismissive about his work: "And I love it now when all these critics say it was the most wonderful thing, because it's a lot of those same guys who, at the time, said it was crap!"[4]

Mick Jagger's Glimmer Twin is Keith Richards, the embodiment of rock 'n' roll's "elegantly wasted" lifestyle. In the annals of rock music, Richards has had few equals in the dominion of self-destruction, his stature heightened by scores of incredible compositions and appearances produced in spite of continuous flirtations with a Reaper yet to conquer him. In other words, Keith Richards knows a thing or two about being wasted and trashed yet going ahead to write one classic album after another without getting mired in aesthetic hair-splitting about the genre his band took to the highest heights. On the well-trodden question of rock and art, the guitarist shrugs, "'[A]rt' is a word that gets bandied around. I don't think that rock 'n' roll songwriters should worry about art. . . . As far as I'm concerned, 'Art' is just short for 'Arthur.' " Elvis Costello talked to the same interviewer, Bill Flanagan, about his work with the same refreshing lack of ego: "[T]he simple truth is some of [my songs] are not that good. Some of them are a load of wank"—English vernacular not for trash, per se, but certainly for wasted essence. Sting's remarks on rock art hinge more explicitly on the trash trope. "[S]ome of my favorite songs are meaningless," he admitted to Flanagan. "I was trying to figure out why I liked songs like 'Da Doo Ron Ron' and 'Do Wah Diddy' and 'Tutti-Frutti.' There's a whole list of songs with just garbage as words that seem to be able to communicate something without necessarily meaning anything."[5] On the topic of "De Do Do Do, De Da Da Da," Sting informed David Fricke that he had "always felt that song had basically been dismissed as garbage"—that it hadn't been heard as more than baby talk—which, ironically, "was the whole idea! I was trying to make an intellectual point about how the simple can be so powerful."[6]

Lou Reed once goaded consumers into trashing one of his titles even before hearing it. *Live: Take No Prisoners* weaves uproarious trash talk monologues into and around riveting renditions of Reed's warhorses. Before getting to the music, however, the buyer has to contend with *TNP*'s hideous cover. (N.B. The digital insert pales beside the analog sleeve.)

TNP regales the consumer with an illustration of an overturned trash can and two swollen garbage bags set against a brick wall leading to an alley. Rubbish floods the foreground, mostly female clothing accessories—beads, lipstick, bracelets, one blue three-inch high heel, a pocketbook, several boas—but also a banana peel, an orange peel, aluminum cans, egg shells, a playing card, and puddles of this and that. In the middle of the trash can, a scuffed doll with orange-red hair and upraised right hand adds a touch of violation to the picture. Near the mounds of rubbish stands, hands on hip and thigh, a muscular male transvestite, head shaved, wearing a short leather jacket (open, collar up, rhinestones flashing), very tight black briefs (zipper pulled slightly down), garters, fish net hose, and black knee-high boots with high narrow heels. This ghoul has either discarded some of these articles or has been scavenging them.

Whatever Reed's intention in marketing this repulsive sleeve design, *TNP* is a unique and effective presentation of garbage as picture-cum-sound. But Reed wasn't the first to combine garbage graphics with trashy music. The sleeve of the Trashmen's *Surfin' Bird* displays the four musicians leaning athwart a garbage truck. The clean-cut guitarists model blue-green suits and black ties. They smile, grabbing their Fenders along with a long-handled industrial broom and a grubby shovel. One of the boys sits atop a trash can; another one dumps a container into the truck. The drummer, Steve Wahrer, grinning at the joke, lounges on the open gate of the dump truck, his right foot resting on two worn tires, his drums nestled among the garbage, the bass drum bearing the name Trashmen. Nothing better, nothing worse. *Surfin' Bird*, then (1963) and now, inspires enthusiasm for its reckless but rock-solid and instantly addictive junk-food program. In 1969, Richard Meltzer invested the "everlasting Trashmen" (the trash paradox in a nutshell) with "infinite wisdom incarnate" in their recording of "Surfin' Bird." Thirty years later, Meltzer wrote that in the early sixties the Trashmen revived a moribund rock scene along with one other "fabulous" band, the Beatles.[7]

It's impressive that the "fabulous" (Meltzer's word) Trashmen gave teenagers a mild case of punk thirteen years before its official appearance. More impressive is that they reinvented rock 'n' roll: "I can't think of those weeks up till Christmas [1963] without feeling an equal rush of Beatles and Trashmen, who together, where *I* lived and breathed, kind of reinvented rock & roll, dead as a donut . . . since, well, before Bobby Darin."[8] Langdon Winner's essay "The Strange Death of Rock and Roll" (1969) foretold half of Meltzer's rapture, expressing the commonplace that the Beatles saved the day. To contextualize his thesis, Winner looked back to Bill Haley before clinching the history lesson with a tweak of the trash trope: "the shy but noble Haley [led] his Comets to victory after victory over the bastions of entrenched Tin Pan Alley bilge."[9] Winner defined one of the great cultural battles of the 1950s when the trashy upstarts of rock 'n' roll music challenged the entrenched banality of Tin Pan Alley.[10]

The other half of Meltzer's argument may seem extraordinary. The one-hit Trashmen and the hundred-hits Beatles on equal footing? The immortal Beatles, the pride of England, brushing shoulders with a self-mocking midwestern novelty act frivolous enough to name themselves after trash collectors? The idea isn't that far-fetched. Meltzer's pairing isn't the only time these mighty Englishmen have been sullied with garbage. Because they were just a rock band, the Fabs weren't/aren't impervious to the taint of rhetorical garbage. In rock 'n' roll music no one comes out clean.

16. Torn and Frayed

Regarding the Beatles, the intrigue of trash talk increases significantly, especially when one of rock's paramount figures cuts down a colleague's work as well as his own achievements. Released immediately after the Beatles disintegrated, Paul McCartney's first solo album, *McCartney*, received good reviews and it breezed to the top of the American charts. Furthermore, the record has dated well. Thirty years after *McCartney*'s appearance, Stephen Erlewine gave it four out of five stars, praising its "endearingly ragged, homemade quality" and its handful of fine pop songs.[1] This estimation seems reasonable. For those looking for quirky but hummable tunes, supplemented by a few masterpieces and marred by one or two clunkers, *McCartney* remains an album worth owning, surely a safe bet compared to much of McCartney's later solo and Wings work.

Nevertheless, John Lennon, speaking with Jann Wenner in 1971, dismissed McCartney's one-man effort as one man's "rubbish."[2] "Maybe I'm Amazed," "Teddy Boy," "That Would Be Something," "Every Night"—mere trash. Ironically, the album's sweetest ballad, an instrumental called "Singalong Junk," is mirrored by a vocal version called "Junk," as if McCartney aimed to make the most of the discrepancy between dulcet music and misleading title in order to flout or befuddle critics inclined to trash him for indulging his gift for mellifluousness. Unlike Lennon, when Erlewine refers to the "throwaway nature" of *McCartney*, the phrase is meant to compliment the product, what with the disc's throwaway quality connoting easygoing melodies and feel. That Paul McCartney, all alone in his rural home studio, was able to interweave a bunch of hook-thick jams and fragments with five or six complete songs worthy of the Beatles themselves (some of them date back to White Album demos), and to top the package off with a respectable drum solo; and that by including these fragments, false starts, and experiments McCartney winked at the disposability of his project while ensuring, through the appearance of some major additions to his canon, both its contemporary popularity and its longevity—that he succeeded at these tasks helps make *McCartney,* despite being released at a time when the sound of *Abbey Road* was still ringing in everyone's ears, a hybrid of merit, a whole in spite of itself, while showing, as a bonus, the former Beatle debunking his own mythic stature.

In other words, *McCartney* invites no invidious comparison to *Let It Be* or other late records by the Beatles. The recording is one of those rare throwaways by a major artist that thirty years later is still not only required but pleasant listening. The same can't be said with a straight face of Lennon's two volumes of "Unfinished Music," *Two Virgins* and *Life with the Lions.* In these avant-trash vanity projects from the late sixties, Lennon descended to the basement of irredeemable disposability. Trash for collectors and completists only. About these unpopular titles Lester Bangs carped, "*Two Virgins, Unfinished Music No. One,* and the distinctly uncatchy Peace jingles on *Wedding Album* were the ego-trips of two rich waifs [Lennon and Yoko Ono] adrift in the musical revolution of the Sixties. . . . Dilettante garbage, simply."[3] Right on, brother. Given his own trashy track record, John Lennon would have gained critical credibility had he suspended his judgment of *McCartney* until hearing *Wild Life,* an album almost as rickety as Lennon's first collaborations with his wife or the couple's later farrago, *Sometime in New York City.*

Lennon had long poked fun at the Beatles. At the height of Beatlemania, he quipped about the adulation that had altered the lives of him and his mates, anticipating in one press conference the title of the Rolling Stones' tune about rock's likeable disposability. To the question "Do you play the same way now as you did?" Lennon replied, "It's only rock 'n' roll." Asked "Do you think you will be writing any songs with Australian themes?" Lennon replied, "No, we never write anything with themes. We just write the same rubbish all the time."[4] Lennon could afford to be lighthearted about his group's performances and albums—nothing he said would have affected sales—and his cheekiness was the tone to take with reporters who weren't in business to keep Lennon's success in perspective. Granted, this wag could be acerbic to a fault; nonetheless, one can't fault him for trying to maintain some sanity through verbal sparring and self-mockery in a world gone mad for English pop stars.

In the 1971 interview with Wenner, however, Lennon began in earnest his dismantling of the Beatles legend. Amidst much whining about how horrible it was being a Beatle and how despicable the Beatles were, Lennon attacked what consistently shows up on polls as one of the top ten albums in rock 'n' roll history: *Abbey Road*. Lennon declared the second side "junk because it was just bits of songs thrown together." The album was "competent" but "had no life in it."[5] The junk on side two includes "Here Comes the Sun," "Because," "Sun King," "She Came in Through the Bathroom Window," "Golden Slumbers," "Carry that Weight," and "The End." (Side one's best-known numbers are Lennon's "Come Together" and George Harrison's "Something.") Lennon's digs may have been caused in part by the bitterness of the Fab Four's breakup in 1970 and the two years of infighting leading up to the final fracture. He unleashes his causticity with the abandon of a man thirsting for catharsis and consequently using harsh words to wrench himself free, partly because of the search for artistic self-realization and partly because of self-loathing, from the trammels of a ten-year tenure at the helm of the world's most visible band.

John Lennon's disavowal of Beatles during the myth-busting therapy dialogues, lawsuits, and albums of 1970 and 1971 didn't change with age. At the time of the book-length *Playboy* interviews conducted by David Sheff a few months before his subject was murdered in 1980, Lennon was a happy family man hitting his stride with a number-one comeback album (*Double Fantasy*, cocredited to Yoko Ono). But he turned scathing in discussing Beatles songs he would never again hear or play. Lennon trashed "I Am the Walrus" ("*They* get away with this artsy-fartsy crap. . . . I thought, Well, I can write this crap, too"), "Sun King" ("That's a piece of garbage I had around")," "And Your Bird Can Sing" ("[a]nother of my throwaways"), and "Birthday" ("a piece of garbage"). "I Wanna Be Your Man," Ringo's feature on *With the Beatles*, is, poof, "a throwaway." "What Goes On" from *Rubber Soul* was "[r]esurrected [from the Quarry Men days] because I never liked to waste anything." "Tell Me Why," the rollicking number from *A Hard Day's Night* that climaxes in exhilarating falsetto harmony ("Is there anything I can do-oo-oo?") just before Ringo's one-bar triplet fill, is something "I just knocked . . . off." Until penning the ballad "In My Life," confided Lennon, everything he wrote was "sort of glib and throwaway."[6]

Lennon picks them off one by one: "Good Morning, Good Morning" ("It's a throwaway, a piece of garbage, I always thought"); "Cry, Baby, Cry" ("[a] piece of rubbish"); "Mean Mr. Mustard" ("That's me, writing a piece of garbage"); "Hey Bulldog" ("It's a good-sounding record that means nothing"); and "Dig a Pony" ("[a]nother piece of garbage"). Even a song that makes Lennon's cut, "Being for the Benefit of Mr. Kite," exists because of its relation to garbage: "The whole song is from a Victorian poster, which I bought in a junk shop." He blames the very early "Tip of My Tongue" on his partner, who Lennon thinks wrote his fair share of trash before going solo: "That's another piece of Paul's garbage, not my garbage." Turning the spotlight on his own solo work, Lennon sniffs at "Tight A$" ("[j]ust a throwaway track") from 1973's *Mind Games;* "#9 Dream" ("a bit of a throwaway") and "Surprise, Surprise" ("[j]ust a piece of garbage") from 1974's *Walls and Bridges;* and "I Know, I Know" ("[j]ust a piece of nothing") from the Lennon *Anthology* released in 1998.[7]

That these volumes of rubbish and junk continue to sell innumerable copies around the globe (the compilation *Beatles 1* topped the chart for weeks in late 2000/early 2001) suggests that Lennon was a better guitarist and songwriter than critic.[8] But allowing that Lennon is right about *Abbey Road* and other Beatles junk, trash appears to be a measure not of worthlessness but of greatness vis-à-vis rock 'n' roll because *Abbey Road,* both sides of it, sets a rock 'n' roll standard of the highest order.[9] Lennon's comments confirm the ease with which trash lends itself to artists who evaluate their own and others' work; moreover, he confirms the concept's relativity, subjectivity, and ambiguity. If trash can be "good," then the Shaggs and the Trashmen can very well be "as good as" the Beatles. But contradicting this simple inversion of the good/bad (jewel/junk, treasure/trash) binary, Lennon and professional critics teach us that to besmirch a rock artifact as trashy may succeed only in challenging apparent assessments of its quality. What matters less than one man's opinion about this group or that album, even if the man is John Lennon, is that trash and related tropes are used so freely in the assessment of rock 'n' roll music that the term's function demands careful analysis as an aesthetic principle in specific cases and in general application. Superficial critical polarities related to rock music can be misleading. The worst stuff may be the best. The most disposable may be the most lasting. Trash might be collectible, nonsense lyrics might be profound, even sublime, and vice versa down the line.

Just as a skeptic concedes that the success of the Beatles proves that popularity and quality can in fact coexist, a weak link in the argument crops up. The late George Harrison, known on occasion to be dour about the Beatles, was reminiscing about the shows the Beatles played to arenas packed with hysterical fans. He told biographer Hunter Davies, "Nobody could hear. It was just a bloody big row. We got worse as musicians, playing the same old junk every day. There was no satisfaction at all."[10] This remark doesn't reveal a Harrison sick and tired of playing the same *great* songs—no, they were all "old junk" by 1965, these hits played and sung out of tune and off-key day after day on stages enveloped in a deafening roar of teenagers unable to discriminate between the harmony and hoarseness of their heroes.

The inevitable contradiction of the contradiction nips at the heels of Harrison's remark. In 1979, Harrison qualified his disparagement of punk rock with a reference to none other than the Beatles: "Rubbish, *total* rubbish. Listen to the early Beatles records. They were simple too, but they still had much more depth and meaning. It was innocent or even trivial, but it still had more meaning than punk, which is deliberately destructive and aggressive." Also worthless to Harrison was disco music, punk's sister act of the seventies: "It's like a recipe. If you want to make a disco hit, just follow the instructions. You have the bass drum, the cymbal, the violin going, and that's disco. Rubbish!" Having distanced himself from punk and disco, Harrison once again spun the trash trope on its axis. In 1983, Harrison debunked the band who so many people have said did so much to change and save the world. "How do you feel about the Beatles' myth today?" asks Geoffrey Giuliano. Harrison answers, "All this stuff about the Beatles being able to save the world was rubbish. I can't even save myself."[11]

Punk: rubbish. Disco: rubbish. Beatles' myth: rubbish. Was George Harrison aware that his own recordings with the Beatles were rubbish too? At least one insider thought so. George Martin, the so-called "fifth Beatle," opened up to *Goldmine* in 1998, telling Ken Sharp that "most of the songs [Harrison] did were rubbish." (Martin didn't specify *Electronic Sound,* the 1969 solo album released on Zapple that Harrison himself cut down in 1987 as a "load of rubbish."[12]) In Martin's opinion, the Quiet Beatle hit his stride late, with "Here Comes the Sun." Forget about "Don't Bother Me," "Taxman," and especially "Only a Northern Song." George Martin wasn't the man to back off from trashing his four charges if they deserved it. The material in *Anthology* was comprised of "little bits of rubbish" releasable only because it would let fans analyze alternate takes, vocal tracks, and demos. When Paul McCartney asked Martin to produce *Tug of War* in 1982, Martin consented only if "Macca" would "just throw away" four of the proposed tunes.[13] He doesn't give the names of these throwaways. Perhaps they showed up on some of Macca's later duds.

In stark contrast to this general trash-troping of/by the Beatles is Walter Everett's two-volume close reading of their albums, surely the most technical of the hundreds of Beatles-related books. Before he gets underway in his song-by-song dissection of *Revolver* and onward (the companion volume covers the Quarry Men to the wizards who made *Rubber Soul*), Everett stakes his ground, often departing from his technical matter with flourishes in a superlative mode. For instance, the Beatles possessed a "supreme" sense of rhythm and in "If I Fell" Lennon mastered a "stunning chromatic effect . . . worthy of Liszt." Everett mixes observations colored by advanced training in music theory and by simple love of Beatles music:

> [I]nnovations are responsible not only for a large aspect of the Beatles' late sound but also for qualities that brought "rock" away from "rock and roll" in the 1960s. But the Beatles went much further than their peers with such borrowings. . . . [T]he haunting

Dorian mode becomes a favorite collection for George Harrison in "Don't Bother Me." Harrison's "Think for Yourself" is a tour de force of altered scale degrees leading to such an ambiguity of scale membership that its tonal quality forms the perfect conspirator with the text's and the rhythm's hesitations and expected turns. . . . [T]he Beatles' remarkable command over such a wide body of tonal resources will soon allow them to venture into the strange worlds of "Only a Northern Song," "Strawberry Fields Forever," and "I Am the Walrus."

"[R]egistral contrasts," "vocal ornamentation," "rhythmic emphasis," "masterful pacing," "command of the structural values of a wide variety of altered scale degrees," "celebrated later lyrics," and "unearthly tone colors" are phrases that roll off Everett's pen, then put through the blender chord by chord and bar by bar.[14] Everett's justifies his superlatives in eight hundred exegetical pages.

The small amount of Beatles music that is disposable is still pretty good. "Hey Bulldog" is a "throwaway" that Lennon liked for a change (compare Everett's claim with Lennon's comments noted earlier). In turn, McCartney liked Lennon's "throwaway line 'It can't get no worse' " in "Getting Better." Everett thinks "Wild Honey Pie" is a "throwaway" in the normal sense—a slight tune. He charitably suggests that McCartney's "throwaway numbers" on the White Album "add some relief to the song order but represent only his idle moments."[15] Faint praise. He salvages something from one of the Beatles' few pedestrian tracks, "If You've Got Trouble": "While this song is a mindless throwaway, it predicts . . . 'Paperback Writer' and 'Rain' to come in 1966."[16] Everett's study of middle-to-late Beatles music confirms by way of rich objective detail the thesis that the Beatles had no equal—not Frank Zappa, not Syd Barrett, not Brian Wilson—in terms of revolutionizing technology in the recording studio.

Everett's text equips us with the wherewithal to indulge in a little Beatles worship to set matters straight after the Lennon onslaught. But Everett's own thrilling performance should not blind us to the fact that the trash trope always has its day. The fourth section (of four) of Philip Norman's biography of the Beatles, accounting for the years 1968 to 1970, is entitled "Wasting." This is conventional history. The Beatles, so it goes, barely survived the recording of *The Beatles,* stumbled through the *Yellow Submarine* soundtrack and curmudgeonly *Let It Be* sessions, and had to declare a temporary truce to pull off *Abbey Road.* Everett writes, however, that "from 1966 onward, their confident and constant drive for originality in the production of studio masterpieces would push the rest of the rock-music world to reset its goals from the ground up."[17] Whether read over, under, sideways, or down, this sentence doesn't describe the process of wasting. Yet Everett himself uses the trash trope once or twice. No band can or should be shielded from it, whether as a point of pride, disgrace, or pure description.

"Why are the Beatles superior?" asked Ned Rorem way back in 1967. He deduced some interesting, if ultimately circular and vague, reasons such as "[t]he Beatles are good even though everyone knows they're good, i.e., in spite of the claims of people under thirty about their filling a new sociological need like civil rights and LSD." A second reason is more abstract: "Our need for them is neither sociological nor new, but artistic and old, specifically a renewal, a renewal of pleasure." Rorem keeps at the question, offering theories about the Beatles and their melodies, their unexpected harmonic changes, and their "making right choices instead of wrong ones," and he defaults to the trash trope in order to fathom a superiority that's finally unfathomable: "It is easy to say that most of their competition (like most everything everywhere) is junk. More important, their superiority is consistent: each of the songs from their last three albums is memorable" (those albums were *Rubber Soul, Revolver,* and *Sgt. Pepper*).[18] Not a satisfying answer, largely because his question is nearly as rhetorical as Meltzer's "What's better/worse than utter trash?" Yet Rorem's is a welcome question because responding to it will keep us forever busy coming to terms with the pleasure of enlisting for argument the big and little things we love about the Beatles—these four things off the top of my head, for instance: Ringo's wash-out ride cymbal work on the closing choruses of "I'm Down," Paul's jaw-dropping bass pattern on "Something," John's sweeping melancholia on the middle-eight of "Yes, It Is," and George's stinging lead on "One after 909."

I do, however, take issue with Rorem's suggestion that the Beatles competed against junk. During the sixties the Beatles recorded and toured among rock 'n' roll bands and solo artists of renown: Chuck Berry, Elvis Presley, the Rolling Stones, Otis Redding, the Who, Gerry and the Pacemakers, the Kinks, Paul Revere and the Raiders, Buffalo Springfield, Love, the Byrds, the Animals, the Bee Gees, Joni Mitchell, the Lovin' Spoonful, Dionne Warwick, the Four Seasons, Janis Joplin, the Hollies, the Doors, the Beach Boys, the Yardbirds, the Velvet Underground, the Band, the Young Rascals, Blood, Sweat and Tears, the Ventures, the Mothers of Invention, Santana, Dusty Springfield, Aretha Franklin, Pink Floyd, Traffic, Bob Dylan, the Zombies, Tommy James and the Shondells, Sly and the Family Stone, Jimi Hendrix, Simon and Garfunkel, the Association, Cream, the Motown roster, and the Stax-Volt roster, not to mention a thousand one-hit wonders. At no other time in rock history was there less junk against which a band could set off its good qualities and make them seem to shine even brighter as if setting a single fine diamond into a tin bracelet. The Beatles were a diamond, some would say the prettiest and rarest, set into a bracelet studded with dozens of other fine diamonds. Conversely, it can be said (but not demonstrated since such things aren't demonstrable) that given the meager competition and the genre's exhaustion today, Beck, Sheryl Crow, and Pearl Jam seem greater than they are and that they might have sunk without a trace in the chart action of 1964–70. It wouldn't be philosophical to insist on the mediocrity of platinum acts such as Dave Matthews Band and Matchbox Twenty because their mediocrity vis-à-vis the sixties acts listed above can't be proved and the prover wouldn't profit at all by the proof even if he succeeded. Twenty-somethings would still sell their souls for a ticket to a DMB show.

Arriving early to the studio one day in 1969 before the rest of the group, Paul McCartney recorded "Her Majesty" in a take or two. During remixes of *Abbey Road*, he asked a recording engineer to delete this fragment. But the engineers "had been told never to throw anything away, so after [Paul] left [John Kurlander] picked [the tape of 'Her Majesty'] up off the floor, put about 20 seconds of red leader tape before it and stuck it onto the end of the edit tape." Later, during a playback, McCartney heard his fragment as it stands now, at the end of side two. Because of accidental editing, or disobedience, or good studio policy, the last note of "Mean Mr. Mustard" became the first fortissimo note of "Her Majesty" and the last note of "Her Majesty" "was left buried in [the] unreleased rough edit of the medley, at the beginning of 'Polythene Pam.'"[19] The throwaway track, all of twenty-three seconds, so incongruous after the symphonic climax of "The End" and the Fab Four's last benediction (about the taking of love being equal to the making of it), crowns and renders utterly distinctive a brilliant musical journey. A trash track is literally the final element in a rock 'n' roll band's final masterpiece.

17. Junk

At the peak of his midseventies fame, Elton John told Paul Gambaccini that *Don't Shoot Me, I'm Only the Piano Player*, spawning the smashes "Daniel" and "Crocodile Rock," was "Elton John's disposable album." At about the same time, Elton elaborated his philosophy of pop. Rock musicians take themselves too seriously, he said, and that's

> a mistake, because in the sense of time we are very unimportant; we're just extremely lucky to be able to be doing what we're doing. I used to do sessions for groups and some of these groups thought they were creating masterpieces, just ordinary pop songs that were not very good. I've always said that pop music was disposable, and it is, and that's the fun of pop music. If it wasn't disposable it'd be a pain in the fuckin' ass.[1]

In the Gambaccini interview, Elton's lyricist Bernie Taupin added, a lot of times it's good to write disposable songs anyway. You can write one or two "classics" that will last and be covered again in a few years' time, but I think a majority of good pop songs nowadays are disposable. They're songs for the time they're in the charts, and three months later they're just completely forgotten and nobody bothers with them again. I think that's healthy in a way. You should always have fresh material coming along.[2]

Paul McCartney echoes these thoughts in his remarks on "Come and Get It": "You see, I believe in throwaway as a great thing. . . . I did a demo for 'Come and Get It' . . . which took about 20 minutes, it was before a Beatles session. . . . I ran in [to the studio] and said 'Just do this, Phil [McDonald, engineer], go on, it'll only take 20 minutes' and I threw it away." This throwaway became a number seven hit in America for Badfinger.[3] A few years later, "Mull of Kintyre," which was also a "throwaway at first," became Macca's biggest solo hit.[4]

Who else but Richard Meltzer could have tortured the idea of the intentional throwaway and the waste track into an aesthetic ideal? As early as 1969 he wrote, "The Waste Track (is what Looking Glass and stuff of that ilk is on the Association's Renaissance album) is not a rock exclusive but a *great* rock exclusive. In other art scenes you gotta wait til guys get senile or too young (or only occasionally) in order to see some wholesome throwaways."[5] He revisited this idea in *The Aesthetics of Rock:*

> The copresence of nonheaven rock stuff on an album, or in a random grouping with the true stuff, is fully allowable, even as the mere waste track, ah the infamous waste track. How else do you preserve "very specialness"? Dionne Warwick averages eight to eleven waste tracks per album; Tim Hardin (with *This Is Tim Hardin*) has even masterfully produced an entire waste album.[6]

From this it can be deduced that an album's waste tracks cause its few good tracks to stand out, which ups the value of the album, and that, surprise, after a couple of spins, the album's waste tracks start sounding good themselves, in fact may become indistinguishable from the hits, just as a wilderness hiker dressed in colorful L. L. Bean duds becomes impossible to distinguish from brown muck when after an hour or so of steady sinking, the poor man is sucked into a patch of Maine quicksand. Case in point are records by the Ventures. Starting in 1960, this instrumental cover combo cranked out dozens of twelve-tune LPs, putting out four albums a year, slowing down only in the eighties. A high percentage of filler—waste tracks—was mixed in with their readings of pop/rock hits. So adept were the Ventures at getting to the basics of songs as complicated as "Strawberry Fields Forever"—they even braved the songbooks of the Carpenters and Jim Croce—that a given album's mortar didn't seem any less outstanding than its one or two sanded, painted bricks. One way or another, an album had been built again and that was fine with Ventures fans able to detect difference among sameness, to savor detail among repetition. The example of the Ventures aside, when one considers the original hit songs deemed disposable by their own composers, Meltzer's hypothesis appears neither sarcastic nor nutty.

A song as important as anything released by Elton John, Paul McCartney, Dionne Warwick, or Tim Hardin is the Velvet Underground's "Heroin." "Heroin" is to alternative rock what "Johnny B. Goode" is to classic rock 'n' roll: foundational. Reed's biographer Victor Bockris expresses an oft-heard judgment of "Heroin": it's "one of the greatest rock-and-roll songs of all time."[7] Maureen Tucker thought it VU's "greatest triumph[,] Lou's greatest triumph too," invariably giving her goosebumps in performance. Yet she grieved that the album version "is a pile of garbage."[8] In these pages, garbage has been bandied about so much that its power to shock may be wearing off. Then Maureen Tucker lets fly that "Heroin," a milestone in terms of rock songwriting, arrangement, and performance, is garbage too. The hoariest fan of rock, even the most devout minion of the Velvet Underground, is shocked anew. "Heroin," a pile of garbage? How can this be?

Here's how. Throughout the original track, Tucker's drums are out of synch with the other instruments. She batters her two tom-toms at a tempo either behind or ahead of the guitars and vocals. This happened not because Tucker lacked good time (her time was superb) or because she was drunk or stoned (she was straight) but because during the recording of "Heroin" she lacked, one, eye contact with Lou Reed, who sang lead, and, two, a studio monitor. Because Reed, John Cale, and Sterling Morrison were plugged directly into the board, Tucker could hear nothing but a "mountain of drum noise."[9] She couldn't compensate by watching Reed's lips as he sang. In bad performance situations, when volume becomes excessive, drummers often focus on the singer's mouth or concentrate on a rhythm or bass line, stabilizing the pulse by correlating internal time and external clues with song form instilled through hours of practice. As the tapes rolled and "Heroin" went into feedback overdrive, Tucker could fasten to no reference points. At one point she stopped thumping altogether.

Tucker's spastic rhythms and the long pause she takes in the last verse are aural serendipity. This is the sound of Art. No one could hope to reproduce it. Tucker's drums-searching-for-the-downbeat meet their match in John Cale's keening viola and Lou Reed's twangy Ostrich guitar. These instruments hurt; they're the breath of Reed's self-nullification. This jarring fragmented take sound-mirrors modern urban existence, saying in effect that injecting heroin is one handy method of coping with it. So what if it kills you? So does everyday life. "Heroin" simulates a jagged and painful rush, debunking the peace that passeth understanding described by users such as Art Pepper: "[T]he demons and the devils and the wandering and wondering and all the frustrations just vanished and they didn't exist at all anymore because I'd finally found peace . . . like a kind of warmth. . . . It was like looking into a whole universe of joy and happiness and contentment."[10] Again:

> The effect was so calming, like suddenly finding yourself lying under the stars in a per-fect little island all of your own creation, where gentle sea-breezes caress the skin and a sweet seductive music comes wafting through the air, like the sound of Javanese bells ringing in strange beguiling tonalities with the voice of a woman singing wordlessly against its rhythm.[11]

But the woman vanishes, the bells go out of tune, the island decomposes, and the gentle breezes turn rough and cold. In "Heroin'"s dissonance, the Velvet Underground captured not the image of "the sweetest little smile on [Keith Richards's] face" as his "head lolled back" in junkie stupor, but Lou Reed's agony when the bliss wears off, when the reality of life strikes back, and when with-drawal turns each cell into a screaming nodule of need for more poison or death itself, which is how Pepper depicts detox in his memoir.[12] In any event, the track was approved as-is, low-budget, in tatters. Tucker's tom-toms thump and bub-ble behind and beneath the ultimate track about addiction. The city Reed aches to escape overflows with garbage, human wastrels, and narcotic junk. Erratic, hectic drumming reproduces the rhythm of that junk-laden city.

To separate the Velvet Underground and trash would be to separate the ner-vous system and the skeleton. It can't be done. They were grounded in "formu-laic trash rock from the early-sixties Brill Building, where Reed had been a staff songwriter."[13] They stole their name from a trashy pulp sex novel. Their divided soul combined "poetry with trash."[14] They "insinuated a rare beauty found only in ugliness and corruption, putting your hands inside the spiritual garbage can that is the subconscious."[15] Iggy Pop testified, "The first time I heard [their first album] I just hated the sound. You know, 'HOW COULD ANYONE MAKE A RECORD THAT SOUNDS LIKE SUCH A PIECE OF SHIT! . . . FUCKING DISGUSTING HIPPIE VERMIN! FUCKING BEATNIKS, I WANNA KILL THEM ALL! THIS JUST SOUNDS LIKE TRASH!'" (original caps).[16] Iggy soon came to his senses and realized what "a fucking great record" he had slagged. The album's "cheap" sound was integral to its beauty. As for being "hippie vermin," the Velvet Underground were anything but. They despised so-called hippies and on a normal day wanted to kill them too. There were no bongos, peace chants, antiwar slogans, hymns to flowers, odes to white birds, or cameos of Allen Ginsberg on Velvet Underground al-bums. While the hippies, clad in tie-dyed organic fabrics, gathered around the Grateful Dead and swayed to the Flower Power sound of It's a Beautiful Day, disciples of the Velvets donned black leather, walked the urban strut, partook of speed and smack (not the hippie's acid and weed), and grooved to music doused with neurosis, not peace, love, and community.

Granted, these stereotypes are revealing only to a point. The Velvet Underground concocted "Sister Ray" (about murder), "Lady Godiva's Operation" (about mutilation), and "Venus in Furs" (about masochism), but they also concocted some of rock's most heartbreaking ballads, and much of their music is poppy, bouncy, funny, and happy. Conversely, the hippies in and around San Francisco had their share of junkies and recorded their share of nasty music. Nonetheless, the mutual loathing of these two types came to a head in a humorous twist on the trope of disposability. The Velvets came west to play some gigs in love town. Sterling Morrison said this:

> San Francisco was rigged. It was like shooting fish in a barrel. The fish being the innocent heads prowling around Haight-Ashbury. We came out there as an unshakable entity. I'd never heard of Bill Graham. In fact, I've never heard of him since. I don't know who he is. I just thought he was an insane slob, totally beneath my abilities to observe. . . . An absolute nonentity. . . . He knew what we thought of him. The day I arrived at his club, I was thrown out. . . . He said, "Get out, get out you s.o.b."[17]

The Velvet Underground were managed by Andy Warhol, the maestro of disposable culture. Warhol installed his discovery in the Factory during its glory days. On the band Warhol foisted Nico, a doom-throated femme fatale whose beauty and Teutonic accent seduced many Factory workers and half the Velvet Underground. On the first disc Nico was permitted to sing the ballads "I'll Be Your Mirror" and "Femme Fatale" and the drone anthem "All Tomorrow's Parties." Warhol packaged his combo with the Exploding Plastic Inevitable, an extravaganza of dancers, slide-show backdrops, and bizarre rock music played at clear-the-seats volume. Andy produced the debut, whose pitiful sales were out of whack with its subsequent acclaim as an album whose influence on rock is beyond calculation; and while Warhol's contribution in the studio was more nominal than actual, he did design the peel-off banana cover. Warhol's philosophy of art can be distilled into ninety-three words, as if it's not worth the trouble to elaborate a Mission Statement for consumers willing and able to pay cash for trend-setting trash:

> *I really believe in empty spaces,* although, as an artist, I make a lot of junk.
>
> Empty space is never-wasted space.
>
> Wasted space is any space that has art in it. . . .
>
> So on the one hand I really believe in empty spaces, but on the other hand, because I'm still making some art, I'm still making junk for people to put in their spaces that I

believe should be empty: i.e., I'm helping people *waste* their space when what I really want to do is help them *empty* their space.[18]

Inevitably, Andy Warhol's creed sheds light not only on the image he projected for the Velvet Underground but on rock 'n' roll music in general and, naturally, on American trash culture. Junk may be junk or it may be art. Either way, Warhol implies, when properly marketed by a space-waster who prefers empty space, it's very good for business and distinctions of quality don't matter much because in the end mass-produced junk will have rushed in to fill up the vacuum of democratic emptiness configured in empty apartments and houses that owners and renters insist on cluttering with pictures, prints, posters, mobiles, wall-hangings, collectibles, and sculptures, not to mention rock 'n' roll tapes, records, compact discs, and videos. Because junk tells us who we are (remember Rathje and Murphy's open book and mirror?) and because the aristocracy of the art world, along with parvenus and philistines, validates trash-art with checkbooks, there's no need to apologize for either purveying or patronizing it. Museums are full of trash, special wings are reserved for it, personal philosophies explicate it. Natural rights, baseball, apple pie, huge gas-guzzling cars, guns, blockbuster movies, strip malls, Disney/Pixar cinema, talk shows, billboards, theme parks, fast food, superheroes, superstars, little pink houses, Andy Warhol's prints of Marilyn Monroe, Elvis Presley, and Campbell soup cans. Rock 'n' roll music. The music of the Velvet Underground too. And garbage . . . heinous beyond description, heavy beyond statistical calculation, beautiful beyond belief. American culture, American garbage, American art.

18. How Long

Garbage engaged Maureen Tucker in one more important way. After the theft of her fifty-dollar kit, she took Reed's advice and ransacked the alleys and streets around the club, coming up with some garbage cans on which to roll and thump: "[We] put some mikes under them. That's what I played for a week or so. The audience loved it. At the end of every night we'd have to clean up the little piles of garbage that got shook loose during the set."[1]

Mo's temporary drums prefigured a trend in F/X cymbals popular among rock drummers since the 1980s. The Avedis Zildjian Company offers a wide range of diameters in its Oriental China Trash (OCT) line (the twenty-inch size retails for about $165). "Every knowledgeable drummer we've asked says that they're what a China should be," the late CEO Armand Zildjian was happy to report, "[b]ut I hate to tell you how long it took. That edge had to be turned just right, and the bell had to be shaped just right. We went through dozens of prototypes."[2] The OCT deploys a clangy crash that jolts listeners with the same panglike shock made by whacking an open car door with the lid of a metal trash can. Zildjian's engineers and craftsmen toiled at this replication. Good-sounding trash isn't cheap.

Another creative use of the trash can as percussion instrument was improvised by audience members at Woodstock '99 who couldn't resist primal expression: "A hundred yards in front of them, a crowd of youths had formed a defiant drummers' circle. They repeated wordless chants and banged on empty 55-gallon metal trash cans. Some danced to the pounding rhythms, others lay on the ground, staring dreamily into the increasingly hazy sky. Several women wielding glow sticks danced naked on the trash cans."[3] Two other journalists saw the same thing: "Almost 200 formed a drumming circle, banging on overturned garbage cans with their hands, chunks of wood, a sledgehammer, an ax."[4] Metal trash cans supply the rhythms for a weekend reconnaissance with atavism.

Garbage cans and bins yield a spectrum of appealing tones. Metropolitan buskers set up minikits made of plastic or metal containers of various sizes, at times supplementing these with a broken cymbal or two, some stands, and an old beat-up bass drum with a dented batter-head. The unsightly pieces hang rickety and limp because they were salvaged from places worse than pawn shops. No matter. Having seen such kits and their performers in crowded locations in downtown New York City, San Francisco, and other big cities, I can attest to the quality of the drumming, to the cool thuds of the junky kits, and to the audience's delight in the intricate cross-patterns the better percussionists elicit from rubbish containers and cracked cymbals. A music-oriented issue of Richmond, Virginia's *Style* had a brief story and half-page photograph of two twelve-year-olds banging away with broken drumsticks on an array of empty upside-down institution-sized tin cans and white plastic buckets. One boy spends his earnings on "junk food and the movies" and on gifts for his mother. He and his partner found their instruments in alleys and storebacks.[5]

A final word about substandard drums. Nick Tosches hails Jackie Brenston's "Rocket 88" for possessing "a sound and a fury the sheer, utter newness of which set it apart from what had come before. In a way, it can be seen as a turning-point." Nick likes Ike Turner's thrashing piano on "Rocket 88," Raymond Hill's "post-melodic saxophone shriekings," Brenston's lunatic singing, and driving home the beat, "Willie Sims's trash-can drumming."[6] Two of a perfect pair: a trash can and the first rock 'n' roll song.

19. Catholic Boy

Before raiding the alley with Maureen Tucker, Lou Reed had had previous experience with rubbish containers. The composer of "Heroin" experienced a "revealing incarnation as a trash collector on Jones Beach, although that assignment only lasted for one day."[1] Provided with a pole terminating in a steel point, Reed was hired to impale and pick up paper cups and other rubbish strewn over his assigned area. Reed gave this job a shot during the year following his departure from the Velvet Underground in 1970. After several years on the road and in the studio, the band didn't break big so they broke up—to be precise, Reed quit and the deserted Velvets limped along for a couple of years before dissolving. Reed's stint picking up litter has its garish counterpart in the cover of *Take No Prisoners*. On this live album with the hideous cover (see section 15), Reed uses the four-minute single "Walk on the Wild Side" as a forum for a seventeen-minute improv based on rock critics he detested, his stage persona, his biases, local celebrities, and the origins of the tune itself, commissioned by producers planning to make a film of Nelson Algren's novel. The band vamps behind the churlish star, who occasionally touches base with the lyrics before taking another stab at stand-up. There's no backbeat. The quirky rhythm settles into the listener's head, anchoring the song while freeing Reed to play his voice off it—much like a jazz saxophonist picking out notes over a rigid rhythm section—with a flow of invective, ribaldry, and tease that crisscrosses the instrumental patterns and makes seventeen minutes pass quickly. Reed elongates triplet phrases, cuts across the downbeat with rushed syllables like a cabbie slashing through three midtown lanes during rush hour, swoops into a punch line and out again when it fails to get much of a response, enjambs dozens of lines, jabs the audience with eighth-note runs, and lapses into midmeasure rests. Think maledictions streaming out of Charlie Parker's horn, not hopped-up melodies. Well into the tune, Reed reminisces for fifteen seconds about his day eight years earlier snagging cigarette butts and orange peels with his device. He laughs off the episode to the amusement of his rapt audience in the Bottom Line that night.

"I like my trash to sound better than anybody else's trash," Lou Reed once said, "because I make records to sell records."[2] His best group and solo work channels a kind of methane burst generated from decomposing trash. He has said that he empties himself out, "so what people see is a projection of their own needs," prompting Peter Doggett to sum him up as a "wastepaper bin for the worries of the world."[3] In the sixties and seventies, certainly, he was never more than a step away from garbage. A verse in one Velvets track (recorded in 1968, released in 1985) is crooned by Reed: "It's hard being a man / Living in a garbage pail."[4] This fantastic self-dramatization is mirrored in Quinn, a character in Paul Auster's *City of Glass*. Quinn spends a spell living in an alley. When it rains, he crawls into a large garbage bin:

> Inside, the smell was overpowering, and it would permeate his clothes for days on end, but Quinn preferred it to getting wet. . . . In one corner there was a gap of six or eight inches that formed a kind of air hole for Quinn to breathe through—sticking his nose out into the night. By standing on his knees on top of the garbage and leaning his body against one wall of the bin, he found that he was not altogether uncomfortable.[5]

(Curiously, Lou Reed and Paul Auster are good friends.)

Does trash attract trash? The singer whom Reed asked to record a voice-over on "Street Hassle" had had a significant experience with trash. Bruce Springsteen's career is an outstanding example of the interrelationship between garbage and greatness in rock 'n' roll. Normally the name Springsteen conjures images of speeding cars, runaway girls, and crazy hard-bitten Romeos pushing their luck to escape the city. We think of lovelorn drifters, sidetracked lovers, listless housewives, and bored teenagers dragging their jalopies for bragging rights to streets on the deserted side of town. We think of loners treading the shoulders of deserted highways in faraway states that resemble the ones in which we ourselves live. We don't think of trash.

But trash figures in Springsteen's personal history. During a rehearsal for *Born to Run*, the Boss's future manager Jon Landau spent "the night on a ratty old couch which, Springsteen told him the next day, had been rescued from a neighbor's trash." No big deal. Neither is a musical reference to trash: Springsteen preferred "the forgotten, sometimes junky hit singles he and his friends had loved when they were kids." Dave Marsh relates that Springsteen's ambition to conquer the planet was modeled on Elvis Presley, "the man who had it all and threw it all away" (echoes of Greil Marcus). By far the most loaded of all Springsteen trash anecdotes happened earliest, when the man who became a superstar was humiliated by direct contact with garbage: "In the third grade a nun stuffed me in a garbage can under her desk because, she said, that's where I belonged."[6]

That was the last time Bruce Springsteen was at the bottom of a barrel! By treating the youngster so badly, the nun may have shaped his future as a rock 'n' roll saint revered worldwide. From a pop-psych or rock-romantic point of view, it's tempting to argue that the man's vocation was set in stone—er, rock— the day the nun subjected the boy to a disgrace no sensitive child cursed, or blessed, with an artistic temperament could ever forget.

20. Sunny

To the roster of masters tainted or burnished by garbage and trash must be added a name invoked in section 1.

During the recording of "Ezy Ryder," engineers Kim King and Eddie Kramer were leaning back in their chairs, swaying to Jimi Hendrix's solo, when they tumbled over. They scrambled back to the board. "[We] brought [the master fader] up full," King recounts, "to make sure we had hit the end of the tune correctly. Actually, we hadn't—there was some garbage there at the end—but Jimi thought the whole thing was hilarious, so we left it in!"[1] This aural garbage, remastered and sequenced with other tunes Hendrix had nearly polished for release, can be heard on the compact disc *First Rays of the New Rising Sun*.

21. Rape Me

It's time to return to Kurt Cobain, an avenging demon who whittled life to a sharp point on which the speaker of each song falls, impales himself, and bleeds nearly to death.

Cobain was born and raised in a violent, trash-strewn culture. Blessed with musical gifts that brought him from Washington State to the summit of the rock 'n' roll mountain, he lent strangled voice to a generation of kids cursed by the dysfunctionalism of postsixties selfishness, despair, and apathy. Legions of his fans hobbled into adolescence and adulthood from broken homes; they went through the motions in dumbed-down schools shoving dull self-esteem curricula down their throats; they rejected the sixties ideals (that is, what remained of those ideals) of their parents; and they weren't much interested in the sacrifices or rewards of careerism. Throughout their teen years they "partied hardy" because oblivion and self-degradation are if not admirable goals then acceptable ways to squander one's youth. Cobain's fans knew all about the spiritual emptiness that accompanies moral collapse. To these fans "family values" were a hoax, a charade, and a con. Embodying this generation, Kurt Cobain happened upon the role of tragic hero.

In Michael Azerrad's account, Cobain's teen years flash by in a collage of chaos, rebellion, vandalism, drunkenness, and uprootedness. The teenager served a musical apprenticeship that by his early twenties blossomed into the composition of blistering rock songs in which Nirvana expressed the trauma of children who had come of age in a society that had trashed them and thrown away their future. This music was dubbed "grunge"—not quite punk, certainly not heavy metal, not exactly hard rock. David Fricke defines grunge as "a music of black celebration rooted in the brutish white blooze of the early '70s, revved up with the chain-saw aggro of late-'70s punk and charged with an exorcising ferocity that is eternally teen-age and, when you get down to it, as old as the blues."[1] Nirvana's grunge was

> "alternative" music that mainstream people could like, too. . . . Not only was the music compelling and catchy, but it captured the spirit of the age. . . . Kurt screams in a code that millions can understand. He communicates in the same scattershot, intuitive way that his generation has been trained to assimilate and to express information, thanks to the usual litany of tens of thousands of hours of television advertising before they were even able to read, lousy schools, the glut of the information age, video games, etc.[2]

Trash figures heavily in Cobain's short life. First of all, trash was a literal reality. Azerrad describes the string of squalid apartments in which the adolescent Cobain crashed. These living quarters housed a subculture of malcontents, junkies, drunks, and dropouts in Aberdeen, Seattle, and other towns. The attitude in each rented hovel was that "if you drank a beer, you could just throw the can on the floor." In one apartment, Cobain told an interviewer, "[t]here was beer and puke and blood all over the carpet, garbage stacked up for months. I never did do the dishes. [My roommate] and I cooked food for about a week and then put all our greasy hamburger dishes in the sink and filled it up with water and it sat there for the entire five months I was there." This orgy of garbage was portable. Trash tagged along with Cobain whenever and wherever Nirvana traveled. The trio's European tour manager complained that the condition of the band's van was unspeakable—to him. Cobain would curl up amidst "all manner of broken equipment and accumulated garbage."[3] Like the inside of the van, the group and its entourage were usually trashed.

Alcohol- and drug-induced trashing originated in the broken homes and unhappiness of a neglected generation. In the early days at a shack where one of Nirvana's first incarnations rehearsed, underage drinkers "used the house as a place to get trashed."[4] Tableaux of depravity reproduced themselves and spread across a nation half in denial, half in despair. From his teen years on, Cobain, no different in these respects than millions of other adolescents, was usually more trashed or hungover than not, Percodan, heroin, acid, drink, and cough syrup being his banquet of help-me-throughs, pick-me-ups, and all-purpose poisons. The years—actually, there weren't that many of them for Cobain—of paying dues before Nirvana became the miracle group from the Northwest were spent in the grip of substance abuse of such intensity that one marvels at death's belatedness. It has been said that teenagers destined to invent grunge inhabited a wasteland created by corporate America and its middle-class minions in the 1980s, at the beginning of which *Trouser Press* despaired that "the majority by far of people who currently consume rock music are buying some of the worst garbage in the history of the form."[5]

Before proceeding with the trash trope in Cobain's tale of woe, it must be noted that self-destruction has involved another type of trashing, with precedents in many performers of whom Keith Moon is the drum major cavorting and stumbling at the head of a procession of carousers being led into exile down Main Street. Moon the Loon wins the rock 'n' roll award for all types of destruction hands-down, and destruction is a word for the act of wasting things in violent ways. This uncontrollable personality had proven himself *the* destroyer of hotel rooms while Kurt Cobain was still in diapers. Celebrating his birthday with some friends in the Royal Suite of a first-class hotel in Denmark, Moon went to work on the well-appointed rooms:

> "First, I must thank you all for being here. Then I should point out that we are occupying the Royal Suite and I suggest that we comport ourselves accordingly. So, dear boys, I give you a toast: raise your glasses . . . and chuck them at the fucking wall!" With that, Moonie hurls his heavy crystal goblet at a beautiful gilt-framed mirror above the open fireplace. A million slivers of glass scatter the area. Then he grabs a half-empty champagne bottle and slings that at a chandelier, which comes tumble-tinkling down. . . . [He] dismantle[s] the entire suite on his own. Ornaments fly out of the windows, which are shut at the time. Elegant tables are reduced to matchwood. Sideboards which are at once lovingly assembled by master carpenters suddenly take on a somewhat two-dimensional appearance. Everything that will burn is stacked into the fireplace and doused in brandy.[6]

This memory comes courtesy of Dougal Butler, Moon's long-time assistant, witness to dozens of such escapades, many recorded in the six hundred pages of Tony Fletcher's biography of Moon. The trash trope in this book mirrors the vacillations of a comic genius whose costume changes and mood swings were as flamboyant as his drum fills, and like those fills, they just kept coming in a torrent of rolls and roles:

- Domestic: In the midseventies, Moon and his girlfriend Annette moved into a "dump" of a house in Sherman Oaks, California.
- Cinematic: In the "insane milieu" of Frank Zappa's film *200 Motels,* which one participant called "a total waste of a half million dollars," Moon "fitted in perfectly."
- Material: Expensive items were bought only to be thrown away: "It was a characteristic that would become increasingly prevalent in his life: obsess-

ing over, buying, playing with, becoming bored with, and then discarding . . . expensive acquisitions."

- Social: Partying with Led Zeppelin in Los Angeles in the late seventies, Moon was "thrown out" of the Comedy Store in Los Angeles.
- Culinary: At an event hosted by the Beverly Wilshire in Los Angeles, Moon showed the guests how to trash a room "in a flash." He "got up and started grabbing all the tablecloths . . . and dragged them off the tables. All the crockery went up in the air. He then went and jumped on the table and got these pink chairs and started smashing the chandeliers. . . . He had gone completely beserk." The damages for this one episode "ran into the tens of thousands of dollars."
- Musical: (1) Alcohol abuse so ruined the sessions of Moon's solo album that producer Skip Taylor had to "throw out" all the vocal tracks and redo them. (2) Annette would "throw away" bottles of the liquor ravaging Moon's skills. (3) One big clue to Moon's uniqueness behind the drums was that he "threw technique out the window." (4) Of the handful of tunes Moon cowrote for the Who, "In the City" was a "throwaway."
- Personal: For an uninterrupted thirteen-year run, Keith Moon was trashed on pills and booze, cocaine too during the last three or four years. He trashed cymbals and custom-made drum sets. He trashed luxury cars. He trashed houses. He wasted his talent, toward the end barely able to hit a drum. He threw it all away.[7]

This is not a morality tale. It's evidence that Keith Moon *was* rock 'n' roll, which is to say the trash trope incarnate. So was Kurt Cobain.

In Moon's riot of waste and destruction lies a stellar precedent in the boomer generation that Cobain and company assimilated into their own rock-trash lifestyle. Destroying hotel rooms was de rigueur for Cobain and bassist Chris (aka Krist) Novoselic. Cobain delighted in rampaging through all rooms—dressing rooms, furnished apartments, whatever cubicle that touring put him in, doing this by his own admission as a form of protest. Before becoming a rock idol, Cobain was well-practiced in destruction. He discovered the joys of vandalism in high school, when "he and his friends would find an abandoned house, or one that was in the midst of being vacated, break in and destroy everything in sight." In 1991, Cobain's "band was fully dedicated to completely destroying their dressing room every night of the tour." Nirvana also declared open season on stage: "The band got drunk before their set at the final show of the tour in Rotterdam. Chris climbed up the P.A. stack at the end of the set, with his trousers around his ankles and a bottle in his hand. Security ran onstage and hauled him down while Kurt trashed everything in sight." In Los Angeles to record *Nevermind,* the band rented furnished apartments. "Naturally," Azerrad relates, "they trashed the place, breaking a coffee table and a framed painted of flowers." Once, Cobain and drummer Dave Grohl pelted their ailing car with rocks.[8]

Did "demographics" play a part in all this? Was there a socioeconomic cause and effect? The argument has been made by those not hesitant to put a stereotype to work. Novoselic's mother summed up Kurt Cobain in one simple word: "trash." Cobain agreed! The family he had abandoned (or who had abandoned him) was, he averred, "white trash posing as middle class." The label wavers between descriptive and discriminatory intent. Producer Bruce Pavitt thought the "white trash" sensibility was elemental to the sound of Nirvana and grunge in general.[9] If trash defines punk, then white trash defines grunge. This should offend no one: the white trash sensibility denotes a (necessary) step in the direction of a genuine rock 'n' roll product. Consider John Densmore's (drummer of the Doors) high regard for Jim Morrison's "cool white trash imagery."[10] It's a compliment, not a temperature reading.

Let us not forget the musical instruments. Nirvana again took a cue from the Who, whose splintered Rickenbackers and overturned Premiers were part and parcel of concert finales.[11] Beginning in late 1988, well before cash from Geffen subsidized Nirvana's predilection, trashing gear brought down the curtain. Destruction satisfied an urge for fun that turned habitual, culminating in more than one "trash-a-thon finale that left instruments and bodies strewn about the stage." This fun-filled aggression directed at expensive inanimate objects is demonstrated by the sound of Cobain demolishing a guitar during the recording of *Nevermind*'s unlisted closer, "Endless, Nameless."[12]

Trashing guitars played once or twice and wrecking rooms rented for the night; dumping grunge on a civilization already rife with garbage: all so fascinating, funny, fun, full of social and psychological meaning, and finally pathetic. On tour in Europe, Cobain sought treatment for a dyspeptic stomach on which he blamed everything from his self-hate to his heroin addiction. Cobain's chronic pain beguiled the diagnosis of every specialist. Reaching a low point (the lowest would be suicide), Cobain stuck his swollen face stuck inside a trash can as putrid gunk streamed from his churning belly. Worn-out and sick, Cobain had consulted a doctor in Scotland, in whose clinic the Guitar/Vocals of a Generation had been reduced to "vomiting and coughing into this garbage can."[13]

It's only rock 'n' roll?

Kurt Donald Cobain, 1967–1994. Beautiful blond boy-man. Rock 'n' roll genius. White-trash superstar. Junkie. Waste incarnate. R.I.P.

22. Take It as It Comes

The garbage syndrome and the high-tech cellular acoustics of the millennium aren't mutually exclusive. One reason for this is that the production of garbage, cultural and real, hasn't diminished. All statistics tell the same tale: exponential increases in garbage disposal parallel population growth, municipal sprawl, and society's indifference toward the environment. Rock star Beck (Hansen) contemplates rock's intersection with this throwaway culture. His comments are best understood with some knowledge of his music. Uniformly, critics characterize it as a mélange of rock idioms laden with reflections on trash culture. Speaking a few years back from the perspective of a rock star contracted to a gigantic image-focused record company, Beck complained, "If you don't fit into someone's mission of what a musical personality should be in 1997, then they'll just make you into it. They air brush out Neil Young's sideburns and give Patti Smith a nose job. People, music, everything in our culture—it's so disposable now." "[M]y generation has been fed a culture that's just so disposable," he said. "I can see that a lot of it is very 1997—stuff that's very of-its-time disposable." Sure, "there *was* disposable culture in the '60s. It's not just a '90s thing. . . . But it seems to be so dominant today."[1]

Because Beck is one of today's apostles of rock 'n' roll, his albums reconstitute Trash America. This artist, concludes Alec Bemis in a review of *Sea Change*, is "a garbageman with a magpie's eyes . . . and although he knows that pop music is disposable, he has finally realized that junk yards have their share of both trash and tragedy."[2] Beck is a pop polymath on the order of Prince, Frank Zappa, and the members of Phish. He has mastered numerous rock genres and found a way to blend them into a coherent whole over the course of several compact discs. Given Beck's concept of disposability and his stylistic breadth, *Mellow Gold, Odelay,* and now *Sea Change* can be described as the rock equivalents of municipal waste transfer stations where recyclers deposit household trash, yard waste, motor oil, newspapers, junk mail, cardboard, tires, bottles and cans, plastics, wood articles, and scrap metal in designated bins. As A. R. Ammons would have it in his poem *Garbage*, recycling stations and landfills are sites of potential transcendence. So are Beck Hansen's records.

Reviewing new product by the Dandy Warhols in 2000, Neva Chonin writes, "Coming from a band whose greatest hit was 'Not If You Were the Last Junkie on Earth,' this album suggests that it's possible to be elegantly wasted for fifteen minutes and survive to eloquently tell the tale."[3] To be "elegantly wasted" is admirable in rock circles because of the example set by glamorous (and invincible) junkies such as Keith Richards, whose remarkable talent didn't seem to diminish as he lived out the full meaning of this phrase during the Rolling Stones' classic years, 1965 to 1972. The archetype of the elegant wastrel has sources in romantic conceptions of decadent beauty or beautiful decadence. Ben Fong-Torres invokes the archetype in a study of Rickie Lee Jones. Her music is distinguished by its "elegance from waste; determination from despair."[4] INXS's 1997 album *Elegantly Wasted* pays further homage to the theme but without putting a positive spin on the condition. Unfortunately, the music of INXS's midtempo title cut doesn't compensate for its thin lyrics, and thus the whole shebang makes a mess of a fascinating concept. Perhaps the band's desultory performance was intended to capture the self-indulgent ennui inherent in a condition that's romantic only up to a point and interesting only in a few exceptional poets, painters, actors, and rock stars.

Another millennial artist of significance is Polly Jean Harvey. A sign of trash is thumbed-up in John Blitzer's review of Harvey's *Stories from the City, Stories from the Sea,* selected as one of the CDNow Web site's top ten "alternative" compact discs of 2000. Blitzer writes, "Harvey alternates between episodes of blistering, trashy, gutter guitar rock, and keyboard ballads of sheer melodic grace."[5] Trashy is good, clean is bad. The trash pocking the emotional terrain explored by P. J. Harvey and Beck serves as a touchstone of excellence in a review of Alice Texas's compact disc *Gold.* The reviewer reports that "frontwoman Alice Schneider casts post-modern imagery and conjures psychic wastelands as memorably as Beck on a bender or P. J. Harvey after a primal-scream session."[6]

Sheryl Crow values the throwaway nature of Bob Dylan's music. "I really understand his knack for creating an arc in his melodies," she says, "because his songs sound so effortless and sort of thrown away; you kind of miss their subtlety."[7] Throwing away songs belies their complexity. Crow has touched on a significant point. In tandem with Dylan's throwaway tunes and throwaway lyrics— Lou Reed once scoffed at Dylan's "marijuana throwaways"—are his throwaway recording techniques, well known in the industry, quintessential examples being *John Wesley Harding,* cut, mixed, finis in six hours, and *The Basement Tapes,* that batch of throwaway half-improvisations that weren't literally thrown away only because either Dylan or one of the Band bothered to turn on a lo-fi tape machine while they were knocking out fragments in a couple of basements in Woodstock over the span of several months in 1967.[8] To this day, fewer than thirty of the hundred-plus cuts (the bootleg edition contains five compact discs) have been officially released, which is another way of saying that most of *The Basement Tapes* have been thrown away after all.

To continue, Steve Huey commends the Cramps (one of whose greatest hits is entitled "Garbage Man") because of a "disposable feel" that "synthesizes classic rockabilly, touches of psychedelia, and lyrical fare . . . into an infectious, gloriously tasteless conglomeration of American trash culture."[9] When people talk about the Cramps, allusion to American trash culture is inevitable. At making trash their trademark, the Cramps have few if any peers, perhaps the Ramones, four alley cats celebrated for honing a "caustic sense of trash-culture humor and minimalist rhythm guitar sound," and Beck, the lone postmodernist celebrated for "creat[ing] music that celebrated the junk culture of the '90s," variegated music whose "trashy, disposable quality" renders it "unique."[10]

In response to a question by Lyndsey Parker, Poison Ivy of the Cramps put the myth of trash to rest in a defensive reaction to insinuations about her band's trashiness: "We see the adjective 'white trash' thrown around a lot to describe what we do, and I think that's a really racist term. . . . Everybody's trash! People call us white trash as they're munching their McDonald's burger. There's middle-class trash, suburban trash, bourgeois trash. You're all fucking trash. We would never, ever sing about white trash as a concept."[11] By universalizing trashiness, Ivy expedites the argument that the Cramps, who are glaringly trashy whether or not Poison Ivy cares to admit it, may be the most representative of American rock 'n' roll bands, an achievement not to be sniffed at.

Moving on, why does Greg Kot, assessing *The Menace* by the English band Elastica in *Rolling Stone,* assign it four out of five stars? Largely because of its trashiness. This album "finds Elastica in an unrepentant mood, scuffing up their terse, trashy guitar rock with fun-house noise." (The trashy P. J. Harvey sound hits pay dirt again.) But there's more garbage to the disc than is found in its guitar track. Elastica *recycles.* Kot approves of the band's "blatant thievery" and "recycled" riffs from a number of sources (the Velvet Underground, Wire, the Stranglers, and others) because Elastica dresses up these purloined riffs in cheeky, smart new fashion. The band's "[g]arbage-can drums, rinky-dink keyboards and corrosive guitars also make a fine mess of all those second-hand melodies. Elastica may not be particularly original, but they're boisterous enough to make that shortcoming beside the point."[12] Elastica proves to Kot's satisfaction that recycling is more than a civic virtue; it can be an aesthetic virtue too.

Can be. Steve Wildsmith isn't impressed with Duran Duran's tendency on *Pop Trash* to "recycle their old material and filter it through the modern sounds of Radiohead, Moby and The Cure." He believes trash "is an apt description" of the album.[13] Self-reflexive album titles can get a band of recyclers into trouble at review time.

Can get. A band that puts the garbage factor up-front is Garbage. Donning this name emphasized and then muddled the discrepancy between expectation and performance. When they formed a few years ago, the only place Garbage could go was up, and their name reflects that joke at their own expense. But Garbage went a long way up. Garbage has done well critically and commercially.

Their second album, *Version 2.0,* was nominated for both Grammy and MTV Awards. These honors demonstrate that accessible and award-winning music can be produced by, well, Garbage. Not all reviews of their work, however, have been favorable. In line with my thesis that in rock music the trash trope has the potential to signify either inferior or superior product, the band Garbage provides an ideal chance to test it, a test made the more interesting because of the group's audacious name. Three reviews of *Version 2.0* will illustrate my point.

The first one, by Ron Sheffield, leads the 28 May 1998 "Trash Mouth Recordings" review column in *Rolling Stone.* Sheffield's four stars are attributable to *Version 2.0*'s stacked melodies and "slippery groove" and to lead singer Shirley Manson's "slinky wit." Sheffield especially admires Garbage's skill as rock robbers:

> They absorb all the sounds they like, whether it's industrial guitar grind or easy-listening fluff, and process them into brand-new kicks. After all, recycling is a pop tradition that's older than the blues, and Garbage aren't shy about being scavengers. . . . They swipe whatever they can use and leave the rest on the floor.[14]

The second review, by David Gates at *Newsweek,* begins by contending that Garbage's first album (1995) was good because of "[c]atchy melodies, sure-fire hooks, tasty, understated guitar, immaculate production," and so on. Meanwhile, *Version 2.0* is ruined by trendy samples, "space-age wheeps," and "calculated showbiz shtik," earning it a D grade.[15] Gates should be congratulated for refraining from making any predictable "puns intended" on the theme of trash and garbage. Alec Foege in *People Weekly* can't resist this temptation. In his rave review of *Version 2.0* (an A grade), he mentions one of the disc's highlights, "Push It," which successfully "recycles" a Beach Boys song, and he concludes with this witticism: the album "[t]rashes the competition."[16] To draw a conclusion from these critics: You can never tell if rock 'n' roll garbage is going to generate a good or bad review.

Sheffield's, Foege's, and Kot's references to recycling are good examples of a metonymic application of the trash trope. Recycling is the metonym, garbage the referent. The metonym assumes that one or more influences have been plucked from the trash heap of past recordings (sometimes a band's own recordings), then recast, reformatted, reconstituted, repackaged, and marketed as brand new for a new era. Accusations of recycling tend to imply skepticism about an act's attempts to be original (generally, a positive goal) and therefore mean that the kind of compliment Greg Kot pays Elastica—despite (or because of) their thieving and rehashing of Wire and the Velvet Underground—isn't typical. The band that recycles too much is the band that lowers its chances of winning over discriminating listeners eager to hear something fresh and willing to wait for it.

Bearing the mark of precursors isn't a weakness in and of itself. Focusing on the birth of punk rock, Jon Savage fixes "[t]he process of recycling waste, that today [1991] is a pop commonplace," around the year 1972, when British and American bands began the retreat into midsixties "barbarism."[17] Knowing what we do of punk/trash, we shouldn't wonder that punk rockers recycled *waste*. Nonpunks recycled nonwaste. Before producing 1967's *Sgt. Pepper's Lonely Hearts Club Band* and *Their Satanic Majesties Request,* respectively, the Beatles had done masterly revisions of Little Richard (covers as well as original compositions like "I'm Down"), and the Rolling Stones had done the same with Buddy Holly and Chuck Berry. No one does it alone; all sounds are to some degree derivative. We can trace a hundred influences back to Elvis Presley. The weakness lies in bearing the mark too obviously, at the expense of adding anything original to a given influence. It's one thing to say that the Rolling Stones draw heavily on Muddy Waters, Slim Harpo, and Robert Johnson on *Exile on Main Street,* which they do to their advantage. It's quite another to say that Wilco draws heavily on *Pet Sounds* and *Revolver* here and there on *Summerteeth,* which they do to their disadvantage. More disadvantageous is Mojave 3's poaching of late-eighties Cowboy Junkies on *Ask Me Tomorrow.* Then again, the Junkies had been caught mixing a half-cup of Hank Williams flour, a few tablespoons of Velvet Underground sedative, and some dashes of Neil Young sugar into their thick dark pudding. Painfully obvious are the recycling of Nirvana (or is that Pearl Jam?) by Nickelback, a band that came out of nowhere in 2002, Idlewild's tendency to reveal their debt to R.E.M., and the Black Crowes' impersonation of Rod Stewart/the Faces/Keith Richards/the Rolling Stones. Belle and Sebastian seem blood related to the Nick Drake of *Bryter Layter.* In some cases the recycling bin is filled with product that's nearly interchangeable. Were these groups less masterful in their postgrunge domains, discs by Catherine Wheel and the Doves would be like cans of Coke and Pepsi tossed into one container. Each brand is fine unto itself but not as unique as commercials insist. Cola drinkers, unless they're just looking for a caffeine rush, don't chase a Pepsi with a Coke. By the same token rock fans are advised not to play *Adam and Eve* and *Lost Souls* back to back. Loaded with four- to eight-minute cuts, these discursive albums are less likely to sound same-y when auditioned a few hours or days apart. The recycled line involved here goes backward like this: the Doves to Catherine Wheel to the Chameleons UK to Echo and the Bunnymen to the Beatles.

The image of recycling as a poor aesthetic strategy is picked up by Jeff Giles in his review of Aerosmith's *Just Push Play.* Giles pillories the record: "[Y]ou've got to listen to the CD several times before you realize how deeply terrible it is. Hectic. Overproduced. Desperate to sound edgy and newfangled." Steven Tyler's lyrics are "gibberish," not to be taken in the sense that James Miller and Philip Norman delight in the "sublime gibberish" of the rockin' 1950s. On the title song, "Tyler recycles his famous directive 'walk this way.' Apparently, he couldn't think of anything else that rhymed with 'f—kin' a!' " [18]

Recycling? No thanks, Aerosmith.

And no thanks Thou. This Belgium band's compact disc *Put Us in Tune* earns a C grade from J. Gabriel Boylan. What works for Elastica (that is, recycling and/or ripping off precursors) fails for Thou, in whose music Boylan finds traces of T. Rex, Yo La Tengo, and above all, Portishead. The CD "is curiously built upon the bulwark of discarded Portishead rhythm tracks." Even its best tune (and it's a very rare album that doesn't have at least one excellent track) is corrupted by "throwaway Casio pop." Boylan works the trash trope a third time in his short review when he decides that Thou's effort "is another one headed for the 99-cent bin." [19]

Almost too self-referential to be true, Throw That Beat in the Garbagecan "literally went from the garbage can to the spinART roster" after A & R man Joel Morowitz "found an unlabeled tape in a giant dump bin of demos . . . and spent five months tracking down the group." [20] To describe this nineties band, Ira Robbins selects the motif of recycling from his junk pile of images:

[L]ooking for culture in all the wrong places, [postwar industrial] Germany has to do its global bit in the abject scavenging and silly recycling of American junk with merry abandon. A quick look at the early scrap operation mounted by this hyperactive Bremen sextet reveals a band name nicked from the B-52s, an album title skimmed off *Pee-Wee's Big Adventure* and a record label named after a Big Star song. The group's colophon, however, is more locally relevant: the anti-fascist symbol of a swastika being dumpsterized. [21]

Adjectives and adverbs used to show the band's strengths are "silly," "madcap," "amazing," "determined," "muscular," "smileyface," "imaginatively loopy," and "unerringly adorable." Not bad for a band whose name honors a garbage can. They know where rock 'n' roll belongs, and Ira Robbins, no pushover, approves. Perhaps the trashed swastika has something to do with his approval—as unique a use of the trash trope in a rock 'n' roll context as can be found in its literature and lore.

Not to worry, however, that the trash trope and its metonyms always sabotage standard denotation. Apology, from Germany, recorded *Pass You By*, reviewed by Matt Average in *Maximum Rock 'n' Roll*. Average employs old-fashioned insult: "Good gawd!! Someone please take this out with the garbage, it stinks!!" The trash trope has done its job. Still, Average keeps at the task for another fifty words. Apology's music is "MOR lite rock for those who have outgrown their 'childish punk days', and go for something a little more . . . 'mature'. Pure pap form [*sic*] a label that will release anything for an easy buck, despite quality (or legality!). Pass this one by indeed!"[22] Matt's trashy little text adds authority to his review and charm to the overall trashiness of *Maximum Rock 'n' Roll*, the more charming and authoritative because you have to wash your hands after reading it.

In these latter days, it comes down to this:

> It's maddening to try to remain conscious of all the punk, pop-punk, hardcore, and emo bands running around these days. And not just the bands themselves; just think of all the CDs, records, videos, tours . . . dedicated to this industry. One could break their brain trying to absorb and filter through the depth and breadth of what's put before them every single day. But most of that is crap. Drivel. Junk.[23]

It's the duty of today's fan to figure out whether today's junk is good or bad; whether or not junk is recycled garbage and whether the recycling process went poorly or well; whether junk is of the throwaway sort as in Thou or the throw-away sort as in the Strokes, a five-man band from New York City who on their debut *Is This It?* play "likable" tunes "with just the right amount of throwaway insouciance to show they aren't trying too hard."[24] Did no one catch them replenishing empty bottles of Ramones with fizzy pop? Imagine the Ramones with a few music lessons, more pinupness, better leather, lighter hooks, an extra member, cooler names, and more hype from the get-go.

Go Strokes!

23. Those Were the Days

The "Night Life: Clubs" writer in the *New Yorker* has at his disposal only a few lines to describe a given band headlining at a given club. Reading an issue in November 1999, I learned that performing at Irving Plaza on the twenty-ninth and thirtieth was Luna, a band that "makes a dreamy kind of music so frankly derivative that it's both disposable and eternal." With the snap of a finger, we're back in Richard Meltzer's better/worse territory of non–mutually exclusive binaries (not to mention the metonymic territory of recycling ["derivative"] just discussed). The writer adds that Luna's record company Elektra "found the band disposable and dropped it."[1]

This notice is one of the most telling pieces of criticism in this book. It's a critique superior to many full-length essays on rock 'n' roll, even superior to many monographs on the genre. It goes well beyond the obvious point that since Luna's style of music has been perfected by so many other artists that it's never going to fade, Luna benefits from the tradition in which they base their own dream pop; and yet Luna themselves are disposable for that very same reason. There's plenty of good dreamy music—so who needs Luna? Yes, the notice goes well beyond these implications. In this anonymous throwaway notice advertising a club date by a little-known band discarded by its record label, the student of rock 'n' roll has nothing less than a theory of a musical form condensed into twenty-five words. The conjunction "and" is a fulcrum between two evenly weighted terms, which also happen to be the two most important words in rock 'n' roll rhetoric, sitting on opposite ends of a plank: "disposable," "eternal." Criticism shows whether the seesaw is rising or dipping in favor of this or that adjective. A few bands are in equilibrium, some tip the plank violently in one direction, some are in playful but steady reciprocal vibration, most are in flux. If so much money, ambition, ego, and, looking ahead, salvation weren't at stake, making rock 'n' roll and criticizing it would be one big recreational moment, lovers (and haters) of trash culture's favorite music larking about in a playground equipped with swings, slides, and other rides, yet littered with cigarette butts, aluminum cans, gum wrappers, and fast food bags. The *New Yorker* notice also underlines the trash trope's role in supplying information to a general readership. Because I have a good idea of what's meant by rock that's dreamy—ten bands leap to mind—and what's meant by rock that's both "disposable and eternal"—scores leap to mind—then I have an idea what to expect when I get around to hearing Luna, whom I plan on hearing, preferably though improbably live.

The disposability factor in rock music is what captures Jeff Tamarkin's attention in his recent review of *Yeah!* (1966) by the Alarm Clocks. "Their one record," he writes with an eye on the seesaw,

> is either as good or as bad as any of 10,000 other regional garage sounds of the day. But the non-essentialness of it all is precisely what makes a disc like this one so essential: This is the real thing, teen-age madness at is finest, captured in its natural habitat—hey, there's even a photo of them playing out of a garage to a mass of gyrating neighborhood loonies.[2]

The Alarm Clocks' record is disposable ("non-essential") but eternal ("essential"). If a record is here today and gone tomorrow, it's possibly classic, potentially eternal.

Today the problem facing rock groups fond of the disposable timbres of the Alarm Clocks, the Cramps, or the Shaggs is to sound disposable too. The challenge for a band worried enough about writing good material and having the chops to deliver it is how to arrange conditions so as to reproduce a "throwaway" sound. The problem goes beyond digital technology. It's also a matter of content and a matter of the genre's very being, its conceptual center. The burden of the past affects everyone who enters a studio with guitars and drums. Rebecca Cole of English Settlement groaned in 2001, "It's so hard to make music with all these giants that came before. There already was a Mingus and a Beatles." Cole's colleague Martyn Leaper doubled Cole's groan: "Everything is disposable; it's here today and gone today. . . . Pop music is pretty much at a standstill. They've sucked everything they possible could out of the '60s, and that's where music has been for the last 10 years: revising old styles." Anyone familiar with rock rhetoric has heard this kind of thing a thousand times. Five years before Martyn Leaper passed sentence on pop, Beck Hansen, rock's supreme bricoleur, had said the same thing about its disposability and indebtedness to the past. He solved the aesthetic problem by making a postmodern virtue out of synthesis and pastiche. Leaper, on the other hand, doesn't know how to escape or outdo the past: "it's the only way I know how to communicate; it's the only music I know how to make."[3]

For the sake of an argument that can't be avoided, let's entertain the idea that rock 'n' roll has been foundering since at least the late sixties, the early seventies at best. Cole, Leaper, and Beck imply this. It's easy for older fans to agree with them. When the Band, the first all-out retro rockers, went "back to basics" on their first two albums in 1968 and 1969, they established to the surprise of many listeners the fact that rock musicians had fallen prey to nostalgia (this confused fans too young to know what nostalgia felt like), and nostalgia can only occur when something important has been over long enough for people to miss it in the context of other losses and intervening experiences. Consequently, today we shouldn't blame digital chill entirely for our inability to get back to an *elusive disposable sound,* just as we shouldn't blame boomers for expecting or wanting more than they get from contemporary rock 'n' roll, or for nagging about the sorry state of the genre when they don't get it, or for declaring the whole thing dead. Nor should we scoff at younger musicians for maintaining that their music is as fresh, bold, and real as rock ever was and for telling boomers to go to hell with their boring canons and patronizing attitudes. We shouldn't even blame the music industry or media for pretending that rock is as healthy as ever, give or take a few knocks on the head from rap and pop. It's the consumer's responsibility to demand good music, not the industry's to volunteer it. An elusive disposable sound needs a certain attitude, something defined by more than adolescence (which isn't in short supply) and its stereotypical agonies and ecstasies. This attitude is evidently irrecoverable. If being a teenager were the only requirement for it, there would still be a million garage bands. Although we have more teenagers than ever before, garage bands are endangered. Nothing has quite replaced them. The attitude needed for an elusive disposable sound would have to include a mixture of innocence and urgency, wonder and risk, all-or-nothing passion and I'm-a-lazy-sod indifference: not the self-conscious or programmed disposability that's instantly detected as factitious by the type of rock 'n' roll witness profiled in section 1. Between the years 1966 and 1969, Bob Dylan *(The Basement Tapes, John Wesley Harding)*, Elvis Presley *(The Comeback TV Special)*, and the Beatles *(Let It Be)* all tried to "get back" to an attitude of this sort. They had seen it vanish within the span of their own relatively brief careers. The rock 'n' roll attitude seems to have been that fragile and evanescent.

Most of today's mainstream bands are disposable in the negative sense. Are Creed, Vertical Horizon, Sister Hazel, Sevendust, System of a Down, Dashboard Confessional, Limp Bizkit, Matchbox Twenty, Third Eye Blind, Blink-182, Stone Sour, Nickelback, and Hootie and the Blowfish tormented by the desire to get back to the garden of disposable, essential, rock 'n' roll? These color-by-number bands are the aural equivalent of designer clothes and "athletic shoes" sold in factory outlet franchises. The shirt and sweater hang well and look great but they were made to last three months at most. The athletic shoes are made to flash rather than to function. The record stores installed in malls stock and sell designer discs to complement the logos emblazoned on the shirt, the athletic shoes, and the sweater. New Age rockers who furnish the digital diversion for post–Generation Xers are too sophisticated for generic jeans, and naked inspiration is out of the question. Any nonchalance they muster on record is prefab and post–Fab Four. Oh, they can play, like the dickens they can play those guitars and drums. Their technique will kill you. Nothing else will.

All these generalizations are implicit in a review printed in *Magnet*, a self-styled alternative music magazine, in 1999. The writer (given the magazine's slant, I assume he's under forty) is interested in what the predigital epoch connotes about what the passage of thirty years has done to rock 'n' roll music. The band reviewed is Big Star. The album is *Nobody Can Dance* (unreleased tracks recorded 1971, released 1999). The writer feels compelled to inform readers that singer-guitarist-composer Alex Chilton had been a member of the Box Tops and that he had cut "The Letter" with them. "Luckily," he writes,

> the band didn't even try [to emulate its studio subtlety] at its Overton Park gig, and the result is Big Star at its erratic best, covering "The Letter" . . . as a bluesy, impassioned throwaway and spitting out "You Get What You Deserve" in all its raw, angry sweetness. Of course, it was a peak the band wouldn't reach again.[4]

The "of course" is, of course, where the writer gives it all away. Lodged in this throwaway transitional phrase isn't just the culmination of a review about Big Star but a three-pronged insight into rock music.

1. An "impassioned throwaway" is well on its way to becoming a band's peak, in live performance anyway. Sometimes the peak is caught on tape. Most of the time it isn't, which makes it more special when it has been.

2. "Raw, angry sweetness" is good. It's easier to give examples of this epithet than to define it. Bob Dylan's "Positively Fourth Street" and "Just Like a Woman." Elvis Costello's *My Aim Is True* and *This Year's Model*. Most of Nirvana. Much of P. J. Harvey. "Raw, angry sweetness" now is as hard to find as a decent turntable in a Circuit City warehouse. Pressed for a reason, I'd say "raw, angry sweetness" doesn't breed well in a factory-outlet, AOL Time-Warner, cyber-cellular-digital, Wal-Mart, Ecstasy, MTV, CNN, SUV, please-don't-offend-me, self-esteem-at-all-costs climate. Sociologists will have to take it from there. Rock 'n' roll is overbred, overripe; its sweetness is that of mealy apple. People who've been feeding on rock for a long time can taste the difference between ripe and mealy music—a mixed blessing because it makes it hard to enjoy the taste of anything anymore.

3. Peaks are a thing of the past. Anyone for the Rolling Stones? Oasis? Pearl Jam? It's been said that the genre passed its own peak long ago, in 1965, 1969, or 1977. Can a later date be taken seriously? All the excellent music released since 1977 doesn't retard the pace of decline, just as the fact that the Sierra Club's membership is up doesn't mean global warming will be reversed.

There thrives, fortunately, an extensive scene of independent, "underground" (the term won't go away even though it's antithesis isn't what it should be, *overground*, but *mainstream*) rock music. Covering much of it is Jack Rabid, publisher, editor, and main writer of *Big Takeover*, now in its twentieth year of covering music that mainstream radio, television, and press ignore. *Big Takeover's* three hundred pages per issue of interviews, features, and reviews contradict the "rock is dead" and "past peak" biases. Although Rabid leans toward relatively unknown punk and postpunk groups, he doesn't slough off rock's big names. He's comfortable reviewing new titles—for example, *Roulette* by Violet Indiana and *A+ Electric* by Crushstory—and old—*Mojo Workout!* by Paul Revere and the Raiders (live, 1964) and *Beatles 1*. This last album brings out the trash trope twice: "It's been fun watching *1* sell several million copies, since the other half-dozen LPs selling similar numbers are so blatantly disposable and worthless—even without being compared to the greatest band ever." Rabid exhorts readers to buy the entire catalog of a band who created "music that will always matter to you, when you're young to when you're elderly, not music made to endlessly throw out when you outgrow it or use it up like old, holey socks."[5]

I quote Jack Rabid because, first, he's not a boomer, yet he loves the Beatles as much as he loves, say, hard-core legends Bad Brains; and because, second, his review applies the trash trope in a 180-degree turnabout from John Lennon's application of it. In an interview with Robert Pollard of Guided by Voices, a rare "lo-fi" band able to tape the *elusive disposable sound,* Rabid declares,

> I don't want to be one of these guys who says, "OK, I'm in my 30s, we only did it right in my era, all the bands suck now." What I'm saying is that too much of what people laud, and in fact what sells, is in fact music that's too temporal. [Temporary?] I don't think people are going to be playing Britney Spears' singles ten years from now. Whereas I think most of us will still be playing some of your records ten years from now. . . . What do you have if you're 16 years old now? Limp Bizkit? Jennifer Lopez? My nephew's 18 and I try and buy him records. . . . I have the damnedest trouble with him. He's into Korn and stuff like that.

Pollard comments, "Well, you've gotta feel sorry for kids these days, they really don't have anything to listen to. When we were kids . . . the shit that they played on the radio was good. It was song-oriented, you know? Now, everything is sort of image and technology-oriented."[6]

How many times must we hear the same thing? Yet Rabid continues to recommend titles to fans searching for rock 'n' roll in a conglomerated market. A consumer must be able to think outside the squeezebox of Sony, Geffen, and BMG. The platinum-on-the-brain pathology of music executives force-fits groups into three or four surefire genres, all digital, all predictable, all as hollow as the center of a compact disc.

24. Rip It Up

In a turn-of-the-century poll listing the top one hundred singles of the rock era, *Rolling Stone* stressed the transient yet enduring nature of the music. "[P]op honors the ephemeral just as much as the lasting," an editor declared. "Pop songs can be trivial and they can be awesome—often at the same time. They can change the world, or they can make you change the radio dial. They make rules and they break them, they play with our emotions, they trigger memories and arguments, and just when you're sure they'll never go away, they disappear."[1] A reader might be pardoned for wincing at the writer's ineptness—the first-person plural "our" tossed in with the second-person "you," "awesome" (instead of "profound") serving as an antonym for "trivial," and the either-or fallacy—but not at his thesis. As if to prove it, the list adds new terms to the lexicon of garbage. Some examples:

Number 10: "I Want It That Way," the Backstreet Boys. One BSB recalled, "When we heard it, we just thought it was wack." This "wack" single spurred a record-breaking pace for the album *Millennium*—specifically, first-week sales of 1.13 million units. By early 2001, *Millennium* had been certified thirteen platinum.[2]

Number 3: "Smells Like Teen Spirit," Nirvana. A demo version "sounded like shit," said producer Butch Vig. Two years later, during preproduction of the Grunge National Anthem, "it fucking blew my mind." It fucking blew another fifteen million minds too.

Number 12: "Where Did Our Love Go," the Supremes. Diana Ross "strenuously complain[ed]" to Berry Gordy Jr. that it "was a piece of garbage." It was originally turned down by the Marvelettes.

Three throwaways, three monsters.[3]

A less reverent poll compiled by the Onion A. V. Club analyzed the "least essential albums of the '90s." All of these albums are of the rock and pop variety. The idiocy of rock polls is the subject of the Onion brigade's satire. Their hacking at scores of titles constituting "the Decade's Most Disposable Recordings" is both edifying and amusing. The authors rip up releases by household names (George Martin's *In My Life*, Fleetwood Mac's *Time*, the Knack's *Serious Fun*) and dredge gunk from the bottom of the barrel, disasters such as *The Best of Shaquille O'Neal, Songs from Ally McBeal Featuring Vonda Shepard*, Joe Pesci's *Vincent Laguardia Gambini Sings Just for You*, and, incredibly, the Least Essential Album by a Cornerback, Deion Sanders's *Prime Time*—albums that it's hard to believe were conceived, contracted, recorded, pressed, hyped, and taken to market. Working the trash trope overtime, the pollsters enlighten readers about dreadful discs fated to clog landfills. Johnny Mathis singing Diane Warren is "a treacly throwaway." Depeche Mode's *Songs of Faith and Devotion Live* is "a disposable cash-in." "Skid Row and Guns N' Roses put out time-wasting covers albums" and Wreckx 'n' Effect "releas[ed] a disposable album of old-school covers such as 'Planet Rock' and 'Da Vapors.'"[4]

The rhetoric of garbage, so easily deconstructed in the bravado of *Rolling Stone*'s best-singles survey and others its editors continually concoct, serves as critical ballast to a ship overloaded with product and hype designed to move even the worst of it out of the hold, onto the docks, into the stores, and into plastic bags. Because polls usually celebrate what's (supposedly) BEST, consumers are conditioned into forgetting how bad rock 'n' roll really is. The Onion scribes repeat a lesson that should have been drilled into the consumer's head in Rock 'n' Roll 101, to wit: *There's no shortage of abysmal, disposable records marketed to steal us blind.* Too many people slept through class the first time.

25. There's a Place

Every one of rock's hundreds of substyles has inherited the trash gene. Yet most of them disguise signs of their inheritance. Some Guthrify it with acoustic guitars and social commentary (folk rock); some put it into big band arrangements (new jack swing rock); some stomp it into the boards of the dance floor (disco); some obscure it in tape loops and F/X (experimental rock); some turn up their noses at it, think twice, and then embellish it in multitracked virtuosity and bombast (progressive and art rock); some cross-dress it in four-inch heels and plaster it with mascara and polish (glitter and glam rock); some wax it for a good ride through the pipeline and pylons (surf rock); some give it a south-of-the-border accent (Tex-Mex); and some dab it with Clearasil (bubblegum). A few substyles openly embrace trash and get good and wasted in the process (frat rock, punk rock, and grunge).

Rock taxonomists face the same problem professionals in other fields face as they try for the sake of expediency to wrestle mutable styles or epochs into place and make them stay put. They have to contend with overlap, exceptions, subjectivity, arbitrariness, pigeonholing, and reductiveness, not to mention the uniqueness of rockers who with each new record stretch the limitations inherent in categories. For example, according to Perry Meisel, Jimi Hendrix trashed the rules on "Purple Haze," the first song on his first album: "Here Hendrix challenges the funky duo behind him . . . to see how well it can maintain the backbeat while he trashes almost every category upon which his performance ironically depends, including at times the groove itself."[1] To trash old categories is to create new as yet unnamed ones. Rock 'n' roll turnover gives the most disposable genre new life. Trashing it rejuvenates it. It's good that critics can't pin down Hendrix (acid blues to psychedelic soul to Latin rock), Radiohead (art rock, synth rock), Beck (seventies-funk rock, rap, folk, hard rock), Dave Matthews (stadium rock, jazz rock), Led Zeppelin (hard rock, metal blues, bardic balladry, "Indian" trance), the Who (power pop, rock opera, synth rock), the Velvet Underground (pop rock, protopunk with traces of doo-wop, soft rock), the Rolling Stones (stoned white blues, drugged folk rock, hard rock, disco rock), or the Beatles (seemingly every category). Because they trash categories that would otherwise reduce them to being defined by only one, the greatest bands and performers are irreducible: in this light, relish not merely the big names just cited but other, alternative masters such as the Flaming Lips, Pavement, Guided by Voices, the Pernice Brothers, Elastica, and Yo La Tengo. Ira Robbins struggles with distinctions and invokes the trash trope (as did Meisel above) when assessing Treat Her Right, which is "[n]ot quite a blues band, not exactly swamp trash and too stylized for basic rock 'n' roll."[2]

Be all this as it may, a trash-rock category became official in the midnineties, originating in France, of all places. Emmanuel Legrand defined trash rock as Gaul's idea of punk added to grunge added to hard-core—got that?—its practitioners taking from the Yankees their Red Hot Chili Peppers and Rage Against the Machine as models and cranking it up from there. The leading exponents of trash rock were/are Mano Negra and Noir Desir, both formed in the late 1980s, both very popular in France, and both unknown in America, probably because the stateside market is already saturated with trash.[3]

26. Rock Show

For better, for worse, trash, literal and figurative, defines rock 'n' roll music. Whether as the stamp of beauty or the confirmation of ugliness, whether as an aesthetic term or a taxonomical heading, whether as a physical element or its spiritual counterpart, garbage or one of its variants characterizes the music better than any other metaphor. In the following passage about the Sex Pistols, garbage ("debris") signifies positive qualities: audience participation and joy, intense bonding with the artist, the freedom to indulge in unfettered fun, and the creative expression of support:

> Even seeing the band only once, as I did at San Francisco's Winterland in January 1978, brought home their consequence with an indelible jolt. That night, Rotten danced— waded, actually—through a mounting pile of debris: everything from shoes, coins, books, and umbrellas, all heaved his way by a tense, adulatory crowd. . . . Rotten rummaged through it all like some misplaced jester. . . . It was the most impressive moment in rock & roll I have ever witnessed.[1]

The higher the pile, the higher the approval rating. Punk junk is love from us to you. But the signifier quickly turns menacing. Discussing the riots marring Bill Haley's British tour in 1957, Philip Norman describes the perpetrator as looking "more like a kiddies' entertainer than a revolutionary leader in whose name a hundred provincial cinemas had been trashed."[2] At a Stones concert in 1964,

> a crowd of drunken Scots . . . started spitting at Brian Jones, offended by his effete image. . . . When they spat at [Keith] Richards too, he stomped on their fingers which were grabbing the edge of the stage, and kicked one of them in the nose. When cries of "Scotland, Scotland" filled the Gardens, the Stones made a quick exit. The stage was rushed, instruments smashed, and the auditorium trashed.

So what's new? Kids go bonkers, trash venues. The ticket buys two hours of relatively legal savage deportment. Hooligans come to howl, litter, carouse, bash bodies, and crunch the metal seats. We know that. It would be naive to say the performers don't help to instigate audience violence and baseless to say they don't at times fall under its spell. What I wish to emphasize is that rock historians can't seem to get in and out of the concert hall without picking up some collateral trash. Referents are packed into representations of disposability that as usual don't settle into comfort zones of good this or bad that. For example, Linda Martin and Kerry Segrave rationalize Pete Townsend's compulsion to crack perfectly good guitars: "Many people, including fans and other musicians, were horrified by this kind of wasteful destructiveness. But few realized that the trashing of assembly-line guitars was basically a reflection of their own disposable society." *Pete was making a statement.* On the Big Beat tour of 1958, they add, it was customary for Jerry Lee Lewis "to completely trash a piano during his set."[3] Simple showmanship? Insanity? A mockery of transubstantiation? A rehearsal for perdition? A glimpse of purgatory? Nick Tosches taps biblical syntax to represent Lewis's antic disposition:

> [W]hen it seemed that the screams had grown loudest and the rushing most chaotic, [Lewis] stood, kicked the piano stool away with violence, and broke into "Great Balls of Fire." As the screaming chaos grew suddenly and sublimely greater, he drew from his jacket a Coke bottle full of gasoline, and he doused the piano with one hand as the other hand banged out the song; and he struck a wooden match and he set the piano aflame, and his hands, like the hands of a madman, did not quit the blazing keys, but kept pounding, until all became unknown tongues and holiness and fire, and the kids went utterly, magically beserk with the frenzy of it all.[4]

The Killer's Pentecostalism leaves a scorched and probably unplayable piano, pieces of its busted keyboard and charred frame hanging off the bridge and cabinet. Tosches elevates the creation/destruction of rock 'n' roll debris into an (anti)sacrament of salvation/damnation. This ritual version of the trash trope is far removed from, say, Lou Reed's trash-can graphics or the Trashmen's photo shoot amid garbage pails. Granted, Jerry Lee Lewis trashed his piano because it was good show business. It was also, however, a method of siphoning or achieving personal and collective guilt, rebellion, defiance, apostasy, mass hypnosis, retribution, and transcendence.

Trash, then, has links with violence, foreboding, even discrimination. A gig in Boston on the same tour turned ugly at the point Chuck Berry (whom Jerry Lee successfully upstaged with his piano flambeau) "was pelted with garbage from the gallery and had to take refuge behind his drummer," an example of a major black rock musician subjected to double doses of prejudice, musical and racial, from his own compatriots.[5] In Italy, it was anti-American sentiment that got the garbage airborne. Jay Dee Daugherty, drumming in Florence for the Patti Smith Group, said the singer provoked the crowd by displaying a massive American flag. The singer's patriotism was (rightly) interpreted as Yankee imperialism. Missiles of trash started striking the musicians. Instantly coming to Daugherty's mind were "all the horror stories about Lou Reed's concerts in Italy being firebombed. So as soon as I saw those things coming, I ran over to this gigantic road case for the B-3 organ and got inside of it, and then when it stopped raining debris, I came out."[6]

According to David Moodie and Maureen Callahan, Woodstock '99 upheld a tradition in which tonnage of garbage is a by-product of large rock festivals. Their field report makes plain that the sequel to the original sixties mudfest was a disaster for anyone expecting even the lowest standards of civility and hygiene. Oppressive heat was the weather's contribution to a second Woodstock rampant with drugs, dehydrated revelers, price gouging, violence, first-aid emergencies, sewage, rape, and squalor. "Around the Monkey Sex Cult compound," they write, "the campgrounds were wrecked. Garbage was strewn everywhere, collecting in fetid piles that began to resemble landscaping in some of the less desirable neighborhoods in Manila." That was Sunday morning. By 1:00 P.M., Moodie and Callahan observe, "[v]ery little trash had been picked up for the duration of the festival, and the entire field before the East Stage was dotted with garbage. Fans picked through refuse to find a clean pizza box upon which to sit." Garbage-hurling was ceaseless and without prejudice. Everyone was a target, from artists and policemen to technical personnel and fellow campers. In one incident a group of teenage hecklers tried to pelt VJ Carson Daly, who fled from the minimob with his tech crew: "Pursuing garbage traced lovely parabolic arcs through the air but failed to hit its mark." Granted, people get excited, especially when they're wired on Ecstasy and insomnia, and given the mass chaos, trash pick up can't be a priority at a festival of this size. But as Moodie and Callahan describe it, the spillover of human waste at this three-day celebration of music was nothing short of revolting: "At least 100 kids dove into a shallow mud puddle near the row of Port-a-Sans closest to the East Stage, largely unaware that they were slathering themselves in human waste." On Saturday, "Port-a-Sans were clogged up and overflowing, and waste streamed into the field; several campsites were suddenly awash in rivers of human waste."[7] Excrement, pizza boxes, broken bottles, plastic bottles, aluminum cans, discarded clothes, and used tampons covered the multiacre site. Perhaps the music was good enough to compensate for the conditions and perhaps the deluge of waste complemented the sound of a civilization going into the Dumpster. The two journalists don't say.

In contrast, it has been said that vibes of communal love and Aquarian oneness ruled at the first Woodstock in 1969, "remarkable not only for its size but for the peacefulness and joy of the event." This event is said to have proved to skeptics that half a million "youths could join together in peace, endure three days of rain and mud, share music, pleasure, and hardship, and live together virtually without violent confrontation." Woodstock '69, they say, was a rare triumph of "dancing day and night, lovemaking and nude bathing, and the feeling of being free with hundreds of thousands of friends." But those youths had to answer calls of nature and they relied on disposable commodities. Waste disposal services at Yasgur's farm weren't equal to the demand. Aerial photographs of the six hundred–acre postfestival site show stretches of trampled meadows strewn with garbage. On the scene at the time, Jean Young wrote that clean up was undertaken in the Woodstock spirit of "flair and fun. A long plastic tube with 'Peace' written on it was stuffed with napkins and other soft materials, and inflated with hydrogen. It took off through the air like a big snake until it was out of sight."

How cute. We're to assume that farmers upcountry welcomed the sight of this monstrosity floating toward them, probably leaking its contents over barns, gardens, cattle, and silos, before plummeting into someone's back forty. Young recalled that another mass of "[g]arbage was collected and then shaped to form the word 'Peace,' which could be seen in its entirety only from the air. One person started designing with bottles as they came in. It was creative-play garbage!"[8] Statements such as this one explain why hippie attitudes of the Flower Power era are so easy to ridicule and even to despise. Young's lack of irony, coupled with the imbecility of thinking that garbage is just another material on which to disseminate peace slogans for the benefit of airborne entities, reveals a la-dee-da complacency about trash that's as reprehensible as the fuck-you attitude that smeared Woodstock '99. Young believes that garbage can be deployed as another sign of universal love. After making tons of trash, we can play in it like toddlers who don't understand the consequences of their actions. It's a sad day when a partisan of rock music has to agree with Bob Larson's fundamentalist judgment that "[t]he garbage-strewn scene of [the first] Woodstock, left a metaphoric testimony to the aftermath of ruined lives that far exceeded the extent of the rubbish covered hillsides."[9] Meanwhile, the offspring of Young's generation, those Woodstock '99 carousers who don't attend weekend concerts in search of unity, took garbage at face value and hurled it to soil others. *Fuck love and peace! Eat trash, dude!*

Young and her generation have long since matured. Today, the garbage generated in the subdivisions in which millions of her brother/sister boomers live in quiet comfort is whisked away and put to rest far from their sight. No one is dumping it in their backyards then teaching their children and grandchildren to shape it into the letters P-E-A-C-E. In trash terms, the two Woodstocks teach three things: (1) The garbage produced at each event was so staggering as to surpass the predictions of promoters. (2) Two generations had different ways of handling the garbage generated during their days of rock 'n' roll revelry. (3) No matter what generation is making it, live rock 'n' roll and trash are symbiotic.

All this talk of garbage pales beside one significant showing of the trash trope at the festival often cited as Woodstock's antithesis, Altamont. The Rolling Stones were there. So were the Hell's Angels (the security detail!) and so was death. So was the Rolling Stones' chronicler, Stanley Booth, who reprinted the courtroom testimony of Paul Cox, who witnessed the security detail at work. After the fatal stabbing of Meredith Hunter, testified Cox, an Angel "grabbed one of those garbage cans, the cardboard ones with the metal rimming, and he smashed him over the head with it, and then he kicked the garbage can out of the way and started kicking his head in."[10] It's only rock 'n' roll, but did he like it?

27. Rock and Roll Music

Because images of trash and tropes of disposability pervade the criticism and culture of rock 'n' roll music, it follows that many rock songs foreground some aspect of trash. In some cases whole songs are based on it. In others a line or phrase will do. Fully aware of the subtexts and aporias inherent in lists—they're marketing strategies, canon-making projects, teaching aids, or personal favorites without much to offer in the way of universal relevance—and fully aware of postmodern theories that reduce vertical lists to rubble (1) because textual meaning is always deferred (the trash trope, rock titles, rock anecdotes: all deconstructible texts) and (2) because representations (verbal, aural, oral, illustrative) can't be stabilized, can't embody transcendental "human values," cannot not repress infinite differences between and among similar entities in a class or genre, can't embody disinterested or unpoliticized authority, and thus can't be prioritized in anything approaching sacrosanct linearity—I nonetheless offer a survey, compiled in the tradition of a nice round number (Top Ten, Top Forty, One Hundred Greatest Albums of All Time, and so forth) and ordered chronologically (1958–2000), of forty songs featuring the trash trope.

I hear someone protesting that my moment of origin is arbitrary. I agree. All origins are. But I had to balance my first choice against the hundreds of tunes that would compete for the other thirty-nine places. Many worthy candidates had to be excluded, including some previous to 1958. Facing practical and theoretical restraints, I decided to lead off with a title dating from rock 'n' roll's golden age. Readers are encouraged to check out earlier rock 'n' roll tunes based on waste, notably 1954's "Wasted" by Wanda Jackson and "Your Cash Ain't Nothing but Trash" by the Clovers and the postwar standard "I Sold My Heart to the Junkman" (1947) by Etta Jones.

My choices range in instrumental/compositional ability and method from the rudimentary to the sophisticated, and in vocal delivery from the articulate to the incoherent. Lyrical quality is assumed to be irrelevant. Few judgments are forthcoming in regard to occurrences of bad grammar, simplistic rhyme schemes, sentimentality, poor taste, or lack of originality. Lyrical content concerns me more than do production, dynamics, instrumentation, and so on, first because I intend to exhibit the frequency and diversity of the trash trope and then to explicate each instance of it, and second because I can't reconstitute the listening experience in words. To comprehend a lyric, listen to the tune:

> Singing patterns which use a unique grain of voice, often one which traditionally would not be accepted as "singing" at all, might be accepted in rock music as a pivotal contribution to the quality of the music. In the same way sighs, whispers, screams and shouts, grunting and other vocal practices might be interpreted in the context of rock as signs of the performer's emotional commitment to the meaning of the music. . . . [I]solating rock lyrics from their performance and subjecting them to any form of content analysis, reduces their compoundness of meaning. Rock lyrics should be examined, according to this view, in conjunction with their performance and the sonic package of which they are a component.[1]

This was written in 1994. Musicologists continue to wrestle with lyrical representation. Writers are physically unable to read their interpretations of a lyric and play musical samples for readers at the same time. I see no solution to this predicament better than giving descriptive and nominal information about the music while discussing what forty lyrical texts communicate about the theme of disposability in this disposable art form.

1. 1958. Sob stories about parents are legion in rock 'n' roll. On hand to establish this tradition was Jerry Leiber and Mike Stoller's "Yakety Yak," the Coasters' first chart topper. A blatting saxophone and jerky shuffle underpin this novelty rhythm-and-blues tune crafted to cross over into the expanding rock 'n' roll marketplace. An endearing irony of "Yakety Yak" is that its humor relies largely on references to garbage, yet nothing's wasted: the thing exhausts itself in one minute and fifty-five seconds. One of the funniest hits to emerge from the rock 'n' roll era, "Yakety Yak" is also a "statement" about what in the sixties became known as the Generation Gap. The composers portray a parent telling his son to do his chores, privileges hanging in the balance. Junior doesn't want to scrub floors? Then he can kiss his rock 'n' roll R & R good-bye. Doesn't want to sweep his room? Forget Friday night. The kid is a male Cinderella dreaming about a sock hop where he's free to dance, sneak some cigarettes, complain about school, and drive off with his gal into the summer night and see how far she'll go. First, however, is the fact of household garbage. Daddy dictates the terms. Cash and a free Friday night depend on whether or not the boy gathers up the trash and puts it where it belongs. In this fifties household (as in many others), rock 'n' roll music was a bargaining chip; it made it easier for the teenager to bear his weak position, and daddy knew it, which is why he threatened to take it away, a mistake since it would only increase the teenager's desire for it. Compared to the punk rock the fifties teenager's own teenagers would dream up twenty years later, "Yakety Yak" comes off as the dumb fun of a prehistoric age. And yet its snappy pulse, nutty verses, and funny refrain ("Don't talk back") articulate indignity and smoldering rebelliousness. Until the boy hauls off the garbage, dusts off his hands, hops into his waiting buddy's jalopy, and roars off to meet the rest of the gang, he won't get no satisfaction. Despite this menacing subtext, "Yakety Yak" sounds like pure innocence.

2. 1964. *Rock music is rubbish:* this conclusion is reached in "The Story of Bo Diddley," one of the first and best tunes whose subject is the history of rock 'n' roll. Recorded by the Animals at the outset of the British Invasion, "The Story of Bo Diddley" compares favorably with Don McLean's "American Pie," the Mamas and the Papas' "Creeque Alley," George Harrison's "When We Were Fab," and the Minutemen's "History Lesson (Part II)," other pop histories. "The Story of Bo Diddley" is propelled by the ur-rhythm pioneered by Bo Diddley:

We hear this pattern roll out of drummer John Steele's warm tom-tom.[2] (The same groove whips up the excitement in "Not Fade Away" by Buddy Holly, "I Want Candy" by the Strangeloves, and "She's the One" by Bruce Springsteen, as well as works by other rockers too numerous to count.) The Animals' saga (at 6:22, it's a long track for the time) surveys the growth of the white rhythm-and-blues and rock 'n' roll scene, touching on the rise of the Beatles, the Rolling Stones, and the Animals themselves. As the tune winds down, Eric Burdon recalls when Bo Diddley and his entourage showed up at a hometown (Newcastle, England) gig by the Animals. Bo Diddley, "the man himself," in the audience! Burdon's delight notwithstanding, he satirizes Jerome Green, Bo's percussionist, and the Duchess, Bo's "gorgeous sister" on these counts: he likes alcohol, she likes sight-seeing. The biggest joke, however, isn't on these visitors but on the Animals and other English combos who can't leave the American blues alone. Oh, that elusive feel, that behind-the-beat backbeat, those stinging punch-drunk guitars, those wolf-wailing harps, those grainy voices of suffering and survival! Bo Diddley versus the Animals: the authentic versus the ersatz. The original, the duplicate. The natural, the studied. The pure, the posed. The black, the white. If nothing else, growing up in a rough town gave the Animals the wherewithal to laugh at their own pretensions, and this self-deprecation is as winning as Steele's syncopations. Bo Diddley listens to the racket and then declares that the Animals' music "sure is the biggest load of rubbish I ever heard in my life." Performed with humility, wit, and charm, "The Story of Bo Diddley" implies that rhythm-and-blues, or rock 'n' roll, as played by white teenage wanna-be's from England, is nothing to write home to Chicago about. The song implies this but sounds mighty fine coming out of the loudspeakers. The same goes for much of what was recorded by the Rolling Stones and the Yardbirds during this period. In this discrepancy—these boys couldn't pull off true electrified blues but they sure as heck could pull off something else—lies much of the song's lyrical appeal. The trash trope comes across as either put-down or pull-up, perhaps both at the same time.

3. 1968. An example of environmental awareness and hybrid instrumentation in rock music, "Fresh Garbage" leads off Spirit's debut record. The group exhorts citizens of Earth to look into their garbage cans, take an inventory of the unconsumed items, and realize that the world itself has become one big bin full of fresh garbage. The first verse is repeated, as if repetition will raise consumer consciousness. If "Fresh Garbage" fails as a protest song, most likely the blame lies in the fact that the group dumps too many influences into the three minutes and thirteen seconds of the tune's three-part arrangement. The first section, in a syncopated four, is bossa nova oriented; section two, also in four, is straight rock; section three is a jazz jam in three, with John Locke soloing on electric piano. Then it's back to the cowbell, conga, and tambourine of section one and the feedbacked guitar and space-age vocals of section two. "Fresh Garbage" is a lively, disjointed hybrid, each element so distinct from the others that the whole ends up less than the sum of the parts. Spirit's signature tune, "Nature's Way," addresses environmentalism a little less didactically and certainly more coherently.

4. 1969. Decentered instruments and pinched off-pitch vocals buoy the lyrics of "That Little Sports Car," the Shaggs' parable of the disappointment that clips high hopes of romance. The narrator sees a sports car driven by a man she knows. She pursues it in her own car, accelerating to intercept him at a gas station, to no avail. He's not there, it's late, she can't figure out where she went wrong, and she concludes that she has "no time to waste." The girl draws a lesson from frustrated desire: "Never do wrong." This bizarre tune yields some old-fashioned New England didacticism (the three Shagg sisters, Dot, Betty, and Helen, were born and raised in rural New Hampshire), and its allusion to waste is one of the most ambiguous in rock 'n' roll. No time to waste doing what? Getting back to work? Getting home? Getting luckier in the pursuit of men in sports cars? Tracking the driver? "That Little Sports Car" claims the distinction of being the first tune in the Trash Top Forty to make wasted time, a popular subject for songwriters, an integral part of the lyrics. To hear these words uttered (no one could pretend that the sisters do anything that resembles singing) in a song without a one count, a two count—without, in short, any beat that could be assigned a number—and without a melody is to experience the full impact of a tank of musical garbage into which a listener's hearing apparatus has been submerged.

5. 1969. "Trash Man" by Jimi Hendrix is an instrumental that languished in the vaults until released with overdubs on the posthumous album *Midnight Lightning*. I have no idea why Hendrix gave the title "Trash Man" (trash = noun? adjective? verb?) to this tremendous throwaway and I have no idea what the original tape sounds like without the contributions by session men with whom Hendrix had never recorded. Steven Roby observes that "Trash Man" was one of about twenty tunes composed and taped (solo acoustic guitar) by Hendrix between mid-1969 and early 1970 for an autobiographical suite that Hendrix named *Black Gold*. The version of "Trash Man" on the archival *Black Gold* demo tapes "bears no resemblance to the version released on *Midnight Lightning*," mainly because (here Roby, who seems not to have heard the tapes, relies on unpublished notes by Hendrix archivist Tony Brown) it's much shorter and it has vocals. What these vocals are Roby doesn't say, probably because Brown doesn't. In any event, at just over three minutes in length, the "Trash Man" we do have isn't an improvisation, and it's certainly equal, arguably superior, to other late instrumentals by Hendrix such as "Tax Free" and "Pali Gap," both resurrected on the compilation *South Saturn Delta* in 1997. Its neometal solos and savage drumming (Allen Schwarzberg answers Jimi's thunder note for note) cry to be heard. As of 2003, however, the song remains unavailable on compact disc. *Midnight Lightning* too is long gone. "Trash Man" in limbo underscores rock waste conceived in terms of premature death, Hendrix's example being one of the worst if judged from the perspective of an artist's lost potential. In "Rock Death in the 1970s: A Sweepstakes," Greil Marcus devised a system for figuring the relative loss to rock culture of each given corpse. In the category of Future Contributions, Hendrix scored a perfect ten.[3]

6. 1969. A third example from 1969 is Bob Dylan's country-rock ballad "I Threw It All Away." Taped in Nashville with the cream of studio musicians,

Dylan plays the part of a man who has learned to value love. To paraphrase: Dylan advises the listener who has been blessed with a gal's love to accept it wholeheartedly, not letting her devotion "stray," because it's a certainty that the cold-hearted person, as the singer once was, will suffer terribly if he throws away such love. So lovely is this ballad that it's impossible to snicker at what in paraphrase must seem to be maudlin lyrics. Trash tropes are scattered throughout Dylan's work, a perennial favorite showing up in 1965 on the hard-rocking blues "From a Buick 6," where Dylan coins the phrase "junkyard angel" to describe a perfectly dependable girlfriend, about whom he barks and boasts to a chugging beat that if he dies, she's the kind of woman who will cover his bed with a blanket.

7. 1969. Second up on Blind Faith's sole album is Stevie Winwood's ballad "Can't Find My Way Home." In the song's haunting chorus, the world-weary Winwood laments two existential problems: he's wasted and he can't get back to where he once belonged. Circularly, one problem causes the other, which in turn perpetuates the first one. "Wasted" describes a condition in which a person's mental, emotional, or physical health has been ruined by excess. Paradoxically, excess empties ("wastes") a person's well-being. The more drugs taken, the more groupies laid, the more money squandered, then the more wasted the person. While telling the tale of one man's loss of direction, "Can't Find My Way Home" also implies that the sixties dream had begun to fade into fuel for nostalgia and that its long orgy had done in many of its participants. Dazed survivors of rock 'n' roll's greatest decade were on the verge of beginning to count and account for the ones who didn't make it. Winwood seems to have sensed how large that count, and how draining that accounting, would be for the survivors and their inheritors alike.

Blind Faith was reissued in 2000. In reviewing it, Jeff Tamarkin took the trash route: "A great band and album even though their cover of Buddy Holly's 'Well All Right' was a weak throwaway and 'Do What You Like' was largely a Baker drum wank."[4] That would be scanned. The album is marred by two throwaways that clock in at twenty minutes, in contrast to four other numbers at twenty-three minutes. Half the album is throwaway and wank. Tamarkin, however, calls it "great." Because of the mutability of the trash trope, Tamarkin is right, even if we disagree with two of his conclusions. The album's obvious throwaway is Eric Clapton's "Presence of the Lord." As for "Well All Right," I admire Blind Faith for tackling it at all.

8. 1970. The lyrics of Paul McCartney's "Junk" are as whimsical as its melody. Parachutes are juxtaposed with sleeping bags, bicycles for two with a jamboree. A sign in the window of a shop tells people to "buy" while the junk out in the yard asks "why"—a low-key comment on the perils of acquisitiveness? This waltz, either rejected or never seriously considered by the Beatles (a White Album demo of "Junk" sweetens 1996's *Anthology 3*), belongs among the elite of McCartney's most cloying tunes, "Yesterday," "Here, There, and Everywhere," "I Will," and "My Love." As well as if not better than any song in the Trash Top Forty, "Junk" proves that images of disposable goods are, when handled properly in the idiom of rock 'n' roll, beautiful to behold. The instrumental "Junk" on the same album adds weight to this proof. "Singalong Junk" is nothing less than ethereal.

9. 1973. The official birth of punk rock was imminent in New York City. Five fellows either by design or accident combined the sounds and styles of the Velvet Underground and the Rolling Stones and took rock one giant step closer to punk. The New York Dolls got glammed up like bargain-basement transvestites and cranked cheap sloppy rock with the swagger of junkies living off a big score. But as the title of their second album indicated, too much happened to them too soon. Only a few fans and fellow freaks got the point behind fashions, mascara, and music packaged to look and sound like sleazy trash. Robert Christgau got it. He thought the Dolls capitalized on "a slight natural effeminacy in the speech patterns and body language of leader David Johansen and bassist Arthur Kane," whose core effect depended on "David's amazing flair for trashy clothes."[5] Aptly, Clinton Heylin gave the title "Trash!" to a chapter on Johansen's group.[6] Kiss, Television, Blondie, Patti Smith, and Talking Heads followed in the wake of the Dolls, who themselves had followed in the wake of the trashy Velvet Underground and trashier MC5. A grandly dysfunctional band—alcohol, heroin, and death stalked them—the New York Dolls lived out rock stereotypes of self-destruction, and they were one of those bands around whom critics on the lookout for something new and obnoxious swarm. Record buyers scorned, ignored, or never heard of them. The tune "Trash" typifies their sound, garish to the point of unpleasantness, with little compensation in the areas of melody, lyric, and instrumentation. In "Trash," the singer declares that he won't pick up trash while demanding (or imploring) an external force not to take away his life, as if his own life could be mistaken for trash. In rock 'n' roll, does music matter? Lyrics? Attitude is where it's at, and Image is the clothing that Attitude drapes over its pose. And that's why the New York Dolls were more interesting as phenomena than as recording artists.

10. 1974. Elton John had attitude *and* musical genius, and so his records sold by the gazillions. One of his number ones, "Don't Let the Sun Go Down on Me," hinges on four components: a Grammy-sized hook, verse-chorus dynamics, high-church harmonies, and walloping percussion. In Bernie Taupin's last verse of this histrionic track—Do we puke? Do we weep?—his partner yanks a singular plea out of the depths of his tortured soul: "Don't discard me just because you think I mean you harm." No one wants to be disposed of like an object drained of beauty or utility, and few singers have voiced the fear of abandonment so well. The word "discard" is the tune's pivot point, the tip of its emotional fulcrum, where the drummer balances his time and the singer focuses the agony that compels his voice to sing to survive—or win Grammys. "Don't Let the Sun Go Down on Me" holds up very well beside two other classic "don't" dirges, "Don't Let Me Down" by the Beatles and "Don't" by Elvis Presley.

11. 1977. "God Save the Queen" was unleashed on the British Empire by four representatives of a youth generation who in the process of making music for their age-group happened to gnash the ears of mild-mannered citizens going about their business in the peppy metropolis and the serene village green. Johnny Rotten sputters and yowls this quintessential assault on middle-class complacency. The Sex Pistols break punk ground on the idea that there's no future for a civilization whose children have been thrown away like "flowers in a dustbin." The incongruity of this image—flowers tossed into a garbage pail by a society that discards even beautiful things without a qualm—reflects the incongruity that defines rock 'n' roll music itself. It's beautiful, it's hideous. It's honorable, it's deplorable. It blooms, it wilts. It should be treasured, it should be thrown away. The Sex Pistols clawed the verities and rent the remnants of an enervated empire that maintained a facade of royal pride while its youngsters scrabbled about with nothing to do but drain the dole, drink pint after pint, shoot smack, mutilate themselves, model wardrobes of trash, and pogo to punk rock.[7] How ironic that punk's partisans turned out to be the conscience of a society unaware or unconcerned that it throws away its greatest resource! Once they found a way to articulate and amplify their dismay in sufficient numbers and to unify around the musical movement dubbed punk rock, England's and America's children scarred themselves and snarled; they said the *f* word on prime-time TV; they arched back, whipped forward, and gobbed into the faces of adults who had abused and abandoned them, saving some of their biggest wads of phlegm for the faces of those rock musicians bloated by gross profits earned off grosser music.

12. 1978. The primary subject of Patti Smith's "Twenty-fifth Floor" is the flesh/spirit dichotomy filtered through the medium of human waste. It begins with a fantasy about making love in the men's room on the twenty-fifth floor of a skyscraper in Detroit. Smith's focus shifts to pollution and the idea that we human beings are unable to turn waste into anything of value. In a climactic mantra following this observation, Smith's trash trope assumes a form hitherto unexpressed, and probably unimagined, in rock music. She announces the possibility that making the attempt to transform waste (now related specifically to human excretion) has preoccupied our species more than any other activity since time immemorial. The singer next implicates mankind in an alchemical process in which we are the base metal ("clay") from whose excretion the alchemist will (or must—Smith's vision is a little fuzzy) refashion us into "solid gold" (an apt term for a rock star to use). Out of this purple punk poetry, eons distant from the nuttiness of "Yakety Yak," Smith locates transcendence in the transformation of the waste that we daily produce within ourselves. Waste, the cousin of trash, is the raw material of divinity. . . . This is one of rock's great original ideas, and Smith's performance of it is astonishing. Heaven is as far away as the bathroom at the end of the hall. Everyone can make it that far. (It's regrettable that Ms. Smith didn't permit me to cite this passage verbatim because needless to say the original is far more expressive than the paraphrase I was obligated to write.)

13. 1979. Pulling off a Prince, a Stevie Wonder, and a Paul McCartney, Marshall Crenshaw plays all instruments and sings all parts on the peppy B side "You're My Favorite Waste of Time." The metaphor "wasted time" has helped many lyricists forge a tune about the futility of desire. In compiling the Trash Top Forty, I passed over dozens of tunes using this platitude, choosing Crenshaw's because he spins it into something new and refreshing. He doesn't fret about time lost in the grip of infatuation possibly because he (or the song's "I") has possessed the partner, and the thought or expectation of future possession will go a long way in consoling an infatuated person. The singer nevertheless seems compelled to rationalize some indiscretion or to veil some irresponsibility bound up in his passion. He sings the title repeatedly, concluding in a choirboy's winning whine that no matter if it's meaningless, ridiculous, wrong, or right, he's got to love his partner for the next two nights, at the very least, because: well, see the title. This reversal doesn't suggest that the singer has come to terms with his rationalization and denial or with his sensuality. If love, more likely lust, causes a person to waste precious time, how good can it possibly be? In short, a tricky lyric best not to take literally.

14. 1980. The Cramps dabble in "extreme trash."[8] In "Garbage Man," a nominee for rock music's best self-reflexive trash trope, they drown in it. The tune kicks off with a wheezing, clattering garbage truck. For three and a half minutes, an onslaught of retro riffs, sneers, echo-drenched effects, ghoulish guitar, and cardboard-box drums pours out of the loudspeakers. In this anthem of kitsch, Lux Interior whines, grandstands, growls, and dares. He dresses down a punk who ain't no punk but a pretender who would rather talk than dig into the "real junk" embodied by the singer of the song, who proudly declares, "I'm the garbage man." Like Dante recruiting Virgil as an escort to boost his own resolve on the trek through the Inferno, Lux Interior invokes the phantoms of the Kingsmen and the Trashmen, the great garbagemen of yore, during this trip through rock garbage: "Oh a Louie-Louie-Louie-Lou-eye / The bird's the word, and do you know why?" While Nick Knox's drums thump a dim-witted tattoo and Poison Ivy's guitar twangs with absurd menace, Lux Interior wheedles cheesy lines that make a virtue out of the trash from which rock 'n' roll music is manufactured and recycled over and over again. Interior's pun on "dumps" (trashy rock music is ideal consolation when a person is "down in the dumps") deflates his mock machismo. Rock's mythic garbageman brings as much garbage as he totes away and in the long and short run he's as gentle and giving as Santa Claus.

15. 1982. The trash trope is a piston in the engine of some of Bad Religion's most moving lyrics. On this hard-core quintet's splendidly titled album *How Could Hell Be Any Worse?*, "White Trash (Second Generation)" critiques American parents responsible for broken homes and wasted children. Credit goes to Greg Graffin for enunciating gripping lyrics over scattershot cymbals and fuzzy guitars. The next year, to buck up potential suicides, Bad Religion cut "You Give Up." To be honest is one step toward winning a punk audience; suicidal self-hate can't be sugarcoated; directness is a gesture of compassion; to say the words others deny or avoid requires courage. It's good, therefore, for fans under drinking age to hear Graffin sing "your life is in the garbage can," a second pairing in the annals of punk/hard-core of a wasted young person and a trash receptacle (see section 21) and an echo of the flowers-in-the-dustbin motif of the Sex Pistols. The tragedy of wasted youth is well-trodden terrain in punk and hard rock music, the first great example found in the bridge of the Who's "Baba O'Riley," when Pete Townsend cries, "It's only teenage wasteland," setting up Keith Moon to punctuate this staggering cry with a huge roll across the tom-toms. Normally a band that lashes out in predictable couplets, Bad Religion often comes up with lines that prick one's brain the way a picador's lance pierces the neck of a bull, as in "What Can You Do?" where Graffin jabs listeners and their complacency with a verbal spear sharpened by the trash trope: "So you waste another day getting older and gray in your head," which is too bad because no happiness lies ahead.

16. 1982. On the Crosby, Stills and Nash album *Daylight Again*, Graham Nash comes to grips with aging and wasted time. "Wasted on the Way" typifies Nash's tendency to preach; he did, after all, compose "Teach Your Children," "Military Madness," and "We Can Change the World." In this sing-along sermon, he croons above a blanket of harmony lyrics about wasted time, compared to water flowing under a bridge—time that must be made up (how?), along with wasted love. (Yet Nash tells us to let this same water "carry us away.") Here we have it, where one strand of popular music of the late sixties and early seventies ended up: wisdom served in abstract chunks via an easy-listener composed and sung by a graying Woodstock-era superstar backed by the cream of L.A.'s studio musicians—wisdom extracted from the garbage can of a generation's failed idealism. "Wasted on the Way" is, like much of CSN's work, pleasant, unchallenging, hard not to hum, easy to chew and digest, an ideal snack for boomers beginning to have problems with their teeth and digestion: instant "classic rock." Just add self-pity. Poised as giant-killers of pretense and self-importance, hard-core bands such as Bad Religion, X, and Black Flag festered and then came roaring out of Los Angeles in the late seventies. This doesn't mean Crosby, Stills and Nash didn't have a right to make music. It means their music would never again keep pace with what mattered.

17. 1982. Two menacing and unsavory applications of the trash trope sully the Birthday Party's *Junkyard*, the title cut and "Big Jesus Trash Can." Leader Nick Cave's jaundiced worldview is slopped across two incoherent outings aching with stinging guitars, tuneless drums, and abrasive vocal cords—"music" by trash rockers who don't give a flying *f* that their creative process stresses to the MAX and then some the delicate organism known as the human eardrum, which didn't evolve over countless eons in order to register the vibrations caused by this junk. In the title track, Cave yelps something about garbage inside a sack of honey, yelps this again and again, topping off this strange image with reference to the king of the titular junkyard. Meanwhile, from "Big Jesus Trash Can," arguably the most off-putting title cited in the pages of this book, come growls about sex appeal and soul mates and a gold suit and Texas oil and trash that smells and a trash can being driven by Big Jesus to the singer's town. Very Cramps. These two cuts add up to hair-raising music that might send one running for cover under late Crosby, Stills and Nash records. Half-dismayed, half-relieved, one arrives at CSN's utopia of haggard harmony only to look down and see pieces of the Birthday Party's music stuck in the grooves of one's soles. What exactly is that stuff?

18. 1985. The Crucifucks left a scar on the body of rock 'n' roll by choosing a group name as outrageous as the Dead Kennedys and by conceiving an eponymous debut featuring a coup de grâce called "Marching for Trash." Searing and sneering in a way that makes the Sex Pistols sound like a lounge act doing Jimmy Buffett covers, "Marching for Trash" runs its course in one minute and twenty-five seconds. Not an ounce of fat sticks to the bones of loathing. The crucifuxion verses march to a frantic shuffle; the choruses shift to an insane straight four. There's not the faintest sign of John Philip Sousa honking a tuba at a football game. The 'fucks beseech a Top Dog to give orders and guidance, if only to have something and someone upon to fix the aforesaid loathing. The tune's sarcasm is exemplary of hard-core punk, the band making fun of all the fools who apparently take orders without a thought of resistance, protest, or reprisal. The whiplash whine of Doc Corbin Dart's voice holds its own against the screech of an overdriven amplifier. Like an oversized child sick of being told what to do and thus throwing an epic tantrum in retaliation, Corbin screams not only that he doesn't have to follow orders after all, but that he's going to take "your world and trash it." Before you can say enough already, it's over. For more of the same, however, the hard-core fan can proceed to "Cops for Fertilizer" and "Hinckley Had a Vision" on the same disc.

19. 1986. Popping up like a dirty bomb on Metallica's *Master of Puppets* is "Disposable Heroes," an antiwar tune in the tradition of Dylan's "Masters of War," Barry McGuire's "Eve of Destruction," Jimi's "Machine Gun," Television's "Foxhole," and Stiff Little Fingers' "Wasted Life" (in which a soldier curses the waste of time and life). Metallica's rhythmic patterns might be supposed to emulate the chaos of hand-to-hand combat. Speed raises the bar of virtuosity: the band bludgeons the listener at warp velocity, a seeming paradox, as they exhaust several time signatures without one rest in eight deafening minutes. Like most heavy metal anthems, "Disposable Heroes" can't be said to have much of a melody, yet it's easy to imagine a stadium filled to the rafters with male fifteen-year-olds bellowing every word as they punch the air above their heads. The song's melodic sophistication is to musical theory what stoning animals to death circa 10,000 B.C. was to food preparation. And yet the virtuosity of drummer Lars Ulrich and guitarist Kirk Hammett is breathtaking, so that as "Disposable Heroes" pumps along, dragging along the unwilling and the half-dead, you want to sing along too. Lyrically, "Disposable Heroes" defaults to abstractions and metonymies familiar to readers of allegory, morality tales, and sixties protest songs, here the anonymous soldier being brainwashed to tramp into a blaze of bullets. In this tune irony doesn't get a foothold on the field of earnestness. The band cries from the point of view of a faceless officer who has an understanding with death that he, death, can take away this twenty-one-year-old son who did as told, killed well, and is now finished. Metallica charges into the fray of banal lyricism like a heavy metal light brigade.

20. 1986. Robyn Hitchcock's "Trash" keeps time with Dylan's "Leopard-Skin Pill-Box Hat," Lennon's "How Do You Sleep?" and Carly Simon's "You're So Vain," three other rock 'n' roll character assassinations. In this easy-paced, nasty rocker, Hitchcock reminds his subject of scorn (an MTV/NBC employee or hanger-on) that wishing he could be Brian Jones and that getting into photographs with Charlie Watts and Iggy Pop isn't sufficient to hide the fact that the scorned one is a loser inferior to Jones's bones and incapable of absorbing any of Charlie's or Iggy's charisma. "You're just trash," Hitchcock concludes, at the risk of alienating listeners who don't know what Hitchcock's target has done to arouse such contempt. Hitchcock so reviles his subject that he's willing to drag poor Brian Jones's skeleton into the act. The nod to Iggy seems less gratuitous. (Jones embodies waste in terms of drug abuse and early death. Iggy Pop embodies waste in terms of drug abuse and survival. In this light, Hitchcock chose his touchstones well.) Hitchcock rolls his tongue over the morsel of insult dictated in each syllable before spitting it into the hated person's eyeball.

In the catalog of rock songs named "Trash," none are as allusive and tantalizing (who's the target?) as Hitchcock's contribution. It isn't, for instance, to be confused with "Trash" on Suede's *Coming Up* (1996). This trash tune soars as if a Britpop band had abducted David Bowie and forced him to sing with them. The success of Suede's cut probably lies in its reversal of Hitchcock's meaning of the epithet. Suede flatters fans tired of being put down for their otherness. Suede understands these kids are breeze-blown litter, trash in everything they wear and do. My reading assumes for the moment that lyrical content is the main attraction of a pop song. In "Trash," however, Brett Anderson puts text to a made-for-the-masses hook, making it likely that a listener of a given age and burdened with a given self-image would be seduced by Suede's form of bonding. "Trash" tells a person in need of a boost that it's okay to be trash; and because "Trash" had all the other elements of a big hit, Suede took it to the top.

21. 1987. The Legendary Stardust Cowboy's "Standing in the Trashcan (Thinking of You)" is a great bad song that doesn't need to knock twice for admission to the TTF. The title alone deserves acclaim. The lyrics continue where the title leaves off. The LSC spins a cocoon of nonsense words around the chrysalis of the title, rhyming "baloney" and "pony" (his next meal), taking note of the scraps of food soiling his boots and spurs, and more or less entertaining listeners with the revelation that his girl, the one I assume he's been thinking about, found him in the said trash can, located far from the fruited plain—to be exact, in a New York City alley. All this and more is set to an atonal one-chord rockabilly bounce.

22. 1988. In 1988, rock 'n' roll had aged eighteen years since Paul McCartney's paean to junk. Punk rock in 1988 had passed the age of ten. Thriving most visibly in Chicago, New York, and Los Angeles, and less visibly in midsized cities and small towns scattered across America, thousands of punks and their tiny labels held fast to the original punk do-it-yourself ideology, and punk rockers continued to decry the worst aspects of American civilization. By 1988, classic punk had evolved into subdivisions such as new wave, goth, early grunge, hard-core, and postpunk in general. In 1988, *junk* referred to (1) objects sold in pawnshops and yard sales, (2) heroin, and (3) trash, litter, and millions of tons of used-up consumer goods dumped legally into landfills or illegally wherever a person could get away with it. In 1988, making mincemeat of preconceived categories and standards of criticism, punk-jazz-funk band NoMeansNo pounced on the third definition of junk. Hands down, their "Junk" wins first prize for the most complex song arrangement in the TTF, not simply because it's scored in 5/4 time. Five/four time is rare enough in rock music; 5/4 whizzing by in a wave of atonal passages is even more rare. In contrast to this instrumental brilliance, "Junk's" unexceptional lyrics preach that human beings have blighted nature and culture. While busy doing to rock form what Picasso did to portraiture, Rob and John Wright clamor that the world is inundated with garbage and—screamed at song's end in voices of passionate disgust—junk. NoMeansNo spins protest into postpunk fracture and squall.

23. 1988. Definitely a good year for alternative rock insofar as it saw the release of Sonic Youth's classic album *Daydream Nation* and "Total Trash," one of the songs responsible for its fame and a shoo-in for this list. This number differs in mood from the LP's prevailing anxiety and dissonance. Still, cryptic lyrics belie "Total Trash'"s tunefulness: something at the top spirals down, "works best" when lost, digs underground, can be brought back, and is "total trash"— and the singer, incidentally, isn't a cow. Despite such opaqueness, "Total Trash" is the most accessible track on a record that a person would be crazy to throw away. Even a mainstream rock fan who chanced upon "Total Trash" might agree. To accuse Sonic Youth of obscurity would be as misguided as to call Leiber and Stoller on the carpet for coining dumb rhymes for peeved teenagers. The song is that good.

Also on *Daydream Nation* is "Providence." This echo-drenched monologue is spoken over a pretty ambient piano pattern packed in a case of rumbling stereo static, an effect akin to jet turbines sucking the last gallons of fuel at thirty thousand feet. A phone message is superimposed over the piano and white noise. Someone is calling Thurston Moore, one of Sonic Youth's guitar players, from Providence, Rhode Island, asking him if he found his "shit," warning him to "watch the motin'" because it messes up your memory. The caller tells Thurston that "we" couldn't find said substance in the van and wonders if he, Thurston, checked the trash can for it. The caller wants to know if Thurston was holding the bag "when we threw out that trash," and if Thurston later dumped the can.

Sonic Youth does audio noir.

Sonic Youth are artists of noise and image and for them *trash* (concrete referent and abstract musical code) is like the primary color red or yellow in a palette. To a layperson yellow is yellow. To an artist yellow encompasses a spectrum of tints and hues, each one selected to represent a mood that resists verbal reconstruction. All of which is to say that Sonic Youth's trash in "Total Trash" differs from their trash in "Providence," where the pairing of Providence (founded by Massachusetts Separatists in the 1630s) and a trash can conveys an image of America's fall from grace.

Two cuts on Sonic Youth's *Experimental Jet Set, Trash and No Star* (1994) revert again to trash imagery, and again I hesitate to interpret its meaning. But it's apparent that longing and self-doubt permeate the silly similes in "Quest for the Cup," where the singer compares himself to a doughnut and burger, directs someone to take out the trash, and questions the use of crying. The next tune, "Waist," doesn't resolve the anatomical pun in several references to waste.[9]

24. 1989. "The television's my best friend / I've been watching since I don't know when," are throwaway lines from Sewer Trout's "Garbage In, Garbage Out." The grooves of this lark were lathed into vinyl during rock's worst lull in creativity since the years 1959–63. With punk mired in its own identity crisis after 1983 or so, countless alternative bands without much originality to sell (not every band could be a Sonic Youth, a Hüsker Dü, or an R.E.M.) and without a chance of either a major label deal or widespread appeal, kept up the indie faith until Nirvana, Pearl Jam, and Soundgarden bounded out of Washington State to save the day—or, some would argue, to ruin things once and for all by going multiplatinum and signaling punk's surrender to mainstream production values. In Sewer Trout's brief chronicle of everyday garbage, the singer bemoans to the churn of primitive chords, trashy drums, and a series of belches his lousy nutrition (beer and chips), his ailments (shingles, colitis, gastritis, premature hair loss), his flab, and the breakdown of a car whose fuel tank he had topped off with Elmer's glue, this same car expiring in a local parking lot. Running time: 2:04. "Garbage In, Garbage Out" is one of Generation X's finest versions of "Summertime Blues." Both are archetypal throwaways, both are fresh and funny, and both are over before you know it.

25. 1989. We're talkin' not about revolution but about rock 'n' roll music as trash. Clearly, "Trash" is the most self-reflexive of titles this side of "Rock and Roll Music" itself. It's also a title waiting to be mined by a misogynist, or someone pretending to be one. Alice Cooper obliges. (I'm not saying the man behind Alice Cooper's mask, Vincent Furnier, was, or is, a misogynist. Rock stars aren't the images they present on stage and disc. Jagger wasn't Lucifer, Bowie wasn't Ziggy, Paul wasn't a walrus, and Bruce wasn't a Vietnam vet. Milli Vanilli weren't even singers. We long ago established that rock is an art form, and art forms presuppose fantasy and impersonation. If anything, Furnier was probably satirizing misogyny.) "Trash" is the title cut of the album *Trash,* and in this case "Trash" trashes a woman who rather inconsistently crawls across the floor of a brothel, wears a big diamond, and drives the most expensive luxury car of all. The characterization is vague but the main idea—that the woman needs a verbal lashing followed by sexual conquest—is clear. The singer knows better than to fall for this femme fatale's public image, a blend of riches and striptease. Lurking behind her silk and fur facade is nothing more, nothing less than trash.

This sexy "peach in cream" shows her true colors in bed, inciting the singer to leer that the touch of the sheets turns her into the trash that any man can have as long as he sweats up the cash. From here, the lyrics of "Trash" go quickly downhill from a level that was already dangerously low. In rock 'n' roll music by man, woman cannot escape unscathed. I repeat, it's called misogyny, and it isn't right, but if you're going to listen to rock 'n' roll, you'd better get used to it.

26. 1992. In "Democracy" Leonard Cohen opts not for misanthropy (this cut appears on *The Future*, whose title cut was chosen as the closing-credits score for *Natural Born Killers*) but for affectionate satire. "Democracy" pulses to hypnotic rhymes about the correlation between national dysfunction and democracy. The poet gives himself a double dose of the trash trope: for one thing, he's as "stubborn" as a decay-proof garbage bag, and for another, he's "junk" even though he offers a bouquet to the United States of America. Because this is a rock song about a nation where brand-name garbage bags are more durable than 50 percent of the marriages, it would have been incomplete without a reference to trash. The twist is that Cohen equates the poet capable of appreciating the beauty of wildflowers with junk, and this junk represents the durability of poetry in a land that trashes with abandon. America is content to trash its poets (technically, Cohen is Canadian and he began his career as a poet and novelist, not a singer-songwriter) as it entertains an illusion of democracy that hasn't been realized. This type of disposability, however, won't stop the poet from holding out flowers to an oblivious populace. Not incidentally, Leonard Cohen first linked garbage and flowers in "Suzanne" (1968), the first song on his indispensable first album, where Suzanne takes a man by the hand for a walk by the river.

27. 1992. There are throwaway lines, and there are great throwaway lines. Pavement specializes in the second type, and they're strewn over the band's four-song extended-play *Watery, Domestic* like litter over the playground in a low-class housing project. These slackers seethe the art of nonchalance. A ragged stew of jolting melodies into which shards of discontinuous lyrics are stitched by Stephen Malkmus's matter-of-fact but passionate vocals, underpinned by Gary Young's cracking slap-happy drumming, the hot-wired guitars of Malkmus and Scott Kannberg, and Mark Ibold's perfectly prosaic bass work, this EP packs two teasing trash tropes in the first two tracks. Among other prime throwaway lines—"Bleacher dates the second prize"; "she's on a hidden tableau"; "I hear the natives fussin' at the data chart"—"Texas Never Whispers" and "Frontwards" include, respectively, Malkmus's plaintive cry that "down my alleyside / I'm just a wasted behind" and that "I've got style, miles and miles / So much style that it's wasted." As they used to say in the 1990s, *whatever.* On the first tune the singer mentions a female who's "so lackadaisical, / Should have been a West Coast bride," a fantastic two-line portrait hinging on an adjective that describes the EP to a tee. Laxness is to Pavement what joie de vivre was to the early Beatles or what slovenliness was to the early Rolling Stones. As the listener's ear tastes the phrase "cherry pickin' favorites," these lines arrest his eyes: "The way the river bends / The woman's bending over me," a metaphor John Donne could have done worse than devise. If it isn't clear whether Malkmus is bragging about his surfeit of style or mourning the fact that so much of it must be wasted, it's because he's doing both at the same time, and the musicians on *Watery, Domestic* bear out his burden in nothing less than the same spirit of toss-off virtuosity.[10]

28. 1993. The voluptuous shuffle "Wasted" by neopsychedelics Mazzy Star threatens to implode into the core of its own lugubrious rhythm. During the first minute, fuzz-tone guitar and thick drums lurch along as if each performer is contesting the other's fidelity to a steady pulse while daring him to play slower to really mess things up. They play out the game for another five minutes, adding lots of clutter, stray logs slipping off a logging truck into the middle of a funeral motorcade. "Wasted" opens strangely: "After I stuck my hands into your ground and pulled out somebody else's son, I felt a little unfortunate, a little mistaken." Hope Sandoval saturates the obscure lyrics with a torch singer's languor, voice, drums, and guitars draining toward the epiphany moaned in the refrain: "I felt like I'd been wasted, all day long, all day long." Sandoval may be the Nico of the nineties. She lulls like a siren begging to be consoled for a personality disorder signaled by inordinate sexual desire and loss of volition. Her voice is a deep plush cushion into which the listener sinks, turning to the singer's embrace, happy to divert the wasted darling from her dismay, even if its causes are hard to fathom, and then to love her before falling off into a dreamless sleep in her arms. To be "wasted all day long" could well mean that a woman's beautiful body has been wasted because it hasn't been loved as it deserves. But an erotic reading of "Wasted" doesn't cancel theses about enervation, ennui, or drug addiction. The guitarist grinds, the drummer splatters fills around the tune's noncommittal backbeat, cymbals splash like ships crashing into rocks, and the tune dribbles to an ending as inconclusive as its beginning. The lyrics don't communicate a precise message so much as darken the melody's luster and as a result draw the listener deeper into the mystery of waste that unfolds as long as the band provides a venue for Sandoval's voice. To hear Sandoval croon is to be hooked and then to look for the hook that made you bleed. The best thing about "Wasted" is that everyone involved in it sounds wasted, on what or by what being unclear, and the mood rubs off on the listener, who can't easily remove that voice and shambling rhythm from his mind.

29. 1993. A magnum opus in the canon of rock trash is Blur's *Modern Life Is Rubbish*. At seventy-three minutes, this concept album requisitions nearly every digit on the disc to shed light on John Bull's anomie and Albion's irrelevance. *Modern Life* employs the wit found on *The Who Sell Out* (like the Who, Blur structured their recording around an intermission and a commercial break) and indulges the pessimism found on *The Rise and Fall of Ziggy Stardust and the Spiders from Mars* (Bowie's closer "Rock and Roll Suicide" is paralleled by Blur's closer "Resigned"). These influences are superseded by one even greater. Take the album's sickly and stuffy characters, its sardonicism, its big hooks, its hum-along choruses, and the music-hall stomp of "When the Cows Come Home" (an unlisted track, except on the inside of the CD case), and presto! Britpop Kinks! On *Modern Life* one encounters the Prufrockian but oddly likeable citizen inhabiting Kinks albums from 1966 to 1969 (Colin Zeal is a dead-ringer for the Well Respected Man). The album title references a voice-over on the opening track, "For Tomorrow." Over the refrain, Damon Albarn chimes that a man named Jim drives to his house in Emperor's Gate, enters, switches on the telly, turns it off, makes tea, and declares "modern life is rubbish." Then a girlfriend drops by and they leave for a drive. The album leaves the reader feeling queasy, as if he had dipped a moldy biscuit into a cup of bad tea and then consumed both.

30. 1993. David Thomas's vocals on Pere Ubu's "Wasted" are enhanced by a melodeon playing waltz time. A melodeon is an accordion.[11] The accordion is a shy creature in the rock 'n' roll jungle. It accents Italian ethnicity in Billy Joel's "Scenes from an Italian Restaurant," lightens the boy's insecurity in "How Can I Be Sure?" (the Young Rascals), brightens the winsome "Tears in the Morning" (the Beach Boys), and decorates "Misguided Angel" (the Cowboy Junkies). Postmodern popsters They Might Be Giants depend on their accordion, as does Moxy Früvous's David Matheson. It lilts the live takes of "Apeman," "Muswell Hillbillies," and "Do You Remember Walter?" on *To the Bone* (the Kinks).[12] John Kirkpatrick's accordion adds busker charm to Richard Thompson's "Poor Little Beggar Girl" and, pumped by Krist Novoselic, hope to Nirvana's "Jesus Doesn't Want Me for a Sunbeam." And is that an accordion sealing the sex pact in "Back Street Girl" (the Rolling Stones)? In rock recordings, aside from novelty numbers, an accordion is about as popular as a glockenspiel, which is scored about as often as an oboe is. Consequently, the waltzing melodeon renders "Wasted" special. The tune's bipolarity also demands comment. Thomas recites two verses about wasted time before muttering, at 1:33, the verb *rock* as if to say it's time to quit messing around with such a lightweight contraption. The band doesn't have to be told twice. Pere Ubu roars to life, constructing cinderblock walls of sound around the stubborn three-count. The melodeon minstrel has been effaced. This movement halts at 2:16, after which a verse is repeated until "Wasted" shuts down for good at 2:37. The arrangement heightens the impact of this study of wasted time, not a unique theme and thus not easy to pull off, because a listener can't help but be jarred into concentrating on the lyrics as the song goes through its mutations. Thomas tugs at the lyric sheet, which grieves over Homo sapiens's reckless and breathless tendency to throw away time. Intense vocals render the process of wasting time the more tragic because of our inability to do anything else with it.

(Time wasting of this sort was the theme seven years earlier in "Time" on the set *Strange Times* by Chameleons UK. On paper the lyrics fall flat—singer Mark Burgess exhorts us to make the most of our time rather than to waste it— but because the band backs these words with passion and a decent melody, the message hits home.)

31. 1994. Beck Hansen's art would be unthinkable without trash to beautify it. (This trademark runs in the family. Beck's grandfather was Fluxus trash artist Al Hansen, d. 1995.) Ecological collapse, alienation, violence, and garbage suffuse *Mellow Gold* (1994). In "Pay No Mind (Snoozer)," a lesson in detachment, Beck reaches into his deep bag of trash tropes, advising consumers to flip off the rock star whose album sales soar "through the garbage pail sky," a fresh metaphor in rock's trash bin of clichés. Another cut, "Beercan," hinges on a metonym of trash familiar to anyone who has ever scanned the shoulder of a highway. "Blackhole" wraps the disc. This ballad almost convinces the listener, who has a right to be skeptical after a program including "Loser," "Beercan," "Soul Suckin Jerk," and "Mutherfucker," that it's okay to hope things will turn out okay as we grope around the black hole of contemporary existence, eyes half on the news, half on the nearest escape hatch. But Beck undercuts his own eleventh-hour rally by remarking that the cloudy world is "open to a waste can." We're rubbish fumbling in the dark. Beck's next major release, *Odelay* (1996), studied social and personal collapse with lethal hooks, deep grooves, and startling images, leading off with those in "Devil's Haircut," where "garbageman trees" mingle with hanging heads, the faces of lepers, and dead ends. Such apocalyptic imagery is Beck's calling card, along with his fusion of styles (rap, folk, hard rock, disco, schmooze funk, psychedelia, and so forth). Weird trash-troping is again evident in the "garbage classes" in "Minus." *Mutations* (1998) continues the trend. "Nobody's Fault But My Own," a dirge about "wasted blues," refers to a "throwaway" and "an open grave."

32. 1994. Napalm Death's "Throwaway" is a natural choice for a trash-title survey. First, how does one explain what their music, dubbed "grindcore," sounds like? Try this. During the midsixties, my friends and I would select an album, set it up on the record player, and then hold our fingers against the side of the platter as the turntable's motor toiled to maintain its designated

RPM. In time, with better turntables we could automatically retard the pitch by switching from 33⅓ to 16 RPM. Altered thus, the voice that crawled out of the three-inch loudspeaker made Darth Vader sound like a chipmunk. The point of this activity was to analyze fast rhythm patterns so as to work them out on our own instruments. Usually, however, the procedure was good for little more than a laugh. Of course, at the time I had no idea that altering the voices on rock albums would be a practice run for comments I would make thirty years later when discussing Napalm Death's contribution to the trash trope. In fact, until a friend E-mailed me a lyric sheet of "Throwaway," I couldn't distinguish one word of English coming from the Altecs. I still can't. Napalm Death's voices drag as if wrung out of the throats of troglodytes grunting in a sci-fi movie's time-reduced dimension or on a planet whose gravity retards all utterance to a lugubrious, larynx-constricted crawl . . . zombie utterances, pitched way low in chunks of hertz; guttural, incoherent, buried not in white noise but, a first for my ears, black noise. If dissonance could be beheld in terms of size, the dissonance on "Throwaway" would be gigantic. Voices freighted with darkness grumble from the back of a dripping cave, echoing with a metallic din. Napalm Death reproduces the growl of a large cavernous creature slobbering over a recent kill. Assuming the lyric sheet is accurate, the verses of "Throwaway" don't cite the title but do throw out some striking images of a "shell with integrity scooped out," a glass eye unable to cry, a retreat from a fatal edge. After everything I've said or implied about Napalm Death, I must add that "Throwaway" is rock 'n' roll music, and I like it, even the words I had to read to understand.[13]

33. 1994. The cover of *Point Blank,* Nailbomb's second installment of ear-crushing metal, presents the photograph of an Asian woman, neck up, about fifty years old, a peasant or laborer of some sort, grimacing because the barrel of a gun is jammed into her right temple. The left hand of the gunman seems to be yanking her hair. This exceedingly unpleasant photograph seems to protest human rights abuses in the Third World, and the music enhances that protest. The opening ear-attack "Wasting Away" is an extreme exercise in extreme negativity, the band screaming about universal pain and the sad fact that citizens of this mad planet can do little but waste away. (Not that a person can comprehend these words without a lyric sheet. See previous entry. Nailbomb could be Napalm Death's angrier kid brother.) Other titles on an album replete with speed-metal clichés such as tuneless howls, gargantuan guitars, battered cymbals, sixteenth-note double bass drum fills, and a sonic boom warehouse production of sky-rending volume are "World of Shit," "Cockroaches," "For Fuck's Sake," "Shit Piñata," "Sick Life," "Religious Cancer," and "Twenty-four Hour Bullshit."

NOTE TO TEENAGERS: Next time your music teacher, minister, mom, or dad tells you rock music is crap, rubbish, demonic drivel, inarticulate trash, and guttural garbage from the gutter with no remote connection to fine art, listen. They're right even if they don't know what they're talking about.

34. 1996. Phish's title "Waste" (on *Billy Breathes*) doesn't prepare us for a sappy ballad in which the singer assures an object of desire that there's nothing he'd rather do than waste his time with her. This kind of reversal—a happy song about waste (and a sappy song by Phish)—is to be expected in the music of a band that has always delighted in messing with the status quo (length of concerts, song structures, stage garb, stage antics). Trey Anastasio confides in fairly banal lyrics that painting, acting, farming, climbing, or running from the law (unrelated activities stuck in throwaway lines) couldn't measure up to the pleasure of realizing a dream by wasting his time with the object of this apostrophe. "Waste" is musically mellow, verbally slight, and thematically extravagant, and it could be accounted a bad song were it not saved by a decent melody and strong musical support. Toward the end, another reversal occurs. Trey now repeatedly implores his beloved to waste her time with him. This is the sound of a man on his knees. "Waste" is a love song whose tender melody and sentimental lyrics (I can't detect a trace of irony in it) are at odds with the title's seeming negativity. Time wasted in romantic matters is for once desirable rather than, the rock norm, regrettable.

35. 1996. Amy Rigby jokes around on her barn-burner "Twenty Questions." The interrogator starts by quoting the opening strums of Dylan's "Subterranean Homesick Blues" and stealing the lick from his "Obviously Five Believers" as her band leaps into a standard rockabilly progression. This song exhibits no musical originality: whence, then, its kick and bite? Rigby's attitude, surely, and her lyrics. These dwell on the immemorial battle between men who give too little and women who want too much. Rigby comes across as exasperated rather than ticked-off, even when she cross-examines her man: "Were you wasting cash on some piece of trash / You picked up at the mall?" Women were deemed "trash" long before Rigby came along (see entry 25), but the two-stroke trash trope—wasting cash on female trash—is new and exciting, and the singer's cattiness is in character with the rest of the words. The final and best joke, however, is on the singer herself: she ain't leaving nobody, and she knows it and he knows it too. An unrelated but wonderful example of the trash trope graces a title on 1998's *Middlescence*. "The Summer of My Wasted Youth" (Rigby could make a career naming records) includes this line: "Summer in '83 / The last time I took LSD / But listening to Patsy Cline / and Skeeter Davis really blew my mind." Brava! A great album title, a great song title, great lyrics, and a great example of the trash trope's ever-shifting role in rock 'n' roll music.

36. 1997. "No Surprises" is the first of the last three wrenching odes on a postgrunge album that proved rock wasn't dead in 1997: *OK Computer* by the magi of Oxford, England—Radiohead. "No Surprises" commences with a simile that does full justice to the theme of garbage in rock 'n' roll and to the theme of alienation in *OK Computer:* "A heart that's full up like a landfill." "No Surprises" is a ballad giving scope to Thom Yorke's dream of enjoying life without bells going off in the night. Yorke moans away his woes in tandem with his innervision of a modest house and a pretty garden in classic retired English rockstar fashion, far from the madding crowd. But the landfill image sticks, and like a landfill encroaching on a green landscape, it taints the ideal. There's malaise in utopia. A second trash reference on *OK Computer* is buried at the bottom of a page of credits printed in tiny letters at the back of the program booklet. The band asks listeners to "please write to us at w.a.s.t.e. correspondence p.o. box 322, oxford, ox4 1ey uk." The same astonishing invitation is printed on *The Bends* (1995) and *Kid A* (2000). To listen to *OK Computer* and then to pick out this address is to be struck with the discrepancy between the profundity of the rock 'n' roll Radiohead composes, performs, and records, and its inevitable, if not instant, disposability.[14]

(Eleven years earlier, Elvis Costello, to a jazz backing—brushes, swing ride, double bass, tinkling 88s—belted out a line comparing his heart to a junkyard. "Poisoned Rose" is music crafted for a smoky lounge on the lonely side of town, best played at 3:00 A.M. It's got everything but glasses clinking and perfunctory applause.)

37. 1998. Marianne Faithfull survived the parties, addictions, binges, busts, and orgies of the sixties and early seventies. Not only did this scandal-scarred chanteuse survive them but she kept recording. In 1998, she released an anthology comprised largely of lugubrious cabaret rock. A typical downer is the previously unreleased "A Waste of Time" (coauthored with Stevie Winwood, author of "Can't Find My Way Home," number 7 in the list). This one seems to have been composed as a kiss-off to the transience of sexual love. Faithfull's meditation on time wasting is galaxies distant from Marshall Crenshaw's and Phish's pop-sappy treatments of it. Acid irony dosed with a dash of contempt is dripped on lyrics that don't waste further time pretending that the affair in question was anything more than a sordid delaying tactic and a matter of "sensual decay," in other words, a waste of time. The song fades as Faithfull croaks a half-hearted attempt at salvaging something from the bitterness of loss. Although it's good to have some company with whom to share happy times, those times are brief, and in the end there's little to show for the interlude and nothing to say about it. In love, you take what you can get, make the most of it, and then watch it waste away.

(In 1995, Southern California punk band Pennywise confronted the futility of life—a far cry from Faithfull's lament about washed-up love—in "Waste of Time." If we agree that most rock lyrics about wasted time are frivolous, then we must admit that these lyrics are rife with existential doubt. Pennywise drills eternal questions into the listener's brain. What's there to show for our time on earth? Where are we headed? Is religion worth the effort? Is a pastoral paradise our eventual home? The best the band can offer is their conclusion that their spirits are broken knowing that human life is a tragic waste of time. [These broken spirits are inconsistent with the band's passionate playing and unexpected accents that make the short song jump with vitality.] Pennywise's commonplace reflections are served up in clean, rapid-fire, and accessible punk pop that also manages to be philosophical. The vocals are mixed way up front and thus can be understood for a change.)

38. 1998. The trio Shellac's place in the Trash Top Forty is secured by "House Full of Garbage," best described as an acidulous seven-and-a-half-minute slow-burn dirge whose last minute or two are dominated by Todd Trainer's thwacking tattoo on unaccompanied snare and bass drum, which eventually ceases according to a whim of its own. (A ceasing is less clear-cut than an ending. You wonder if Trainer will come back to torture you some more.) When Trainer takes over the tape, it's as if Shellac's tornado of guitars—actually, "House Full of Garbage" is a relatively subdued cut on a record of brain-scraping aggression—had cleared the sky, swirled off to trouble the deadly dusk, and abandoned the drummer to limp off in unison with dazed, bleeding survivors. Hear them lurch through jagged shards of time. "Imagine a man so proud," drawls Steve Albini about a homeowner whose self-reflective "monument" is the mountainous amount of garbage he amasses. Is this Shellac's way of saying *imagine no possessions* without getting accused of making, and construed as endorsing, a more specific allusion to a forestalled utopian age?

39. 1999. Korn will be remembered as a popular neometal band from the California desert. Showcased on the compact disc *Issues* is "Trash," an aggressive midtempo hate song written to stoke the vanity of postmodern adolescents seized by rage. His voice twisted as if fallen angels were battling for control of hell in his throat, Jonathan Davis shouts, to the cannonade of bass, drums, and guitars, that he despises each moment he spends with the song's "you," a person whose feelings he "rapes." He can't help it—can't help lying, hating, raping, cursing ("fuck" gets a good airing), or throwing away ("I just throw you away") this poor person who hangs around despite all his attempts to run away. Except for the interesting fact that the singer apologizes even as he damns his conscience and the person who has stimulated it, that's basically it: a brutal statement of adolescent ambivalence smack dab in the middle of the postmodern age. Forty-five years after Elvis Presley pointed his feet in the direction of a studio on 706 Union Avenue, Memphis, Tennessee, Korn's three minutes of rock 'n' roll trash screams defiantly, *"We're still rockin' and rollin' and sellin' CDs by the million and lovin' every second at the top. If you don't like it, fuck you!"*

40. 2000. Marilyn Manson's "Disposable Teens" is the kind of walloping hard-rock tune, technically a shuffle, that confirms the thesis that in rock 'n' roll music little has changed in terms of topic and attitude. At the millennium there's more swearing, more self-marketing, more self-importance, more cynicism, more make up, and more money . . . but the ur-texts keep coming back retreaded for a larger, more wired, more medicated, more jaded, and probably more confused fourteen-year-old audience. A performer such as Manson has to try harder to be heard and seen above the ruckus and road show financed by the hip-hop industry, as well as to provide a persona different from previous masked marvels of rock 'n' roll like the cartoon men in Kiss or spectacular cracked actors like Alice Cooper and David Bowie. Manson's music, at least as it comes across in "Disposable Teens," is so derivative as to preclude criticism of derivativeness being less than a primary concern of the band's production team and management. In other words, who cares? I'd bet the Beatles catalog on compact disc that the kids who purchase Marilyn Manson product couldn't give a damn about the history of rock 'n' roll and the fact that it has all been done before. Manson's fans probably don't care (or know) much about the achievements—which happened upwards of thirty years ago now—of groups such as Black Sabbath (*The Osbournes* television series notwithstanding), Aerosmith, the Dead Kennedys, and Manson's hard rock, hard-core, metal, and thrash precursors in general. (Actually, a main source for "Disposable Teens" could be a relatively subdued rock act, the Pretenders, and their rock-shuffle single "Message of Love.") A goodly number of kids aged twelve to nineteen crave an icon suitably violent and grotesque on which to project their unarticulated self-loathing and loathing of authority. A buzz, a buzz, their identities for a buzz. There's nothing wrong with that. And so it is good that Marilyn Manson exists to provide a buzz on *Holy Wood (In the Shadow of the Valley of Death)*, one of whose tunes—"GodEatGod," "President Dead," "Coma Black," and "Count to Six and Die" are others—is "Disposable Teens." Manson sets a trash-trope standard for the Columbine nineties and the ecstasy/OxyContin zeros. Eddie Cochran is still bugged about having the summertime blues, but now, wearing macabre makeup and assuming a wild nom de rock, his inheritor has honed a homicidal, suicidal edge. Sardonic thanks are extended to Mom and Dad (think of all the kids living vicariously through this brilliant maneuver!) for bringing about the "bitter end" of the "fucking world." Manson gets around to rhyming "evolution" and "revolution," to writing off God, and to telling his parents they're "full of shit" (another score with the kids who would love to talk like this to their folks). The rant finally resolves itself on the title phrase repeated several times. The more one says it, the more believable it might be. "Disposable Teens" almost makes parents like me want to be fifteen again if only to feel Manson's mosh-pit emotions of self-pity, self-hate, disenfranchisement, self-righteousness, and fury one more time—or for the first time.

In 1995, Mr. Manson recorded another hate song with a trash title on the EP *Smells like Children*. "White Trash" is an acoustic campfire parody based on chords strummed at the top of each line. Manson enters Alice Cooper (of "Trash") territory on this filthy ode to a white trash teenage girl who gladly assumes knee position in order to pleasure the singer. She's his little queen (now Chuck Berry is dragged into the song), a porn queen in the making (isn't this thrilling?) who likes oral sex, likes it "mean," most likely because Manson needs a word to rhyme with "queen." A twenty-six-year-old man plays with images of teen pornography and comes up way short of offensiveness because it doesn't seem as if he knows what he's talking about. He might as well be a thirteen-year-old fan of his own wretched lyrics. He could have built a better song with alphabet blocks.

Marilyn Manson.

Yakety-yakety-yak.

There is no Trash Top Forty. This list isn't an illusion but it's not the real (or only, or final) thing either. This particular TTF is descriptive, not prescriptive, and its selections invite more commentary than I've been able to give them. Like all lists, it will inspire disagreements with my readings and choices. Regarding these choices, space limitations have forced me to overlook dozens of examples of the trash trope in the rock 'n' roll archives, such as famous ones whose absence the reader will possibly question: Jim Morrison growling that a higher power won't pardon us for "wasting" the sunrise (permission to quote this line was declined by the Doors' management). Lou Reed sniping about Beardless Harry, "a waste," who's having trouble scoring dope in Manhattan. Mick Jagger slipping into Lucifer's shoes and threatening to "lay your soul to waste." Bob Dylan informing a lover that she "wasted" his valuable time. Keith Morris yelping "I was so wasted" in Black Flag's forty-eight-second punk watershed "Wasted." Ian Dury emptying the garbage can on his own head, reflecting that he could have been a doctor, a lawyer, a teacher, a poet, an officer, or a ticket collector, but instead "chose to play the fool" in a rock group: "What a waste!"[15] The trash trope is there, spilling out of loudspeakers, an endless supply continually replenished, bits and pieces of rock 'n' roll waste, hunks of garbage, bags of trash, all out in the open and all unseen like the litter along the streets of the nearest bad side of town.

The motif of garbage in rock lyrics, rhetoric, and packaging moves in and out of the genre like garbage trucks circulating noisily day after day in neighborhood after neighborhood. Scraps (a line, an image) or heaps (a title, a dedicated lyric) of the trope attract the eye (the ear) as the trucks rumble by (as the song plays out). Even a truck's empty cradle contains the grease marks of a thousand leaky and squashed bags of trash. (The trope stains the genre; all strains bear the grease mark.) The community as we know it would cease to exist if the garbageman never made another round. Just so, rock 'n' roll would cease to exist if censors cleaned it up or musicians stopped lugging amplified garbage through the streets of sound.

The trash trope is a fixture of rock 'n' roll music whether or not we acknowledge it. When a guest walks into a host's home for the first time—let's imagine a comfortable four-bedroom home in an exclusive suburb of a major city—he compliments the layout, room sizes, furniture, appliances, decorations, carpets, wall hangings, curtains, billiard table, home theater system, and picture frames. He doesn't root underneath the kitchen sink to take a gander at the garbage receptacle. He doesn't inspect the garbage disposal. He's not curious about the color of the trash bins in the garage. Like the toilets, garbage receptacles are in constant use but never mentioned in aesthetic terms or in polite company even though families can't live without the accessories that funnel off waste. Similarly, when listening to a rock song, one doesn't think of it as a function or figure of trash. But the trash is there. It may stink like Thom Yorke's landfill and it may smell sweet like Johnny Rotten's flowers. I haven't tried to convince readers that trash is the only or even the main theme in rock music. I've argued instead that much of the meaning and spirit of the musical genre that defines the trash culture of modern civilization lies in the ubiquity of literal and figurative garbage.

28. The End

Pianos and guitars, hotel rooms, apartments, stages, record covers, personalities, addicts and drunks, rock styles and sounds, demographics, throwaway tunes that never come back and throwaway tunes that last forever, lyrics, actual compact discs and their flimsy jewel boxes: all trash, garbage, waste, and so much rock 'n' roll rubbish. In what frame of mind, in what appropriate mood—reverence, horror, pity, outrage—does one add to this inventory a bus that should have been junked but that, instead, to save the promoters money, was crowded with blue-fingered rock 'n' rollers (who became legends, almost to a man) on a winter tour of the American Midwest? How does one add a single-engine airplane chartered during this tundra tour to make the ordeal a fraction easier for three of its exhausted performers? Where put a little commuter craft that one minute took off from an icy runway into an icy sky and a few minutes later had been reduced to a heap of jagged scrap metal, its four passengers mangled beyond recognition?

The Beechcraft Bonanza carrying Buddy Holly, Ritchie Valens, the Big Bopper, and the twenty-one-year-old pilot is rock 'n' roll's crowning piece of trash. The black and white photographs of it are enough to make one sick. No matter how one turns the page to figure out its original geometry, this hunk of mutilated metal, with the serial number N3794N stenciled clearly along the wing on which the wreckage lies like an abstract sculpture commissioned to update the allegory of Icarus; this mass of fractured aluminum, with its rear wing flopped over like a broken tin wafer and its gashed fuselage exposing nothing but once-humming innards now crushed, sundered, bent, and choked silent; this jagged remnant that began its last flight as a well-maintained, tip-top little airplane, ready to serve farmers, surveyors, sightseers, and the occasional troupe of rock stars, now at dead rest beside a barbed wire fence in the midst of a stubbly field of stripped corn, with a thin layer of snow adding a coda of isolation to a timeless frozen landscape in which man's aerodynamic technology seems as pitiful and fragile as it did thousands of years ago to the Greeks—this too, no matter how one studies its battered angles, is rock 'n' roll music.

There have been plenty of other fatal collisions and tragic disasters, more than enough rock 'n' roll wreckage to study. The airplane in which twenty-five-year-old Randy Rhoads was a passenger when it went down in flames. The 1983 black Corvette Stingray in which drummer Rick Allen was speeding the night his left arm was sheared off. The car in which twenty-one-year-old Eddie Cochran perished. The airplane in which thirty-year-old Jim Croce lost his life. The motorcycle cracked up by twenty-four-year-old Duane Allman. The helicopter that turned out to be Stevie Ray Vaughan's coffin. The airplane in which twenty-two-year-old Aaliyah was robbed of life. The airplane that wiped out half of Lynyrd Skynyrd. Survivor Billy Powell's words about this particular crash forever fuse the bond between tragedy and trash. Approaching impact through palm trees "felt like being hit with 150 baseball bats while rolling down a hill in a garbage can."[1]

The description of debris after a fatal accident conveys something of the loss represented by rock 'n' roll's tragedies, the most vivid and heartbreaking perhaps being the Buddy Holly disaster, possibly because, as one of the first, it struck down one of rock's great innocents and original geniuses, a young artist of exceptional potential, a performer beloved by fans, a new husband with a lifetime of fame and fortune lying before him. Going down with this youthful passenger were seventeen-year-old Ritchie Valens and twenty-eight-year-old J. P. Richardson (the Big Bopper), two fine young rockers . . . and Roger Peterson, the pilot, too, all victims of the mysterious crash.

Preliminary to the catastrophe, as an appetizer to the feast of death, was a series of bad buses hired to transport these three men and their fellow performers on the Winter Dance Party tour of 1959, scheduled to crisscross Minnesota, Wisconsin, and Iowa in cruel conditions. Philip Norman explains that

> the bus in which they started their journey lasted only a few hours on the icy highways before grinding and sputtering to a stop. . . . The second bus proved little better than the first and, likewise, had to be replaced after barely a day's journey. A third was summoned up, but it, too, quickly fell by the wayside—as did a fourth, a fifth, and, unbelievably, a sixth, and a seventh. They were indeed a sorry load of *clapped-out junk,* with engines unequal to the appalling road conditions, and heaters which barely mitigated the ferocious cold that seeped through their ice-blank windows. (italics added)

The buses were such "clapped-out junk" that one musician suffered frostbite. Such junk that all of the rockers, traveling hundreds of miles each day and night, toiling from gig to distant gig, shivered and nursed aching backs. Such junk that Holly and some others decided to charter an airplane to save time getting to the next show four hundred miles away. A chance to defrost, do some laundry, call home, sleep in a bed. Less than twenty-four hours later, Buddy Holly and his two fellow musicians were dead.

In the end, when officials had finished their investigation of it, the wreckage of the Beechcraft Bonanza was repurchased from the Civil Aeronautics Board by Jerry Dwyer, the owner of the air service and the plane itself before it crashed. In 1996, Dwyer "disclosed that he had the remains of N3794N transported to a secret location in the Iowa wilderness and given decent burial."[2]

What a waste!

There's no way to avoid trash, literal or conceptual, in rock 'n' roll, the musical barometer, one might say, of America's penchant for disposability. When one factors into the aesthetics of rock trash the premature death of rock musicians from Buddy Holly to Layne Staley (dead of heroin/cocaine injection on the anniversary in 2002 of Kurt Cobain's death), the trope assumes tragic scope. As usual Richard Meltzer gets it right. The deceased is Lester Bangs, thirty-three years of age. Meltzer felt "jagged fucking anger (at a waste of life, life-force, and relative inconsequentials like 'talent' and 'genius')."[3] On the same note, the late George Harrison, himself wasted by cancer before reaching sixty, invoked waste in the context of Mark David Chapman's assassination of John Lennon: "It was such a waste, some stupid person."[4] Can anyone doubt that many other people have said the same thing—"What a waste!"—on hearing the news of another rock 'n' roll casualty? No one can, which is my cue to begin the second part of this study of the theme of garbage in rock 'n' roll music. "Wasted" will analyze waste vis-à-vis morbidity and death in rock 'n' roll culture. From the trashy sounds of many a rock tune to the wasted lives of many a rock 'n' roll artist, the garbage motif—concrete, critical, lyrical, and human—is central to the feeling, vitality, and meaning of rock. Paradoxically, without this element of disposability permeating it, rock 'n' roll would not have lasted as long as it has. Largely because it is trash through and through, rock music might live, if not forever, then for as long as our civilization continues to produce stupefying quantities of garbage.

I wanna dedicate it to everybody that's died and that's gonna die. Don't give up hope.
—Jimi Hendrix, concert patter following performance of "Machine Gun," 31 December 1969

Rock will die (petrified into a cliché) if its hegemonic line is strong and stiff enough to repress all Others in its efforts to establish a pure origin and canon. If and when rock can be unambiguously defined, then it will be dead.
—Johan Fornäs

Part 2 Wasted

29. Another One Bites the Dust

Romantic love is one of the main themes of rock 'n' roll music; no wonder then that death is also central to the genre. The pathos and intensity of Eros lie in their relationship to Thanatos. Love is all the sweeter because of the bitterness of death. The rareness and evanescence of the former are rendered more precious by the inevitability of the latter. Love gives to us tongue-tied, rapidly aging, degenerative human beings the wherewithal to feel as if we can defy death. By seeming to rejuvenate us in the blink of an eye, love provides us with the illusion that we fragile mortals can thwart the imminence of dissolution. Whenever we say to someone, "I will always love you" (à la Dolly Parton) or "my heart will go on" (à la Celine Dion), we mean to say that through love we'll elude the clutches of mortality. We take it for granted that in the beginning, the fifties, rock 'n' roll was largely an idiom by and through which adolescents expressed their feelings about fast cars, big waves, square parents, school, work, and above and beyond all these concerns, the thrill and curse of being in love. Moreover, we all know that as rock music matured, it took on additional subjects such as ecological collapse, political unrest, social upheaval, and the perils of conformity. But death has been present from the outset. While unsurpassed as the clarion trumpet of youthful joy, rebellion, innocence, and love, rock moonlights as the dissonant foghorn of agony, loss, and death.

At the same time that love and death can be set in opposition to each other, they can be seen as reversible or interchangeable. Anyone who has loved romantically knows that such love, by virtue of being one's salvation and the preeminent stay against the tribulations of life, is invariably the source of bitter disappointment . . . a type of death to the sufferer of unrequited or lost love. No wonder then that like every other art form in the West, rock 'n' roll represents death as well as it represents love and that it has immortalized on plastic and tape countless aural images of emotional, psychological, and physical forms of death.

This much is obvious. What may not be so obvious are the sophistication, subtlety, range, and passion with which rock musicians have addressed the subject of death. The library of rock 'n' roll music, in large part the province of hormone-crazed teen cretins and sex-addled (more likely sex-starved) misfits, would be unimaginable without its meditations on the carnage wrought by the

Grim Reaper. He stalks the ranks of rock musicians, having clipped the budding careers and lives of numberless performers and writers. No living-in-the-fast-lane rock 'n' roller has to hope he dies before he gets old (as Pete Townsend so aptly expressed what his drummer achieved after indulging in years of excessive behavior) because the chances are fair to middling that a rocker's lifestyle will take care of the trouble of aging or dying without the intervention of hope or prayer.

Which for a moment brings us back to Elvis Presley, the king of the wasteland and the incarnation of rock's many antitheses. Ghosting for a few of Elvis's bodyguards (the West brothers and Dave Hebler) late in the King's life, Steve Dunleavy wrote, "Presley is a mass of paradoxes, contradictions, complexities. His generosity vies with his selfishness; his sunny moments battle with his black moments; his demand for excitement clashes with his easy acquiescence to boredom."[1] Enhancing this portrait is Albert Goldman's assessment of rock's

> classic American figure: the totally bifurcated personality. Always professing his undying love and loyalty to Ma, Country, and Corn Pone, always an unregenerate southern redneck who stopped just short of the Klan and the John Birch Society, [Elvis] was also the first great figure in that devolution of American society that has led to the narcissistic, anarchistic, junked-up heroes of the world of rock and punk. . . . [H]e registers both poles of the American schiz with perfect clarity. What makes him so appalling and alarming—but, again, so *echt Amerikan*—is his incredible innocence and self-righteousness, his stunning incapacity to recognize or even sense subliminally the total contradiction that informs his being. Accustomed to living in two worlds simultaneously, the day world of the squares and the night world of the cats, he embraces disjunction as the natural and inevitable condition of human existence. It is this Janus-like existential stance that makes him appear so often an enigma[, a] being who found himself alive at a time when the national values pointed in divergent directions and who reacted by rushing off in both directions at once.[2]

As with Elvis, so with rock, split in halves like a record album. Rock music is at once a salvation and a betrayal; an outcry of autonomy and the fake orgasmic moan of someone whoring for the corporations; an occasion for amateurs to bang out some chords and smash some drums, and for virtuosi to play patterns of stupefying intricacy; a bona fide field of musicology and a waste of the scholar's time; an immense pleasure and a big bore. Rock is transcendent music and it's trashy noise. It's ageless art and it's washed-up entertainment for postindustrial masses dead to feeling, sensation, and spiritual uplift.

Given the second half of the last binary, why would any aging fan of rock 'n' roll music—a music initially created by and marketed to youngsters for whom the question of rock's relative vitality has probably always seemed irrelevant—

want it to live forever by pretending it thrives in the first decade of the twenty-first century? If the pat psychological answer is because listening to rock music distracts the forty-plus fan from thinking about the onuses of adulthood and the onset of age, then these middle-aged devotees of the genre would do well to keep in mind the myth of Tithonus, the beautiful boy for whom the infatuated goddess Aurora secured eternal life but not eternal youth. Borrowing the boy's voice, the poet Tennyson writes, "And after many a summer dies the swan. / Me only cruel immortality / Consumes: I wither slowly in thine arms, / Here at the quiet limit of the world, A white-hair'd shadow roaming like a dream / The ever-silent spaces of the East."[3] This allegory of the human subject yearning for eternal youth has a counterpart in rock 'n' roll. To maintain their youthful appearance so as to compete against the in-synch kids pursuing careers in rock music, many of rock's elder stars have turned, just like millions of others in their age group, to the magic of aerobics, face-lifts, eye jobs, and implants. Contrary to such efforts made to delay or offset the body's decay, our elder stars usually leave the impression that rock 'n' roll becomes more wrinkled and uncomely each year. Rock's youthful look has been seen to assume the creepy postsurgical gaze apparent in recent photographs of Cher and Michael Jackson. But even the majority of young groups, those with bodies and faces still unmolested by time, seem old and recycled, desperate for new riffs in a medium saddled with clichés. They tour to promote albums whose packaging is more exciting than the music within. And when twenty-two-year-old rock singers take on world-weary voices, which they often do, they simply sound ridiculous. Once everything was new; now it just seems to be. To switch metaphors, it's as if the rock 'n' roll young bands are producing were an exhausted horse resisting all attempts to be mounted, much less ridden, one more mile across a desert. The beast—rather, the once-beautiful boy Tithonus—wants to lie down and die in peace.

These generalizations lead to yet another antithesis. Death helps to ensure the vitality of rock 'n' roll even as it dwindles into its dotage. Delete the songs alluding to or focusing on death, and you've gutted the genre. Rock 'n' roll can't thrive without death rearing its head in its songbooks and biographies. The best parable of rock immortality–cum–human frailty originates in Memphis, Tennessee, a good place to turn when taking stock of rock's present condition. Annually, legions of admirers troop to Graceland to pay homage to the once and future King. Greeks never traveled with more alacrity to the oracle in Delphi, and Muslims never toiled more devoutly across the burning sands of Arabia to al-Haram mosque in Mecca. Twenty-five years after dying, Elvis Aaron Presley lives, a divinity breathing life into the recording and tourist industry and, consequently, into American culture.[4] We would die without him.

Ah, Elvis! Ah, humanity!

30. All Things Must Pass

The paradoxes mount. For instance, the trope of disposability in the creation and criticism of rock 'n' roll music is balanced by the miracles of digital technology that ensure rock's material durability. Compact discs aren't biodegradable. They don't decompose. Whereas the life span of a vinyl platter's distortion-free sound was short, a compact disc can reproduce mint sound forever. Unless mishandled, digital discs won't deteriorate; unlike records, they won't warp, skip, wow, flutter, or distort. They won't snap, twist, and jam as do tapes "eaten" by malfunctioning tape players. To a person burdened by hundreds of scratchy long-plays, someone unsentimental about the old days when it always seemed the stylus needed replacement, compact discs still seem so advanced and so superior to vinyl that he may fail to ponder this question: What happens when longevity isn't commensurate with merit?

With the advent of the Internet and what some observers predict will result in the diminishing importance of the major record labels, it seems possible in the digital age that the rock 'n' roll canon, perpetually online and expanding like the universe, will be accessible to everyone.[1] Rare oldies, 45s, and LPs will become the ghosts of a collector's dim past, and new stuff—most of it trash—will last many generations. And yet despite the technostamp of timelessness, the aesthetics of waste will always characterize rock 'n' roll. The vast amount of it will be recorded, distributed (or not), consumed (or not), and forgotten within days. In proliferation of sameness, it will survive.

This point may sound circular, but rock 'n' roll, because of its disposable nature, is a wonderfully wasteful medium. This expresses not the tautology that its disposability makes it wasteful but that its wastefulness makes it wonderful. In celebrating and feeding off waste, rock resembles the phoenix: in undergoing the twin activity of conception and consumption it regenerates itself time and time again. In the abstract, the concept of waste helps us to understand why rock's evanescence is one of the genre's most endearing qualities. But in the concrete, specifically in the flesh, the idea of waste is anything but endearing or wonderful. Why? The answer is self-evident. Because real people are involved. To spectators and consumers, these people, publicly known as rock musicians, may seem unreal, never quite alive, not palpable—fantastic talents, larger-than-life representations transmuted into merchandise by packaging and image manipulation, quasi-divine projections of the universal infatuation with celebrity and big bucks, familiar but foreign faces pictured on the cover of an LP or CD, on a television special, or on the video screens planted around a modern stage. The electronic representation of their presence makes it seem they can't die because they aren't alive, not like you and me, in the first place.

This view, arguably cynical, prevails over the one that conceives in exceptional cases a nation or world of fans mourning the loss of a beloved figure, such as Elvis, John Lennon, or Kurt Cobain, as if they were mourning one of their own dead relatives. Such exceptions aside, it has been remarked that today's mainstream rock 'n' roll seems so distant from its populist roots and values, so far from innocence, so far from providing a reason to idolize any of its practitioners, that one marvels at rock music's ability to hold an audience. On bad days, a fan curses the flood of new radio-friendly titles. He bemoans rock's corruption by moneyed interests. He sickens at the thought of logo-minded and image-focused youth markets scarfing up, along with Mountain Dew and Visa commercials, trivial, reductive, and superficial best-of polls and *Where Are They Now?* episodes on MTV and VH1.[2] In short, on bad days he laments rock music's disinclination either to get another life or die. On worse days, he turns his back on rock and loads the machine with classical and jazz discs. On the worst days, he gives in to the temptation to step over the edge of the "Rock Is Dead" pit and fall to the bottom, where rock's coroners have convened to share their notes. Showing a mixture of courage and disgust, these coroners have put their ears to rock's chest, looked up at the vigil keepers, and reported the absence of a beat. They have lifted the spell. Tithonus is dead.

Many interested parties go to great lengths to deny or refute the allegations of rock's death, such as writers for rock tabloids and supermarket glossies, producers in the video industry, and young rock musicians who crank out dull disc after dull disc; people not quite knowing, for whatever reason, that the first and only indispensable condition of rock 'n' roll music is that it must . . . well, *rock*. Maybe it is, maybe it isn't—but for many of the faithful who grew up with it, rock isn't only dead but, I repeat, has been dead for a long time, expiring at some point on the timeline they themselves drew to chronicle the rock music that meant the most to them as they matured. Consequently, death dates shift relative to the listener's personal chronology, the generation's collective memory. In general, however, the traditional version is that rock 'n' roll had been in the throes of premature death since as early as 1960. With Eddie Cochran (d. 1960, age twenty-one) and Buddy Holly (d. 1959, age twenty-two) deceased; Elvis bouncing back from his two-year absence in the armed forces and hustling for good roles in Hollywood; Jerry Lee Lewis (wasted by scandal) switching from rock to country; and Little Richard and Chuck Berry abjuring the devil's music for religion and being sent to jail, respectively, rock was speeding toward an early grave. We've heard it a million times—rock's resuscitation commenced in 1963 with the advent of the Beatles, the Rolling Stones, the Kinks, and others, and so on, and so on.[3] And then it died, definitely died, in 1970 or so. Of course, since the definition kept changing—see section 2 in "Trashed"—and since no one could foresee the marvelous music to come out during the years following one death notice after another, it was easy enough for a sixties through nineties critic, deprived of the benefit of the hindsight we enjoy, to pronounce rock, or rock 'n' roll, or one of its subgenres—rockabilly, punk, grunge, or alt rock—dead at any given time in what has turned out to be a fifty-year history, and to ignore the fact that there always are and always have been at least ten new albums a month worth purchasing at list price.

The rock-is-dead debate, the oldest, most fruitless, and most boring debate in rock history (challenged only by the debate over whether or not drug use made artists such as Hendrix, Dylan, Cobain, Barrett, Lennon, Evan Dando, Bob Mould, and Gibby Haynes better composers and musicians) continues to get press. In 1999, a journalist quipped in *Newsweek* that the mass sales of Kid Rock, Everlast, Eminem, and Limp Bizkit—all "the King's heirs"—prove that "[r]ock isn't dead, it's just moving to a hip-hop beat."[4] Topping the "million mark" seems to be the mainstream writer's, and mainstream society's, measure of rock's health. The more informed editors of the alt-rock magazine *Magnet* spoke their piece about rock death in a fall 2001 issue, where an article named "Rock Solid" profiled "six young bands providing life support in 2001." The editors asserted that "rumors of rock 'n' roll's death have been greatly exaggerated."[5] Nonetheless, when the article was published, the chances were good to excellent that no more than a few hundred thousand people would ever hear the recorded music of the six anointed bands: Black Rebel Motorcycle Club, the White Stripes, the Strokes, the Burning Brides, Tight Bro's from Way Back When, and the Sights. (The White Stripes and the Strokes did proceed to garner significant popular and critical fame, reaching millions of people on the strength of the compact discs *White Blood Cells* and *Is This It?* and sold-out concerts.) But not hearing these bands doesn't prove that rock 'n' roll is dead. It shows instead that, as in a lake coming back to life after years of pollution, the most interesting and strongest bands resemble fish disporting in the lake's depths and inaccessible recesses, far from the activity of run-off sluices, recreational boats, shoreline swimmers, vacationing anglers, and weekend refugees from the city. A fan patient and ready to do some research and take some risks will find that he can still go broke buying all the newly released reasons to believe.

Recently, James Miller revisited the midseventies, when most baby boomers attended the funeral of rock 'n' roll. By the 1980s,

> the rock world as I came to know it professionally seemed to me ever more stale, ever more predictable, even boring.

What had seemed mysterious to a nine-year-old boy . . . became, to the adult critic, a routinized package of theatrical gestures, generally expressed in a blaze of musical clichés. . . . I believe that the genre's era of explosive growth has been over for nearly a quarter century. Like such other mature pop music forms as the Broadway musical and the main currents of the jazz tradition, from swing to bop, rock now belongs to the past as much as to the future.

For this reason Miller ends his study in 1977, coincident with the passing of Elvis Presley (and, I might add, the high-water mark of punk), "because by that time, in my view, the essence of rock and roll . . . had been firmly established."[6] Miller implies that in rock music as in politics, the reign of a king, queen, emperor, czar, or president (King Alfred, Queen Elizabeth I, Queen Victoria, Napoleon, Peter the Great, John F. Kennedy) defines the epoch it spans.

A funny and sad reflection on the death of rock was penned by Mick Farren in 1982. The radio stations are playing nothing, Murray the K has just died, and "as if this isn't bad enough, I wander out to the bar and run into a living legend who informs me that he/she has been forced to take a day job. . . . I've been hearing that rock is dead for as long as I can remember, but this is ridiculous."[7]

It doesn't matter if Miller, Farren, or anyone else is right or wrong. On the topic of the death of rock, the quality of rock, the future of rock, the canon of rock, I change my own mind daily. Rock allows such contradictions—it contains multitudes. For our present purposes, what matters is twofold: one, that the death debate actually lends vitality to the form (to ask if rock is dead means someone cares enough to take its pulse); and two, that a primal curse or brand stigmatizes rock 'n' roll. Its mark of Cain is waste, waste not solely in the terms examined in part 1, but waste taken to the next level, the morbid, mortal, and tragic level. It's no mystery why books about the premature deaths of rock stars feed the maw of the rock-write trade. Keith Moon giving up the ghost at the age of thirty-one; John Lennon being shot to death in the prime of life; Randy Rhoads dying at age twenty-five in an airplane whose pilot was playing a senseless prank; Stevie Ray Vaughan immolated in a flaming helicopter; John Bonham literally drinking himself to death in a marathon binge; Martin Lamble being killed in a car crash after a gig; Buddy Holly boarding the doomed plane— some sensational cases. Each star's epitaph is the same: *What a Waste*. Our own morbid curiosity can't leave the cemetery without a long backward look over a writer's shoulder at the causes of interment.

Let's not forget too that some of the greatest rock acts have broken up, wasted their potential, squandered their talent and chemistry, and more or less died prematurely. Since such bands failed to reach their peak (their peak as imagined by fans whose projection in this regard is admittedly vague), some of them failed—here our judgment stands on more solid ground—to reap the rewards of fame. Wire, Joy Division, the Velvet Underground, Love, Buffalo Springfield, Nirvana, Mission of Burma, Big Star, Television, the Sex Pistols, maybe even the Beatles, are among the best examples of good to great bands that as a result of being wasted by either external circumstances or internal pressures (or both) threw away more than they or we can ever know—and this self-trashing is arguably a good thing aesthetically because tragedy and incompleteness heighten the luster of their achievements. In terms of romantic fragmentation, this point will be discussed further later.

That convincing cases have been made and are still being made by the best and brightest rock critics for the death of rock 'n' roll, despite the fact that this topic has been beaten to death for well-nigh forty years now, underlines the motif and renders it doubly touching. Dead, buried, and finished . . . yet like Elvis constantly reborn in our imaginations as lean, mean, and clean again, rock 'n' roll hangs on. It has become tiresome and pointless to theorize further about its viability. Sometimes, on good days, it sounds younger than yesterday. But sometimes, contrary to our hopes, dreams, and needs, the Elvis image fades and taking its place is a counterimage of a prune-faced Tithonus pathetically tuning a guitar and croaking a rock song into a cordless microphone. He sounds beaten to blandness by age. So what? Thousands of new rock 'n' roll compact discs released annually give the impression not that the young at heart still enjoy making rock albums but that rock's heyday is today and could reach greater heights tomorrow. The contradictions can drive you mad.

31. Shattered

And so death is implicated in the aesthetics of rock waste. So is disease. Identifying a "mal du siècle" sickness inherent in European romanticism, Henri Peyre suggests that

> it is likely that, in the future, at the beginning of every new century, men will feel that they are afflicted by the same malady and will display their restlessness as their privilege and as a sign of being special, just as at the end of every century (from 1970 onwards, the twentieth century has begun to use these terms lavishly), men will think that their times are characterized by decay and will analyse with secret pride their own decline. Actually, like so many other aspects of romanticism, the one characterized by wailing, cursing existence, making a show of anguish, and continually wishing, quite sincerely moreover, for death . . . did not disappear from Europe, and especially not from France, once the so-called romantic movement was over.[1]

Symptoms of this mid-nineteenth-century malady are found in European culture between 1760 and 1789, and, explains Peyre, they began to reappear in the 1970s. To all students of rock music, Peyre's shrewd insight must surely strike a familiar note because the sickness he describes is apparent in the work and attitude of many important rock musicians beginning as early as the 1960s, rockers who as descendents of the "dark" side of Old World romanticism were avatars of anguish and/or discontent and/or self-destruction. Some of these rockers were terminally ill with this Old World affliction. The faces of Brian Jones and Jim Morrison spring instantly to mind, followed by any one of a number of photographic images of the tortured visage of Janis Joplin. In the process of making beautiful music, these three haunted giants did a lot of wailing, cursing, taking of hard drugs, gnashing of teeth, and wishing for death. After 1965, their contemporary romantic John Lennon had plenty of bad days too, as did Lou Reed, both men, however, pulling through and finding more and more reasons to live (barring year-long lost weekends and serious bouts with substances and creative blockage) in the late seventies, the decade that didn't see the survival of an artist fitting Peyre's template to a tee, the acutely morbid composer and singer of fixin'-to-die lullabies, Nick Drake. Circa 1973–79, brush strokes of morbid romanticism color the careers of many premier punk rockers not generally known for suicidal tendencies but also not known for embracing straight-life domestication or for backing away from bodily risk, including Patti Smith (who broke her neck in performance) and Iggy Pop (who set new world records for personal wear and tear), but not including (because he was suicidal and therefore even more morbidly romantic than Patti and Iggy combined) Darby Crash of the Germs, dead of heroin overdose at the age of twenty-one, 7 December 1980, one day before the assassination of John Lennon at age forty.

Morbid-romantic aspects of the fairly dismal eighties had kicked into gear a few months before these two catastrophes with the very bad news of the suicide by hanging of archromantic Ian Curtis, fronting on the strength of his end-game vocals and drear songbook the Mancunian misanthropes Joy Division (later New Order); and the decade proceeded to feature the work of other rock musicians plagued by Peyre's malady: the Fall released more than ten albums in the 1980s; X's classic albums were cut (and cut ears) in the 1980s; the death-infested Pretenders cranked out at least two strong albums before 1985; the Chameleons UK raised the stakes (or hammered them in?) in the soul-wrenching masterpiece *Strange Times* in 1986, and that meant at least two morbid classics in "Tears" and "Soul in Isolation"; while Bad Brains, Hüsker Dü, the Replacements, the Dead Kennedys, and Bad Religion—tumultuous bands steeped in anguish, self-abuse, and rage—helped hard-core and postpunk music reach critical mass in the dull eighties. (In contrast, the relatively bright eighties Paisley Underground movement revived the trippy side of sixties romanticism.) Yes, the hair-band (Bon Jovi, Def Leppard, Duran Duran) and thou-shalt-dance eighties (Madonna, Bronski Beat, Milli Vanilli, Wham!) produced in spite of itself some morbid rock 'n' roll indispensable to anyone interested in listening to wasted youth giving lessons on a society going to waste.

But the inevitable period of stagnation in the rock life cycle in the 1980s was blasted to smithereens when morbid romanticism turned feverish in the 1990s. Kurt Cobain and Nirvana are the decade's main diagnostic case, but far from the only one. In one way or another, sickness or death afflicted Alice in Chains, Pearl Jam, Stone Temple Pilots, the Red Hot Chili Peppers, and Sublime. The best work of bands of this caliber calls to mind the screams, moans, and imprecations of an intensive-care wing of patients drenched in spit and sweat; flushed, pinch-cheeked patients damning through the use of yowling guitars and battered drums the virulence of the disease laying them to waste, all of them caught in different stages of the national epidemic and making music out of the trauma. Bikini Kill, Team Dresch, and Sleater-Kinney roared out of the Northwest with Riot Grrl voices of protest and confusion, striking a narrow path between rock pathology and rock plenitude, while "shoe-gazing" standard-bearers Lush were shattered by the unexpected suicide of their drummer Chris Acland in 1996, and Hope Sandoval of Mazzy Star crooned mood-indigo tunes ideal for slitting one's throat while fantasizing about having sex with a singer slouching on pillows of despair. Hundreds of rock's casualties fill the gurneys of the morbid-romantic mortuary and hundreds of rock's near misses have spent a night or two in the morbid-romantic emergency room or rehab center. Morbid-romantic rock is what's recorded and staged when rock musicians go to waste and drag their music down with them.

Again, Romantic French authors suffering pangs of "mal du siècle" morbidity textualized this effect, a little artificially it seems, generations before the advent of rock 'n' roll. Peyre believes "[t]here is undoubtedly some affectation in the awe-inspiring attitude of melancholy" evident in the work of Chateaubriand and his contemporary European romantics. But Peyre doesn't question Chateaubriand's sincerity: "there was a blend of sincerity and love of verbal ostentation which made the writer exaggerate the expression of an impression."[2] The deeply morbid *Atala* (1801) and *René* (1802) are allegories of the id (incestuous desire) and the superego (the saving grace of Christianity) in which the mental and physical health of their protagonists is strained to the point of collapse. The sublimity of Nature—no better backdrop for a trip into neurasthenia—also looms in the narratives, which take place in the Old World and the New. In the first, traveling across Virginia, the Indian Chactas, in love with Atala (who for the sake of her dying mother has taken a vow of virginity), visits a tribal burial ground situated among

> a great forest of pine trees. The trunks of these trees were red streaked with green, and rose without branches to their tops, resembling lofty columns which formed the peristyle of this temple of death. The atmosphere was permeated with a religious resonance like the muffled roar of the organ beneath the vaults of a church. But within the depths of the sanctuary, nothing could be heard but the hymn of the birds glorifying the memory of the dead in eternal celebration.

It gets worse. Atala takes poison because the attraction to her brother Chactas has weakened her vows. Chactas, "rolling wildly over the ground, twisting [his] arms and biting [his] hands," observes in horror, "It was in vain that [the hermit saint who has befriended the couple] tried to bring succor for Atala's anguish. Fatigue, sorrow, poison, and a passion more deadly than all poisons together were combining to spirit this flower away from our solitude."[3] Atala's death is the kind one would expect a radiant Indian maiden to suffer in a morbid-romantic parable of pathological repression. It's a fact neither more nor less morbid that years afterward Chactas uses the bagged bones of his beloved as a pillow. *René*, the shorter fiction, is perhaps more horrific. Ever on the move, the noble René is another lost soul of Gaul. He and his sister, Amelia, alone in the world, are in love. He sublimates his unholy passion by embarking on a directionless search. She retreats into the confines of the family château. René reflects,

> Total solitude and the spectacle of nature soon brought me to a state almost impossible to describe. . . . I was furiously driven by an excess of life. Sometimes I blushed suddenly and felt torrents of burning lava surging through my heart. Sometimes I would cry out involuntarily, and the night was disturbed both by my dreams and by sleepless cares. I felt I needed something to fill the vast emptiness of my existence.

The desire for Amelia, who treats her "forbidden passion" for her brother by taking holy orders (the ritual puts him into a "deathlike stupor"), undoes René: "For some time I struggled against my malady, but only halfheartedly, with no firm will to conquer it. Finally, unable to find any cure for this strange wound of my heart, which was nowhere and everywhere, I resolved to give up my life."[4] But he doesn't die. He goes instead to America to be swallowed up in vast solitudes that parallel his misery.

Examples could be multiplied to trace a like blend of melancholy, affectation, and ostentation in the pages of morbid-romantic writers such as George Lippard, Edgar Allan Poe, and Herman Melville, three nineteenth-century Americans masters of nonfiction, fiction, and verse. Lippard, for example, was a prolific, swashbuckling, charismatic—in a word, Byronic—figure who died in 1854 at the age of thirty-one (of tuberculosis). According to one scholar, this caped, long-haired radical novelist, stands for this extreme end of gloomy fiction, and thus his texts limned "some of the most demonic, blasphemous moments" in American culture.[5] In *The Quaker City* (1845), a sensational narrative about seduction and murder in Philadelphia, Lippard unleashed page after page of morbid eroticism that would surpass rock 'n' rollers in the midst of a sex-and-drug debauch. *The Quaker City* drags the reader into a dungeon of intrigue, rape, near incest, seduction, flight, pursuit, torture, murder, madness, revenge, guilt, betrayal, alcoholism, midnight terror, disguise, and all-purpose apocalypse. The text provides a barometer by which we can gauge all gothic and sensational fiction, in addition to all works of morbid romanticism no matter what the medium, including rock 'n' roll. One passage of scores will suffice, a description of a corpse laid out in a dissecting room:

> From head to foot, along the trunk and over each limb, that corpse was all one cankering sore, one loathsome blotch. Features on the face there were none; brow and lip and cheek were all one hideous ulcer. The eye-balls were spotted with clotted blood; the mouth a cavern of corruption; the very hair was thick with festering pollution. It was the corpse of a man who had died from that terrible of all diseases, the most infectious of all epidemics, a curse at whose name beauty shudders and grave science grows pale—the small-pox. Better to look into the plague-pit where man and woman and babe lay mangled together, one reeking mass of quick lime and gory flesh, then [*sic*] to have gazed upon that corpse extended on the Dissecting table before the eyes of five hundred living men![6]

Just the sort of thing we're used to reading in Edgar Allan Poe. (In fact, Lippard was Poe's personal friend and loyal supporter, one the few, and came to his fellow writer's aid during one of his last crises.) Poe succeeded above and beyond his contemporaries in channeling morbidity into literary art. If you substitute the name "Poe" with "Lou Reed," the rock artist to whom all these morbid-romantic roads are leading, you'll find A. Robert Lee's assessment of the author of "Ligeia," "Alone," "Ulalume," "The Valley of Unrest," "The Raven," and *The Narrative of Arthur Gordon Pym* fits Reed, the composer of "Black Angel's Death Song," "I Can't Stand It," "The Gift," "Sister Ray," "Lady Godiva's Operation," and *New York*:

> To the one side he remains the vulgarian, the mere dabbler in sensation, a fraudulent and frequently tiresome maker of effects. . . . He never rises above himself, ever a provincial and juvenile mind. To the other side, he beckons as a great custodian of inner unease and doubt. His writing at best shows him a canny, wonderfully alert and agile

imagination, full of the most startling feats of invention. Which is to acknowledge that Poe goes on sponsoring a range of responses, dismay at his flatnesses, amazement at his genuine ingenuity and power.[7]

Such ingenuity and power are in full bloom in "The Fall of the House of Usher" (1839), a tale in which Poe's narrator analyzes "that morbid condition of the auditory nerve which rendered all music intolerable to the sufferer [Roderick Usher]." On every level and in every detail, "Usher" is Poe's master class in "insufferable gloom," capable of eliciting in the reader, as the sight of the dilapidated Usher mansion does in the narrator, "an iciness, a sinking, a sickening of the heart—an unredeemed dreariness of thought which no goading of the imagination could torture into aught of the sublime." Here, where "[a]n air of stern, deep, and irredeemable gloom hung over and pervaded all," Edgar Allan Poe reaches a summit in morbid short fiction.[8] Similarly, in the album *Berlin* Lou Reed reaches a summit in morbid rock 'n' roll. Whereas hypochondria, impotence, repression, anorexia, self-pity, and self-loathing contaminate the hero of Poe's tale, drug addiction, infidelity, physical abuse, nymphomania, and suicide mangle the couple in Reed's *Berlin*. An anguish of nostalgia and a yearning for plenitude wash like black mist over each narrative. *Berlin* is powerful because a depressing but spellbinding tale is told via shattering songs written by a brilliant songwriter and performed by a studio full of rock masters who understand the nuances of every lyric and, parlaying their grasp of dynamics, heighten the emotions and bring out the textures of bittersweet melodies. The album apotheosizes the concept of death, or human waste, the epitome of rock's trash trope. Masterpieces aside, Poe and Reed have other things in common. Both simultaneously shocked and fascinated their fellow citizens; both considered themselves rare originals toiling among thousands of frauds and hacks; and both saw their work dismissed as humbug and con artistry, as self-indulgent exercises in depravity, as elaborate contrivances, even as perverse melodramas composed by sick men shuffling about in a world besieged by the diseased, the dying, and the dead.

(N.B. The previous passage was drafted in 2000; it was revised and polished for publication in December 2002. A few days after completing it, I learned about the imminent release of *The Raven*, Lou Reed's homage to Edgar Allan Poe. Rarely is a writer blessed with concrete proof, courtesy the artist under scrutiny, of an insight. Unable at this time to closely read *The Raven*, I can at least report that in the style of *Songs for Drella* [1990] and *Magic and Loss* [1992], *The Raven* is a song cycle based on Reed's involvement with real human beings, now deceased. As in his apostrophes to Andy Warhol, Doc Pomus, and Rita [no surname] in the earlier albums, Reed is inspired, this time by his idea of Edgar

Allan Poe as a prophet of perverseness, to contemplate philosophical subjects such as the suffering artist, identity crisis, bereavement, and the downside of fame. In *The Raven,* Reed adds to this list the encroachments of old age [see, for instance, the not-particularly-Poe-like "Who Am I?"] and thoughts of personal dissolution. Supplementing Reed's core rhythm section of Mike Rathke, Fernando Saunders, and Tony Smith is a fascinating group of special guests ranging from Laurie Anderson and David Bowie to the Blind Boys of Alabama and Steve Buscemi. Whether or not Reed properly sets Poe to rock music, the listener must decide. Certainly, the listener who expects Reed to pillage Poe's texts for lyrics will be disappointed. Most of "The Raven" itself, recited by Willem Dafoe over a soft electronic drone, is rewritten by Reed to include some diction to which modern audiences can relate. In short, Reed at times collaborates with Poe. Otherwise, it's his show, many songs lacking any allusions to Poe's oeuvre whatsoever. One hears power ballads, funk workouts, epic rock with generic lyrics. One doesn't hear "To Helen," "The City in the Sea," or excerpts from "Ligeia" adapted to rock 'n' roll music. Further validating my pairing of Reed and Poe, the rocker resurrects a song from *Berlin,* "The Bed," a dirge to end all dirges and thus one of the best examples of why the names Lou Reed and Edgar Allan Poe can—indeed, should—be uttered in the same breath. [Note added March 2003.])

To multiply evidence of morbid-romantic precedents in rock music would be to digress. Instead, let's switch gears from literature and apply Professor Peyre's comments on Chateaubriand to a leading rock 'n' roller who fought through plenty of morbid-romantic spells and cataloged his melancholia with precision and power, seeming sincerity too, despite moments of affectation. John Lennon. Not the John Lennon of the brimming-with-glee "A Hard Day's Night" or "Ticket to Ride"; not even the John Lennon of the cheerfully self-doubting "I'm a Loser" or "Help!" And definitely not the John Lennon chin-deep in the uxorious pleasantries captured on his last album, *Double Fantasy.* The best example of Lennon's morbidity at work is, hands down, 1970's *Plastic Ono Band.* The performances on this record, more than any of Lennon's grimmest sides with the Beatles—"Yer Blues," "I Want You (She's So Heavy)"—or solo—"Cold Turkey," "Jealous Guy"—are poised between histrionics and catharsis, theatrics and therapy, boasting and breakdown. Morbid rock 'n' roll, where obsessive self-analysis goes hand in hand with an ecstasy of anguish, is the product of a self-conscious recording process before it reaches an audience of sympathetic but inarticulate listeners.

Plastic Ono Band begins in a cemetery and ends in a haunted mind. The artist's mother occupies both places. Implication: agony begins and ends with

Mother. Thus it is that "Mother" instigates Lennon's trial of catharsis. In this dire cut, a grown man regresses into the clutches of unresolved Oedipal agony. The mighty ex-Beatle reverted to scared little boy clings to the tatters of hope decades after both parents have abandoned him, his mother twice, first by leaving her little boy to be raised by his Aunt Mimi, second by getting killed in a freak pedestrian accident during her son's teenage years. Preceding "Mother" is a sound effect from what could pass as a fifties Dracula movie: distant church bells, slow, dreamy, an aural metonym for a graveyard enshrouded by the foliage of vast elm trees and weeping willows, bats flitting and squeaking in the gloom, ghostly fog draped over the tilted stones. By the third and last verse of "Mother," Lennon is screaming for his parents to stay, to come home. He whistles in the dark on the next cut, the delicate "Hold On" ("It's gonna be alright / You're gonna win the fight), then turns nasty in "I Found Out."[9] The rock star has found enlightenment on the far side of fame, and is he ever angry about it. One of Lennon's revelations is that the verities with which his belief system was stoked are bankrupt rhetoric. Lennon hacks at the hypocrisy of the homilies that have brought him at the age of thirty to seek relief in Primal Scream therapy, of which this album was the artistic counterpart. The assault on bourgeois wish fulfillment is reinforced in the antifolkie "Working Class Hero," where the singer concludes that everyone's a "fucking peasant" slobbering at the trenchers of vicarious stardom. Side one closes with "Isolation"—pianissimo verses, fortissimo bridge: the teddy boy disjointed by fear and paranoia inches toward agoraphobia. "Remember," the album's operative verb, starts round two. In this piano thumper, the man regresses further into infantile rage directed at the egregious values of England's fathers and mothers. Lennon cuts it off at four minutes and thirty seconds by inserting the album's second sound bite, an explosion signifying an attack on the Houses of Parliament by Guy Fawkes in 1605. (The actual plot was foiled at the last minute.) A love song follows: brief respite. Then Lennon cranks up "Well Well Well." This scream session makes the consolation of love sound as torturous in its intensity as the loneliness that makes that same love indispensable for survival. The solipsism of "Look at Me" (one of the few derivative songs in Lennon's catalog, "Look at Me" is a close cousin of "Julia") paves the way for "God," Lennon's renunciation of heroes, archetypes, idols, divinities, and religions. Lennon exposes them as scapegoats or crutches for individuals—your average Beatles fan, for instance—too starstruck, too deluded, or too weak to know themselves as more real than every false idol combined. Lennon renounces Buddha, Jesus, Kennedy, Elvis, "Zimmerman," and the Beatles, replacing these phantoms with him and Yoko Ono. But he's not finished. Morbid-romantic masterpieces don't end happily.

The album fizzles off to the murky chords of "My Mummy's Dead," in which "Three Blind Mice" is lyrically retooled in line with Lennon's encounter with the specter of dead mother.

"We still live in the age of Romanticism," declares Camille Paglia in *Sexual Personae,* and a "Byronic youth-culture flourishes in rock music, the ubiquitous American art form." Paglia's thesis posits that the roots of rock 'n' roll are discoverable not in (or not only in) rhythm and blues but in the "effeminate heterosexuality" and "annoyingly self-congratulatory modern youth culture" embodied by the charismatic author of *Don Juan.*[10] Paglia's mating of George Gordon, Lord Byron and Elvis Presley, spanning a scant four pages, stands as rock criticism of the highest order not only because it's smart but also because it breaks ranks with dusty accounts of how the country blues became the electric blues, which became rhythm and blues, which became rock 'n' roll.[11] This may be what transpired but there's more to the story and this is where romanticism comes in. Paglia believes Elvis Presley and Lord Byron were two larger-than-life men of "epochal narcissistic glamour." They stand side by side like identical twins of the flesh and spirit separated at birth, and not because each seduced hundreds of women or because each of their perfect bodies eventually gave way to fat. Byron's persona was that of the "glamorous sexy youth of brash, defiant energy," and this pose, according to Paglia, defines the rock 'n' roll attitude. Elvis had it too, in abundance. Elvis also had the emblematic sneer, the counterpart to Byron's disdainful upturn of lip. In common were early style "brooding menace" and, the stamp of maturity, "urbane magnanimity." Paglia remarks a further parallel in Byron's late interest in Oriental costume and Elvis's late indulgence in his "nearly Mithraic" wardrobe of sashes, studded belts, and swooping capes. Moreover, she digs up roots of rock music in the "darkly daemonic mode" of the tormented verses of Samuel Taylor Coleridge, forebear of Paglia's beloved Rolling Stones.[12]

But the most in-depth study of rock 'n' roll as romanticism is Robert Pattison's *The Triumph of Vulgarity: Rock Music in the Mirror of Romanticism.* Presumably, anyone having the slightest acquaintance with the romantic movement (what one learned in a high school English class would suffice) should be able to see, if not with Camille Paglia's clairvoyance and scope, that rock 'n' roll is the legacy of nineteenth-century romanticism. (I'm assuming the same person would know something about rock music.) Yet it would be a mistake to presume too that Pattison has written a superfluous book.

Pattison excels when, among other things, he discusses the rock star's drug use and death wish; when he analyzes the rock star's determination to stay young forever, his emotionalism, and his role-playing; when he analyzes rock 'n' roll as a projection of white fantasies of black culture; when he catalogs rock's "quest for the infinite" reachable through the libido, its Blakean and Whitmanesque frenzies and verbosities, and its narcissism and solipsism; when he describes the paradox that "[r]ock celebrates pastoral and primitive utopias while swathing its stars in polyester jockstraps and arming itself with the latest devices of electronic technology."[13] All this he does very well, citing innumerable artists, from the Rolling Stones to the Meat Puppets, from Van Morrison to Tom Verlaine, from Billy Joel to Soft Cell. Rock is the liturgy of vulgar pantheism, he writes, and

> the creeds of Jefferson, Emerson, Poe, and Whitman provide its Bible. The essential points stressed again and again in rock's liturgy are the growing, healthy self, the infinite extent of human energy when freed from restraint, the corrupt and inhibiting nature of the world's social organizations, the equality of men at the level of feeling, the aversion to institutions, especially political and class institutions, and the inestimable value of allowing each self to make its own approach to the infinite.

Aside from the fact that it emphasizes the other side of morbidity, this passage is inconsistent with Pattison's thesis that above all rock music is the final word in vulgar pantheism. Pantheism is "abysmally indiscriminate—or said another way, it is infinitely tolerant," and "vulgarity is untranscendent." Pattison embodies the pedant and the curmudgeon. In him lies a scholar who would enjoy rock 'n' roll if only it didn't exasperate him so much. At one point he faults rock for having

> vulgarized the Romantic obsession with youth. The vulgarization lies not only in the mass audience rock reaches with its Romantic conventions nor in the loud presentation it gives to the sublime concerns of Romantic art. In rock, the grand questions which refined taste has made the object of conscious and painful deliberation are handled with instinctive and cheerful abandon. What Wordsworth treated with studied craftsmanship, rock manhandles with reckless spontaneity. By its nature, rock *cannot achieve the poetic finish*, the historical awareness, or the rational depths of great Romantic poetry, because these all require the imposition of transcendent order on the materials of feeling. Rock's vulgarity subordinates reason to emotion, denies transcendence, and exalts perpetual youth.[14] (italics added)

Despite the link between rock music and romanticism, Pattison seems to forget they're not equivalent terms. One is a medium, the other is a sensibility. His ideas sometimes break down and his arguments falter on hypostatization because he wants rock to be something it isn't. Since an equivalence can't be forced between Bruce Springsteen and Percy Shelley, or between John Lennon and William Wordsworth (in the end, the names don't matter that much), Pattison faults rock for being that which it isn't, never was, and never intended to be.

In other words, his revelations notwithstanding, Pattison falls into the trap of judging rock by standards to which it never aspired. For all I've said about the motif of garbage in rock 'n' roll, I've said or implied as much about rock's contradictions, one of which is that rock's trashiness doesn't mutually exclude rock's "poetic finish." *Revolver, Pet Sounds, Forever Changes, The Velvet Underground, Five Leaves Left, Meddle, Pour Down like Silver, Another Green World, Station to Station, Aja, Armed Forces, More Songs about Buildings and Food, Strange Times, Sweet Old World, In Utero, OK Computer, The Soft Bulletin . . .* but why continue? Great on their own terms and "poetic" to boot, it's a given that these albums aren't comparable to William Wordsworth's "Intimations of Immortality," William Blake's *The Marriage of Heaven and Hell,* S. T. Coleridge's "Christabel," and Herman Melville's *Pierre.* Its weaknesses aside, *The Triumph of Vulgarity* is the smart bet to remain for a long time the number one guide to rock as romanticism and as such it demanded acknowledgement in the present context.

Going back to page one, our chain has been a black platinum necklace made up of these interchangeable links: rock 'n' roll music, literal garbage, figurative trash, waste, wasted rock musicians, romanticism, and morbid romanticism. The charms attached to these links are rock's morbid-romantic masterpieces. One has been displayed, *Plastic Ono Band.* Let's slip on a more attractive one and see how well it hangs.

The melancholy so familiar to students of romanticism emanates from much rock 'n' roll music. This melancholy, however, needn't depress even the most empathetic or sympathetic listener. After spending two hours being serenaded by Alice in Chains, a listener left with ringing ears isn't certain to shoot dope or to shoot himself. I've listened to Nick Drake's *Pink Moon* dozens of times and on my worst days have yet to buy a coil of rope. Instead of the misery strummed into each chord taped by Nirvana and Joy Division, awe, possibly elation, could well be aroused in the person auditioning the mechanically reproduced voice of an imminent suicide, the music acting like a rock 'n' roll hypodermic injecting sweet sound into an aural mainline, alleviating the listener's own malady. Certainly "malady" is an ideal word—vague enough to cover a lot of ground but specific enough to indicate dysfunction—with which to analyze morbid rock 'n' roll. Like "malaise," malady connotes a general ailment, taking in everything from discontent and anxiety to depression and despair, from paralytic ennui to fixation on suicide. Ironically, by appealing to someone gripped by one of these moods, morbid albums can assuage the victim, at least momentarily. If desired, the victim can then return for another dose of relief. Freud partially explains this pattern (for "art" substitute "rock music"):

At the head of [the] satisfactions through phantasy stands the enjoyment of works of art—an enjoyment which, by the agency of the artist, is made accessible even to those who are not themselves creative. People who are receptive to the influence of art cannot set too high a value on it as a source of pleasure and consolation in life. Nevertheless the mild narcosis induced in us by art can do no more than bring about a transient withdrawal from the pressure of vital needs, and it is not strong enough to make us forget real misery.[15]

That's why we keep buying rock 'n' roll albums: to moderate our "real misery" with fresh resources, cutting back with music the misery that advances from all directions like toxic kudzu.

Freud contradicts the conventional wisdom about sad or blue albums of the Leonard Cohen or Nick Drake stripe—that listening to them will increase a depressed person's depression and thus hasten his steps toward psychosis or suicide. Depending on the person, the opposite could happen, at least until listening to such albums becomes addictive. These are generalizations, of course, but, extrapolating Freud, if a person feels really bad, he could do worse than to spend an hour or two engrossed in *Pink Moon* or Nico's *The End*. Their darkness could well restore some portion of the sufferer's light and hope. Should depression return, another bout with desolate discs could follow. It seems, then, that morbid rock 'n' roll can prove therapeutic. Nonetheless, it's widely believed that this class of albums tends to entangle miserable listeners further in their misery, thus jeopardizing their mental health. On this mistaken pretext, Ira Robbins warns buyers about *Berlin*: it's "one of [Reed's] best, although not recommended for depressives or would-be suicides."[16] This warning begs the question of audience implicit in the critique of any rock album: in this case, aside from rock reviewers, rock historians, and Reed completists, who else but depressives and would-be suicides would want to listen to *Berlin*? But the motif of waste as expressed in the beauty of morbid rock music is my theme, the trash trope turned into a musical sensibility, not the psychology of consumers.

For his concept album of decadence and death, Reed chose his location well. Curiously, reviewers of the record haven't examined the setting. The implication of the cliché (Berlin = decadence) has satisfied them. It doesn't satisfy me. I began this book with a warning about the complacent acceptance of clichés. And although the plot of *Berlin* could have transpired (has transpired) in every Western metropolis, Lou Reed didn't name his record *Topeka, Portland, La Paz, Marseilles, Los Angeles* (L.A. punk band X took that honor in 1980), or *Myrtle Beach*—or *New York* for that matter, and there are plenty of junkies, sex freaks, suicides, neglected children, and men of good fortune living in New York City.

By the same token, Reed's *New York* album couldn't have been named *Berlin* even though New Yorkers have the same problems that Berliners do. James Joyce didn't name *Dubliners* to suggest that his tales of Dublin weren't universal but to emphasize that Dublin was the only place he could set this particular book. Likewise Reed and Berlin. Consequently, we should know something about Berlin before analyzing *Berlin*.

It's a vast and complex subject, but I'll simplify it here. The city of Berlin began making its reputation as a center and symbol of European dissolution as early as the late nineteenth century, this decline hastened by the upheavals, revolutions, and other calamities produced by World War I. By 1919, with German social, financial, and political life in a shambles, pornography rings, homosexual hideouts, prostitution, sex bartering, sadomasochistic cults, and the spread of narcotics (morphine, cocaine, heroin) were firmly, if illegally, established throughout Berlin, which in dozens of other ways had been and would continue to be celebrated as one of Europe's most progressive and sophisticated cities, bursting with art and culture. Germany's emergency constitution of 1919, which codified the policies of the new Weimar Republic, was ineffectual in the face of the economic punishment meted out by the Treaty of Versailles, including the reparations demanded of the German people by the victorious nations.[17] The fabric of so-called "decent" middle-class society had been shredded and rent. Many people gave up. Moral collapse coincided with the economic mayhem best exemplified by Germany's fabled inflation crisis. Alex de Jonge argues that the terrible effects of defeat in war coupled with internal political instability had undermined traditional bourgeois German values, but that it was the hyperinflation of the year 1923 that "finished the process so completely that in the end there were no such values left."[18] What value could citizens lay on anything when 1 trillion marks equaled a halfpenny and when a simple meal would cost millions of marks? Before stabilization took place, between 1924 and 1929, hyperinflation decreased the value of the mark to less than a quarter-trillionth of a dollar.[19] Daily life for thousands had become a theater of horrible absurdity. From 1923 and on, tragedy was fated for Berlin specifically and Germany in general, whose future included the rise of Adolf Hitler and the Third Reich, the devastation caused by World War II, the commencement of the cold war, the fear and paranoia caused by the Berlin Blockade, and the construction of the Berlin Wall.

In the 1920s, foreigners looking for affordable fun swarmed into Berlin because their money could buy so much against the devalued mark. Whereas Berliners were beaten down by economic hardship, tourists and expatriates would show up, rent rooms for nothing, and wallow in luxury. They could buy up pricey consumer goods, speculate freely, eat and drink heartily, play to their heart's content ("party hardy" in today's lingo), and indulge in a spectrum of pleasures for sale in a demimonde where any type of erotic practice could be conducted and every sexual impulse gratified, and where the appetite for cocaine and other drugs could be easily satisfied since by the early 1920s narcotics "formed an integral part of the social life of Berlin." Jonge believes "the inflation that destroyed traditional German values was also largely responsible for the creation of that new, decadent and dissolute generation that put Berlin on the cosmopolitan pleasure seeker's map, and has kept it or its image there ever since."[20]

In this vein, one historian refers to "the hectic hunger for amusement which had befallen Berliners" since the end of the war, indicating euphemistically that "[t]he whole trend seemed to be a constant flight from yesterday, from tradition, from Prussian order and habits into a world of noise, permissiveness, jazz and, it must be said, unreliability." In a sentence of conspicuous understatement, Alexander Reissner sorrows over the fact that "[l]ittle men . . . dance[d] with languid young ladies in new night clubs."[21] More recently, Frank Whitford notes that in these new nightclubs, cafés, and bathhouses,

> every imaginable sexual fantasy could be realized. . . . [S]uch establishments did much to establish Berlin's international reputation as the bawdiest, most licentious city in Europe. Its cabaret acts were outrageously explicit. Its brothels were well publicised. The tables in its dance-halls were furnished with telephones to permit assignations between customers who had never met. In its clubs, pubs and doorways girls, rent boys and entire pharmacopoeias of drugs, especially cocaine, could be had for less than the price of a decent dinner.[22]

Giving visual expression to Berlin's panorama of lust, deformity, greed, crime, illness, anger, deviance, boredom, and folly was George Grosz's *Ecce Homo* (1923), the examination of which is good preparation for a spin of Reed's *Berlin*. Grosz's macrocosm of suffering and depravity, depicted in one hundred black-and-white and color prints, and Reed's microcosm of marital strife and addiction, recorded in ten rock 'n' roll songs—these studies of Berlin go together well despite the passage of fifty years separating each artist's interpretation. Many of Grosz's prints—for instance *Marital Scene* (an enraged husband advances with raised fist on his falling wife), *Café* (hideous patrons huddle at tables, engrossing their particular demons), and *Athlete* (a man with bottle and glass sits beside a gramophone; behind him, a nude woman lies spread-eagle on the bed)—prefigure the traumas of Reed's song cycle. Other prints, notably *Sunday Morning*, bring the Reed fan back to the start of his career, specifically to the first song, "Sunday Morning," a ballad of all things, on the first Velvet Underground album.

Several paintings by Grosz's contemporary Otto Dix rival if not surpass Grosz's atrocity exhibition of a Berlin/Weimar steeped in pleasure and vice, for example, *Le salon I* (1921), *Annonciation* (1921–23), *Trois filles de joie* (1926), and *Le grande ville* (triptych, 1927/28), stunning studies of sexuality and cynicism. Illicit street media inundated Berlin during the years that Dix put high art in the service of social commentary. A cornucopia of soft-porn images peddled during Berlin's naughtiest decade were collected by Mel Gordon and published in 2000 under the banner *Voluptuous Panic: The Erotic World of Weimar Berlin*. To supplement the visual documentation, Gordon organized a directory of the venues available to Berliners on the prowl in the twenties, places to accommodate nudists, lesbians, gays, transvestites, and curious straights; places to be whipped, chained, dominated like an animal, half-raped, tied up, and double-dipped. "The Great Inflation complicated Berlin's sexual folkways," declares Gordon, "but did not really alter them. The so-called moral collapse had already occurred. Erotic amusements, prostitution, and narcotics were all readily available before the inflationary madness." What changed was that the influx of "bargain-seekers" came roaring into town with money that straitened Berliners couldn't afford to decline. To be blunt about it, "during the inflation in Berlin, five dollars could buy a month's worth of carnal delights. The most exquisite blow-job or kinky dalliance with a fifteen year-old never cost more than thirty cents, or 65 million 1923 marks."[23]

Naturally, Grosz's, Reissner's, Whitford's, Dix's, and Gordon's deviant metropolis has much in common with the Berlin that Lou Reed visited in his imagination (the album was recorded in London) in the midseventies in his bid to make a rock 'n' roll masterpiece. It might not be the real city, or the whole city, or the city as it actually existed in 1973, much less 1923—historically, Berlin has incorporated both tolerance and decadence, freedom and license, sophistication and deviance, imperial attitudes and radical agitation, self-expression and perversion—but as the art and history books confirm, it was a choice setting for a rock 'n' roll tale of sickness and woe.[24]

- Side One: "Berlin," "Lady Day," "Men of Good Fortune," "Caroline Says I," "How Do You Think It Feels," "Oh, Jim"
- Side Two: "Caroline Says II," "The Kids," "The Bed," "Sad Song"
- No bonus tracks on compact disc. None needed to increase its value.

Berlin opens in a nightclub. The first seconds of the first track reproduce the howl of an anguished male, whose voice fades into the chorus of a ghostly group-sing of "Happy Birthday" (the carousers seem to sing "Happy Birthday, dear Caroline"), capped by some dying whistles and applause, and succeeded by a cabaret pianist noodling a 12/8 introduction to "Berlin" proper. The piano sets up the first line whispered, not quite sung, by Reed, thus giving life to the character who I deduce—it's impossible to be sure—is the album's main speaker, an unnamed narrator (although we later learn his name is probably Jim). Reed's decision to keep the narrator anonymous is a tactic that presents a problem far more significant than whether or not *Berlin* is autobiographical. For one thing, the composer/singer's interest in (or distance from) his persona/narrator and his hellish plot can be confused with the main narrator's own interest in (or distance from) the same hellish plot in which he participates. Furthermore, several times *Berlin*'s point of view jumps from one I to another I, even crossing gender. A given narrator comes face-to-face with a source of anguish, steps back from it, assesses it, and negotiates it while the coolness of denial and the heat of infatuation wrestle for dominion. For the "viewer" of this "film for the ear" (producer Bob Ezrin's tag), *Berlin* is from top to bottom and from left to right a narrative striptease: a person can't help but watch while struggling with a voyeurism that needles his curiosity, inflames his senses, and goads an unsatisfied need to touch something dangerous, irresistible, partly hidden, and fully forbidden. *Berlin* beckons like an aural strip joint, a cabaret, or a red-lit den of iniquity. The most self-contained Puritan would feel a tug to listen, to peek inside, and then, heart in hand and morals left on the sidewalk, to pass through the door of debauchery. *Berlin* is very alluring "bad" art, not at all the *Sgt. Pepper* of the seventies, a hip comparison reportedly made by a reviewer trying to put it into context, but rather the *White Light/White Heat* of that punk-mangled, disco-deranged decade. Good listeners will be seduced by Reed's bad art, crafted to drag the audience into upheavals experienced by characters walking, if not staggering, on the wild side.

The male speaker tells a tale of being tormented and doing some tormenting in return. At the start, in "Berlin," he pieces together a memory of Caroline (a.k.a. Alaska and Lady Day), the tale's female protagonist. The narrator recalls Caroline, his dead lover (wife?), standing, two inches under six feet, beside the Berlin Wall. What better place for Reed to place and then measure up his doomed character than next to the infamous wall constructed in 1961 by the Russians intent on keeping their communist comrades in and their capitalistic foes out? Peril, anxiety, paranoia, surveillance, and the threat of battle are signified by Caroline's proximity to the Wall, the quintessential cold-war construct that connected Berlin's fortified sectors, armed patrols, and checkpoints. At the outset of Reed's saga, two depressing facts are shared: first, Caroline's already dead and sorely missed by the narrator; and second, the album's events will take place near the twentieth century's main symbol of separation and strife, a wall 155-kilometers (ninety-six miles) in length, pitted with twenty bunkers and monitored by 302 watchtowers, cutting through a city renowned as much for libertinism as for cosmopolitanism. Tone, character, plot, and scene are set for a spiral into the basement of a seventies version of Sodom, and Lou Reed is a choice cicerone for those brave enough to follow.

Whereas the whispery prologue "Berlin" lures the listener into the narrator's nostalgia—"We were in a small café. . . . Oh honey, it was paradise"—the second tune cuts back to Caroline's waywardness and the anxiety it causes the speaker.[25] The song "Lady Day" brings into play the legendary self-abuse of Billie Holiday (d. 1959, aged forty-four) as a tonal and thematic reference point. Like the first lady of jazz, Caroline is both singer and addict. Furthermore, she's given to abusive relationships and self-destruction. Had her career been familiar to rock fans and had she had a familiar stage name, Reed could have availed himself of yet an earlier female model of self-destruction, Anita Berber, a cabaret dancer popular in Weimar Berlin who "mourut jeune [1928] après une vie faite de plaisirs et d'excès."[26] In any event, the point about music and abuse is made and it sticks. Whenever Caroline walks down the street and hears music percolating from inside a club, she answers the call to go inside and take the stage. "It had to be that way," moans the narrator. His pleas are no match for Caroline's need to sing. Beseeching his very own Lady Day to desist for his sake is futile. A beautiful image that might have burst from the brain of Ezra Pound is a splotch of color between the narrator's recollection of Caroline's club cameo and his plea that she stop tormenting him: her hotel had "greenish walls / A bathroom in the hall," and all the narrator could say when she walked away was "no, no, no." Two songs, two sets of walls, the second set tinted sick-green, the first cold war–gray.

"Lady Day's" musical support—organ, tom-toms, cymbals, strings, horns—ranks among the album's most dramatic, conveying the speaker's worries as his repeated cries of "no" reach terrible heights. "No" puts his jealousy and insecurity into one curt syllable. If Reed's flat vocals, varying little throughout the record, unnerve the listener, the foil created by the sweeping melodies and bravura, at times almost baroque, arrangements is responsible. They ask more from the singer than the singer is willing, able, or smart enough to give. Reed's monotone and Ezrin's rich arrangements at once dampen each other and enliven the whole. Neither dominates.

Berlin's score is anchored in the virtuosity of drummers Aynsley Dunbar and, on two tracks, B. J. Wilson. Many tunes boom and crash with deep-shell tom-toms, thick snares, and wide-diameter cymbals. At no point in Reed's thirty-year corpus do his percussionists whack the kit with such color and flash—not, be it stressed, arbitrarily or self-servingly because neither drummer sacrifices the beat or feel to showmanship. Chops are in the service of emotion and musical syntax. Artfully punctuating the text with syncopated figures, Dunbar and

Wilson also stick close to the emotional dynamics of Reed's impersonations, shading moods, lighting corridors of the heart and soul, smashing a window here, crying there. Whatever needs doing, these two drummers deliver, whether humoring the singer's distress in "How Do You Think It Feels" and "Oh, Jim" or animating his self-congratulation in "Sad Song" and his studied indifference in "Men of Good Fortune."

Drumming as melodic as it is rhythmic is a feat not often achieved in rock 'n' roll. The bassists follow the drummers. The notes plucked by Jack Bruce and Tony Levin fix the tempo while embellishing the narrator's descent into darkness. From enervated junkie ballad to wired S-and-M rock 'n' roll, *Berlin*'s production is at one moment clanging (the first thirty seconds or so), then spectral ("The Bed"); big with brass and funky, even swaggering ("Oh, Jim"), then languid and resigned ("Caroline Says II"); stately but sarcastic ("Men of Good Fortune") as well as confessional but soaring ("Lady Day"). In the words of Peter Doggett, "[T]he whole dramatic ensemble is set against a magnificent instrumental backdrop, at one minute lush like a Stravinski tone poem, at another sliced to the bone so there is nowhere to hide from the reality of love and death."[27] Sitting between Reed's voice and Ezrin's rockestra, the listener works out an aesthetic opinion and emotional response to a work whose signature is dazzling incongruity.

In terms of plot, character, and setting, my reading has been, and will continue to be, literal. Reed's ambiguity makes it possible, however, to read Lady Day as a person other than Caroline. At least one critic thinks "Lady Day" evokes Billie Holiday in order to enhance the album's mood, not to advance its plot. But it's also possible, though unlikely, that Lady Day may be a girlfriend or prostitute to whom the narrator, or perhaps the mystery man Jim, is attached despite his involvement with Caroline—thus the cheap hotel (the kind with a communal bathroom) and Lady Day's complacence. Another possibility is that Caroline is in fact Lady Day *and* one of these—that is, a girlfriend or a prostitute—*and* a professional (or amateur) singer, and that "Lady Day," along with other songs on side one of the vinyl version, may have been composed with an eye on building erotic tension in preparation for violent release later on. (This is why the LP is preferable to the CD.) *Berlin* is all the more tantalizing because Reed steps in and out of several points of view, donning half-realized masks, alluding to several unnamed "you"s, even adding a track of children wailing for their mother. Reed's parsimony with names manages to confuse his most attentive critics, but this was probably not the idea. The idea was to deepen the narrative texture and to make us think. Upon hearing Reed's *Berlin* way back when, Robert Christgau nagged that it was "horseshit" and a "lousy story" about "two drug addicts" trapped "in thrillingly decadent Berlin."[28] Steve Simels loved this record about "an American expatriate and his vicious German speedfreak wife."[29] Other listeners have decided that the deadly liaison is between an American woman and a German man—her drug and sex connection, not her husband. Still inconclusive. Victor Bockris assumed that the male's nationality is American and said nothing about his profession. In "Caroline Says I," the fourth track, the narrator calls Caroline "my Germanic Queen" and later "a German Queen," more than enough evidence, I suppose, for us to agree on Caroline's nationality and/or for someone somewhere to construe, if his imagination were sufficiently fevered, a tragedy of homoerotic love between the narrator and a transvestite named Caroline, a German one to be sure, thus adumbrating Lou Reed's three years cohabitating with a man/woman named Rachel. Yes, much is possible. Uncertain identities and Reed's vague pronouns add mystique to events that occur in the bedrooms and nightclubs of Berlin, actions filtered through the mind of a cuckolded, volatile, grieving lover/husband/father, a probable drug addict, and a definite algolagniac.

The narrator's jealousy has no bearing on the meaning of "Men of Good Fortune." In this sullen meditation on good and bad luck, the singer expresses his indifference to the materialism of wealthy men. Men of poor beginnings mean just as little to him. "Men of Good Fortune" is the musical equivalent of someone shrugging his shoulders, the implication being that the speaker's indifference to both rich and poor men renders him superior to both. It's the musical equivalent of a man who has drugged himself into detachment. Detachment alleviates the pain caused by his attachment to a woman who within a few songs will have slashed her wrists and died. Relaxed verses merge into choruses in which Aynsley Dunbar revels in fills, these barrages contradicting the singer's semblance of self-control. He batters every drum on his kit and works the cymbals for everything they're worth. Dunbar continues the campaign of chops in "Caroline Says I," where a rapture of strings and backing vocals belies the singer's awareness of the humiliating fact that Caroline belittles him and dallies with him. He's a toy, certainly not a man (on a later tune, his manhood dwindles even further, as he takes the role of Caroline's "Water Boy"), and he's worried that his tormentor might make good on her promise to go out and get satisfaction with someone else. He's right to worry.

Suspense increases as side one fades away on repetitions of an ominous subordinate clause: "When you're looking through the eyes of hate. . . ." But what foreshadows this desolate acoustic coda from "Oh, Jim"? The maelstrom of "How Do You Think It Feels." This number is a series of rhetorical questions posed by the narrator (perhaps Caroline) as he (she) nears breakdown. The "you" is asked to imagine what it's like to be awake for five days, "hunting" for something, fearing sleep, to imagine what it's like "to always make love by proxy." (Some biographical critics believe Reed's alleged midseventies speed addiction is the song's subject.) Each stanza is a question or a conditional clause, fragment upon fragment, a speed-freak's syntax, sentences undone by insomnia, paranoia, jealousy, and desire. Reed's sexy grunts don't make it to the lyric page. Neither does the white-light lead guitar twisting lines over the top of the blatting horns and swinging drums, all of which say as much as the singer does.

"Oh, Jim" fades in on Dunbar's intricate triplet groove (*Berlin* is a record that all double bass drum freaks will want to check out). Then it struts along to some of the funkiest horns in Lou Reed's canon—not rubber but leather soul. The first part of the tune is a slinky, lowdown track. Jim speaks to himself, he speaks to Caroline (and Reed speaks to himself), leering and lashing out at so-called friends dispensing pills and laughing at her (him) on stage while they ask for an autograph. Reed snarls, "And when you're filled up to here with hate . . . Beat her black and blue and get it straight." The swaggering horns bear up the singer's cockiness, contempt, and rage, and then step back for the album's best guitar solo, which bridges the song's first and second, shorter, part. As a lonely strummed acoustic picks up where the burning lead fades, Caroline finds her voice. Jim's stage-mad floozy is crushed between self-abuse and the abuse of men, one (Jim, appearing now to be a man other than the main speaker) having broken her heart by deserting her (the main speaker doesn't do this), the other getting ready to beat every trace of libido out of her body. Confusing, to be sure. The relative fun and games of side one are over. Jim's departure/abuse is Caroline's turning point. She either can't or won't live without him. "Oh, Jim" closes by drawing the curtain open wider on the spectacle of grief and loss. In other words, flip the record to side two.

Four songs comprise side two of *Berlin* and in succession they put the finishing touch on Caroline's comedown. In the crawling "Caroline Says II," the woman gains another nickname, Alaska. These events occur in "Caroline Says II": someone beats Caroline to the floor; she applies makeup to her eye (covering a bruise? primping for another lover?); she reproaches the narrator; she makes it clear that she's not afraid to die; she tells the narrator she doesn't love him anymore; she takes speed; she punches out a windowpane; and, bearing down on her lip, she concludes that life with what's-his-name "is a bum trip." The point of view continues to be tricky. The narrator drawls, "She put her fist through the window pane . . . It was such a funny feeling." What was? And who felt it? What exactly is a "funny feeling"? The song's last line, blurted out with all the passion a junkie can muster, which isn't much, is equally tricky: "It's so cold in Alaska" (repeated twice). Another throwaway line, or a great rock poet's image of a woman's emotional distance from her man? Woe betide this nymphomaniac for betraying the father of her children!

There are two main lineages in rock 'n' roll music. From what single source they originate is as impossible to trace back as it is to trace back the source of any origin, any transcendental sign in any art form, any lexicon. Rockologists can't even agree on the name of the first rock 'n' roll, much less rock, record. But if at the beginning of language, or creation itself, was the Word, uttered by divine providence to transmute space and chaos into nature and order, at rock 'n' roll's beginning was a Word that split in two at conception. A set of fraternal twins was born. One twin went the party route, the other one headed straight for the funeral.

Party Music: "Goin' to a party, meet me out after school"—"Yes, we're going to a party party"—"Let's have a party tonight."[30] The Move. The Beatles. Elvis. **Funeral Music:** "Hope I die before I get old"—"Yes I'm lonely, want to die; if I ain't dead already, girl you know the reason why"—"I see a line of cars and they're all painted black."[31] The Who. The Beatles. The Rolling Stones.

All strands, traditions, branches, and styles of rock 'n' roll music have evolved from the impulse to give a party or to hold a funeral. As in all things human, the middle ground, the hybrid, the mixture is more common than the extreme, but usually a band's sensibility, either fun or dysfunction, is apparent. The most popular rock 'n' rollers thrive in this middle ground. For example, Bruce Springsteen is a musician inhabiting the middle ground and attracting vast numbers of adoring fans. He has written his share of gloomy numbers, but when one of his happy hits blares from the PA, the house cheers and dances. Even his gloomiest album, *The Rising*, Springsteen's response to post-9/11 New York City, has "Mary's Place" (a lark) to balance out "My City of Ruins" and other dirges.

Springsteen knows when enough of each feeling is enough. So do the Rolling Stones. They attend funerals but are just as willing to throw a good party on record; moreover, their sense of humor lightens many a load. Listen, for instance, to "Dear Doctor," "Dead Flowers," or "Some Girls." Their classic study of fun/dysfunction is *Exile on Main Street*. Drugs and alcohol seem blended into the record's vinyl, which is another way of saying that the subtext of self-destruction mutes the joy in tracks such as Keith's "Happy" or Mick's "Rocks Off," the stallion kick that starts the debauch. A few years before *Exile*, the Doors had lurched from funeral to funeral, instilling their most brooding music with enough pop sweetness to endear themselves to millions of disciples who weren't reading Nietzsche and plotting to murder their fathers. The Beatles, the Kinks, and the Who, to finish off the major sixties bands, as well as Dylan and Hendrix, worked both sides of the dichotomy. As then, so now: the most popular bands stick toward the middle (Radiohead, Sleater-Kinney, Wilco) not only because they themselves aren't manic-depressive but because that's where most of their audience lives.

So it shouldn't mystify people that pessimists such as the Velvet Underground or Joy Division never caught the ear of the masses. Only a simpleton would fail to ascribe this failure to causes other than morbidity alone, from bad timing to bad marketing, or from each band's premature demise to each band's delight in dissonance. The instrumental stamp and lyrical content of a band (or solo artist) relay its (or his) sensibility, and bands as radically negative as the Velvet Underground and Joy Division simply can't compete with the masters of both domains.[32] Any humor they muster is black and cynical—for example, "The Gift" by the Velvet Underground. It's equally difficult for party bands to make a career out of more than one or two hits. The Village People, anyone? The Strangeloves? The Swingin' Medallions? The record bins are bursting with collections of party favorites by long-defunct bands or artists. Hordes of twelve-year-olds might patronize groups selling dum-dum happiness—the Monkees, the Bay City Rollers—but not so hordes of adults; and since kids rapidly outgrow their infatuations, the happy-face bands who one day are locker-liner favorites are the next day thrown out with half-filled tubes of pimple cream.

Party/funeral is a dichotomy and therefore is a sitting duck for deconstruction. A party can quickly turn into a funeral. Imagine, say, a backstage party with the members and entourage of Van Halen, Guns N' Roses, or Mötley Crüe. Conversely, some funerals are the pretext for a party. Since space constraints don't permit me to deconstruct my own dichotomy, I ask the reader to accept it as a descriptive concept. Descriptively, *Berlin* is clearly a staple in the funeral tradition. The trope of waste I've been analyzing in relation to rock 'n' roll dysfunction and death is bound to the funeral tradition the way blood-stained bandages are bound to an accident victim who happens to be physically attractive. *Berlin* is that victim. It's a beautiful body disfigured by trauma. *Berlin*'s obvious precedents are found in the albums of Lou Reed's own Velvet Underground, it being understood again that this disfigured canon is profoundly beautiful. The Velvet Underground and Lou Reed, however, didn't invent morbid-romantic or funereal rock 'n' roll.

As I contemplate the party/funeral binary, I'm listening to Bobby Goldsboro's "Honey," number one in 1968, the twelfth tune of fifteen on a collection called *The Best of Tragedy*. Trifles from beach blanket–bingo movies weren't the only tunes to chart during the years 1958–64. Kids surfed, cut school, drag raced, and made out. They also attended funerals or were the occasion for one. The dates of these fifteen songs of tragedy are 1958 (two), 1960 (four), 1961 (one), 1962 (one), 1963 (one), 1964 (four), 1967 (one), and 1968 (one). Growing up on Long Island, Lou Reed absorbed such music. These hits and many others were like bricks and steel pipe collected by the artist in the construction not only of an aesthetic but also of a repertoire. The requiem set in Berlin that Lou Reed wrote and recorded in 1973 rose like a gothic edifice (an overgrown Chelsea Hotel, shall we say) out of a seedy neighborhood, where dozens of broken-down tenements had already set a tone of collective decay. *Berlin* wasn't the first building on the block but it was one of the most accomplished and most disconcerting. It stood out. It marked the skyline. It *made* the skyline. Still, an expert who inspects the contents of "Sad Song" on *Berlin* will detect the spectral presence of Goldsboro's "Honey" in it. Even though Bobby Goldsboro doesn't express regret at having failed to rape and beat Honey, and even though he doesn't regret the time he has wasted thinking about his angel, his sentiments in "Honey" are much the same sentiments in "Sad Song," on which I will focus in a moment.

These comments are by way of finishing the discussion of *Berlin*. When we left off a few paragraphs ago in "Caroline Says II," we were eavesdropping in the master bedroom on an embattled couple. At that time Caroline was, in no particular order, biting her lip, smashing windows, descending further into addiction, and hurting men while being hurt in turn. She wasn't doing much in the way of mothering. Reed now turns his attention to the children, who suffer as a result of their mother's neglect.

Helping to deepen the hue of their suffering, to intensify the horror of the album's plot, and to jab the listener now finding himself either benumbed by the album's unfolding misery or anxious to detach himself from it, "The Kids" has children—Bob Ezrin's, the rumors say, tricked into the role—wailing "Mommy." (See comments earlier on John Lennon's "Mother.") "The Kids" also has *Berlin*'s most beautiful melody and most moving lyrics. It's one cut removed from Caroline's suicide. Backed by acoustic chords soon poked by the bass's counterpoint, the male narrator, now the Water Boy, reveals that Caroline has lost custody of her children because she's a bad mother. He drones on about Caroline's drug use and roster of lovers. "The Bed," up next, will confirm the Water Boy's paternity of Caroline's children. It doesn't appear, however, that the authorities are giving the father custody of his own children. No matter. Jealousy and vindication preoccupy the Water Boy, not his own unsuitability as a parent. It can't be pleasant to enumerate the unspeakable things his partner did with a girlfriend from Paris and then with a Welshman who, having arrived by way of India, stayed on for awhile, and it can't be pleasant to recall Caroline's misconduct (quite without parallel) in Berlin's alleys and clubs. In short, this "miserable rotten slut" turned down no one. And so Caroline's punishment, losing her children, gratifies the Water Boy (much of whose own viciousness we must surmise) even though it punishes them too. He probably thinks, *The slut is getting her due, so let the kids wail.*

Lest readers forget who deserves much of the credit for the atmosphere of tension/release on *Berlin*, I advise them to heed B. J. Wilson's drumming on "The Kids." The cut's half-ponderous, half-lilting 12/8 time signature offers a canvas on which to inscribe a spectrum of triplets, press rolls, syncopated footwork, well-timed crashes to punctuate vocal end lines, and half-choked hi-hat hisses executed between passages of bone-shaking backbeat. Wilson and company keep it up as the kids begin wailing and continue wailing for another twelve measures. Suddenly Wilson and his ensemble truncate the torture on one last cry of "Mother!" Reed has orchestrated this cutoff like a cannibal who has decoyed human prey into a bog that pulls the dupe down to the waist. To the chords of a blue guitar, Reed croaks the Water Boy's refrain: his heart overflows, he's tired, he has nothing to say.

"The melancholic," says Sigmund Freud,

> displays . . . an extraordinary diminution in his self-regard, an impoverishment of his ego on a grand scale. In mourning it is the world which has become poor and empty; in melancholia it is the ego itself. The patient represents his ego to us as worthless, incapable of any achievement and morally despicable; he reproaches himself, vilifies himself and expects to be cast out and punished.[33]

The Water Boy is a hybrid mourner-melancholic, a worst-case scenario for the psychologist's couch. For a brief moment he brings this period of mourning to an end. Meanwhile, seduced by eight minutes of "The Kids," listeners—Reed's "prey," startled to find how deep the tale has sucked them in—can do nothing about the bog in which they're stuck except to hope they make it through to some other side. To do this requires a six-minute slog through "The Bed" and a seven-minute slog through "Sad Song."

"The Bed" achieves another superlative in Lou Reed's songbook. In his thirty-plus-year career, Reed has mastered both head-splitting and gossamer levels of volume. Leading examples of Reed's hushed hits are "Candy Says" on *The Velvet Underground*, "Waiting for My Man" on *Take No Prisoners*, and "Dreamin'" on *Magic and Loss*. "The Bed" is still more quiet than these whispered melodies of death. *Berlin*'s penultimate tune hangs in the midnight air like a black silk drape separating the dying from the dead in a smallpox ward. Shhh. Peaceful. Caroline is dead. The survivor surveys boxes of the dead woman's trinkets and notes the bed where she slept, where she conceived children, where she took lovers, and "where she cut her wrists / That odd and fateful night."

Shaking off the spell of music, whose pulse has become nearly inaudible, we may be excused for believing that the greatest rock 'n' roll music ever made is that of a genius, allegedly a junkie at the time, singing the plight of wasted characters peopling his imagination.

But it's not over. Rising from the darkness, a layered female keen ushers in a coda to calamity entitled "Sad Song." The chorale acts like a breeze wafting through the fetid closeness of the smallpox ward. The drape moves. Light and health are returning; the plague drifts back to the mysterious place from whence it came; recovery is on the horizon. "The Bed" is behind the narrator, behind us. The narrator survived, the audience too. And the kids? We aren't told what becomes of them.

"Sad Song" revisits the horn-powered dynamics of side one. Lyrically, it's the narrator's last shot at self-vindication. The nostalgia he musters one more time—he compares the Caroline in his photo album to Mary, Queen of Scots—is neither bitter nor maudlin. It's an example of what Svetlana Boym terms "reflective nostalgia," in opposition to "restorative nostalgia." "Restorative nostalgia," she writes, "manifests itself in total [actual, concrete] reconstructions of monuments of the past, while reflective nostalgia lingers on ruins, the patina of time and history, in the dreams of another place and another time." It dwells, asserts Boym, and this assertion is borne out in *Berlin*, "on the ambivalences of human longing and belonging," and in the mind of a romantic it "calls [the absolute truth] into doubt," expressing itself "in elegiac poems and ironic fragments." In the reflectivity of the narrator of *Berlin* lies a morbid-romantic quality of insisting "on the otherness of his object of nostalgia from his present life and [keeping] it a safe distance."[34] But almost as strong as this insistent nostalgia is the narrator's ambivalence about his former passivity. Determined to "stop wasting my time" thinking about a dead woman who broke his heart, he concedes a weakness—a more self-respecting man "would have broken both of her arms." Hindsight is everything. The Water Boy will do what he must in dealing with the woman's death. He poses like a solid citizen of the German (or American) bourgeoisie to whom has been revealed the insight that a man's children and home can get in the way of seeing the nature and extent of his mistakes. Maybe he's a good man after all, or maybe we listeners are so weary of hearing him sob that we take his epiphany without a murmur of protest.

Toying with incongruity to the end, Reed fashions "Sad Song" into the happiest track on the program. "Happiest" is a relative term (here, it's reminiscent of the larking allegro of Mozart's bleakest chamber work, the quintet K. 516), never more so than when Lou Reed is at the controls. The fluty melody gives wing to the narrator's reveries, yet drummer Dunbar's backbeat couldn't be more sluggish, suggesting that someone isn't buying the narrator's change of tone. It's all so happy that it's pathetic and so pathetic that it's sad after all. The most orchestrated of any title in Lou Reed's canon, "Sad Song" is roped to a corpse. It's as if morticians tug at Caroline and find her too stiff and heavy to pull from the bed. Finally the body tumbles free from the mattress and is dragged across the floor and out the portico to the hearse, her poor head banging on every descending step. Once the singer breaks free from whatever mental burden he has struggled to lift and dispatch, the boys burn up the chart. Dunbar funk-fries the rhythm while the swirling strings, buttressed by a batch of singers singing "sad song," whip up a dance macabre in which morbidity cuts in on melodrama. "Sad Song" persists until somebody in the studio has the good sense to bring it home. All effort ceases and *Berlin*'s conflicts are resolved on a woodwind's soothing toot.

It's easy to get bogged down in an analysis of *Berlin* because its force of gravity is so high. It's the planet Jupiter in a rock universe of moons and asteroids. Jupiter and *Berlin*, in their respective orbits, are superdense entities. Their extreme gravity exceeds the gravity produced by lesser entities in their respective systems. Science has shown that extreme gravity will pull an object down, compress it to a tiny point, annihilate it—and a person is an object. An extravagant comparison, perhaps, but hyperbole helps to describe the impression made by *Berlin*. Moreover, *Berlin* like Jupiter is gorgeous. Full-page illustrations of Jupiter are suitable for framing, what with its famous red spot (whose area is twice the size of Earth, incidentally), or its ochre oceans, or its burnt-umber steppes of hydrogen, vast beyond human grasp. The planet is smeared, banded, streaked, and splattered with tints of hangover orange, frostbite blue, toxic green, and deep-space red. This vast gas-whirling planet offers, if we judge by Space Probe images, an orbicular display of Mark Rothko's palette. (Rothko, a good name to cite in the context of *Berlin* and morbid rock in general. The innovator of the massive rectangular color fields was both a suicide [one February morning at the age of sixty-seven he slashed his wrists in the studio] and a long-suffering victim of severe depression and alcoholism.) The program on *Berlin* whirls in and out of melodies either richly embroidered or stripped to bare nerves, storms or breathes quietly, and rotates on an axis of despair, relegating the soul to outer darkness where otherworldly beauty glimmers into view.

To my knowledge nothing in the galaxy of rock 'n' roll rivals *Berlin* in the terms I've been using, which isn't to say there aren't other sublime planets in the night sky. Recordings by Bob Dylan, Mazzy Star, Neil Young, Leonard Cohen, Joy Division, the Cowboy Junkies, Nico, Red House Painters, Smog, and Nick Drake can bring a person to the windowsill, as it were; and if among these major artists of morbid rock no title sustains *Berlin*'s level of morbidity, density, and beauty (although Joy Division's *Closer* comes close), there's more than enough music to reward a vigil spent gazing at them.

For example, many of Nick Drake's entries on *Pink Moon* are airy, brief—understatements that take a minute or two to hint at a monumental solitude implied in any definition of clinical depression, the composer too close to the end of the line to bother with rules of proportion. (*Pink Moon*, the third of Drake's original three albums, is twenty-eight minutes in length, distributed over eleven numbers. Drake overdosed on antidepressant medication two years after recording it, aged twenty-six.) In the manner of a romantic fragment poem—see Schlegel, Coleridge, Shelley—*Pink Moon*'s quantity isn't commensurate with its quality. Paradoxically, therein lies its power. The album is literally a perfect waste of time. Granted, the record isn't technically a romantic, or for that matter a classical, fragment, not as scholars define the fragment genre. Nevertheless, it falls far short of the time span audiences expected of an LP in the seventies and thus qualifies for fragment status in folk-rock circles. Marjorie Levinson's study of the romantic fragment poem yields insights the rock critic could use to explain the appeal of *Pink Moon*. She teaches that the "irresolution" of an intentional or accidental romantic fragment "is experienced as against [an] ideal integrity and extensiveness that it presumably could, would, or should have realized."[35] In lay terms, the record is stupendous but, alas, over before you know it, leaving one to imagine where a less troubled Drake could have expanded and polished his material. In other words, the listener (or reader, or viewer) of a romantic fragment must finish the abbreviated work in the workshop of his imagination. At its best the romantic fragment initiates a "complementary moment of ecstatic reception in the beholder or reader, which resurrects the artist's invisible, internal moment of inspiration"—this according to Monika Greenleaf in a study of fragmentation in Pushkin.[36] Turning back to Nick Drake, we're struck aesthetically by the fact that his throwaway finale, *Pink Moon*, follows the function of fragmentation, not fulfillingness (apologies to Stevie Wonder), and invites the listener to complete, intellectually and emotionally, a masterpiece abandoned by the master after he has etched a few haunted faces and limned a few drear landscapes.

Thomas McFarland speaks in *Romanticism and the Forms of Ruin* of the "diasparactive" facts of existence—incompleteness, fragmentation, and ruin, "the diasparactive triad" responsible for crumpling human beings into pieces of "agonized individuality, wracked grotesquely out of their plane." Diasparaction is most thoroughly mirrored, McFarland writes, in romantic texts, where restlessness, homelessness, dissatisfaction with present existence, and the longing for reunion with an absent reality are "an index to a prevailing sense of incompleteness, fragmentation, and ruin." McFarland's masters are classic European names: Coleridge, Novalis, Shelley, Lamartine. Were he pulling names from the rock milieu, his masters would be the acts on the roster discussed in this section: Lou Reed, Leonard Cohen, Nico, Ian Curtis of Joy Division, and so on. Musicians such as Ian Curtis and Nick Drake can be grouped in yet another special category: premature extinction. "Early death," says McFarland, "is not merely early demise—it is a diasparaction that emphasizes the sense of incompleteness and fragmentation." This being the case, then Drake's death at twenty-six is, like Franz Schubert's death at thirty-one, "existentially diasparactive no less than Keats's still more tearingly early death at twenty-five."[37] "Tearingly," "agonized": modifiers denoting radical unhappiness. On *Pink Moon*, self-annihilation and McFarland's three elements of diasparaction—incompleteness, fragmentation, ruin—aren't in the air, they *are* the air. "Now I'm darker than the deepest sea," Drake sings on "Place to Be," "now I'm weaker than the palest blue." Theoretically, the person wincing to the songs collected on the fragmented album called *Pink Moon* collaborates, as it were, with the late minstrel's solitary struggle against diasparaction by reviving the ecstatic possibilities inherent in Nick Drake's painfully creative depression.

So much for the fragment, but three-pronged diasparaction blooms darkly in full-length works of morbid-romantic rock 'n' roll. On *Time Out of Mind*, where fragmentation has been banished, Bob Dylan is relentlessly negative, carrying on the tradition of Europe's "No Exit school of Dark Romanticism," a state of being, explains Robert Hume, where "wretchedness" and the "acute discontent without prospect of alleviation" nurtured art that was "morbid, gloomy, bitter." This kind of phraseology doesn't make marketing copy for Grammy-winning albums of the year, but Dylan pulled it off in 1998, perhaps because there's a quietude about the record that consumers construed as serenity. Hume indicates that "[a]n author"—substitute "composer"—"caught in the No Exit syndrome will grow fascinated with pain, evil, and paradox," and at times this sense of evil "is offset by ironic devaluation or travesty in an attempt to relieve the existential misery which gives rise to the writing in the first place."[38] These factors are to Dylan's *Time Out of Mind* (and the whole of Dylan's extensive catalog) what rubber products are to an automobile, not its main component but essential to its propulsion. Wasted love and wasted time take on allegorical import in the troubadour's confessions, outcries, calls for help. Dylan is that oldest of allegorical characters, Everyman. "I'm walking through streets that are dead," the album's first lyrics, prep us for a diagnosis of sickness, loss, homelessness, and encroaching night ("It's not dark yet, but it's getting there"). On this record, whose setting is "the dark land of the sun," Dylan comes off like a wordsmith done in by romanticism or like a poet too exhausted for flippancy ("ironic devaluation") or for masquerading behind double entendre. "I'm sick of love; I hear the clock tick," he drawls on "Love Sick," and every song to follow boasts similar lines of freeze-dried eloquence: "I've been down to the bottom of a whirlpool of lies"; "I'm twenty miles out of town, cold irons bound"; "Somehow my memory's in a ditch so deep"; "Up over my head nothing but clouds of blood"; "I wish someone'd come and push back the clock for me."[39] *Time Out of Mind* is arguably rock's most dire study of unrequited love (the main reason it scored the Grammy?), which to most men and women is proof that an evil principle is active in the universe. Dylan's flurry of metaphors hooks up with leisurely riffs and grooves able to absorb the shock of his shredded voice. The tracks pound ("Cold Irons Bound"), lilt ("Not Dark Yet"), or somnambulate ("Highlands," at seventeen minutes, is nearly the length of *Pink Moon*). Drenched in blues and throwaway lines, *Time Out of Mind* is, cherish the paradox, diasparaction at its finest.

Joy Division's *Closer* isn't bad either. Lyricist and singer Ian Curtis, depressed, epileptic, hanged himself shortly after its release, which is another way of saying that the record is about as diasparactive as they come. Its morbidity factor redlines the peak level—ten. Bernard Albrecht's guitars and Peter Hook's bass lash the listener like whips wielded by gladiators driving victims into the center of the Colosseum. Do we watch or look away? Indeed, from what standpoint are we viewing the spectacle? In other words, at what point does Ian Curtis's experience become our own, not a vicarious event or performance recorded for our amusement? On song after song, the drummer's wet hi-hat slaps into birth a dismal tattoo that chokes and hack-coughs until the song exhales its last breath. The first song, "Atrocity Exhibition," with the immortal lines "This is the way, step inside," is remarkable for giving the impression of white noise splashing like hot tar on the surface of the rhythm section's obsessive-compulsive pattern. On "Isolation," Ian Curtis wrings the neck of his solitude while on "Passover" he confides that he has been waiting for a crisis, has lost his balance in the interim, has acknowledged the lies surrounding him, and wonders what's in store. That would be "Colony," where Curtis's diction includes "harm," "lunacy," and "dislocations." He means it, man. Joy Division keeps pushing, pushing, pushing at dread, Curtis working from a corner. He mourns ineffective therapy in "Twenty-four Hours," his voice cracking as he cowers under the lash of self-laceration and visions of dissolution, death ever closer, the specter of further seizures perched like the Raven on his shoulder. The album's most alarming effect is the ritard that drags "A Means to an End" to its end on four measures of Stephen Morris's bass/snare/hi-hat figure. *Closer* is a funeral record par excellence, and it proves the point that rock 'n' roll makes an aesthetic virtue of waste, that waste is a multifaceted trope and theme giving life to some of the most despondent yet most beautiful records of all time.

Beautiful, despondent: Mazzy Star, for instance. Mazzy Star records morbid songs almost too exquisite for the listener's good. Add half of *Among My Swan* to three-quarters of *So Tonight That I Might See*, and, to revive the galactic metaphor, a new planet will appear to brighten one's loneliest night. (Neither album is wholly satisfying as is.) The dopey, lurching "Wasted" on the latter disc epitomizes the spirit of morbid-romantic waste examined in section 27, number 28, and more than implies this imperative: Behold the radiant renderings of/by wasted human beings in the music of rock 'n' roll. Drink deep from the well of depression and despair. Mazzy Star's feathery dirges, embellished with tambourines, at times giving way to fuzz-drone dissonance, don't make up an ample body of music; however, they do sustain the tradition of rock's morbid sensibility and its continued popularity among audiences.

Morbid rock 'n' roll (or alt country, to be technical) is the order of business yet again on a perfect work of art, *The Trinity Session*, cut in one take, live, by the Cowboy Junkies. This record is the equivalent of dipping a drugged infant into a current of cool blue water, giving him a taste of disaster, showing him how good it feels, not agitating him, not dropping him even as the band drowns him in black sound. We are that drugged infant, and we neither gasp for air nor kick in terror as the laser crosses the surface of the compact disc. The album's moribund program, despite its tonal coherence, isn't monotonous for so much as one 4/4 measure. The listener snuggles into the melancholia propelling tunes such as "To Love Is to Bury" (about burying a lover near a river because he liked it there), "Postcard Blues" (about longing for the touch of the only person who can assuage the singer's mental "white heat"), "Dreaming My Dreams with You" (about getting over someone, someday), and "Two Hundred More Miles" (about coming to grips with being a musician who wastes his life on the road—a new twist on the trash trope). Critics fall over themselves praising Margo Timmins's "haunting" vocals, quite rightly too, to which praise it might be added that her brother Peter's drumming is what a physician's catheterization technique is to a critical case in the cardiac ward: following procedure requires the utmost delicacy and decisive action on the doctor's part. *The Trinity Session* is akin to a life-saving experience and is best appreciated when the Cowboy Junkies fan has that cut-my-throat feeling. In a word, transfixing.

I've commented on a few shining examples in a dark genre. I could have spent my time as profitably on the Doors' debut, Neil Young's *Tonight's the Night*, Smog's *The Doctor Came at Dawn*, Red House Painters' *Songs for a Blue Guitar*, perhaps Black Sabbath's *Paranoid*, or Iggy and the Stooges' *Raw Power*, whose opening rave is "Search and Destroy" and whose closing jaunt is "Death Trip." Also exemplary is Nirvana's *In Utero*, which offers, like Nick Drake's and Ian Curtis's small output, a gaze into the ripped-open mind of an imminent suicide, Kurt Cobain. Whereas the Cowboy Junkies float along a river of despair leading to who knows where, Nirvana hammers and slashes at life in psychotic fury. Along these lines, in 1992 Nirvana's colleagues Alice in Chains concocted *Dirt* as a blaring testament to member Layne Staley's addiction to junk. Not to be overlooked is Leonard Cohen's discography, morbid folk rock's premier sourcebook of depression, much too extensive for analysis here, although Cohen's 1968 debut, *Songs of Leonard Cohen*, should be mentioned as the place to start. Another morbid-romantic must-have is Nico's *The End*, a monodrone spiderwebbed with electronica and strangled vocals, which are enhanced at times by a piano dripping notes in a dungeon and at other times by a harmonium hanging chords in the attic of a decaying gothic mansion.

32. The Last Time

This part concludes with a template and an outline, both of which, like the party/funeral dichotomy discussed earlier, are meant to be taken as suggestive and descriptive, not dogmatic and prescriptive. My main point in this part has been to illustrate the aesthetic value of the trash trope in representations of wasted human beings and the morbid states of mind that afflict them. The evidence shows that a considerable number of rock musicians are hurrying to a funeral from which they may never return. Before and while running off in that direction, some (like so many before them) for the last time, many of these artists articulate their anguish in albums that consumers buy, unwrap, cue up or insert, and enjoy. These recordings appeal to a wide range of consumers, not simply to unfortunate souls with lives marred by morbid nostalgia, untreated epilepsy, manic-depression, or attempts at suicide. Consumer variables (numberless) and demographics (complex) are outside my expertise. My purpose, therefore, is not to explain why *Berlin* might "work" for a person who has no particular gripe against the world, his girlfriend or spouse, or himself, or why a Nick Drake threnody was licensed by executives at Volkswagen for an ad campaign on television. Let psychologists and marketers work out these mysteries. Although I take for granted the universal instinct to self-destruct, my focus hasn't been the mechanics of the death wish; no, it has been trash and rock 'n' roll music and the manner in which trash is signified as waste in relation to human existence and how morbidity is the mood that defines the rock artist's descent into a darkness that yields so much white light. The following template and outline conclude the argument that rock 'n' roll music, morbid romanticism, and death are cold-irons bound to each other for as long as the form—poor poor pitiful Tithonus—can drag itself another mile.

Template

What we see repeatedly in morbid-romantic albums are the following traits, half or more showing up on the genre's leading titles, and most if not all showing up on the best of these.

1. The singer/narrator contemplates an indifferent or cruel world, curses it, or recoils from it in horror and disgust; or he looks in the mirror, hates what he sees, and punishes himself accordingly.
2. The singer/narrator sets and sustains a morose tone, sometimes supplementing it with aggression.
3. The singer/narrator is tormented by nostalgia.
4. The singer/narrator projects the worst parts of himself into various characters.
5. The singer/narrator attempts, with feeble results, to lighten his gloom with humor or vivacity.
6. The singer/narrator is torn between a struggle against oblivion and a desire for it.
7. The singer/narrator's vocals are lugubrious, compressed, or drained, sometimes atonal.
8. The singer/narrator's emotional nakedness incites audience sympathy.
9. The singer/narrator's experience seems at best unmerited, at worst tragic.
10. The singer/narrator's suffering has universal significance.
11. Production ranges from simple to extravagant and is rarely if ever tainted by melodrama, sentimentality, self-pity, or kitsch.
12. The pulse of rock 'n' roll music, no matter how muted, can be detected.
13. A ray of hope penetrates the darkness.
14. The audience realizes that waste, understood in terms of depression, morbidity, and death, is a rich source of inspiration/sublimation for rock 'n' roll musicians.

Outline

A classification of death in rock 'n' roll reveals the subject's width and breadth. (Classifying morbid romanticism, a far more difficult task, would require different headings and wouldn't list, as do the headings that follow, songs, albums, and titles dealing exclusively with death.) Limiting my entries to five per category or three per subcategory—laughable but doable—I offer this basic taxonomy to suggest the significant presence of death in rock music. Under some headings, Odds and Sods (XIII) for example, it would impossible to list every pertinent track, and while to fill out Motor Vehicles and Death might not daunt the compiler, the categories Love and Death and Loneliness and Death would have him gathering scores, even hundreds, of titles, never finishing the task if he intended to account for everything now and once in print.

I. Album Titles
   A. *Funeral in Berlin* (Throbbing Gristle, 1981)
   B. *Give Me Convenience or Give Me Death* (the Dead Kennedys, 1987)
   C. *Reek of Putrefaction* (Carcass, 1988)
   D. *One Foot in the Grave* (Beck, 1994)
   E. *To the Faithful Departed* (the Cranberries, 1996)
II. Animals and Death
   A. "Old Shep" (Elvis Presley)
   B. "Monkey Gone to Heaven" (the Pixies)
   C. "Horse Latitudes" (the Doors)
   D. "Meat Is Murder" (the Smiths)
   E. "Eat Your Dog" (Bad Religion)
III. Bands and Death
   A. The Dead Boys
   B. Death Cab for Cutie
   C. Megadeth
   D. Suicidal Tendencies
   E. My Life with the Thrill Kill Kult
IV. Bravado and Death
   A. "My Generation" (the Who)
   B. "Death Trip" (Iggy and the Stooges)
   C. "Stay Away" (Nirvana)
   D. "Too Tough to Die" (the Ramones)
   E. "I Get Lonesome" (Beck)
V. Children and Death
   A. "Kill Your Sons" (Lou Reed)
   B. "Dead Babies" (Alice Cooper)
   C. "Tears in Heaven" (Eric Clapton)
   D. "Mother's Lament" (Cream)
   E. "I Kill Children" (the Dead Kennedys)
VI. Homicide
   A. Assassination
      1. "Abraham, Martin, and John" (Dion)
      2. "He Was a Friend of Mine" (the Byrds)
      3. "The Day John Kennedy Died" (Lou Reed)

B. Odds and Sods
   1. "Sister Ray" (the Velvet Underground)
   2. "Guilt" (Marianne Faithfull)
   3. "Down by the River" (Neil Young)
C. Psychosis
   1. "Psycho Killer" (Talking Heads)
   2. "One of These Days" (Pink Floyd)
   3. "Midnight Rambler" (the Rolling Stones)

VII. Humor and Death
A. Animals
   1. "The Continuing Story of Bungalow Bill" (the Beatles)
   2. "Boris the Spider" (the Who)
   3. "Werewolves of London" (Warren Zevon)
B. Homicide
   1. "Smackwater Jack" (Carole King)
   2. "Papa Loved Mama" (Garth Brooks)
   3. "Let's Lynch the Landlord" (the Dead Kennedys)
C. Odds and Sods
   1. "Pictures of Lily" (the Who)
   2. "I Think I'm Going to Kill Myself" (Elton John)
   3. "The Gift" (the Velvet Underground)

VIII. Loneliness and Death
A. "Dead Souls" (Joy Division)
B. "How Soon Is Now" (the Smiths)
C. "Death of a Clown" (the Kinks)
D. "I Don't Live Today" (Jimi Hendrix)
E. "Tombstone Blues" (Bob Dylan)

IX. Love and Death
A. "A Sailor's Life" (Fairport Convention)
B. "I Would Die 4 U" (Prince)
C. "Without You" (Harry Nilsson)
D. "Whipping Post" (the Allman Brothers)
E. "Died for Love" (Richard and Linda Thompson)

X. Martyrdom
A. "It's Alright, Ma (I'm Only Bleeding)" (Bob Dylan)
B. "Joan of Arc" (Leonard Cohen)
C. "Calvary Cross" (Richard and Linda Thompson)
D. "Ballad of John and Yoko" (the Beatles)
E. "Precious Angel" (Bob Dylan)

XI. Motor Vehicles and Death
  A. "Leader of the Pack" (the Shangri-Las)
  B. "A Day in the Life" (the Beatles)
  C. "Teen Angel" (Mark Dinning)
  D. "Long Black Limousine" (Elvis Presley)
  E. "Wreck on the Highway" (Bruce Springsteen)
XII. Nature and Death
  A. "Watch It Die" (Bad Religion)
  B. "Five Years" (David Bowie)
  C. "Chumming the Oceans" (Archers of Loaf)
  D. "A Hard Rain's A-Gonna Fall" (Bob Dylan)
  E. "When the Music's Over" (the Doors)
XIII. Odds and Sods
  A. "Funeral for a Friend" (Elton John)
  B. "Endless Sleep" (Jody Reynolds)
  C. "She Said She Said" (the Beatles)
  D. "John Barleycorn Must Die" (Traffic)
  E. "A Public Execution" (Mouse and the Traps)
XIV. Society and Death
  A. "In the Ghetto" (Elvis Presley)
  B. "Livin' for the City" (Stevie Wonder)
  C. "London Calling" (the Clash)
  D. "Dead City" (Patti Smith)
  E. "Eve of Destruction" (Barry McGuire)
XV. Substance Abuse and Death
  A. "Heroin" (the Velvet Underground)
  B. "Needle of Death" (Bert Jansch)
  C. "Tonight's the Night" (Neil Young)
  D. "Street Hassle" (Lou Reed)
  E. "Hand of Doom" (Black Sabbath)
XVI. Suicide
  A. "Dress Rehearsal Rag" (Leonard Cohen)—slit wrists
  B. "Pineola" (Lucinda Williams)—gunshot
  C. "Pink Turns to Blue" (Hüsker Dü)—hanging
  D. "Rusholme Ruffians" (the Smiths)—jumping
  E. "Rock 'n' Roll Suicide" (David Bowie)
XVII. Tributes
  A. *Songs for Drella* (Lou Reed and John Cale on Andy Warhol)
  B. "Candle in the Wind" (both versions) (Elton John on Marilyn Monroe and Princess Di)

C. "Sleeps with Angels" (Neil Young on Kurt Cobain)
D. "Love Kills" (the Ramones on Sid Vicious and Nancy Spungen)
E. "Back on the Chain Gang" (Chrissie Hynde on James Honeyman-Scott)

XVIII. War and Death
A. "Machine Gun" (Jimi Hendrix)
B. "Ohio" (Crosby, Stills, Nash, and Young)
C. "Foxhole" (Television)
D. "Orange Crush" (R.E.M.)
E. "The Unknown Soldier" (the Doors)

When we first started out, our fans were JUST A MESS—it was like early Christianity. It was the ugliest chicks and the most illiterate guys—people with skin problems, people with sexual problems, weight problems, employment problems, mental problems, you name it, they were a mess.

—Iggy Pop

I made rock my religion; that was my church.

—Robert Pollard

Part 3 Saved

33. Rock and Roll

My high school and college teachers taught a lesson on rock 'n' roll music as a means of arousing the class's interest in "real" poetry. Other than the Beatles, the sources of their tutelage were Paul Simon and Bob Dylan, two "poetic" folk rockers whom these earnest teachers tamed the minute they institutionalized them. Dylan's radicalism couldn't withstand the worshipfulness of a first- or second-year teacher who insisted the lyrics to "Blowin' in the Wind" or "The Times They Are A-Changin'" merited the label *poetry*, and we students were hardly in a position to dispute the wisdom of our preceptors. Whereas daring instructors might have tapped "Like a Rolling Stone" or "Tombstone Blues" for examples of internal rhyme and implied metaphor, my rather duller teachers opted for the preciosity of "Richard Cory," which tied in neatly with Edwin Arlington Robinson's warhorse; for the sentimentality of "The Dangling Conversation," which alluded to Robert Frost and Emily Dickinson (impeccable company); for the yearning of "For Emily (Wherever I May Find Her)"; or for the tidy versifying that pervaded *Bookends*. Later generations of instructors availed themselves of Cat Stevens, the Indigo Girls, Jim Croce, Carly Simon, Jackson Browne, and other pop poetasters sporting a flair for inoffensive, tender lyrics. Given the amount of self-delusion shown by teachers involved in such lessons (as if they were saying to their students, "Look how cool I am and look how neat poetry is! Your favorite folk-rock and pop musicians write *poetry* but you thought it was simply words to a song!"), one would think the idea of teaching "rock poetry" would have expired when punk roared into town: punk rock, which can count among its many other contributions to society its making rock lyrics off-limits to teachers who when pressed to choose between relevant lessons and job security have got to be concerned less about whining, profane, and iconoclastic teen music than about classroom order, parental values, and administrative surveillance. Schools function best not when the white noise of the Stooges, the Slits, X-Ray Spex, the Damned, the Clash, Black Flag, Bad Brains, and Team Dresch, not to mention new model punks such as Eminem, is blasting out of classrooms up and down the hall, but when the school's functionaries—whether motivated by sternness or solicitousness—confiscate Sex Pistols records and Sid Vicious T-shirts, and strip Darby Crash, Tupac, Marilyn Manson, Metallica, Sevendust, and Stone Temple Pilots pictures off the inside of lockers. If they can't legally do it, they probably wish they could. Not that there ever were (or today are) an excess of nefarious totems of this sort to confiscate or strip. How many school kids actually listen to truly alternative, truly antisocial, truly dangerous music? In the vast majority of lockers, the worst a vice principal will unearth (not counting cigarettes, condoms, and assorted prescription drugs) are the compact discs and the likenesses of the harmless entities—accent on perfect teeth, perfect bodies, big hair, and big poses—in heavy rotation on MTV that month.

But to encourage the continuation of the rock curriculum in public schools, the Rock and Roll Hall of Fame and Museum in Cleveland, Ohio, offers a slew of outreach programs for students. Their Web site notes that their many programs are "appropriate" for several disciplines in the humanities (that is, they will somehow tie into the content of nonmusic courses) and require about ninety minutes of the student's time. From kindergarten to grade twelve, there's something for everyone, all in neat ninety-minute packages: seminars on rock's roots, women in rock, Vietnam in rock, John Lennon's life and work (would those ninety minutes include his role in the Beatles too?), and the most risible, although most predictable, topic of all, multiculturalism and rock (to accommodate grades four through twelve). Now, while youngsters are imbibing a very short and correct version of rock 'n' roll music, teachers interested in incorporating this historicized music into their curricula can sign up for their very own summer programs (K-12) to help them meet their course objectives. (Workbook, lesson plans, shuttle from the Radisson, and daily box lunch included with tuition.) All this learning activity takes place in the meeting rooms of a *musée* de rock jammed with artifacts hinged high on walls or positioned just-so behind unbreakable glass: vintage guitars, metal pieces from vehicles in which stars lost limb and life, report cards, apparel, perhaps old socks too, on eternal display for gawking tourists. John Strausbaugh slips the trash trope (never more unhappily met) into his report from this site dedicated to memorializing youth, fun, decadence, and death: "The visitors push their strollers and their wheelchairs past rows and rows of this junk, pausing briefly, staring blankly, and then stroll on, obediently, following the signs, traveling the chutes-and-ladders system of escalators and stairs that eventually dumps them, with a terrible inevitability, in the gift shop."[1] One museum, one sentence, two explicit trash tropes. A third one, implied, is the gift shop. Rock 'n' roll's cruelest irony may be this: that the museum designated to safeguard rock's treasures makes instead an eternal virtue of junk, construed by curators and tourists alike as priceless artifacts, without knowing it. It's ironic too that they don't take what they do ironically. We might as well dedicate a wing in the Smithsonian to the exhibition of America's beautiful garbage dumps, past and present.

According to Drew Lindsay's report in the January 1999 issue of *Teacher*, the lecturers at the Hall of Fame's summer session that year included Paul Friedlander, Bob Santelli, and Jonathon Epstein, three scholars, historians, and pedagogues who urged participants to use rock music, primarily because, to quote Friedlander, "[t]he study of rock will teach kids critical analytical skills, and it will bridge the generation gap that makes teachers seem like aliens to students and vice versa." Santelli declared that, in the classroom, rock music "saved" him—a parody of my imminent correlation of rock 'n' roll and salvation—because it was the only, or best, way for him to reach bored adolescents. Epstein, a sociologist, champions rock music because it's "a repository of clues about who [the students] are," and consequently we can use the form to understand and communicate with them.[2] These and other members of the institute shared lesson plans and facilitated group discussion. Bands mentioned in Lindsay's article are user-friendly names from days of yore. The lecturers are, after all, baby boomers, which is to say they grew up during rock's Golden Age and must therefore be expected to proselytize with the music they know best. Nonetheless, surprises do pop up, notably one teacher's incorporation of Rage Against the Machine in a unit on *The Grapes of Wrath*.

These methods signify reactionary thinking—the more ironic given that rock musicians, even when they're indebted to a precursor (and they all are), thrive (or, as the inductees in the Hall of Fame did during their heydays, thrived) on doing new things by pushing against the constraints of an old form, while the rock teachers seem content doing the same old thing within the same old form—and are the more grievous because they so thoroughly fetter a genre that to flourish must be free of cinderblock architecture (as exhibited by the average public school) and bells clanging out fifty-minute intervals of adolescent progress toward graduation day. An uglier irony is that once upon a time rock music flourished precisely *because* of this cinderblock-and-bells ideology. That makes two counts against teaching it in prepackaged units and workbooks. A third count, the most obvious, is that as soon as one tries to teach rock 'n' roll music, the teacher alienates (and not merely because of the condescension inseparable from the act) many students, whose eyes glaze in anticipation of thematic approaches to ancient names such as Elvis Presley, Bob Dylan, and John Lennon. (A teacher can't be expected to start his unit with Nickelback and Linkin Park.) The names might as well as be Bach, Mozart, and Chopin, and the course a history, with "appreciation" the objective, of classical music.

It seems to me that in the rock museum's workshops, presumed to be on the cutting edge of rock 'n' roll pedagogy, a (probably unconscious) meretricious motive seems to be at work: to teach teachers how to make the most of rock music so as to involve students in literature because God knows not many, if any, other art forms interest these media-addled progeny of a jaded culture. But does no one taking classes at the museum see the absurdity of co-opting rock 'n' roll in order to reach high schoolers who are both long conditioned to the commercial saturation of this music and its paraphernalia (tour T-shirts, MP3s, posters, tattoos, and fashions) and fully capable of understanding it without interference from adults who don't "dig" what they "dig" and possibly don't know that the idiom "dig" is forty years out of date? Does no one see that this is one of the few disciplines that teachers should leave alone? That one of its immanent messages is, always has been, and always will be "fuck school"? Apparently, they don't see this, not in Cleveland, and not in those places to which the museum's summer participants return to put their new tactics to the test.

Rock has been co-opted as a blend of heuristic and a bribe, not the less insidious because the co-opting agent "means well." One such agent, teaching at a high school in the Midwest, offered in 1999 (and perhaps still offers it) an elective named "The Poetry of Rock."[3] The lyrics of "The Wind Cries Mary" from Jimi Hendrix's firestorm debut album *Are You Experienced?* assisted the teacher in his explanation of Poe's techniques in "The Raven." Jimi Hendrix and Edgar Allan Poe. Other than morbid sensibility, what common ground do these American artists inhabit in terms of prosody, style, theme, atmosphere, or medium? One wonders if our teacher has ever listened to *Are You Experienced?*, an album—rather, a traumatic experience: it blew the minds of sixties kids just as Nirvana's two albums blew the minds of nineties kids—whose whole point is to induce personal liberation through freaky living and behavior. If a sixteen-year-old (who needed assistance) were initiated into the mysteries of "Third Stone from the Sun" or "I Don't Live Today" from the same album, he might be tempted to skip school the next day, maybe for good, and he certainly would be within his rights according to the spirit of the album if he refused to take a quiz on its lyrics. Even if it's true, as Lindsay says, and I'm not convinced it is, that "rock seems a perfect medium through which teachers can excite kids about learning," one faces an insurmountable problem inherent in combining rock 'n' roll and conventional high school protocol.[4] In a system whose operations depend at least as much on conformity and negative reinforcement as they do on official mission statements sanctifying independent thinking and self-esteem, how can one of its functionaries be expected to handle subject matter that condones adolescent rebellion? To succeed would be to fail—to throw up his hands before drawing the blood of one grade from the kids—because that functionary would have to account for the fact that most teenagers want to be either set free, saved, or sedated; they don't want to be quizzed. Failing grades would be a good sign and no grades would be better; and much as I hate to admit it, wrecking the classroom (a class project perhaps, inspired by the climaxes in school films such as Jean Vigo's *Zero de Conduite* [1933] and Alan Arkush's *Rock 'n' Roll High School* [1979]) would be best—but try telling that to guidance counselors, principals, school boards, state accreditation officials, and parents.

From what I recall as a high school student, the lyric-as-poem unit typically diluted the artist, whose music was taken from the radio waves and harnessed to help an adolescent *earn credits* based on whether or not he could fathom the imagery or structure of a tune that seemed to any real lover of rock 'n' roll or folk rock out of place in a classroom, which many students perceive, without expressing it quite this way, to be an irreducible locus of systemic repression, the perfect breeding ground for passive aggression. Bob Dylan spat out in "Tombstone Blues" something about "old folks home in the college" and "useless and pointless knowledge." Educators listened to Dylan selectively. In a class I took as an undergraduate, a professor of English, an expert in Shakespeare, used class time to interpret the stanzas of "Desolation Row," a text that, though unprecedented in rock music, didn't seem on par with the Bard's creations. "Digging" Dylan's allusions to Ezra Pound, T. S. Eliot, and Ophelia (implication: such allusions vindicate the intelligence level of rock musicians and render some rock music appropriate for college-level analysis), the professor dug up nothing concrete. In fact, Dylan's verbal wildness undercut the professor's objective, which was to reveal the subtleties of the best blank verse ever penned in the English language. Employing Dylan to elicit interest in Shakespeare didn't and couldn't work. It made Dylan seem drug fueled, pretentious, and verbose, and it implied that lyrically Shakespeare was comparable to rock stars, an absurdity. Neither genius came out ahead.

Again, this kind of thing was in the air. In *Beowulf to Beatles and Beyond*, David Pichaske poured "I Am the Walrus" into a chapter on image, chasing this shot of the Beatles with a draught from "Kubla Khan" and *Romeo and Juliet*. He blended Billy Joel's "My Life" and Robert Browning's "My Last Duchess," drained Carly Simon's "You're So Vain" into a beaker of verses by Jonson, Cowper, Emerson, Housman, Langston Hughes, and Ginsberg, and sipped the "poetry" of "Oh! Darling" by the Beatles. To object to this mix of poem and rock lyric isn't to say that many lyrics aren't, well, lyrical and that they weren't intended by their composers to be lyrical. Perhaps not as ably as Coleridge and Browning, composers draw on metaphor, metonymy, persona, tension, anaphora, irony, paradox, rhyme, onomatopoeia, and other rhetorical devices. Think of the blend of alliteration (*l*s, *d*s, and soft *t*s) and assonance (short *i*s and long *a*s) in the astonishing line in Warren Zevon's "Werewolves of London" describing a short elderly female who's "mutilated" by the monster (my permission request to quote the eight words that comprise this line was declined by one of the song's three publishers); or think of the astonishing paronomasia peppering the misogyny and misanthropy in Elvis Costello's first three long-plays. But these examples are rare exceptions of advanced wordplay. Reading rock lyrics aloud or silently confirms one's suspicion that most lyric sheets, aside from clarifying slurred lines (Michael Stipe c. 1982–87) or lines buried in the mix (Mick Jagger, *Exile on Main Street*), are like good, solid scaffolding in an open space without a building to support: useless.[5]

My own turn at this game came as a student teacher at a rural school in northern New York. I offered, years before the midwesterner did, "The Poetry of Rock" as an elective. A good number of pupils signed up because it looked to be a gut course taught by a local college boy who probably didn't know the first thing about discipline, which was in fact the least of my problems. I quickly discovered that my knowledge of rock 'n' roll and my first-year enthusiasm weren't enough to convince these country teens that excerpts from *Tarantula* or the words to "Mr. Tambourine Man" made sense or even mattered to them in the way they mattered to me, the young idealist trying to enlighten the masses in a course that in 1974 still seemed innovative.

My groovy elective's chance of success was undermined by a contradiction to which I was oblivious: it was part of a curriculum. This contradiction didn't seem to bother my gung ho supervisor or my, at first, curious students. The institution had vested in me the power to require my students to study the poetry of rock 'n' roll because, damn it all, it was good for them, good because understanding the fine points of verse improves one's critical thinking skills, broadens one's worldview, increases appreciation for language arts, and so on, and so on. But I learned soon enough that Bob Dylan's music didn't sound right when played in a room full of plastic desks, fluorescent fixtures, and gum-chewing teenagers taking notes at nine o'clock in the morning. As for the periodic bell, a novice teacher finds out by the end of day one that students wait for nothing, not even the closing bars of a masterpiece over which he may be rhapsodizing, when that bell tolls. It signifies a cigarette, the dash to smooch a boyfriend lounging by a locker, a five-minute chance to cram for next period's quiz.

To make matters worse, my students (and, to be fair, they were attentive and polite) were perplexed by my fanciful interpretations of text that to this day perplex much older and wiser readers and listeners. It also dawned on them that the business of setting up the record player, the fumbling with LPs, and the passing out of another pile of printed lyrics allowed for extra time to gab or fuss, even to arrive late to class. The rigmarole became routine before the first week ended. And of course the pupils knew they couldn't be examined on the material. All they had to do for an A was appear to sway to the teacher's weird choice of music, write a few personal response papers, and concoct a standard-fare report on a rock 'n' roller who was in mothballs. When they got home they could listen to what they liked. There were exceptions to such passiveness. One pimpled lad who wore an American flag patch and who boasted about his father's collection of hunting rifles grumbled about "fags," "commies," "hippies," and other long-haired scum with nothing better to do than stage antiwar demonstrations—you know, undesirables who listened to Dylan's strange and subversive (my word, not his) music. Pupils bewildered by songs that might have liberated them from the oppressions of laissez-faire capitalism joined with the militant kid in complaining about impenetrable (my word, not theirs) music on the order of "A Hard Rain's A-Gonna Fall" and "Ballad of a Thin Man." But neither were the more mellifluous and less abstract Paul Simon and Art Garfunkel, whose music I also "taught," safe from adolescent disapproval grounded in common sense. Richard Cory? "Obviously crazy." "Anyone that rich who would kill themself was wacko." "What a dumb song."

My curriculum didn't backfire so much as fizzle out. Cordially but firmly, most of the kids had allied themselves against the teacher who tried to take them to higher moral ground by studying the youth anthems—his youth anthems—not of the day but of five to ten years earlier. The irony that I was one of Them, the enemy, a new kind of authority, the older generation at twenty-one years of age, sunk in gradually. "Meet the new boss, same as the old boss": having thrilled to these lines, I had failed to apply them to myself.[6] My ignorance and arrogance were more disquieting than the lad's vehement defense of his daddy's mores. So much for the revolutionary spirit of rock 'n' roll in the public school! Dylan's snarl was muzzled by self-conscious handling of vinyl and paper and Simon's urbane charm turned wimpy. The so-called "poetry" on which the class focused once a song ended never materialized. Granted, "Richard Cory" caused predictable discussion about suicide and the perils of materialism (my word, not theirs), but deep down even I, the teacher responsible for all this silliness, didn't believe that Paul Simon's adaptation of Edwin Arlington Robinson's original text was worth a second look (or listen) in the forum where I first tried out the teaching trade.

But outside the classroom, Simon's tune *was* worth a second listen, as were, one hopes, the other tunes mined by me and other well-meaning but slightly soft-headed teachers let loose to ladle out chunks of smorgasbord curricula in the 1970s. This is why I never quite lost my pedagogical interest in rock 'n' roll. I believed a place for it existed. It had to. After all, a teacher teaches adolescents. Rock is an adolescent form. It was even whispered that rock could "save" a person, save him from ennui, despair, identity confusion, a broken heart, self-pity, and a hundred other adolescent (and, it turns out, adult) afflictions. Therefore, my logic concluded, teachers should teach rock 'n' roll. Despite this logic, the more I taught, the less I "used" rock to "demonstrat[e] the *relevance* of poetry

and poetic criticism to a generation that is [was] highly skeptical about everything its fathers and grandfathers found worthy studying" (italics added).[7] I had
lost my idealism regarding its place in the classroom, its wonderful relevance be
damned; my conviction that study units pertaining to rock 'n' roll lyrics could
be justified on any grounds ("reaching students" included) had crumbled. At
the same time, I referred to it constantly in my lessons on literature, even though
with each passing year fewer and fewer students could hear my allusions in their
heads, even when those allusions were to active bands, not mainstream, whom
I assumed students would know something about. But they turned out to be
the last to know. Ironically, their teacher was informed about the punk rock,
shoe-gazing pop, hard-core, grunge, and Britpop that their generation(s) had
invented not for me and my age group to catalog, shelve, and access in an ever-
expanding library of rock, but for them to enjoy. Generally, no matter what the
course level, my rock allusions were no different from my allusions to literary
and historical figures, to paintings and artists, to foreign countries, and to famous buildings and natural sites. Students who might be amused to hear me
date myself by saying in a given context—perhaps, paradoxically, to illustrate
the impossibility of proving an opinion like this in a postmodern classroom—
that the Beatles were the greatest band ever (why even bring up other candidates: the Kinks, the Velvet Underground, Pink Floyd, the Ventures, the Rolling
Stones, the Ramones, U2, Nirvana?) had of course never heard more than several
of their number-one hits and thus had no idea how deep their albums went;
and yet only a paltry handful of them had heard, which would have justified
their amusement at my expense, what I considered the best indie rock of the
era at hand. The vast number of students tended (and tend) to be as clueless
about "their" music as they were (and are) about "mine," which, incidentally,
usually included (and includes), discounting hip-hop, what theirs *should have
been* at the time. Ultimately, the joke was on the babies, not the baby boomer,
who, however, wasn't inclined to laugh at anyone's musical taste or ignorance
because it wasn't amusing seeing class after class of young Americans take for
granted a body of work, an art form, a medium, a way of life, and an avenue to
physical gratification and spiritual ascendancy: that is, rock 'n' roll music.

One day everything clicked in a college classroom where I was teaching
"Paul's Case," Willa Cather's touching study in 1905 of adolescent dysfunction.
In the fictional Paul, a version of the "problem students" Cather herself had
dealt with during her years as a high school English teacher, I saw past and
present versions of teenagers suffering alienation and sexual confusion and acting out their hostility and rebelliousness in self-destructive behavior, a no-win
situation for both the authority figure empowered and expected to discipline
the child just this side of man- or womanhood and for the child him- or herself.

It was impossible to read "Paul's Case" without thinking that Cather's protagonist would have been an ideal candidate for salvation via the glories of rock music. This realization was an important step toward conceiving the broader thesis presented in these pages, to wit: that the disposable musical trash labeled rock 'n' roll—a popular music shot through and through with throwaways, junk, and garbage—provides the individual (most likely a young person) with nothing more or less profound than the materials for reaching a state of grace, a momentary one, of course, but repeatable. *But Is It Garbage?* has documented many of rock's contradictions; and within the context of the trash trope—for example, the throwaway lyric or guitar lick is often the classic to keep, or the artist composing songs the sober fan can treasure is often a junkie who throws away his sobriety, talent, and life—rock 'n' roll fans are continuously forced to make sense of them. The final contradiction to which we've been headed since the first page is this one: that human beings can be saved by a disposable art form. There are many ways of saying it. *Infinitive subject:* To listen to trashy rock music is to be saved. *Imperative:* Listen to rock 'n' roll music, the counterpart of a garbage dump, and save yourself. *Conditional sentence:* If it weren't trash, not only would it not be worth saving but it wouldn't save us anyway. *Verbose compound-complex periodic sentence:* A genre that its detractors have continuously tried to "throw away" (discredit, dilute, ban) through twin campaigns of censorship and disparagement, even though it would be society's assimilation of rock 'n' roll, not the repression of it, that would curtail the music's revolutionary impact; this genre, notwithstanding commercialism, formularization, and, above all, inherent disposability, is yet, at this late date, capable of inspiring musicians to create and merchandise artifacts that must and will be heard by a considerable sector of society; and it will continue in the foreseeable future to save the souls of the fans who seek it out, buy it, listen to it. *Fragment:* Trashed, wasted, saved.

Hyperbole? Let Ken Viola's testimony help us decide. Writing in an ideal contemporary medium for rock commentary—liner notes commissioned for remastered CD reissues/box sets—Viola explains (foreshadowing a plot element in "Paul's Case") that in 1967, at the tender age of fifteen, he cut school in New Jersey and "hopped on a plane to Los Angeles" for the express purpose of seeing Buffalo Springfield perform because he had recently missed their concert in Manhattan. Viola had been smitten by the Springfield's first album, about which thirty-five years later as an adult he writes: "From the beginning . . . I was bathed in the awareness that the writer and the singer and these players UNDERSTOOD. I felt a connection so powerful; I will never forget that moment of transcendence. . . . The music, the playing, the fabric it created. . . . That music saved my life. I was only 14."[8] The (in)significance of school in Viola's reminiscence must be emphasized. When it came to a choice between school and Buffalo Springfield, truancy was nothing. Age was nothing. Distance, nothing. Disciplinary action, nothing. Buffalo Springfield, the boy's synonym for *salvation*, was everything.

In my comments up to this point, I've expressed a negative view of the educational system, not because I'm unaware of wonderful teachers, staff, programs, campuses, and students, and not because I'm unaware of the infinite value of a good education, but because I wish to examine "Paul's Case," which, aside from the rock texts that will appear in the remaining pages, is where my argument about rock's potential to save comes together, largely because school in "Paul's Case" is so hateful to Paul that he makes stupid decisions in the effort to escape it. Hopping on an airplane isn't an option for him; hopping on a train is. But the train of temporary freedom doesn't whisk this teenager to a rock show in Los Angeles. It whisks him to his death in the frozen outskirts of New York City. Going back in time and training the spotlight on a troubled high school student lacking the emotional outlets that teenagers today take for granted will, I trust, put rock's power to save in a new light for anyone who either doubts it or never gave it a thought. Moreover, it will make it easier to read Viola's statement— "That music saved my life"—without giggling at his naïveté, or the present author's, and without demeaning his experience as a trivialization of genuine spiritual conversion. I'm not submitting that the gist of Viola's liner note rivals the *Confessions* of St. Augustine and Paramahansa Yogananda's *Autobiography of a Yogi*, but neither am I brushing it off as the nonsense of a starstruck juvenile delinquent making a mockery of the miracle of divine intercession as chronicled by the world's great saints and divines. In any event, the two types of conversion aren't comparable because rock fans aren't saved by God and they're not saved the same way monks and born-again Christians are. They're not swept away, or "swallowed up" and "annihilated" (as the Puritan preacher Jonathan Edwards purported to be), in one flashing crisis (although they can "lose themselves" in the music), and they need constant doses of the saving power. They feel bliss, they may even leave their bodies, but they don't see God. Their visions are no less sweet and radiant for being unheavenly. Rock fans do depend, however, on similar figurative language to represent their rapture, and they shouldn't be patronized for dealing in the same tropes that eye-shining mystics deal in.

"Paul's Case: A Study in Temperament" is set in Pittsburgh, Pennsylvania, circa 1900, the month November. Paul (no surname is supplied) is a student at Pittsburgh High School, and he has just been suspended. No one knows what to do with him. "Disorder and impertinence" are the main charges, but no one can pinpoint where his transgressions begin and end.[9] Disrespect for authority, a contemptuous attitude, and flippancy—these are the vague charges and for these the teenager must answer as the tale opens with a teacher conference in medias res, the adults falling "upon him without mercy, his English teacher leading the pack." The omniscient narrator relates that Paul possesses a "hysterically defiant manner" and that he exudes "physical aversion" in proximity to his teachers. Neurotic tics afflict him. His lips are "continually twitching," even in sleep. He raises his eyebrows in a manner that offends adults. The "abnormally large" pupils of Paul's eyes suggest an addiction to belladonna, a drug so named because Italian women would apply a drop in their eyes in order to dilate their pupils and thus, theoretically, beautify themselves, making the insinuation of Paul's addiction not far off the mark because his aesthetic self-consciousness—vanity is too weak a word to ascribe to him—is pronounced. (Of further interest is that because belladonna has been used since ancient times as a sedative, poison, hallucinogen, and ingredient in other drugs, the reference to it positions Cather as something of a prophet in terms of foreshadowing the effects wrought on today's teens by "recreational" drugs that no matter how well-publicized the risks they annually ingest by the millions. Paul, incidentally, isn't addicted to belladonna or any other drug, but fast-forward to 2000 and the lad would have gobbled Trazadone and Ecstasy by the handful.) Throughout the "inquisition," the lad deploys an arsenal of passive-aggressive mechanisms: smiling continuously, toying with his buttons, jerking his hat, and shrugging his shoulders, each gesture of "hysterical brilliancy" irritating his interrogators. As if to give a flourish to his otherness, if not to needle his teachers further, Paul wears a red carnation in his lapel, to his teachers the ultimate symbol of a dysfunction too elusive (or abhorrent) to name. The exposition of "Paul's Case" insinuates that Paul's sexuality is on trial too. The masculinity of this "hysterical" lad is in doubt but either none of the masters can put their finger on it or none of them want to broach so delicate a topic. It would be hard enough to broach it in today's "open" society even if a lawsuit were guaranteed not to ensue. After the boy mocks his tormenters by bowing on his way out of their presence, they face the fact that their combined wisdom is baffled by "something about the boy which none of them understood."[10]

Paul runs off to Carnegie Hall, where he works as an usher. It's here that his aesthetic sympathies, represented by the carnation, become more obvious. For instance, in the gallery he "loses himself" while staring at a "blue Rico." A cast of the Venus de Milo, however, elicits "an evil gesture" from the boy, more evidence of his sexual orientation. When the symphony begins, Paul tingles with "a sudden zest of life" that the music prolongs all evening, and at concert's end he tries to sustain this euphoria by following the female soloist to her hotel, which he doesn't enter, loitering in the cold to visualize the "mysterious dishes" and the "green bottles in buckets of ice" she will enjoy, important details because they reveal Paul's unappeased appetite for exotic foods and stimulating beverages.[11]

At last he returns to Cordelia Street, Cather's metonym for dullness and drudgery. "After each of these orgies of living," we learn, "he experienced all the physical depression which follows a debauch; the loathing of respectable beds, of common food, of a house penetrated by kitchen odours; a shuddering repulsion for the flavourless, colourless mass of every-day existence." He nears home "with a shudder of loathing," sensing that Father waits, lording over a house that generates in the prodigal son "a morbid desire for cool things and soft lights and fresh flowers." Paul is besieged by ugliness, a poor relationship with his father (his mother died before his first birthday), problems at school, self-importance belied by low self-esteem, and sexual needs he's unable to sublimate. That he's gay—this allegation becomes indisputable as the evidence unfolds—makes life infinitely more unlivable, especially in light of his father's expectations of him. Paul is expected to marry before he's twenty-five, work for the company, save his earnings, sire children, attend church, be a good citizen and husband, and so on. Worshipping at the shrine of Beauty isn't one of the father's priorities for the son.[12]

Paul creeps into the cold basement to spend a bad night in a makeshift bed. Fantasies about being killed by his father and the fear of rats melt into Sunday afternoon on the steps outside Paul's house, where a clerk "to one of the magnates of a great steel corporation" chats with Paul's father. This twenty-six-year-old clerk, his "wild oats" behind him, has sired four children, who like his "angular" wife, are "near-sighted." Having curbed his youthful appetites, this clerk is the paragon Paul's father holds up "daily" as a "model" and "pattern" for his son to emulate. In this passage Cather satirizes the homilies of bourgeois life so mercilessly that our sympathy shifts to Paul, even though there's much about him that's obnoxious. Her skill in undercutting our misgivings about this teenager is one of the miracles of "Paul's Case," neither a ham-fisted satire nor a pity party for the protagonist. And by now, the reader familiar with the Kinks will have remarked the parallel between Paul's aestheticism ("there was something of the dandy about him") and loneliness and a string of satires and soul-searchings composed by Ray Davies in the midsixties: "Dedicated Follower of Fashion," "A Well Respected Man," "Dandy," "Too Much on My Mind," "I'm Not Like Everybody Else," and "Dead End Street." Other songs by other bands—"And the Cradle Will Rock" (Van Halen), "We Gotta Get Out of This Place" (the Animals), "I Don't Wanna Go Down to the Basement" (the Ramones), "Father and Son" (Cat Stevens), "My Dad Sucks" (the Descendents)—will also have popped up. Undoubtedly, of further interest to rock fans would be that Paul's fear of locking horns with the paterfamilias was experienced by the sixteen-year-old

Bruce Springsteen. After slipping out of the house for a night on the town, "I used to always have to go back home. And I'd stand there in that driveway, afraid to go in the house, and I could see the screen door, I could see the light of my pop's cigarette. . . . [T]he old man he'd catch me every night and he'd drag me back into the kitchen" for a lecture about his son's waywardness.[13]

There's a place, where Paul can go, when he feels low, when he feels blue: "It was at the theatre and at Carnegie Hall that Paul really lived; the rest was but a sleep and a forgetting. This was Paul's fairy tale, and it had for him all the allurement of a secret love." Lacking musical aptitude himself, Paul finds happiness in the role of spectator. Opera bewitches him. (In one of the text's subtle erotic touches, Cather observes that Paul "jerked at the serenade from *Rigoletto.*") Paul the dandy. Paul the aesthete. Paul the sybarite. Passive-aggressive Paul. Rebellious Paul. Paul in the closet, going mad. Compelled by immaturity, intensity of repression, singular aestheticism, and instinctive elitism, Paul detests the world of "Sabbath-school picnics, petty economies, wholesome advice as to how to succeed in life," a world that, beginning sixty years later, rock 'n' roll bands too numerous to count would cut to shreds. An American Adam against the grain, Paul yearns for "starry apple orchards that bloomed perennially under the limelight." Again, beginning sixty years later, such dream visions would be depicted by rock musicians detaching themselves either from the memory of childhoods spent in colorless neighborhoods, boring schools, and unhappy homes defined by the failure to communicate, or perhaps from terra firma in general; for example, Bob Dylan's "Mr. Tambourine Man," Pink Floyd's "Matilda Mother," Stevie Wonder's "Visions," Björk's "There's More to Life Than This" and "One Day," Radiohead's "Exit Music (For a Film)," Sparklehorse's "Comfort Me," and the Byrds' "Fifth Dimension," where, in line with the theme of teaching I've been pursuing, Roger McGuinn sings, "I opened my heart to the whole universe and found it was loving. And I saw the great blunder my teachers had made."[14]

When our hero is expelled from school, put to work in an office, and barred from Carnegie Hall, the velocity of disaster jumps into high gear. Paul had become the victim of his own "fervid and florid inventions" insofar as acquaintances, officials, and parent concur that "Paul's was a bad case." The second part of the tale is signaled by Paul's arrival in January by train in Newark, New Jersey, thence to Manhattan, where clothiers, haberdashers, and jewelers at Tiffany's beckon. Now a fugitive, he purchases his new goods out of the thousand-dollar wad embezzled from his job at an accounting firm. Next he bluffs himself through the registration at the Waldorf, settles into his suite, sends for violets and jonquils, takes a hot bath, and, emerging from his toilette "in his new silk underwear, and playing with the tassels of his red robe," luxuriates in the triumph of his heist.[15]

Cather inseminates "Paul's Case" with double entendres on onanism and homosexuality. The "bewildering radiance" of New York City and the "enchanted palace of the hotel" produce in Paul "a spasm of realization" as he burns "like a faggot in a tempest." Autoerotic imagery infects the very champagne he guzzles, described as "cold, precious, bubbling stuff that creamed and foamed in his glass." Paul is content to "watch the pageant" as long as he can indulge in like opulence: "Nobody questioned the purple; he had only to wear it passively." But he isn't completely passive. He spends twenty-four hours in the company of "a wild San Francisco boy, a freshman at Yale," returning to the hotel at seven in the morning. Paul awakes at two o'clock in the afternoon, hungover from this escapade. Fifty years too soon, the rock 'n' roll lifestyle has begun.[16]

Despite hangovers and overstimulation, during his week at the Waldorf the youngster experiences peace. But then he reads in the papers that a posse is bearing down on him. Naturally, this information revives his worst fears, namely that "the tepid waters of Cordelia Street were to close over him finally and forever. The grey monotony stretched before him in hopeless, unrelieved years." As if to squeeze dry the fleeting time, he drinks "recklessly," justifying his behavior as that "of one of those fortunate beings born to the purple." Paul is unsuited, however, to fight the world, which "had become Cordelia Street," the worst fate imaginable for a boy with his taste for things purple, aromatic, and intoxicating. In his final hours, the teenager achieves if not serenity then a few moments of calm: "he had looked into the dark corner at last and knew. . . . He saw everything clearly now." By cab to ferry to train to carriage, Paul reaches railroad tracks near a snowbound field outside Newark. His red carnation droops. A second epiphany occurs the moment he leaps in front of an oncoming train: "the folly of his haste occurred to him with merciless clearness." This act seals the lid on Paul's case.[17]

"Paul's Case" is an indictment of middle-class values, an assessment of art in the land of philistines, a gesture of sympathy for teachers unable to fathom a student's perverseness, a portrait of a young man without talent or courage, and something Willa Cather couldn't have planned or foreseen. Her tale is evidence, by virtue of its absence, of the healing power of rock 'n' roll music. "Paul's Case" sketches the agony of a teen misfit yet doesn't fit onto a shelf of other adolescent classics such as *The Catcher in the Rye* (1951), *Lord of the Flies* (1954), *The Bell Jar* (1963), *The Chocolate War* (1974), and *Dead Poets Society* (film, 1989), in which rock 'n' roll, if overlooked by the authors as a source of comfort for their heroes, was at least available to real teenagers at the time of each title's respective publication. In this view, a hole gapes at the center of Paul's life, the more pitiful to the modern reader able to perceive that emotionally and psychologically Paul would have found strength, solace, and salvation in rock music. In this regard—that is, as a prerock fictional character in tune with the rock 'n' roll sensibility—he may be unique, certainly ahead of his time. In contrast, it's impossible that the personal problems of other famous literary teenagers of the prerock era—for example, Romeo, Juliet, Huck Finn, Anne Frank, Jo March, Jane Eyre—could have been solaced by the music of P. J. Harvey and the Rolling Stones. Or when one thinks of Clarissa Harlowe (she turns nineteen during a life-threatening crisis) in Samuel Richardson's *Clarissa* (1747–48) resorting to rock tunes for relief, the absurdity of anachronism cuts the thought in two. Paul is an anachronism waiting to happen, not impossible to happen.

"Paul's Case" doubles as title and multivalent metaphor. First of all, the boy is a "head case," probing which a psychologist would detect Oedipal issues made the more severe since Paul's mother "abandoned" her infant son. The psychologist would make much of the mother's absence in the diagnosis of Paul's inability or refusal to channel his antisocial tendencies, which he can verbalize no better than can school personnel, and to coexist with his father without lying constantly, dreading him, defaulting to passive-aggressive behavior, and finally committing a felony. The psychologist would delve into the knot of narcissism and aggression at the core of Paul's dysfunction. Paul is also a case for school counselors to pick at. This student's folder is thick with documentation of disciplinary action for "[b]ad moods, passivity, lack of motivation, and unfocused attention," symptoms of a schoolroom disease termed "psychic entropy" in contemporary jargon. "As they attempt to follow both instincts and social directives," write Mihaly Csikszentmihalyi and Reed Larson, "adolescents find themselves in a labyrinth of difficult and confusing choices. Just when the path seems clear, they run into another wall."[18] Paul's last wall is a ten-ton locomotive. The case might also connote a suitcase, hurriedly stuffed with emergency clothes and cash. (Actually, the runaway carries no luggage on the red-eye from Pittsburgh; he purchases cases at a store on Broadway.) A case for the police to solve resonates in the title, as does a lapidary connotation: clerks at Tiffany's don't throw a gentleman's merchandise into a paper bag. Furthermore, in a different place, better time, Paul's case would open up to reveal an object that would do a lot more for him than silk underwear, silver, banknotes, and mental profiles: an electric guitar. A Kramer, say: fire-engine red with turquoise-studded strap. Something eye-catching.

But before we turn him into a rock star—or better yet, into a manager in the mode of Brian Epstein, the tortured homosexual whose "real thing was the *flair*"—we need to look closer at the case of Paul's homosexuality, which connotes "medical and legal overtones [because] in 1905 discourse on homosexuality was couched almost exclusively in terms of criminality or psychopathology."[19] I've claimed Paul's unhappiness stems largely from his homosexuality. Imagine coming out of the closet in Pittsburgh High School in 1905! Imagine confiding a secret of this magnitude to a father who has all but scheduled the births of his grandchildren! Claude Summers surveys the commentary on Paul's "disease" (by 1905 standards), tying it into Edwardian aestheticism and Cather's disparagement of Oscar Wilde, before concluding, "the cause of Paul's unhappiness and suicide is not his homosexuality but his inability to integrate [it] into real life. This inability is itself the result of the homophobia that pervades his society and that he himself internalizes."[20] Such internalization tears a breach between Paul and "normal" life at school, at home, and at work. Perhaps unable to admit the truth to himself, Paul goes through the paces with no satisfactory outlet—attending operas merely helps him tread water—for his sexual urges and his overactive imagination; he becomes increasingly detached from those helping him toe the line.[21]

I must stress that in the present context Paul's homosexuality isn't important in and of itself; instead, it's important as a sign of his difference. That said, his hang-up could have been any one of hundreds that make teenagers feel like freaks of nature—a bad case of acne, say, or an inability to make a varsity squad on which one has set one's sights. Of course, each such case must be assessed on its own terms. Regarding Paul's personality disorder, no matter how little or much homosexuality may have affected it, I'd like to take Summers's assertion that "Paul's depression is reminiscent of the neurasthenic morbidity associated with aestheticism and decadence" and bring this point back into the arena of rock 'n' roll, keeping in mind my earlier discussion of morbid romanticism and waste.[22] Basically, Paul is a morbid romantic in the making and his "case" diagrams the same waste evinced in the life and art of Nick Drake, Ian Curtis, and other musicians ravaged by incurable depression. Indeed, that Paul might have been solaced if not saved by rock 'n' roll music is made more poignant by the fact that his self-image was "wasted" by psychoemotional handicaps. A weird likeness between Paul and a rock star who was not clinically depressed, who was not homosexual, and who was not motherless must be mentioned. This star was dragged down by demons that to this day elude explanation. During the trial of Brian Jones for the possession of drugs, three psychologists testified that the twenty-six-year-old Rolling Stone was "deeply distressed, anxious, and a potential suicide"; that he was "emotionally unstable, with neurotic tendencies . . . vacillat[ing] between a passive, dependent child with a confused image of an adult on the one hand, and an idol of pop culture on the other"; and that he "might well make an attempt on his life."[23] The doctors were right. Jones had a year left to live. And, "Oh, yes, Brian was always a dandy."[24]

Although many scholars have failed to address, even to acknowledge, homosexuality as a source of Paul's pain, they've pointed out a different problem: Paul isn't an artist and yet he thrives on artistic beauty. According to Phyllis Robinson, Cather, who spent ten years in Pittsburgh, told friends that Paul, though based on two boys she taught, embodied her own "hunger and frustration . . . in the unhappy boy's flight from the drab reality of his daily life and in his instinctive reaching out for beauty."[25] Whereas Cather not only appreciated art but created it, Paul, gripes Robinson, was not so blessed: "Paul may have had the sensitivity of an artist but, unlike his creator, he was without discipline, without direction and, saddest and most hopeless of all, he was without talent."[26] Though impossible to deny, this commonplace is superficial because it doesn't allow for sublimation through spectatorship. It implies that while the more fortunate artist finds satisfaction in creative expression (a sop to suicides like Cobain, Drake, and Brian Jones, and a joke to men like Joseph Conrad and John Lennon for whom being an artist was torture), the audience will always come up short. Still, his aestheticism is so strong—he commits a felony to feed it—because Paul *does* possess the artistic instinct. Unfortunately, he never discovers his art. This is because his art, rock 'n' roll music, hasn't been invented yet.

Having accused others of reducing "Paul's Case" to platitudes about artistic satisfaction and frustration, I'm aware of the charges to which I expose myself when arguing that rock 'n' roll music would be sufficient to save Paul, or any other teenager for that matter, from life's conflicts. Paul's problems are, after all, quite mundane and common. Yet so insurmountable are they in his mind that he kills himself to escape what is summed up in a street address: "Cordelia Street." Moreover, I've stipulated that rock music has saved adolescents who, like Paul, can't negotiate the maze in which adolescence abandons them, and as such, "Paul's Case" has occasioned a meditation on rock 'n' roll and grace. At the very least, listening to rock music may have helped to delay his suicide for a few years. (Since homosexuality isn't a sickness, I'm not implying rock can "cure" it. It can, however, provide a closeted teenager with an emotional outlet.)

Rather than speculate further on this argument—which, frankly, is less important than the bigger issue of how the metaphor of trash is enriched and completed by the metaphor of being saved—let's gather more testimony of the sort Ken Viola has given about Buffalo Springfield's effect on him.

Start at the top. The Beatles have sold more albums in the United States than any other recording act—106 million units as of November 1999.[27] In December 1999, the editors of *Rolling Stone* voted the Beatles the most influential artists of the century and the best rock band, while the magazine's readers chose the Beatles as the best combo, placing three of their titles in the top four of the ten best albums. Inevitably, Lennon and McCartney were elected the best rock songwriters.[28] Stuck in his room on Cordelia Street, Paul would have been comforted to learn that as teenagers these two immortals lost their mothers and that rock music assuaged their grief.

Paul McCartney's mother, Mary, died of breast cancer when her son was fourteen years old. Barry Miles relates that Paul "dealt with his grief by focusing his attention on his music."[29] His first song, penned the same year about his deceased mother, was "I Lost My Little Girl," a song unfamiliar to most people because the Beatles never recorded a serious version of it. They did, however, release serious versions of a masterpiece, "Let It Be," also inspired by McCartney's mother. "Let It Be" is remarkable for blending hymnal prayer with rock instrumentation without sinking into sentimentality. McCartney's loss attains a sacramental spirit of acceptance.

The other half of rock's premier partnership, John Lennon, lost *his* mother at seventeen. The impact of this calamity—his mother was hit by a car minutes after visiting her son, who was raised by his aunt—on Lennon's art is evident in three laments recorded in 1968 and 1970: "Julia" (his mother's name) on *The Beatles*, "Mother" on *Plastic Ono Band*, and "My Mummy's Dead" from the same album. But rock 'n' roll had solaced Lennon long before he composed these dirges. "Cynthia [Lennon] saw music come to be Lennon's salvation"; Brian Epstein urged Lennon to write as therapy; and McCartney "cajoled" his friend to compose for the same reason. Ray Coleman believes these influences, along with the birth of Julian a few years later, saved the Beatle from self-destruction.[30]

Patti Smith's account of being saved—thrilled to the core, sexually aroused, enlightened—by rock 'n' roll begins in 1965, a fabulous year for the Fabs and an incredible year for rock in general: *Bringing It All Back Home; Highway 61 Revisited; Kinda Kinks; Help!; Rubber Soul; For Your Love; My Generation; The Rolling Stones, Now!; Out of Our Heads.* Salvation for Smith came in the guise of five lads of unprecedented scruffiness and menace. The eighteen-year-old girl hears her father yelling at the television set:

I ran in panting. I was scared silly. there was pa glued to the tv screen cussing his brains out. A rock'n'roll band was doing it right on the ed sullivan show. pa was frothing like a dog. I never seen him so mad. but I lost contact with him quick. that band was as relentless as murder. . . . five white boys sexy as any spade. their nerves were wired and their third leg was rising. in six minutes five lusty images gave me my first glob of gooie in my virgin panties.

That was my introduction to the Rolling Stones. they did Time is on my side, my brain froze. I was doing all my thinking between my legs. I got shook. light broke, they were gone and I was cliff-hanging. like jerking off without coming.

Pa snapped off the tv. but he was too late. they put the touch on me. I was blushing jelly. this was no mamas boy music. it was alchemical. . . . . blind love for my father was the first thing I sacrificed to Mick Jagger.[31]

Meanwhile, Jagger's partner Keith Richards had been a shy thirteen-year-old boy on whom "[t]he spirit of rock and roll appeared to have an immediate effect." Strained relations with his father were reflected in the son's boredom in school. "[T]hey manage to turn the whole thing around and make you hate 'em," he said years later. "I don't know anyone at school who liked it. I wanted to get the fuck out of there. The older I got, the more I wanted to get out."[32] Richards's expulsion coincided with the discovery of the guitar, Chuck Berry, American rhythm and blues, and American folk music. He eventually coauthored a supreme songbook fairly bursting with antidotes to the humdrum existence of teenagers living on Cordelia Streets in every corner of the Free World and indispensable to grown-ups not ready to die. In 1990, Guy Chadwick, leader of the House of Love, wrote a homage to the Rolling Stones and the Beatles that gets just right the effect any favorite group (the Stones and the Beatles happened to reach more people than do most groups) has on the dazed and confused teenager scrounging for a fraction of reason to feel proud of himself. The Beatles and Stones heal cuts made by rules at school, make a kid proud to be seventeen, make "it good to be alone."

Paul Williams interprets rock as "a healing music. It has a unique power to aid the individual listener in the process of locating himself or herself amidst the confusion and complexity of the modern world."[33] Taking another tack, Donna Gaines claims world history itself is easy to understand thanks to a scurvy three-chord genre: "First there was the Bible, then Marx, and then there was rock 'n' roll." Elaborating on this unique trinity, she puts her finger on the healing power of rock music:

[H]ow else can we explain the everyday excrement [of Auschwitz and human vanity], where the only hold on life that teenagers feel they have left is suicide (ending it) or procreation (starting it). And there are the betrayals: friends who die too young, lovers who turn out to be assholes, people we believe in who stick it to us. In the minutes that lie between the hurt, anger, and confusion and finding the guts to call a friend, what do I do? You got it—I stick my head inside my speakers.[34]

Billy Corgan shares another inspirational tale. Jon Wiederhorn sums up Corgan's difficult days in grades nine through twelve:

As a teenager [living from age three with his great-grandmother, then two grand-mothers, then his divorced dad and stepmother, and finally his stepmother], he was fraught with insecurity and unhappiness, which he endured by reading a lot. At age 15, he picked up his first guitar and quickly discovered the cathartic power of visceral power chords. But his goth haircuts and alternative-before-alternative-was-mainstream listening habits made him a pariah, and after school, he would return straight home and practice in his room alone for hours on end.

"You walk into high school with a pretty open mind, and you quickly realize where you exist on the food chain," he says.

The purpose of rock 'n' roll, says the Smashing Pumpkin, is "to heal. To help people to see soulfulness in a technological society." [35] "When you're fifteen years old, it's everything. It's like God, like a religion, and when you get older it isn't the same. The energy of music will always be the energy of the kids." [36]

Among the tenets of rock 'n' roll—it's loud, rebellious, rough around the edges, vulgar, disposable—perhaps the most pervasive one is that it's by and for "the kids." Jeremy Larner pontificated in 1964 that "rock 'n' roll is doubly help-ful to the adolescent: it simultaneously socializes him and provides a relatively harmless outlet for anti-social feeling." In the same watershed year, Stuart Hall and Paddy Whannel credited pop tunes for "reflect[ing] adolescent difficulties in dealing with a tangle of emotional and sexual problems. . . . They express the drive for security in an uncertain and changeable emotional world." Ed Ward thinks Chuck Berry's "Johnny B. Goode," "the story of rock and roll Everykid, gave hope to all those who knew that rock and roll had given them a new way out of the miseries of teenagerhood, poverty, and any and all dead-end situations." Jann Wenner has called this mode of expression the "sound": "The sound comes to life as a vehicle to express a generation's restlessness. Rock and roll becomes a teenager's sanctuary from the adult world, a badge of identification with its own lingo." "For teens who formerly made public compromises so that their private views could remain intact, here was a music that permitted public expression of introspective rebellion," writes Herbert London about why early rock 'n' roll was a boon to millions of unhappy youths. (In contrast, what musical outlet does Paul have? A grand opera once in awhile. One peek at Kiss, Alice Cooper, or the Butthole Surfers, and Giuseppe Verdi would be history.) Tracing the ori-gins of rock 'n' roll, London says something else redolent of Paul's case circa 1905: "[w]hile the adolescent has always felt like an outcast, trapped between the worlds of childhood innocence and adult maturity, there had been no true means of expressing such fears and concerns." [37]

Come 1954, there *was* a true means of expressing such fears and concerns, and it was still there forty years later, 5 April 1994, Doomsday, when Kurt Cobain shot himself to death. *Cobain,* essays collected soon after the disaster, is a book Paul would have devoured between classes, before another parent-teacher conference, or in his bedroom at night while blasting Pearl Jam, Imperial Teen, Sonic Youth, Pennywise, and others on headphones so as not to disturb his sisters and dad. (Headphones: a teenager's godsend. Björk praises this device in song as saving her life and lulling her to sleep.)[38] Just as Paul ached to experience the glamour of the prima donna; just as he was seduced by life in the fast lane for a week in Manhattan; just as he was overwrought, pissed off, cynical, lonely, ignorant, and suicidal, so Cobain's bio would have nourished him. At least one key aspect of Paul's own past is repeated in that future history.

Insofar as young Kurt was persecuted there because of his uniqueness, Aberdeen, Washington, bears striking resemblance to Cordelia Street. Unless all Cobain biographers have romanticized their subject's cursed boyhood, Aberdeen seems to be a town rife with suicide and alcoholism where girls and boys yearning for something beautiful suffocate unless they fight back with everything they have and, with luck, keep their self-respect and dreams intact. Aberdeen "recognized [Kurt's] otherness and wanted to batter him for it."[39] He got through his childhood and early teens, according to Michael Azerrad, mainly because he "listened to nothing but the Beatles until he was 9," after which he began to embrace Led Zeppelin, Kiss, Black Sabbath, and the Sex Pistols.[40] School was a disaster, of course. Cobain was a born artist-vandal-rebel interested neither in mundane activities such as football nor in a logging career. He hated jocks, policemen, brain-dead woodsmen, and stupidity.

> Like many youthful misfits, he found a bracing refuge in the world of rock & roll. In part, the music probably offered him a sense of connection that was missing elsewhere in his life—the reaffirming thrill of participating in something that might speak for or embrace him. But rock & roll also offered him something more: a chance for transcendence or personal victory that nothing else in his life or community could offer. Like many kids before him, and many to come, Kurt Cobain sat in his room and learned to play powerful chords and dirty leads on cheap guitars; he held music closer to himself than his family or home, and for a time it probably came as close to saving him as anything else could.[41]

David Fricke backs up Mikal Gilmore's statement by tagging Kurt Cobain the John Lennon of Generation Hex, "someone who genuinely believe[d] in rock & roll salvation."[42] To listen to master-class pop like "Smells Like Teen Spirit," "Rape Me," "Territorial Pissings," and "Scentless Apprentice"; to hear Cobain scream out the lining of his lungs while hewing hummable melodies from ear-piercing chords; to hear Krist Novoselic pounding out turbine-thrust bass lines that pump the heart to greater ecstasies of liberation and rage; to hear Dave

Grohl pouncing, nimbly and heavily at the same time, on the thick snare, deep toms, and massive cymbals of his traumatized drum set—to hear all this is to cruise the high road to salvation.

But what if you're not in the mood for Nirvana's "relentless barrage of thundering, fuck-you grunge-pop anthems"?[43] Salvation comes in a thousand sounds. Talking about Lou Reed's band of malcontents, addicts, hippie haters, and drone makers, Philip Milstein wishes "I'd had the Velvet Underground with me in high school. I could have held my head up so much higher. Anyone could have called me anything and it wouldn't have bothered me, because I had the Velvet Underground, and thus I *knew*. I envy those high school kids who do have the Velvets. They're luckier than the rest of us." His turning point came as a college freshman

> hunting around for something new, something different from the Beatles/Stones/ Beach Boys/Elton John axis I'd theretofore known. Pick up this odd green two-record set, *1969 Live . . . the Velvet Underground*, some more mystery. This silly cover, little information again, "Special Price—Contains 103 Minutes of Music." A good deal. Ah-hah, there it is! That moment, that pivotal moment when you decide to purchase your first Velvet Underground record, sound unheard. There is no turning back.

The pivotal moment—when you know you've been saved. Even better for Milstein than unearthing *1969* was discovering the Velvet Underground's first album: "If there were 40 minutes in my life that I'd like to have back again, I'd have to choose the first time I heard the banana album."[44] On the same wavelength is Ellen Willis, observing that the Velvet Underground fashioned from harsh dark music "a metaphor for transcendence, for connection, for resistance to solipsism and despair."[45] Not bad for a band saturated with junk and trash! These big claims are given weight in Donna Gaines's account of a friend headed for suicide until saved by the band behind "Heroin" and "Sister Ray": "In high school, Anthony overdosed from recreational Thorazine. The next week he was voted president of the school's honor society. He tells me that if it were not for Lou Reed, he would have done himself in long ago."[46]

Teenagers have been well served by songs written with their low self-esteem in mind. Alice Cooper's *Love It to Death* rushes into the ring with "Caught in a Dream," "I'm Eighteen," and "Long Way to Go," three knockout punches. Of these cuts, the second one works at the ambivalence of being eighteen, when a lad (many lassies go through this stage too) doesn't know what he wants, feels trapped at home and school, and can't explain his confusion. Six years later, the Sex Pistols delighted the seventeen-year-old set with "Seventeen." The hell with work—all Johnny Rotten's punk teen needs is speed because he's "a lazy sod . . . a lazy sod." Try teaching that in the Poetry of Rock course! Six years after the

Sex Pistols battered England with songs like "Seventeen," the Replacements of Minneapolis, Minnesota, softened the blow in their reflection on sexual identity in "Sixteen Blue." Composer Paul Westerberg was adored by troops of kids who, like the sixteen-year-old in the song, were between boy- and manhood, were unsure of their sexuality (am I gay?), and agreed with Westerberg that their "age is the hardest age."

What if the boy-man *is* gay? Queercore understands. A strain in the punk revival of the eighties and nineties, queercore slices the jugular of gender prejudice and oppression. The gay's stereotypical effeminacy is booted out the door and the door is ripped off its hinges. A leader of the pack is Pansy Division, ruffling the calm waters of conformity with queercore standards such as "Fuck Buddy," "Bill and Ted's Homosexual Adventure," "Two Way Ass," "Rock and Roll Queer Bar," "The Cocksucker Club," and "Smells Like Queer Spirit." Gays (and straights) enjoy the queercore efforts of the Queers, God Is My Co-Pilot, and Team Dresch ("Fagetarian and Dyke," "Hate the Christian Right!"). If it isn't stocked in the local franchise record shop (and it isn't), fans can go online to buy Glen Meadmore's *Hot Horny and Born Again* from Pervertidora Records in San Francisco, the discography of Tribe 8 ("dyke punk rock that works hard"), and the product line of Phranc, "your favorite all American Jewish lesbian folksinger."[47] Links to "queer" magazines and services pepper these Web sites. Swelling the roster of gay rockers are mainstream stalwarts such as the late Freddie Mercury of Queen, Boy George, George Michael, and Elton John.

I've been analyzing Paul's homosexuality as a sign of difference rather than as a "condition" with its own apparatus of artistic and political implications. At one point I grouped it with adolescent acne and a poor showing on the high school try-out field, facts of life that teenagers magnify into proof of their worthlessness. This wasn't done condescendingly, as if to equate a gay boy's inner strife with a straight boy's inability to throw a football. It was done to universalize Paul, certainly, but also to sharpen the reader's sense of the despair a teenager of an exquisite sensibility exacerbated by "criminal" sexual desires would have suffered in 1905. It would have been bad enough in 1955. John Gill's chapter on Elvis Presley in *Queer Noises* corrects those who tend to romanticize fifties rock 'n' roll (as some of my references and I seem to do) as a medium that gathered every last American teenager to its pulsing bosom:

> Rock'n'roll may have been pushing at the barriers of conventional morality . . . but mostly it reflected the moral consensus, certainly as far as deviant sex was concerned. . . . [R]ock'n'roll was essentially heterosexual in its subject matter. . . . As a small controlled teen explosion, rock'n'roll had to work out its own obsessions with boy meets girl before it could begin even to contemplate the possibility of boy meets

boy or girl meets girl. . . . [P]op's *langue d'amour* remained resolutely fey and coy even about respectable heterosexual dalliances.[48]

In the fifties Paul would have to have learned to decode the gay signifiers in the lyrics and stage moves of rock's gay performers (such as Little Richard and Johnnie Ray) because, Gill notes, nothing explicit would come out of the mouths of gay and lesbian rock musicians until the midseventies, by which time performers could emerge from the closet without destroying their careers. In all this talk of gay connectiveness, it behooves me to stress that there's no reason to believe our Everyteen (Paul) wouldn't have enjoyed the music of straight rockers just as straights (teetotalers and churchgoers among them) have been known to enjoy the music of homosexuals, junkies, and alcoholics.

The gay/straight binary quickly gets tedious. Art doesn't discriminate. And so, before concluding Paul's case for good, some final remarks on salvation.

- Paul loved opera. Few teens do—or did until Pete Townsend composed an opera about a deaf, dumb, and blind pinball wizard named Tommy. Good as that record was, imagine Paul's delight at unwrapping and cueing up the Who's second rock opera, *Quadrophenia,* about which the composer declared, "[I]t's about a young screwed-up, frustrated idiotic teenager. Like us."[49] Townsend's art doesn't discriminate. General adolescent malaise subsumes individual sexual agon. Paul would have listened to "The Real Me," "Drowned," "I've Had Enough," and "The Dirty Jobs" for hours at a time, perhaps side by side with the pimply kid and the unsuccessful quarterback. Bonus for Paul: Townsend's protagonist dreaded the thought of going home.
- The life of Lou Reed's five-year-old Jenny was saved by the rock 'n' roll broadcasted from a radio station in New York City. See "Rock and Roll," third tune on *Loaded* by the Velvet Underground.
- Having turned to rock music for "survival, and [living] it down in their souls, night after night," Bruce Springsteen and his fellow musicians were empowered to save the lives of others, Dave Marsh, for instance, and God only knows how many other individuals on whose behalf Marsh speaks: "I believe that rock and roll has saved lives, because I know that it was instrumental in shaping my own. . . . Rock saved my life."[50]
- In 2001, Adam Franklin of Toshack Highway entitled an EP *Everyday, Rock'n'Roll Is Saving My Life.* He moans in the title track that while a woman breaks his heart, rock saves him, day after day.
- Richard Sorrell begins an essay published in an academic journal thus: "Like Lou Reed's 5-year-old Jenny, my life has been frequently saved by rock & roll." He concludes with the insightful tautology that "each new

generation of young people will re-create rock & roll, or a new version of popular music . . . so that they too can claim that their 'lives were saved by rock & roll.' "[51]

- Don McLean's "American Pie" exists mainly to validate rock's grace, as does the Lovin' Spoonful's "Do You Believe in Magic?"

- Writing from Cordelia Street, Bob Larson rants that rock music "is a collective noun referring to an unprecedented twentieth century phenomenon that may well be an instrument in the destruction of our Western political, moral, and spiritual foundation."[52] Rock is "the devil's diversion." Larson is only half right. We can't deny that rock is synonymous with drug addiction, excess, egomania, sex, self-absorption, dissolution, garbage, and death. Nevertheless, we must inform Larson that "you got to go through hell before you get to heaven."[53] Larson doesn't understand that the more he damns rock 'n' roll, the more full of grace it appears because the one state can't exist without the other to balance it and thus derive its own meaning from it. But Larson's damn/save binary doesn't quite work. The better binary for rock music is waste/save.

- Steve Huey, reviewing *Never Mind the Bollocks, Here's the Sex Pistols,* marshals these modifiers: "confrontational, threatening, rabid, foaming, bitterly sarcastic, daring, grating, snotty, roaring, ranting, and positively transcendent."[54] Once upon a time, this positively transcendent record blew out every window on Main Street and knocked over every mailbox on Cordelia Street.

- In "Rock 'n' Roll/Ega," cult hero Daniel Johnston witnesses in his warbling alto, accompanied by solo acoustic guitar interrupted by crashing electric guitars and drums, the inrush of grace: "I was alone as lonely could be / I laid asleep and turned on the radio / The music to me was like a dream / Oh that rock 'n' roll it saved my soul. . . . My heart looked to art and I found the Beatles / Oh God, I was and am a true disciple."

Amen.

34. The End

A reader protests.

"Do you expect me to accept this business about transcendence with a straight face?

"Are you ignorant of the fact that complicit in your thesis that rock 'n' roll can 'save' a person is an archaic 'power-of-art' ideology that a postmodernist audience will find insupportable at best and ridiculous at worst?

"Have you never heard of deconstruction, which has done in the transcendental signification of language, demonstrating that there's nothing outside of text—'il n'y a pas de hors-texte' in Jacques Derrida's phrase—and that the Western fixation on 'presence' presupposes a fixation on a logocentric center that exists neither in 'books' nor rock 'n' roll records; that apparent meaning is multivalent, not univocal, as well as always already deferred, under erasure, playing freely, crisscrossed with traces, and contingent on the arbitrariness of difference, not to mention *différance* (delay, dispersal, difference): never at one with itself or any transcendent absolute, and leading, sign by sign, to the dead end of aporia?[1] Have you not heard that your *transcendent* rock music, like any other discourse, implies 'an infinite regress, leading ultimately to the abyss of nothing and nowhere'?[2] That the author, the 'composer' too, is 'dead' and has been dead for the past twenty years or so?

"Have you never heard of New Historicism and multiculturalism, whose practitioners have leveled canons, recuperated the Other, and pinpointed the hegemonic discourse implicit in your aesthetic distinctions and hierarchical musical agendas? Are you ignorant of Marxism, which has shattered all ideals of your so-called 'art,' exposing it as an elitist preoccupation bound head to foot to oppressive class relationships, to the commodification of imagination, and to the piracies of unbridled capitalism? Don't you know that rock music, like literature, 'is determined by the primary means of production, technological and intellectual, and is necessarily an instrument in the class struggle for political control'?[3] And have you been deaf to the manifestos of feminism, whose representatives had to fight for decades against the misogyny entrenched in all facets of culture, including the fantastically macho Boys-Only Club of rock 'n' roll music before females at last began in recent years to gain parity with overtly sexist male rock stars and record company executives?

"A short lecture courtesy Fredric Jameson. 'We are left with that pure and random play of signifiers that we call postmodernism, which no longer produces monumental works of the modernist type but ceaselessly reshuffles the fragments of preexistent texts, the building blocks of older cultural and social production, in some new and heightened bricolage.' 'The former work of art, in other words, has now turned out to be a text, whose reading proceeds by differentiation rather than by unification.' 'The autonomous work of art thereby—along with the old autonomous subject or ego—seems to have vanished, to have been volatilized.' Jameson states that "we find ourselves confronted henceforth with 'texts,' that is, with the ephemeral, with disposable works that wish to fold back immediately into the accumulating detritus of historical time.' The end result is an inability 'to organize an analysis and an interpretation around any single one of these fragments in flight.'[4] You seem unschooled in such theories.

"And so, in terms of 'transcendence' and other superannuated assumptions about 'art,' albeit cleverly conflated with garbage, do you have anything to say about these facts of postmodern life?"

I reply.

In the end every beautiful theory mentioned is blowing in the wind because everyday people (and every day, people) talk about rock 'n' roll music in terms of salvation, transcendence, and, lest we forget, trash. This too is a fact of postmodern life. The hundreds of examples scattered throughout *But Is It Garbage?* prove this. But let's listen to one more voice, not as formidable as Derrida's or Jameson's, borrowed from the lowest pop culture source this side of a high school kid's Xeroxed (and forbidden) newsletter on hard-core punk and antischool politics: a webzine. Joanna Lux rhapsodizes about the album by Neil Young to which I referred long ago in section 2. She writes, "Everything I needed to know about life I learned from a Neil Young song, and *Live Rust* is the Holy Grail. . . . *Live Rust* is musically and lyrically prophetic. From paradise and sin to forgiveness and death, Young reaches depths few dare to plumb."

"The Holy Grail"—Lux's words, not mine. And such words are as vital in the "discourse" of rock 'n' roll music as are and would be the words of the Marxist Theodor Adorno, the deconstructionist Paul de Man, the feminist Mary Daly, or the New Historicist Stephen Greenblatt—brilliant, profound, revolutionary voices, true, whose admirers are free to apply their theories to rock 'n' roll at any time—but these words are not, however, the final say on this subject. Perhaps more to the point is that in the end it should be clear that what I've done in this essay is not to reject the postmodern sensibility at all but to embrace it from the first sentence of the first section where instead of negating the "meaning" of salvation—granted, a transcendental sign—I imply that the concept is a multivalent, even subversive representation: Jesus, Jimi: each has saved men and women starving for spiritual consolation. Moreover, this salvation is rooted not in divinity but in trash and trashed human beings. The Ramones weren't gods but they saved—well, how many individuals? More than Mary Daly or Paul de Man did. Two other postmodern maneuvers: I've written about a marginalized "art form" that isn't taken seriously by the priests and proponents of high culture to whom you'd be better off quoting Jameson and others; and I've deconstructed a trope, specifically the trash trope. Rock 'n' roll music is trash, garbage, and junk—all deconstructible figures of speech—represented in word, flesh, and deed. But precisely because of its inherent disposability and its connection to waste, rock 'n' roll music is, or can be, "transcendent"—saying which, I realize, is to privilege yet another figure of speech that as such can be (and was) deconstructed in turn, thus bringing us back to trash, my initial term in the trash/transcendence binary. Dwelling on the deconstruction of transcendence and the reinscription of the trash trope—or should that be the other way around?—the rock 'n' roll fan hears the voice not of Derrida or de Man but of Paul McCartney howling (in present tense) about a game he played as a lad in the 1940s in a playground in Liverpool: when he reaches the bottom of the slide, he returns to the top, stops, turns, rides down again until reaching the bottom, where he sees "you again."[5] In like fashion we can return to trash as often as we wish, ride the slide, climb the ladder again—waste ourselves if so inclined, rummage through the stinkiest or sweetest pile of garbage available, throw up into the heap or, with luck, eyeball something worth saving, something that will save us and help us transcend the confines of the Cordelia Street we might be fated to call home.

Yes, I have heard of postmodernism, and I like it. But in the end, it must be said, rock 'n' roll saved me too.

APPENDIX   Section Titles

Preface. "Start Me Up." The Rolling Stones, Rolling Stones Records, 1981.

I. Trashed

1. "It's Now or Never." Elvis Presley, RCA, 1960. Baby boomers have to testify now because time's running out.

2. "It's Still Rock and Roll to Me." Billy Joel, Columbia, 1980. The Piano Man pokes fun at those who would divide rock into categories. From the Fugs to Fugazi; from Kenny Rogers and the First Edition to Sleater-Kinney; from Dino, Desi and Billy to Dinosaur Jr.; from New Riders of the Purple Sage to Red House Painters—it's all rock 'n' roll music.

3. "Do It Again." Steely Dan, MCA, 1972. In summarizing the thesis and methodology of *But Is It Garbage?*, I refer to Ralph Waldo Emerson for the second time in the book, writing, "To drink once again at the Emersonian fount, I suggest that an elite corps of rock musicians fulfills his conditions for acknowledgment as 'liberating gods.' " Oops! I had done it—used Emerson—again.

4. "Give the People What They Want." The Kinks, Arista, 1981. From the album of the same name, Ray Davies skewers the same pop music consumerism that Theodor Adorno critiqued. Ray Davies satirizes mass taste in "Give the People What They Want," where families watch reruns of John F. Kennedy's assassination ("Look Mom, there goes a piece of the President's brain!"). Forty years earlier Adorno phrased it thus: "The promoters of commercialized entertainment exonerate themselves by referring to the fact that they are giving the masses what they want. This is an ideology appropriate to commercial purposes: the less the mass discriminates, the greater the possibility of selling cultural commodities indiscriminately. Yet this ideology of vested interest cannot be dismissed so easily. It is not possible completely to deny that mass-consciousness can be molded by the operative agencies only because the masses 'want this stuff.' But why do they want this stuff?"[1]

5. "Isn't It a Pity." George Harrison, Apple, 1970. Yes, it is.

6. "Reflections." The Supremes, Motown, 1968. The lyrics of this pop song have nothing to do with my reflections on the trash trope.

7. "Big Yellow Taxi." Joni Mitchell, Reprise, 1970. Mitchell satirizes progress through the metonym pavement.

8. "Over and Over." Fleetwood Mac, Reprise, 1979. I fine-tune my thesis, ask new questions, deepen the argument, and raise the stakes. Corkscrewing around the topic, I reinforce it while tightening my grip on the other sections.

9. "Bad Boy." The Beatles, Capitol, 1964. A Larry Williams rocker covered on *Beatles VI.*

10. "It's All Too Much." The Beatles, Apple, 1969. In a short review of *Yellow Submarine,* Richie Unterberger uses the trash trope twice: (1) "It's All Too Much" is one of four

"pleasant throwaways" on the soundtrack. (2) A plan to release an EP including these four throwaways was "ultimately discarded."[2] The relevance of this title to this section lies in this sentence: "The music is too much for words, especially tame ones."

11. "Graceland." Paul Simon, 1986, Warner. Other possibilities for this section were Bruce Springsteen's "Pink Cadillac," Bo Diddley's "Cadillac," and "Liar Liar" by the Castaways because I call Elvis a liar after quoting a Vegas monologue in which he insists he's drug-free.

12. "Tell It Like It Is." Aaron Neville, Collectables, 1967. Good critics do.

13. "Total Trash." Sonic Youth, DGC, 1988. Self-explanatory.

14. "Vicious." Lou Reed, RCA, 1972. The word is Frank Sinatra's. It's one of several insults he hurled at rock 'n' roll music, which, as I explain, he felt was "the most brutal, ugly, desperate, vicious form of expression it has been my misfortune to hear."

15. "Fame and Fortune." Elvis Presley, RCA, 1960. I write this: "The bulk of [the rock] repertoire is *not* here to stay because it manages at best to beguile a fleeting moment. As if aware of this, some bands seeking fame and fortune . . . are able at the same time to mock or deflate their own ambitions."

16. "Torn and Frayed." The Rolling Stones, Rolling Stones Records, 1972. John Lennon tears and frays the Beatles.

17. "Junk." Paul McCartney, Capitol, 1970. See section 27, number 8.

18. "How Long." Ace, Anchor, 1974. This title refers to the late Armand Zildjian's claim that his company's production of a trashy sounding "China" cymbal took a long time to develop. China cymbals emit a pangy, clattering tone. Whereas a good strike on a standard crash cymbal washes over you in a quick shower of bright brassy sound, a good strike on a China cymbal fractures your head with a metallic assault. Chinas are used more often in fusion set-ups than rock. They aren't heard at all in the work of the major sixties and seventies rock drummers. All this has nothing to do with the theme of infidelity in Ace's "How Long."

19. "Catholic Boy." Jim Carroll, Atco, 1980. This section concludes with the anecdote about Bruce Springsteen being humiliated by a nun.

20. "Sunny." Bobby Hebb, Philips, 1966. This is obviously an ironic application of a title to a section, referring as it does to Jimi Hendrix's posthumous album *First Rays of the New Rising Sun*. The thought of Jimi's corpse doesn't add sunshine to one's day.

21. "Rape Me." Nirvana, DGC, 1993. The section deals with pain, destruction, and death.

22. "Take It as It Comes." The Doors, Elektra, 1967. A phrase to keep up the reader's morale as he trolls through the text's morass of trash. Take it as it comes because it keeps on coming.

23. "Those Were the Days." Mary Hopkin, Apple, 1969. A meditation on rock music then and now.

24. "Rip It Up." Little Richard, Specialty, 1957. Little Richard's title wasn't meant to conjure the image of a rock critic ripping up groups and solo performers.

25. "There's a Place." The Beatles, Parlophone, 1963. This section picks on a subgenre of rock music, trash rock, which "became official in the mid-nineties, originating in

France, of all places." Rock 'n' roll has given provincial Americans a rare chance to look down on citizens of France. Have you ever heard of a French rock 'n' roll band or singer? Neither have I.

26. "Rock Show." Paul McCartney and Wings, Capitol, 1975. This section investigates the trashing that occurs at rock concerts and festivals.

27. "Rock and Roll Music." Chuck Berry, Chess, 1957. Self-explanatory.

28. "The End." The Doors, Elektra, 1967. Leading into the morbidity of part 2, this title refers to the epic ending the Doors' debut, not the penultimate tune on the Beatles' swan song.

II. Wasted

29. "Another One Bites the Dust." Queen, Hollywood, 1980. Black humor.

30. "All Things Must Pass." George Harrison, Apple, 1970. The unending debate, no matter how pointless or dull, about the death of rock 'n' roll can't be overlooked in a discussion about waste.

31. "Shattered." The Rolling Stones, Rolling Stones Records, 1978. *Berlin,* I write, "is told via shattering songs written by a brilliant songwriter and performed by a studio full of rock masters." On the final cut of *Some Girls,* Mick Jagger riffs on the decadence of New York City and its shattering impact on him. "Shattered" also alludes to heroin, a drug that may be on hand in *Berlin*'s mise-en-scène.

32. "The Last Time." The Rolling Stones, London, 1965. The phrase is embedded in a sentence about running toward funerals.

III. Saved

33. "Rock and Roll." The Velvet Underground, Atlantic, 1970. To my knowledge no song better expresses the thought that rock 'n' roll music saves lives.

34. "The End." The Beatles, Apple, 1969. With the Beatles' epigram about taking and making love, the Beatles, the sixties, and the second wave of rock 'n' roll music ended.

NOTES

Preface

1. Coleridge 495.

I. Trashed

1. It's Now or Never

1. John Strausbaugh doesn't credit baby boomers for inventing rock 'n' roll music: "Although boomers would later appropriate the notion of youthful rebellion, as well as assign to themselves all credit for rock 'n' roll, it was in fact teens in the 1950s—not baby boomers, mostly, but Parsons's war babies—who created the first 'youth rebellion' and were the audience for the origins of rock 'n' roll, a 'youth music' that was created, it's curious to remember, by men born in the 1930s (Elvis, Little Richard, Buddy Holly, Jerry Lee Lewis) or even 1920s (Chuck Berry)" (13).

2. Of rock 'n' roll's many beginnings, the traditional one (Elvis Presley, the Sun Sessions) was for Nick Tosches the end of it: "by the summer of 1954 . . . the cycle was already complete, the beast of rock 'n' roll had been tamed for the circus of the masses, by the time Elvis (another dead fuck) came along. . . . In 'Milkcow Blues Boogie,' his third record, made in December 1954, raw power has already turned to schmaltz" (*Unsung Heroes* ix).

3. Jefferson, "To Benjamin Rush" 1124; "To William Short" 1436.

4. Milstein, Kostek, and Messer 141.

5. In 1993, a few thousand spectators saw the original Velvets on their brief reunion tour in Europe. The rest of us got the chance to buy an overpriced, lackluster double-CD of the tour.

6. Henderson 218–19.

7. Emerson, "An Address Delivered before the Senior Class in Divinity College" 80.

2. It's Still Rock and Roll to Me

1. Gracyk 6–7, 13, 12.

2. Fornäs 111–12, 113.

3. Bomp Records 33, Bombardier 24.

4. Young, "Sedan Delivery."

3. Do It Again

1. Molesworth 7, 8.

2. Ammons 28.

3. Emerson, "The Poet" 461.

1. Of these stars, Harold F. Mosher Jr. draws on Paul Simon to conclude that the "drama, irony, ambiguity, and symbolism" of many rock or folk-rock tunes "put them in the tradition of 'serious' poetry," as do their "imaginative, original, and sometimes quite extravagant forms" (175). In other words, rock is Art.

2. In section 2, I refer to Tesh to suggest that the definition of rock 'n' roll can be bent only so far.

3. Gracyk 156, 164.

4. Adorno 437–38, 439, 441, 458, 442, 443, 459.

5. Steve Albini is a scourge of the rock industry, leading radically anticommercial bands such as Shellac, Rapeman, and Big Black and producing countless others. The Minutemen, the pride of San Pedro, California, in the 1980s, did nothing by the corporate book. Wire was/is (they have disbanded and regrouped several times in their career) an English art-punk band that released two acclaimed "punk" albums in the late seventies, *Pink Flag* and *Chairs Missing,* neither of which courted or conquered a mass audience in Adorno's sense of the term.

6. Gendron 25.

7. Adorno 458. Fine studies of rock and marketing include Dannen, *Hit Men* (1991); Goodman, *The Mansion on the Hill* (1998); Stokes, *Star-Making Machinery* (1976); Denisoff, *Solid Gold* (1975) and *Tarnished Gold* (1986); and Garofalo, *Rockin' Out* (1997).

8. Gendron 26, 27, 30.

9. Gracyk 156.

10. Scruton 504, 505, 491, 493, 505.

11. Ibid. 501, 499.

12. Regev 87, 88, 91, 96, 97, 98. Jon Landau's "Rock and Art," penned in 1968, sniffed the rat of formalism and pretense in "art" and backed off from it. His anti-Emersonianism is apparent in the essay's last clause: "rock musicians are not the new prophets" (134). Yet look at the prophet he went on to produce: Bruce Springsteen.

5. Isn't It a Pity

1. Poovey 615, 616.

2. Strasser 199–200.

3. Ibid. 14–15.

4. Sawyer 52.

5. Donald Reed 29.

6. "Lighting Disposal" 287.

7. Solomon 73.

8. Environmental Protection Agency (henceforth epa), "Household Hazardous Waste."

9. epa, "Collecting Used Oil"; "Industrial Waste Management."

10. Anita Hamilton reports, "Every year an electronic trash heap nearly as tall as Mount Everest is tossed into garbage cans, stashed in garages or forgotten in closets. Some 500 million PCs will be rendered obsolete by 2007 in the U.S. alone" (70). John Dvorak opines, "[I]n most cases, PCs are merely chopped up and sent to a dump. . . . And let's not even touch on the older printers and other peripherals, let alone the billions of plastic CD-ROMs and old floppy discs ending up in landfills" (91).

11. Elliott 26.

12. EPA, "Environmental Fact Sheet."

13. Greengard 69.

14. Sam Martin 59.

15. Ibid. 59, 62.

16. Alexander 59.

17. Sam Martin 60.

18. "Michigan Representative" n.p.

19. Broydo 19.

20. Kantor et al. 2.

21. Sam Martin 59. This figure of 200 million tons is consistent with statistics published by the EPA and various reporters. During the past fifteen years, totals of domestic solid waste, expressed in pounds discarded per person per day, have ranged from 2.9 to 8 pounds (Rathje and Murphy 49).

22. My calculations are based on statistical charts in EPA, "Municipal Solid Waste in the United States."

23. Rathje and Murphy 11.

6. Reflections

1. An example of *waste* as insult: the rock critic "C.A." trash-tropes John Tesh's album *Discovery* thus: "Unblushing waste of perfectly good notes" (46). April Long uses the same trope to make the opposite point in the review of *The Photo Album* by Death Cab for Cutie: "Not a single track, nor note, is wasted" (96).

2. Marcus, *Mystery Train* 114–15.

7. Big Yellow Taxi

1. *Trash* refers to dry discards (for example, newspapers and cans); *garbage* refers to wet discards (for example, yard waste, offal); *refuse* includes wet and dry discards; and *rubbish* "refers to all refuse plus construction and demolition debris" (Rathje and Murphy 9). Technically, discarded record albums, album sleeves, tapes, plastic cases, compact discs, and jewel boxes are trash.

2. In 2000, compact discs led sales with an 86 percent share; cassette albums sold a meager 8.4 percent; cassette singles were expected to be discontinued within a year or two; and vinyl albums barely registered at two million units shipped ("First-Half CD Shipments" n.p.). The same year, Gordon Masson reported total sales of all music compact disc sales at 2.4 billion units (10).

3. Aldersey-Williams 40–41.

4. Horowitz 1. On saturation shipping, see Meyer 83, 87. Horowitz's statistic of 200 million returns in the system at any given time seems high in light of the total number of albums sold in 1983, the year compact discs showed up in record stores. In that year, writes Ken Armstrong, the Recording Industry Association of America reported nationwide LP sales of 210 million units. Armstrong's article is about the problems libraries have faced in getting rid of albums—conservatively, tens of millions all told—to which patrons no longer listen (1).

5. Global Environmental Change 1.

6. Celestial Harmonies.

7. Denby 80. More than six billion compact discs had been sold when this essay appeared in 1996.

8. Goldberg 20.

9. Peter Newcomb calculated the sale in 1990 of 286 million compact discs generating twelve thousand tons of waste (82).

10. In 1990, James E. Ellis reported, "CD boxes contribute far less to America's waste problem than even deodorant or toothpaste packaging." Ellis claimed that long boxes were in fact recyclable and that they accounted for "less than six hundred-thousandths of 1% of the weight of all garbage produced in the U.S. annually" (30).

11. Verna, "Confusion's the Rule" 86.

12. Verna and Newman 99.

13. Spahr 6.

14. "New Life for Old CDs" 23.

15. Nunziata and Lichtman 85.

16. Gillen 12.

17. Tyler Maroney's exposé of jewel boxes begins, "We all hate CD jewel boxes. They're hard to open, their hinges snap, and those little plastic hubs that hold the disk inevitably break" (54). See also Steve Martin's satire on jewel boxes, "Designer of Audio CD Packaging Enters Hell."

8. Over and Over

1. The poster is reproduced in Russo 35.

2. Zappa's opinion is cited in Susan Orlean's profile on the Shaggs, which begins with this sentence: "Depending on whom you ask, the Shaggs were either the best band of all time or the worst" (72).

3. Chuswid 1–2. Jimmy Guterman and Owen O'Donnell muse, "[T]he Shaggs are . . . fundamentally awful, yet you can't help loving them" (191).

4. Christgau, *Any Old Way* 110.

5. Guterman and O'Donnell back up this judgment in pages 249–52.

6. Poe, "Charles James Lever" 311, 312.

7. VH1.

9. Bad Boy

1. Meltzer, *A Whore Just Like the Rest* 145. Unless noted otherwise, all citations for Meltzer are from this book.

2. *Their Satanic Majesties Request* by the Rolling Stones, *Self Portrait* by Bob Dylan, *Wild Life* by Paul McCartney and Wings, *Having Fun with Elvis on Stage:* albums by superstars savaged by critics.

3. Meltzer 76, 77.

4. Ibid. 186.

5. Ibid. 387.

6. Ibid. 245, 8, 555.

7. Ibid. 534, 537, 535.

8. As of this writing, predictions of the compact disc's replacement by MP3s and other forms of technology are common.

9. Meltzer 537.

10. Ibid. 554, 556.

11. Hall and Whannel 311.

12. Meltzer 558, 568.

10. It's All Too Much

1. Bangs, *Psychotic Reactions and Carburetor Dung* 302, 303. Unless noted otherwise, all citations for Bangs are from this book.

2. Ibid. 10, 32.

3. Ibid. 39.

4. Ibid. 46.

5. Shepherd 171. Shepherd says punk's throwaway line helps to "focus the attention . . . on the thoroughly alienated, quasi-schizoid individual it has produced—the individual who has been told he is so worthless he might as well not bother investing his singing with any great sense of self." Compare with the Ramones, Kurt Cobain, and Radiohead's "Creep."

6. Bangs 296.

7. Meltzer 243.

8. Stax 49.

9. Shaw 17, 21.

10. Norman, *Rave On* 112, 119.

11. Stax 78.

12. Robbins 807.

13. Gilmore, "Brothers" 131.

14. James Miller 77, 78.

15. Gracyk 102, 151–52.

16. Carson 445.

17. Christgau, *Any Old Way* 102–3.

11. Graceland

1. Marsh and Swenson, eds. 281, 280, 282, 366, 67.
2. Marsh, *Louie Louie* 5, 200, 5–6.
3. Robbins et al. 681, 679, 488, 3.
4. Robbins 213.
5. Carr and Farren 130.
6. Goldman 324–25.
7. Guralnick, *Careless Love* 538, 543.
8. Tosches, "Elvis in Death" 208.
9. Goldman 35, 31. On the Colonel's living quarters: "When you enter the Colonel's private quarters, you are assailed by a barrage of the same visual static. The rooms resemble a junk shop. They are crammed with chatzkahs, bric-a-brac, curios, mementos and gimmicks from floor to ceiling" (34).
10. Marcus, *Dead Elvis* 47–48, 64, 71, 192–93.
11. Marcus, *Mystery Train* 209.

12. Tell It Like It Is

1. Guterman and O'Donnell 101.
2. Ibid. 11.
3. Bangs 99.
4. Heylin, *Bob Dylan* 169, 168.
5. Guterman and O'Donnell 177.
6. Weberman, "The Art of Garbage Analysis" 114. See also *My Life in Garbology:* "After recovering from my shock and joy at finding an actual hand-written letter by my favorite poet in the trash can, I pulled myself together and began digging deeper, just barely aware that I was opening up the first chapter of a brand new science. I confess, though, that the overpowering odor of decaying food, raw onions, dirty diapers and dogshit was a strong argument for turning back. Nevertheless, I pushed onward because I knew that 'the answer was blowing in the wind' " (2).
7. Guterman and O'Donnell 160, 61, 64, 131, 12, 193. The companion volume to *The Worst Rock-and-Roll Records of All Time* is Guterman's *The Best Rock-and-Roll Records of All Time.* The trash trope pops up in his affection for the "trashy vitality" of the Rolling Stones (4) and his approval of the fact that the Sex Pistols "trashed as many of rock's traditions as they could" (167). He's glad Neil Young "threw away a certain career as a folk-rock/country-rock heartthrob for a more treacherous mixture of hard rock and hard turns" (54).
8. Bradley Smith 4.
9. Christgau, *Christgau's Record Guide* 381.
10. Burchill and Parsons 45, 46, 53, 54.
11. York 33. York inserts a photograph of "*That* Tony Parsons. *That* Julie Burchill" (128). They received "more hate mail than all the other writers together" at *New Musical Express* (34).
12. Burchill and Parsons 74.

13. Ibid. 61.

14. "The Fifty Most Essential Punk Records" 108–12.

15. Burchill and Parsons 64.

16. Duncan 240.

17. Carson 445.

18. Angio et al. 14–15.

19. Ramone and Kofman 20.

20. Strummer and Jones 3. A few years later, Strummer blamed punk's dismal state on fans who "wanted it to stay the same. . . . Now they got what they deserved: a lot of rubbish, basically" (Garbarini 104).

21. Burchill and Parsons 59, 66.

22. Bloom, "Notable and Quotable" 30. Junk food fueled Janis Joplin. Bill Graham remembers her asking him to get a bite to eat with her after a show. They "went to an all-night place where you could get food. She had some booze; we got some cheese and salami and crackers and Oreos—just garbage food" (163).

23. Bloom, *The Closing of the American Mind* 77, 64. Bloom averred that the rock 'n' roll industry cleverly "discovered a few years back that children are one of the few groups in the country with considerable disposable income" (76). Disposable income buys disposable music. J. D. Considine uses junk food imagery to dispense with AOR bands such as REO Speedwagon, Styx, Journey, and Foreigner: "At best, the music is a sophisticated test of its own limits; at worst, it's musical junk food, overly sweet and utterly non-nutritious" (11).

24. Burchill and Parsons 84, 85, 86, 91, 93.

13. Total Trash

1. Swirsky 153.

2. Strummer and Jones 4.

3. Wallis and Malm 166.

4. Wicke 145, 138, 144.

5. Savage 279.

6. McNeil and McCain 46, 299, 122, 149, 190, 299.

7. Marcus, *Lipstick Traces* 5. "[J]unk shops, car boot sales and warehouse clearances can still be a haven for the sussed record buyer," says Angus Batey in an article encouraging fans to browse "junk shops, second-hand furniture shops, even rubbish dumps—anywhere you can pick records up" (18).

14. Vicious

1. Falconer cover.

2. Kane.

3. Martin and Segrave 19, 21, 47, 50, 225, 157, 46–47.

4. "Rock 'n' Roll" 34.

5. "Rock and Roll and Riot" 16.

6. Robbins et al. 532.

15. Fame and Fortune

1. Regarding the "trash or smash" radio spot, see Reece 17; regarding the Trash-O-Rama tour, see Bitar 38.

2. Townsend 388, 393.

3. Jagger 47.

4. Gilmore, "The Rolling Stones" 90.

5. Flanagan 207, 253, 305.

6. Sting 295.

7. Meltzer 45, 551. Lagwagon continues the visual tradition on the sleeve of *Trashed* (Fat Wreck, 1994). An empty mayonnaise jar, a Budweiser can, a bottle of gin, an orange peel, and other trash form a circle around the band, posing dead center.

8. Meltzer 551–52.

9. Winner 38.

10. James Miller situates this conflict in radio programming of the midfifties: "most of the time, [programmers] feared, people, if left to choose for themselves, would choose junk—a betrayal of the industry's avowed commitment to good taste and high musical standards" (55).

16. Torn and Frayed

1. Erlewine, *All Music Guide* 254.

2. Lennon, interview 133.

3. Bangs, rev. of *Plastic Ono Band*, 18.

4. Giuliano 21, 22.

5. Lennon, interview 145.

6. Sheff 156, 173, 152, 160, 145, 151, 164, 151.

7. Ibid. 155, 169, 171, 172, 173, 155, 164, 180, 182, 183, 181.

8. Lennon lacked objectivity and admitted as much after Sheff asked, "You don't agree that the Beatles created the best rock 'n' roll that's been produced?" "I don't. I mean, then you get into the definition of what is rock 'n' roll, what is best, all that. But the Beatles, you see—I'm too involved in them artistically. I can't listen to them objectively" (61). In the 1971 interview with Wenner, Lennon confessed, "You know, we all say a lot of things when we don't know what we're talking about. I'm probably doing it now, I don't know what I say. . . . I'm just a guy that people ask all about things, and I blab off and some of it makes sense and some of it is bullshit and some of it's lies and some of it is—God knows what I'm saying" (136).

9. *Abbey Road* ranked number eight on vh1's "One Hundred Greatest Albums of Rock 'n' Roll."

10. Davies 214.

11. Giuliano 145, 149.

12. Harrison 163. Equally rubbishy, thought Harrison, was John Lennon's *Life with the Lions: Unfinished Music No. 2.*

13. Sharp 267, 271.

14. Everett, *The Beatles as Musicians: "Revolver" through the "Anthology"* 15, 18, 19, 20.

15. Ibid. 156, 106, 188, 198.

16. Everett, *The Beatles as Musicians: The Quarry Men through "Rubber Soul"* 289.

17. Norman, *Shout!* 307; Everett, *The Beatles as Musicians: "Revolver" through the "Anthology"* 5.

18. Rorem 154, 155.

19. Lewisohn 183.

17. Junk

1. John and Taupin 290; Fong-Torres, "Elton John" 196.

2. John and Taupin 290.

3. Lewisohn 11.

4. McCartney, interview by Timothy White 144.

5. Meltzer 48.

6. Meltzer, *The Aesthetics of Rock* 66.

7. Bockris, *Transformer* 71.

8. Milstein, Kostek, and Messer 133.

9. Ibid. 133.

10. Pepper and Pepper 84–85.

11. Kent, "The Four Ages" 247. Kent thinks junk ruined Iggy Pop: "[I]n no time at all the guy was a full-tilt junkie, as were most of the rest of the band. This in turn prompted a number of very ugly episodes, and after most of the Stooges' equipment got pawned for junk and Iggy had overdosed several times, the group dissolved" (247).

12. Kent, "Twilight in Babylon" 139. Kent quotes Ian Stewart's opinion that "Keith's drug problem was turning him into 'a walking bloody tragedy . . . a terrible waste of talent' " (131–32). Interested listeners should note that Alice in Chains focused an entire album on heroin addiction. *Dirt* (1992) is dissonant, clattering, painful music.

13. Duncan 100.

14. Mary Harron quoted in Julià 175.

15. Julià 175.

16. McNeil and McCain 18.

17. Sterling Morrison quoted in Bockris and Malanga 47.

18. Warhol 143, 144.

18. How Long

1. Bockris and Malanga 37.

2. Van Horn 110, 112.

3. Wartofsky A1.

4. Moodie and Callahan 92.

5. Nieman 16.

6. Tosches, *Unsung Heroes* 139, 142. Steve Calhoon of Skeleton Key has taken the idea of trash percussion to new heights, using propane tanks, movie reels, pots and pans, even

a child's wagon to drive the group, which takes "delight in trying to find beauty in the garbage" (White 3).

19. Catholic Boy

1. Bockris, *Transformer* 182.
2. Lou Reed quoted in Wrenn 100. Reed had an ear for superior trash. On "I Wanna Be Black," he tried to attain the superior disposable sound of Marvin Gaye's guitarist: "his throwaways are riffs that people would give their left ball for" (Wrenn 100).
3. Doggett 95.
4. Velvet Underground, "I Can't Stand It."
5. Auster 177.
6. Marsh, *Born to Run* 117, 127, 74, 11.

20. Sunny

1. Hendrix, liner notes.

21. Rape Me

1. Fricke, "Heart-Shaped Noise" 127.
2. Azerrad, *Come as You Are* 226–27.
3. Ibid. 43, 36, 201.
4. Ibid. 45.
5. Farren 52.
6. Butler, Trengove, and Lawrence 57.
7. Fletcher 449, 297, 293, 513, 476, 431, 528, 563, 181.
8. Azerrad, *Come as You Are* 40, 189, 169.
9. Ibid. 59, 16, 71.
10. Densmore 238.
11. The opening sequence of *The Kids Are Alright* presents the Who performing an explosive "My Generation" on the Smothers Brothers' television show. Keith Moon had rigged the bass drum with explosives, which he triggered during the mayhem at the end.
12. Azerrad, *Come as You Are* 110, 177. See page 177 in Azerrad for a photograph of the smashed guitar.
13. Ibid. 207.

22. Take It as It Comes

1. Hansen 94, 97.
2. Bemis 221–23.
3. Chonin 74.
4. Fong-Torres, "Rickie Lee Jones" 320.
5. Blitzer.
6. Mills 82.
7. Sheryl Crow quoted in Scapelliti 44.

8. Lou Reed quoted in Jones 36. Reed justifies "all that junk" in *Sally Can't Dance* on the pretext that "it's still Lou Reed" (64). Spitz 389.

9. Huey, "The Cramps."

10. Robbins et al. 532; Erlewine, *All Music Guide* 31.

11. Parker.

12. Kot 110.

13. Wildsmith 13.

14. Sheffield 188.

15. Gates 67.

16. Foege 43.

17. Savage 82.

18. Giles 73.

19. Boylan 36.

20. Verna, "Label Puts New Spin" 81.

21. Robbins 749.

22. Average n.p.

23. Agneta 209.

24. Cateforis, rev. of *Is This It?* 216.

23. Those Were the Days

1. "Night Life: Clubs" 22.

2. Tamarkin, rev. of *Yeah!* 108.

3. Valania 16.

4. Berkowitz 64.

5. Rabid, rev. of *Beatles 1* 179.

6. Rabid, "Chasing Pollard Crazy" 157.

24. Rip It Up

1. "Pop 100" 59.

2. "Back Street Boys."

3. "Pop 100" 69, 64, 70.

4. Phipps, Rabin, and Thompson.

25. There's a Place

1. Meisel 119.

2. Robbins et al. 688.

3. Legrand. Dave Marsh foreshadowed France's trash rock: Springsteen's "No Surrender" is "updated Sixties trash rock" (*Glory Days* 153). Reebee Garofalo refers to New York prepunk as "trash rock" (308).

26. Rock Show

1. Gilmore, "Life and Death" 150.

2. Norman, *Rave On* 173.

3. Martin and Segrave 132, 126, 76.

4. Tosches, *Hellfire* 145.

5. Norman, *Rave On* 194. In his autobiography, Berry mentions neither incident.

6. McNeil and McCain 369.

7. Moodie and Callahan 86, 87, 76, 74, 79.

8. Young and Lang 126.

9. Larson 120.

10. Booth 365.

27. Rock and Roll Music

1. Regev 96.

2. Drum Bum.

3. Roby 198; Marcus, "Rock Death in the 1970s" 59–78.

4. Tamarkin, rev. of *Blind Faith* 107.

5. Christgau, "(If I'm Acting Like a King That's Because)" 187, 188.

6. Heylin, *From the Velvets to the Voidoids* 72.

7. "The Sex Pistols were the catalyst for a genuine youth phenomenon. Punk . . . stirred the imagination with galvanic music, inventive dress and relevant personal politics which truly reflected the lifestyle, hopes and frustrations of a generation" (Coon 127).

8. Savage 606.

9. For a close reading of Sonic Youth's instrumentation (no lyrics discussed) in "Total Trash," see Cateforis, "'Total Trash'" 39–57.

10. This entry is dedicated to Derek Krissoff.

11. "The accordion we now use is actually by origin and definition a 'melodeon' because a pull out of the bellows gives a different note than a push in on the same button. . . . The word melodeon for our part is now considered obsolete" (Miller and Miller).

12. Thanks to Professor Tom Kitts, coeditor of *Living on a Thin Line: Crossing Aesthetic Borders with the Kinks* (2002), for fielding my question about the accordion on these tracks. Kitts wagers, in the absence of detailed liner credits, that the accordion (perhaps a keyboard function) is played by Ian Gibbons, who plays it on "Muswell Hillbillies" and "Do You Remember Walter?" Apparently instructing Gibbons to use it, Ray Davies says "accordion" twice before the band digs into "Muswell Hillbillies," Dave Davies first adding that somebody has to go fetch it.

13. The "friend" is my elder daughter, whom I thank for tracking down the lyrics that eluded me.

14. Radiohead, liner notes.

15. Doors, "The Wasp (Texas Radio and the Big Beat)"; Velvet Underground, "Run Run Run"; Rolling Stones, "Sympathy for the Devil"; Bob Dylan, "Don't Think Twice, It's Alright"; Black Flag, "Wasted"; Ian Dury and the Blockheads, "What a Waste."

28. The End

1. Lynyrd Skynyrd LS-2.
2. Norman, *Rave On* 259–60, 199.
3. Meltzer 319.
4. Marcus, *Dead Elvis* 184.

II. Wasted

29. Another One Bites the Dust

1. West, West, and Hebler 90.
2. Goldman 349.
3. Tennyson 90.
4. Elvis Presley Enterprises grosses more than $700 million a year and the King's record sales have surpassed the one billion mark (Phillips 55, 54). In 1997, 750,000 tourists visited Graceland (Brown 62). That year, Melinda Newman and Chris Morris outlined a flood of videos, remastered discs, deluxe box sets, television specials, books, fan clubs, and academic conferences devoted to Elvis. The twenty-fifth anniversary of his death, which occurred during the composition of this book, was accompanied by much commercial fanfare.

30. All Things Must Pass

1. The question posed by Reid Kanaley is, "Could Napster, MP3 audio, home networks, Internet radio, broadband connections, and ever-expanding computer power kill the compact disc?" The answer is yes. The music lover's future will entail not the collection of CDs but the manipulation of hardware and software.

2. Paul Peterson exposes the incompetence typified by VH1's special in 2000, "The One Hundred Greatest Women of Rock." Instantly the producers err by listing Billie Holiday at number six. Peterson's tally finds that "in addition to Holiday and [Dinah] Washington [at number forty-eight], there are another fifteen non-rockers on the list, making 17% of the list consist of non-rock performers. Ella Fitzgerald (13!), Sarah Vaughan (50), Lena Horne (62), Eartha Kitt (89), and Peggy Lee (93) are all legendary jazz and pop vocalists who are inexplicably on this list." Peterson questions the inclusion of blues and country names such as Ruth Brown (number sixty) and Tammy Wynette (number seventy-three). Peterson would delete these singers and add Wanda Jackson, Connie Francis, Lesley Gore, Irma Thomas, Lulu, and Marshall Chapman, classic rockers beneath the notice of VH1's bungling compilers.

3. As recently as fall 2000, Louis Menand repeated this history, concluding that "by the time the Beatles arrived, in February, 1964, the rock-and-roll component of the American pop scene was nearly moribund" (245). Earlier obituaries include one by Lester Bangs, who traced the seeds of doom to 1968, "finally culminating [in 1976] in the ascendance of things like disco and jazz-rock, which are dead enough to suggest the end of popular music as anything more than room spray" (224). In 1971, Peter Guralnick

wrote that rock 'n' roll expired at the end of Sun Records' reign. An affluent American white middle class consumed this once-rebellious product, which by the late sixties had become a music of nostalgia. American culture had subsumed and tamed "a liberating act" (*Feel Like Going Home* 175, 34, 35).

4. Croal 60.

5. Cost et al. 49.

6. Miller 17, 19.

7. Farren 48.

31. Shattered

1. Peyre 72.

2. Ibid. 77, 78.

3. Chateaubriand, *Atala* 53, 63.

4. Chateaubriand, *René* 96, 108, 106, 98.

5. David S. Reynolds 192.

6. Lippard 441.

7. A. Robert Lee 15.

8. Poe, "The Fall of the House of Usher" 325, 317, 321.

9. Lennon, *John Lennon/Plastic Ono Band*.

10. Paglia 358, 359.

11. There are hundreds of such accounts. A reader new to the field should consult Cohn, *Rock from the Beginning*; Tosches, *Hellfire*, especially pages 57–58 and 86–87; Gillett, *The Sound of the City*; Ward, *Rock of Ages*; Escott, *Good Rockin' Tonight*; Guralnick, *Feel Like Going Home*; and Miller, *Flowers in the Dustbin*. Those wishing to take the representative-man route should start with Guralnick's two-volume biography of Elvis Presley, *Last Train to Memphis* and *Careless Love*.

12. Paglia 364, 357, 361, 362, 358.

13. Pattison 112, 126.

14. Ibid. 173, 27, 6, 102.

15. Freud, *Civilization and Its Discontents* 27–28.

16. Robbins et al. 543.

17. Because the Weimar Constitution "was a politically contrived instrument, never commanding deeply rooted loyalty, never defining a true national consensus," it was powerless to stem radical opposition. "[T]he German Republic, precariously improvised to assure the armistice while heading off Bolshevik revolution, was racked for especially its first five years by political riots and murders, Communist uprisings, separatist plots, and attempted *coups d'état* . . . which drove the government from Berlin to Stuttgart and was broken only by a general strike . . . and the abortive National Socialist putsch in Munich in 1923, led by Adolf Hitler" (Detwiler 180).

18. Jonge 93.

19. Detwiler 181.

20. Jonge 102, 101.

21. Reissner 121, 122.

22. Whitford 1.

23. Gordon 24.

24. *The Weimar Republic Sourcebook,* edited by Anton Kaes, Martin Jay, and Edward Dimendberg, documents the Weimar epoch's "panoply of political, economic, social, and cultural models" in "[p]olitical blueprints, practical and utopian; cultural experiments, elitist and popular; social initiatives, progressive and reactionary," and "a frantic kaleidoscope shuffling of the fragments of a nascent modernity and the remnants of a persistent past" (xviii).

25. Lou Reed, *Berlin.* All citations from *Berlin* are derived from Reed, *Lou Reed, Pass Thru Fire.*

26. Died young after a life full of pleasure and excess (Michalski 57). The rest of the caption to a portrait of Berber by Otto Dix reads: "Anita Berber, actrice, danseuse de cabaret et reine de la bohème berlinoise était une de ces personnalités-types de son époque, dont Otto Dix tenait tant à faire le portrait. Dans le Berlin du début des années vingt, elle était aussi populaire que Marlene Dietrich." (Anita Berber, actress, cabaret dancer and queen of bohemian Berlin, was one of the personality types of her epoch, whose portrait Otto Dix was bent so much on doing. In Berlin at the beginning of the 1920s, she was as popular as Marlene Dietrich.) This exotic figure is named in Peter Jelavich's *Berlin Cabaret:* Berber was "[n]otorious for bisexuality and cocaine addiction in her private life, but respected for the artistry, passion, and intensity of her performances" (164). Reports from vice squads reveal that Berber's stage show gave oglers plenty of posterior and labia over which to drool.

27. Doggett 87.

28. Christgau, *Christgau's Record Guide* 322.

29. Simels 102.

30. The Move, "California Man"; Beatles, "Birthday"; Elvis Presley, "Party."

31. Who, "My Generation"; Beatles, "Yer Blues"; Rolling Stones, "Paint It, Black."

32. But we can't overlook the Velvet Underground's *Loaded,* where Lou Reed's love of pop shines. The few dark moments on *Loaded* are beautiful too.

33. Freud, "Mourning and Melancholia" 246.

34. Boym 41, xviii, 13.

35. Levinson 25.

36. Greenleaf 27.

37. McFarland 5, 4, 11, 13. McFarland notes that "early death not only afflicted Schubert and Keats but became almost a norm: by suicide, as with Chatterton, by misadventure, as with Shelley, by disease, as with Byron." From there, McFarland lists other casualties of diasparactive romanticism: lives broken by drugs, insanity, and other ways of dying "in little pieces" (15, 16).

38. Hume 123, 124.

39. Dylan, "Love Sick."

III. Saved

33. Rock and Roll

1. Strausbaugh 184.
2. Lindsay 29–30, 30. Friedlander wrote *Rock and Roll: A Social History*. Santelli was vice president of education and public programming at the museum and is now an executive at Experience Music Project. Epstein edited *Adolescents and Their Music*.
3. In 1969, Richard Goldstein published *The Poetry of Rock*. David R. Pichaske published *The Poetry of Rock: The Golden Years* in 1981. In 1999, a poetry of rock course would seem to be passé at best, reactionary at worst.
4. Lindsay 31.
5. Pichaske, *Beowulf to Beatles and Beyond*. "Rock was meant to be heard, not seen," wrote Richard Goldstein, adding, "all rock lyrics are altered by versification" and separated from their music many are "reduced to drivel" (xi). Good vocalists transform trite lyrics by singing with sincerity, passion, dynamics, and charisma. "I Want to Hold Your Hand," words a seventh-grade boy with a crush on the girl in the next row might scrawl to her in a secret in-class note, is a tour de force when the Beatles belt it out in three-part harmony; its melody, harmony, beat, and words give goose bumps to grown men who've heard it five hundred times. But it isn't poetry.
6. Who, "Won't Get Fooled Again."
7. Pichaske, *Beowulf to Beatles and Beyond* xiv. Pichaske's preoccupation with "relevance" led to side-by-side readings of Jim Croce and Thomas Hardy.
8. Viola 20, 21.
9. Cather 243.
10. Ibid. 243, 244.
11. Ibid. 245, 246, 247.
12. Ibid. 248. After I presented a draft of this section at a conference, a man introduced himself and congratulated me for noticing what he thought everyone else seems to have missed, that Paul is gay. This scholar informed me that he, being gay, should know. But others had noticed this too. See Claude Summers, "A Losing Game in the End."
13. Ibid. 250, 243; Marsh, *Born to Run* 13.
14. I began the paragraph by paraphrasing the Beatles, "There's a Place"; Cather 251.
15. Cather 253, 254.
16. Ibid. 256, 257.
17. Ibid. 258, 259, 259–60, 260.
18. Csikszentmihalyi and Larson 21, 20. Contributing to Paul's problem, these scholars might say, is that "schools are essentially machines for providing negative feedback" (198).
19. McCartney, interview by Julia Baird 304. Other flamboyant rock managers/agents, straight and gay, have been Andrew Loog Oldham, Malcolm McLaren, and David Geffen, "fortunate people born to the purple" so envied by Paul. Summers 109.
20. Summers 110.
21. Paul "could not remember the time when he had not been dreading something.

Even when he was a little boy, it was always there—behind him, or before, or on either side. There had always been the shadowed corner, the dark place into which he dared not look" (Cather 255). Just before the suicide, he looks into this corner "and knew. It was bad enough, what he saw there, but somehow not so bad as his long fear of it had been" (259–60).

22. Summers 112.

23. Dr. Anthony Flood, Dr. Leonard Neustatter, and Dr. Leonard Henry, quoted in Booth 282.

24. Aronowitz 627.

25. Robinson 125, 126. James Woodress observes that the crime in "Paul's Case" was modeled on the case of two boys from Pittsburgh who stole money from an employer and then squandered it in Chicago. They were pursued and brought back, and their parents reimbursed the employer. During her Pittsburgh years, Cather occasionally visited New York City, which impressed her as much as it impressed Paul (174). Hermione Lee writes that Cather "drew [Paul] from a boy she once had in a Latin class in her Pittsburgh teaching days, a restive, nervous show-off, always trying to attract attention." This "Paul" didn't jump in front of a train (21). Lee says nothing about Paul's sexuality. More important to her is Cather's lesbianism.

26. Robinson 126.

27. Gundersen's figures are from the Recording Industry Association of America.

28. "Picks" 256.

29. Miles 21.

30. Coleman 108, 109.

31. Patti Smith, "Jag-ahr of the Jungle" 186.

32. Bockris, *Keith Richards* 27, 29.

33. Williams 121.

34. Gaines 85, 86.

35. Wiederhorn 100, 39.

36. Corgan.

37. Larner 47; Hall and Whannel 280; Ward 180; Wenner 13–14; London 24, 25.

38. Björk, "Headphones."

39. Gilmore, "The Road from Nowhere" 113–14.

40. Azerrad, "Inside the Heart and Mind of Nirvana" 38.

41. Gilmore, "The Road from Nowhere" 115.

42. Fricke, "In Utero" 54.

43. Mundy 29.

44. Milstein, "Notes from the Velvet Underground," *The Velvet Underground Companion* 10, 11.

45. Willis 117.

46. Gaines 89.

47. These blunt mottos can be found at the self-styled "ultimative Punk and Underground Search Engine," <http://www.casmira.com>, and at <http://www.mrlady.com>.

48. Gill 81, 83.

49. Barnes 104.

50. Marsh, *Born to Run* 31, xvi.

51. Sorrell 81, 89.

52. Larson 121.

53. Steve Miller, "Jet Airliner."

54. Huey, "The Sex Pistols" 358.

34. The End

1. Derrida 158.

2. Kernan 79.

3. Ibid. 86.

4. Jameson 96, 31, 77, 78.

5. Beatles, "Helter Skelter."

Appendix

1. Adorno 458.

2. Unterberger 29.

WORKS CITED

Adorno, Theodor W. "On Popular Music." *Essays on Music.* Ed. Richard Leppert. Trans. Susan H. Gillespie. Berkeley: University of California Press, 2002. 437–68.

Agneta, Neal. Rev. of *River City High Won't Turn You Down,* by River City High. *Big Takeover* 49.22.2 (2001): 209.

Aldersey-Williams, Hugh. "The English Patent." *New Statesman* 28 Feb. 1997: 40–41.

Alexander, Judd. *In Defense of Garbage.* Westport, Conn.: Praeger, 1993.

Ammons, A. R. *Garbage.* New York: Norton, 1993.

Angio, Joe, et al. "Who Let the Dogs Out?" *Time Out New York* Feb. 2002: 13–17.

Armstrong, Ken. "LP Scratches Its Way Out of Libraries: Down to a Last Haven, Vinyl Slowly Fades Out." *Chicago Tribune* 23 Nov. 1994, north sports final ed.: 1.

Aronowitz, Al. "Over Their Dead Bodies—Memories of Brian and Jim." *The Penguin Book of Rock and Roll Writing.* Ed. Clinton Heylin. New York: Viking, 1992. 626–32.

Auster, Paul. *City of Glass.* New York: Penguin, 1987.

Average, Matt. Rev. of *Pass You By,* by Apology. *Maximum Rock 'n' Roll* May 1995: n.p.

Azerrad, Michael. *Come as You Are: The Story of Nirvana.* New York: Main Street/ Doubleday, 1994.

———. "Inside the Heart and Mind of Nirvana." *Cobain.* Ed. Holly George-Warren. New York: Rolling Stone Press, 1994. 32–39.

"Back Street Boys." Rock on the Net. 3 July 2001 <http://www.rockonthenet.com>.

Bangs, Lester. Rev. of *Plastic Ono Band,* by Yoko Ono. *The Rolling Stone Record Review: The Authoritative Guide to Contemporary Records.* Vol. 2. New York: Pocket, 1974. 18–20.

———. *Psychotic Reactions and Carburetor Dung.* Ed. Greil Marcus. New York: Knopf, 1987.

Barnes, Richard. *The Who: Maximum R and B.* New York: St. Martin's, 1982.

Batey, Angus. "Yeah, We Got the Junk." *Mojo* May 2001: 18–19.

Bemis, Alec Hanley. "Junk-Yard Angel." *New Yorker* 14/21 Oct. 2002: 220–23.

Berkowitz, Kenny. Rev. of *Nobody Can Dance,* by Big Star. *Magnet* June/July 1999: 64–65.

Bitar, Marcelo Fernandez. "Sony Puts Argentina into 'Trance.'" *Billboard* 30 Sept. 1995: 38.

Blitzer, John. "The Ten Essential Alternative/Indie Albums of 2000." 4 Jan. 2001 <http://www.cdnow.com>.

Bloom, Allan. *The Closing of the American Mind.* New York: Touchstone, 1987.

———. "Notable and Quotable." *Wall Street Journal* 2 May 1983: 30.

Bockris, Victor. *Keith Richards: The Biography.* New York: Poseidon, 1992.

———. *Transformer: The Lou Reed Story.* New York: Simon and Schuster, 1994.

Bockris, Victor, and Gerard Malanga. *Up-Tight: The Velvet Underground Story.* New York: Omnibus, 1983.

Bombardier. Advertisement. *Big Takeover* 49.22.2 (2001): 24.

Bomp Records Advertisement. *Big Takeover* 49.22.2 (2001): 33.

Booth, Stanley. *Dance with the Devil: The Rolling Stones and Their Times.* New York: Random House, 1984.

Boylan, J. Gabriel. Rev. of *Put Us in Tune,* by Thou. *Philadelphia Weekly* 11 April 2001: 36.

Boym, Svetlana. *The Future of Nostalgia.* New York: Basic, 2001.

Brown, Corie. "Look Who's Takin' Care of Business." *Newsweek* 18 Aug. 1997: 62.

Broydo, Leora. "Truth in a Jar: Good Things Don't Always Need Packages." *Mother Jones* Sept.–Oct. 1996: 19.

Burchill, Julie, and Tony Parsons. *"The Boy Looked at Johnny": The Obituary of Rock 'n' Roll.* London: Pluto Press, 1978.

Butler, Dougal, Chris Trengove, and Peter Lawrence. *Full Moon: The Amazing Rock and Roll Life of the Late Keith Moon.* New York: Morrow, 1981.

C.A. "Disgraceland: The Worst Records of the Year." *Stereo Review* Feb. 1997: 46.

Carr, Roy, and Mick Farren. *Elvis: The Illustrated Record.* New York: Harmony, 1982.

Carson, Tom. "Rocket to Russia." *On Record: Rock, Pop, and the Written Word.* Ed. Simon Frith and Andrew Goodwin. New York: Pantheon, 1990. 441–49.

Casmira.com. 6 July 2004 <http://www.casmira.com>.

Cateforis, Theo. Rev. of *Is This It?* by the Strokes. *Big Takeover* 49.22.2 (2001): 216.

———. " 'Total Trash': Analysis and Post Punk Music." *Journal of Popular Music Studies* 5 (1993): 39–57.

Cather, Willa. "Paul's Case: A Study in Temperament." *Willa Cather's Collected Short Fiction 1892–1912.* Vol. 2. Ed. Virginia Faulkner. Lincoln: University of Nebraska Press, 1970. 243–61.

Celestial Harmonies. *In the Gardens of Pharao, Aguirre* (1983), by Popol Vuh. *2000 Celestial Harmonies Compact Disk Catalogue.*

Chateaubriand, Francois-René de. *Atala.* Trans. Irving Putter. Berkeley: University of California Press, 1980.

———. *René.* Trans. Irving Putter. Berkeley: University of California Press, 1980.

Chonin, Neva. Rev. of *Thirteen Tales from Urban Bohemia,* by the Dandy Warhols. *Rolling Stone* 31 Aug. 2000: 74.

Christgau, Robert. *Any Old Way You Choose It: Rock and Other Pop Music, 1967–1973.* New York: Cooper Square, 2000.

———. *Christgau's Record Guide: Rock Albums of the Seventies.* New Haven: Ticknor and Fields, 1981.

———. "(If I'm Acting Like a King That's Because) I'm a Human Being: New York Dolls." *Grown Up All Wrong: Seventy-five Great Rock and Pop Artists from Vaudeville to Techno.* Cambridge: Harvard University Press, 1998. 187–200.

Chuswid, Irwin. "The Shaggs: Groove Is in the Heart." *Songs in the Key of Z: The Curious Universe of Outsider Music.* Chicago: A Cappella, 2000. 1–11.

Cohn, Nik. *Rock from the Beginning.* New York: Stein and Day, 1969.

Coleman, Ray. *Lennon.* New York: McGraw-Hill, 1984.

Coleridge, Samuel Taylor. "1812–13 Lectures on Belles Lettres." *Lectures 1808–1819 on Lit-*

erature. Vol. 5 of *The Collected Works of Samuel Taylor Coleridge.* 23 vols. Ed. R. A. Foakes. Princeton: Princeton University Press, 1987. 493–95.

Considine, J. D. "AOR Rock." *Musician Player and Listener: The Year in Rock 1981–82.* Ed. John Swenson. New York: Delilah, 1981. 11–15.

Coon, Caroline. *1988: The New Wave Punk Rock Explosion.* New York: Hawthorn, 1977.

Corgan, Billy. "Smashing Pumpkin Interviews." *ABC Spanish Magazine* 11 Nov. 2002 <http://www.starla.org/articles/spanish.htm>.

Cost, Jud, et al. "Rock Solid." *Magnet* Sept./Oct. 2001: 49–54.

Croal, N'Gai. "Long Live Rock 'n' Rap." *Newsweek* 19 July 1999: 60–62.

Csikszentmihalyi, Mihaly, and Reed Larson. *Being Adolescent: Conflict and Growth in the Teenage Years.* New York: Basic, 1984.

Dahl, Shawn, ed. *Rolling Stone Raves: What Your Rock and Roll Favorites Favor.* New York: Rolling Stone Press, 1999.

Dannen, Fredric. *Hit Men: Power Brokers and Fast Money Inside the Music Business.* New York: Vintage, 1991.

Davies, Hunter. *The Beatles.* New York: McGraw-Hill, 1978.

Denby, David. "My Problem with Perfection." *New Yorker* 26 Aug./2 Sept. 1996: 64–83.

Denisoff, R. Serge. *Solid Gold: The Popular Music Industry.* New Brunswick, N.J.: Transaction, 1975.

———. *Tarnished Gold: The Record Industry Revisited.* New Brunswick, N.J.: Transaction, 1986.

Densmore, John. *Riders on the Storm: My Life with Jim Morrison and the Doors.* New York: Delta, 1991.

Derrida, Jacques. *Of Grammatology.* Trans. Gayatri Chakravorty Spivak. Baltimore: Johns Hopkins University Press, 1976.

Detwiler, Donald S. *Germany: A Short History.* Carbondale: Southern Illinois University Press, 1976.

Dickerson, G. W. "Solid Waste: Trash to Treasure in an Urban Environment." *New Mexico Journal of Science* Nov. 1999: 166.

Doggett, Peter. *Lou Reed: Growing Up in Public.* London: Omnibus, 1992.

Drum Bum. Lessons. 1 Sept. 2002 <http://www.drumsdatabase.com/bodiddley.htm>.

Duncan, Robert. *The Noise: Notes from a Rock 'n' Roll Era.* New York: Ticknor and Fields, 1984.

Dvorak, John. "Our Legacy: Computer Junk." *PC Magazine* 6 Feb. 2001: 91.

Elliott, Victoria Stagg. "Needles Used at Home Need a Place to Go." *American Medical News* 26 Feb. 2001: 26.

Ellis, James E. "Should Compact Disks Come in Compact Boxes?" *BusinessWeek* 24 Dec. 1990: 30.

Emerson, Ralph Waldo. "An Address Delivered before the Senior Class in Divinity College, Cambridge, Sunday Evening, July 15, 1838." *Ralph Waldo Emerson: Essays and Lectures.* New York: Library of America, 1983. 73–92.

———. "The Poet." *Ralph Waldo Emerson: Essays and Lectures.* New York: Library of America, 1983. 445–68.

Environmental Protection Agency. "Collecting Used Oil for Recycling/Reuse." March 1994. 3 Feb. 2001 <http://www.epa.gov/epaoswer/non-hw/recycle/recy-oil.pdf>.

———. "Environmental Fact Sheet: Recycling Grass Clippings." July 1992. 3 Feb. 2001 <http://www.epa.gov/epaoswer/osw/citizens.htm>.

———. "Household Hazardous Waste: Steps to Safe Management." 3 Feb. 2001 <http://www.epa.gov/epaoswer/non-hw/household/hhw.htm>.

———. "Industrial Waste Management." 25 June 2003 <http://www.epa.gov/epaoswer/non-hw/industd/index.htm>.

———. "Municipal Solid Waste in the United States: 1999 Facts and Figures." July 2001:2. 25 June 2003 <http://www.epa.gov/epaoswer/non-hw/muncpl/mswfinal.pdf>.

Epstein, Jonathon, ed. *Adolescents and Their Music: If It's Too Loud, You're Too Old*. New York: Garland, 1994.

Erlewine, Stephen Thomas. *All Music Guide: The Definitive Guide to Popular Music*. 4th ed. Ed. Vladimir Bogdanov, Chris Woodstra, and Stephen Thomas Erlewine. San Francisco: Backbeat Books, 2001.

Escott, Colin. *Good Rockin' Tonight: Sun Records and the Birth of Rock 'n' Roll*. New York: St. Martin's Press, 1991.

Everett, Walter. *The Beatles as Musicians: The Quarry Men through "Rubber Soul."* New York: Oxford University Press, 2001.

———. *The Beatles as Musicians: "Revolver" through the "Anthology."* New York: Oxford University Press, 1999.

Falconer, Ian. "A New Low." Cartoon. *New Yorker* 5 March 2001: cover.

Farren, Mick. "Of Grammys, Death, Radio and the Egg McMuffin." *Trouser Press* June 1982: 48, 52.

"The Fifty Most Essential Punk Records." *Spin* May 2001: 108–12.

"First-Half CD Shipments at All-Time High." *Consumer Electronics* Sept. 2000: n.p.

Flanagan, Bill. *Written in My Soul: Conversations with Rock's Great Songwriters*. Chicago: Contemporary Books, 1987.

Fletcher, Tony. *Moon: The Life and Death of a Rock Legend*. New York: Spike/Avon: 1999.

Foege, Alec. Rev. of *Version 2.0*, by Garbage. *People Weekly* 15 June 1998: 43.

Fong-Torres, Ben. "Elton John: The Four-Eyed Bitch Is Back," *Not Fade Away: A Backstage Pass to Twenty Years of Rock and Roll*. San Francisco: Miller Freeman, 1999. 185–96.

———. "Rickie Lee Jones: Say Good-bye to That Slinky Black Dress." *Not Fade Away: A Backstage Pass to Twenty Years of Rock and Roll*. San Francisco: Miller Freeman, 1999. 319–23.

Fornäs, Johan. "The Future of Rock: Discourses That Struggle to Define a Genre." *Popular Music* 14.1 (1995): 111–25.

Freud, Sigmund. *Civilization and Its Discontents*. Trans. and ed. James Strachey. New York: Norton, 1961.

———. "Mourning and Melancholia." *The Standard Edition of the Complete Psychological Works of Sigmund Freud*. Trans. and ed. James Strachey. Vol. 14. London: Hogarth, 1957. 243–58.

Fricke, David. "Heart-Shaped Noise." *Cobain.* Ed. Holly George-Warren. New York: Rolling Stone Press, 1994. 124–27.

———. "In Utero." *Cobain.* Ed. Holly George-Warren. New York: Rolling Stone Press, 1994. 54.

Friedlander, Paul. *Rock and Roll: A Social History.* New York: Westview, 1996.

Gaines, Donna. "Sylvia's Husband." *The Velvet Underground Companion: Four Decades of Commentary.* Ed. Albin Zak III. New York: Schrimer, 1997. 85–93.

Garbarini, Vic. "Rude Boys: An Interview with Joe Strummer and Robert Fripp." *Musician Player and Listener: The Year in Rock 1981–82.* Ed. John Swenson. New York: Delilah, 1981. 102–7.

Garofalo, Reebee. *Rockin' Out: Popular Music in the U.S.A.* Boston: Allyn and Bacon, 1997.

Gates, David. Rev. of *Version 2.0,* by Garbage. *Newsweek* 1 June 1998: 67.

Gendron, Bernard. "Theodor Adorno Meets the Cadillacs." *Studies in Entertainment: Critical Approaches to Mass Culture.* Ed. Tania Modleski. Bloomington: Indiana University Press, 1986. 18–36.

Giles, Jeff. "A Great New Aerosmith CD? Yeah, Right, Dream On." *Newsweek* 12 March 2001: 73.

Gill, John. *Queer Noises: Male and Female Homosexuality in Twentieth-Century Music.* Minneapolis: University of Minnesota Press, 1995.

Gillen, Marilyn A. "CD, Jewel-Box Recycling Under Way at Some Plants." *Billboard* 22 May 1993: 12, 102.

Gillett, Charlie. *The Sound of the City: The Rise of Rock and Roll.* New York: Pantheon, 1983.

Gilmore, Mikal. "Brothers: The Allman Brothers Band." *Night Beat: A Shadow History of Rock and Roll.* New York: Picador, 1998. 115–39.

———. "Life and Death in the U.K." *Night Beat: A Shadow History of Rock and Roll.* New York: Picador, 1998. 150–64.

———. "The Road from Nowhere." *Cobain.* Ed. Holly George-Warren. New York: Rolling Stone Press, 1994. 112–18.

———. "The Rolling Stones' Journey into Fear." *Night Beat: A Shadow History of Rock and Roll.* New York: Picador, 1998. 72–91.

Giuliano, Geoffrey. *The Lost Beatles Interviews.* New York: Plume, 1994.

Global Environmental Change. Report, 14 Dec. 2001: 1.

Goldberg, Michael. "The Battle over the Box." *Rolling Stone* 28 June 1990: 20.

Goldman, Albert. *Elvis.* New York: McGraw-Hill: 1981.

Goldstein, Richard. Preface. *The Poetry of Rock.* Ed. Richard Goldstein. New York: Bantam, 1969. xi–xii.

Goodman, Fred. *The Mansion on the Hill: Dylan, Young, Geffen, Springsteen, and the Head-on Collision of Rock and Commerce.* New York: Vintage, 1998.

Gordon, Mel. *Voluptuous Panic: The Erotic World of Weimar Berlin.* Venice, Calif.: Feral House, 2000.

Gracyk, Theodore. *Rhythm and Noise: An Aesthetics of Rock.* Durham: Duke University Press, 1996.

Graham, Bill. Interview by Michael Goldberg. *The Rolling Stone Interviews: The 1980s.* Ed. Sid Holt. New York: St. Martin's, 1989. 159–67.

Greengard, Samuel. "Getting Rid of the Paper Chase." *Workforce* Nov. 1999: 69.

Greenleaf, Monika. *Pushkin and Romantic Fashion: Fragment, Elegy, Orient, Irony.* Stanford: Stanford University Press, 1994.

Gundersen, Edna. "Beatles on Top of the Century." *USA Today* 9 November 1999.

Guralnick, Peter. *Careless Love: The Unmaking of Elvis Presley.* Boston: Little, Brown, 1999.

———. *Feel Like Going Home: Portraits in Blues and Rock 'n' Roll.* Boston: Little, Brown, 1971.

———. *Last Train to Memphis: The Rise of Elvis Presley.* Boston: Little, Brown, 1994.

Guterman, Jimmy. *The Best Rock-and-Roll Records of All Time: A Fan's Guide to the Stuff You Love.* New York: Citadel, 1992.

Guterman, Jimmy, and Owen O'Donnell. *The Worst Rock-and-Roll Records of All Time: A Fan's Guide to the Stuff You Love to Hate!* New York: Citadel, 1991.

Hall, Stuart, and Paddy Whannel. *The Popular Arts.* New York: Pantheon, 1965.

Hamilton, Anita. "How Do You Junk Your Computer?" *Time* 12 Feb. 2001: 70–71.

Hansen, Beck. Interview by Mark Kemp. *Rolling Stone* 17 April 1997: 58–64, 94, 97.

Harrison, George. Interview by Timothy White. *Rock Lives: Profiles and Interviews.* New York: Holt, 1990. 151–74.

Henderson, David. *'Scuse Me While I Kiss the Sky: The Life of Jimi Hendrix.* New York: Bantam, 1981.

Hendrix, Jimi. Liner notes. *First Rays of the New Rising Sun.* MCA, 1997.

Heylin, Clinton. *Bob Dylan: The Recording Sessions 1960–1994.* New York: St. Martin's, 1995.

———. *From the Velvets to the Voidoids: A Pre-Punk History for a Post-Punk World.* New York: Penguin, 1993.

Horowitz, Is. "$50 Million Returns Bite Stirs Action." *Billboard* 9 June 1979: 1, 106.

Huey, Steve. "The Cramps." Artist Direct Network. 2 April 2001 <http://ubl.artistdirect.com>.

———. "The Sex Pistols." *All Music Guide: The Definitive Guide to Popular Music.* 4th ed. Ed. Vladimir Bogdanov, Chris Woodstra, and Stephen Thomas Erlewine. San Francisco: Backbeat Books, 2001. 254.

Hume, Robert D. "Exuberant Gloom, Existential Agony, and Heroic Despair: Three Varieties of Negative Romanticism." *The Gothic Imagination: Essays in Dark Romanticism.* Ed. G. R. Thompson. Pullman: Washington State University Press, 1975. 109–27.

Jagger, Mick. Interview by Jonathan Cott. *The Rolling Stone Interviews 1967–1980: Talking with the Legends of Rock and Roll.* Ed. Peter Herbst. New York: Rolling Stone Press, 1981. 44–50.

Jameson, Fredric. *Postmodernism, or The Cultural Logic of Late Capitalism.* Durham: Duke University Press, 1991.

Jefferson, Thomas. "To Benjamin Rush, with a Syllabus." 21 April 1803. *Letters. Thomas Jefferson: Writings.* New York: Library of America. 1984. 1122–26.

————. "To William Short." 4 August 1820. *Letters. Thomas Jefferson: Writings.* New York: Library of America, 1984. 1435–40.

Jelavich, Peter. *Berlin Cabaret.* Cambridge: Harvard University Press, 1993.

John, Elton, and Bernie Taupin. Interview by Paul Gambaccini. *The Rolling Stone Interviews 1967–1980: Talking with the Legends of Rock and Roll.* Ed. Peter Herbst. New York: Rolling Stone Press, 1981. 288–98.

Jones, Allan. "Don't Make Me Cry—There's Only One Lou Reed." *Melody Maker* 13 May 1978: 34–36, 64.

Jonge, Alex de. *The Weimar Chronicle: Prelude to Hitler.* New York: Meridian, 1978.

Julià, Ignacio. "Feedback: The Legend of the Velvet Underground, the Fully Revised Version (1986–1996)." *The Velvet Underground Companion: Four Decades of Commentary.* Ed. Albin Zak III. New York: Schrimer, 1997. 175.

Kaes, Anton, Martin Jay, and Edward Dimendberg. Preface. *The Weimar Republic Sourcebook.* Ed. Anton Kaes, Martin Jay, and Edward Dimendberg. Berkeley: University of California Press, 1994. xvii–xx.

Kanaley, Reid. "Experts Say Compact Discs May Become Extinct Due to New Technology." *Philadelphia Inquirer* 18 Jan. 2001: n.p.

Kane, Dan. "Marilyn Manson Postpones Concerts: Claims Respect for Victims, but Denies Blame." *Repository* 29 April 1999.

Kantor, Linda Scott, et al. "Estimating and Addressing America's Food Losses." *Food Review* Jan.–April 1997: 2.

Kent, Nick. "The Four Ages of a Man Named Pop: Pictures of Iggy." *The Dark Stuff: Selected Writings on Rock Music, 1972–1995.* New York: Penguin, 1994. 244–66.

————. "Twilight in Babylon: The Rolling Stones after the Sixties." *The Dark Stuff: Selected Writings on Rock Music, 1972–1995.* New York: Penguin, 1994. 126–54.

Kernan, Alvin. *The Death of Literature.* New Haven: Yale University Press, 1990.

Kitts, Thomas M., and Michael J. Kraus, eds. *Living on a Thin Line: Crossing Aesthetic Borders with the Kinks.* Rumford, R.I.: Rock 'n' Roll Research Press, 2002.

Kot, Greg. "Menace to Propriety." *Rolling Stone* 17 March 2001: 110.

Lagwagon. Album cover. *Trashed.* Fat Wreck, 1994.

Landau, Jon. "Rock and Art." *It's Too Late to Stop Now: A Rock and Roll Journal.* San Francisco: Straight Arrow, 1972. 129–34.

Larner, Jeremy. "What Do They Get from Rock 'n' Roll?" *Atlantic* 214.2 (1964): 44–49.

Larson, Bob. *Rock and Roll: The Devil's Diversion.* McCook, Nebr.: Bob Larson, 1967.

Lee, Hermione. *Willa Cather: Double Lives.* New York: Pantheon, 1989.

Lee, A. Robert. Introduction. *Edgar Allan Poe: The Design of Order.* Ed. Robert A. Lee. London: Vision, 1987. 7–15.

Legrand, Emmanuel. " 'Trash' Overflows in France: New Bands with Noise, Attitude." *Billboard* 14 May 1994. 1, 108.

Lennon, John. Interview by Jann S. Wenner. *The Rolling Stone Interviews 1967–1980: Talking with the Legends of Rock and Roll.* Ed. Peter Herbst. New York: Rolling Stone Press, 1981. 128–55.

Levinson, Marjorie. *The Romantic Fragment Poem: A Critique of a Form.* Chapel Hill: University of North Carolina Press, 1986.

Lewisohn, Mark. *The Beatles Recording Sessions.* New York: Harmony, 1988.

"Lighting Disposal." *American School and University* Nov. 1998: 287.

Lindsay, Drew. "So You Want to Be a Rock and Roll Teacher." *Teacher* Jan. 1999: 29–32.

Lippard, George. *The Quaker City; or, The Monks of Monk Hall: A Romance of Philadelphia Life, Mystery, and Crime.* Ed. David S. Reynolds. Amherst: University of Massachusetts Press, 1995.

London, Herbert I. *Closing the Circle: A Cultural History of the Rock Revolution.* Chicago: Nelson-Hall, 1984.

Long, April. Rev. of *The Photo Album*, by Death Cab for Cutie. *Mojo* April 2002: 96.

Lux, Joanna. Rev. of *Live Rust*, by Neil Young. *Inkblot* 11 Nov. 2002 <http://www.inkblotmagazine.com/rev-archive/Neil_Young_Live_Rust.htm>.

Lynyrd Skynyrd. Interview by John Swenson. *Billboard* 5 Dec. 1998.

Marcus, Greil. *Dead Elvis: A Chronicle of a Cultural Obsession.* Cambridge: Harvard University Press, 1991.

———. *Lipstick Traces: A Secret History of the Twentieth Century.* Cambridge: Harvard University Press, 1990.

———. *Mystery Train: Images of America in Rock 'n' Roll Music.* Rev. ed. New York: Dutton, 1982.

———. "Rock Death in the 1970s: A Sweepstakes." *Ranters and Crowd Pleasers: Punk in Pop Music 1977–92.* New York: Doubleday, 1993. 59–78.

Maroney, Tyler. "Why Is CD Packaging So Godawful? (First Great Questions of Our Age)." *Fortune* 8 Nov. 1999: 54.

Marsh, Dave. *Born to Run.* Vol. 1 of *The Bruce Springsteen Story.* New York: Thunder's Mouth, 1996.

———. *Glory Days.* Vol. 2 of *The Bruce Springsteen Story.* New York: Thunder's Mouth, 1996.

———. *Louie Louie: The History and Mythology of the World's Most Famous Rock 'n' Roll Song.* New York: Hyperion, 1993.

Marsh, Dave, and John Swenson, eds. *The Rolling Stone Record Guide.* New York: Rolling Stone Press, 1979.

Martin, Linda, and Kerry Segrave. *Anti-Rock: The Opposition to Rock 'n' Roll.* New York: Da Capo, 1988.

Martin, Sam. "Recycle This Article." *Mother Earth News* Dec. 2000/Jan. 2001: 59–60, 62, 94.

Martin, Steve. "Designer of Audio CD Packaging Enters Hell." *New Yorker* 19 April 1999: 53.

Masson, Gordon. "World Sales Remain Stagnant." *Billboard* 29 April 2000: 10, 22.

McCartney, Paul. Interview by Julia Baird. *The Lost Beatles Interviews*. Ed. Geoffrey Giuliano. New York: Plume, 1994. 289–305.

———. Interview by Timothy White. *Rock Lives: Profiles and Interviews*. New York: Holt, 1990. 122–50.

McFarland, Thomas. *Romanticism and the Forms of Ruin: Wordsworth, Coleridge, and Modalities of Fragmentation*. Princeton: Princeton University Press, 1981.

McNeil, Legs, and Gillian McCain. *Please Kill Me: The Uncensored Oral History of Punk*. New York: Grove, 1996.

Meisel, Perry. *The Cowboy and the Dandy: Crossing over from Romanticism to Rock and Roll*. New York: Oxford University Press, 1999.

Meltzer, Richard. *The Aesthetics of Rock*. New York: Da Capo, 1970.

———. *A Whore Just Like the Rest: The Music Writings of Richard Meltzer*. New York: Da Capo, 2000.

Menand, Louis. "Why They Were Fab." *New Yorker* 16/23 Oct. 2000: 236–46.

Meyer, Frank. "CBS Cuts Returns Policy, Catalog Prices in Bid to Ease Disk Blues." *Variety* 5 Sept. 1979: 83, 87.

Michalski, Sergiusz. *Nouvelle Objectivité: Peinture, Arts Graphique et Photographie en Allemagne, 1919–1933*. Köln: Taschen, 1994.

"Michigan Representative Reintroduces Bottle Bill to Keep Containers from Landfills." *Solid Waste Report* 8 March 2001: n.p.

Miles, Barry. *Paul McCartney: Many Years from Now*. New York: Holt, 1997.

Miller, James. *Flowers in the Dustbin: The Rise of Rock and Roll, 1947–1977*. New York: Simon and Schuster, 1999.

Miller, Larry, and Mike Miller. "History of the Cajun Accordion." 14 Sept. 2002 <http://www.meloche.net/acchist>.

Mills, Fred. Rev. of *Gold*, by Alice Texas. *Magnet* Sept./Oct. 2001: 82.

Milstein, Philip. "Notes from the Velvet Underground." *The Velvet Underground Companion: Four Decades of Commentary*. Ed. Albin Zak III. New York: Schrimer, 1997. 9–12.

Milstein, Philip, M. C. Kostek, and Katherine Messer. "The Maureen Tucker Interview (1980–90)." *The Velvet Underground Companion: Four Decades of Commentary*. Ed. Albin Zak III. New York: Schrimer, 1997. 120–69.

Molesworth, Melanie. *Junk Style*. New York: Stewart, Tabori and Chang, 1998.

Moodie, David, and Maureen Callahan. "Don't Drink the Brown Water." *Da Capo Best Music Writing 2000*. Ed. Peter Guralnick. New York: Da Capo, 2000. 72–97.

Mosher, Harold F., Jr. "The Lyrics of American Pop Music: A New Poetry." *Popular Music and Society* 1 (1972): 167–76.

Mr. Lady.com. 6 July 2004 <http://www.mrlady.com>.

Mundy, Chris. "Nirvana vs. Fame." *Cobain*. Ed. Holly George-Warren. New York: Rolling Stone Press, 1994. 26–30.

Newcomb, Peter. "Waste Treatment." *Forbes* 8 July 1991: 82.

"New Life for Old CDs." *Audio* June 1999: 23.

Newman, Melinda, and Chris Morris. "Elvis Anniversary Brings Renewed Promotional Push." *Billboard* 16 Aug. 1997: 1, 81–82, 88.

Nieman, Carrie. "What I Do." *Style Weekly* 8 May 2002: 16.

"Night Life: Clubs." *New Yorker* 29 November 1999: 22.

Norman, Philip. *Rave On: The Biography of Buddy Holly.* New York: Fireside, 1997.

———. *Shout! The Beatles in Their Generation.* New York: MJF, 1981.

Nunziata, Susan, and Irv Lichtman. "Discarded CDs in Landfills Seen as Threat to Ecology." *Billboard* 11 May 1991: 5, 85.

Olster, Stacey. *The Trash Phenomenon: Contemporary Literature, Popular Culture, and the Making of the American Century.* Athens: University of Georgia Press, 2003.

Orlean, Susan. "Meet the Shaggs." *New Yorker* 27 Sept. 1999: 72–77.

Paglia, Camille. *Sexual Personae: Art and Decadence from Nefertiti to Emily Dickinson.* New York: Vintage, 1991.

Parker, Lyndsey. "The Cramps: Don't Cramp Their Style." mylaunch Music. 25 March 2001 <http://www.launch.com/Promotional/The_Cramps.html>.

Pattison, Robert. *The Triumph of Vulgarity: Rock Music in the Mirror of Romanticism.* New York: Oxford University Press, 1987.

Pepper, Art, and Laurie Pepper. *Straight Life: The Story of Art Pepper.* New York: Da Capo, 1994.

Peterson, Paul. "The Missing Women of Rock: A Commentary on VH1's 100 Greatest Women of Rock." Popular Culture Association/American Culture Association of the South Convention. Sheraton Hotel, Nashville, Tenn. 5 Oct. 2000.

Peyre, Henri. *What Is Romanticism?* Trans. Roda Roberts. Tuscaloosa: University of Alabama Press, 1977.

Phillips, Andrew. "Elvis the Immortal: He Reigns Supreme Twenty Years after His Death." *Maclean's* 18 Aug. 1997: 54–57.

Phipps, Keith, Nathan Rabin, and Stephen Thompson. "The Least Essential Albums of the Nineties: The Onion A. V. Club's Guide to the Decade's Most Disposable Recordings." 31 July 2000 <http://www.theavclub.com>.

Pichaske, David R. *Beowulf to Beatles and Beyond: The Varieties of Poetry.* New York: Macmillan, 1981.

———. *The Poetry of Rock: The Golden Years.* Peoria, Ill.: Ellis Press, 1981.

"Picks." *Rolling Stone* 16–23 Dec. 1999: 256.

Poe, Edgar Allan. "Charles James Lever." *Edgar Allan Poe: Essays and Reviews.* Ed. G. R. Thompson. New York: Library of America, 1984. 311–20.

———. "The Fall of the House of Usher." *Edgar Allan Poe: Poetry and Tales.* Ed. Patrick F. Quinn. New York: Library of America, 1984. 317–36.

Poovey, Mary. "Cultural Criticism: Past and Present." *College English* 52.6 (1990): 615–24.

"Pop 100." *Rolling Stone* 7 Dec. 2000: 59–107, 122.

Rabid, Jack. "Chasing Pollard Crazy: A Beer Soaked Afternoon with Guided by Voices Leader Robert Pollard." *Big Takeover* 48.22.1 (2001): 55–62, 153–59.

———. Rev. of *Beatles 1*, by the Beatles. *Big Takeover* 48.22.1 (2001): 179.

Radiohead. Liner notes. *OK Computer.* Capitol, 1997.

Ramone, Dee Dee, and Veronica Kofman. *Lobotomy: Surviving the Ramones*. New York: Thunder's Mouth, 1997, 2000.

Rathje, William, and Cullen Murphy. *Rubbish! The Archaeology of Garbage*. New York: HarperCollins, 1992.

Reece, Doug. "Flip/A&M Hoping Rock Fans Will Warm to Cold." *Billboard* 1 Nov. 1997: 12, 17.

Reed, Donald. "Air Bag Recycling." *Automotive Engineering* Oct. 1993: 29.

Reed, Lou. Album cover. *Live: Take No Prisoners*. Arista, 1978.

————. *Lou Reed, Pass thru Fire: The Collected Lyrics*. New York: Hyperion, 2001.

Regev, Motti. "Producing Artistic Value: The Case of Rock Music." *Sociological Quarterly* 35.1 (1994): 85–102.

Reissner, Alexander. *Berlin 1675–1945: The Rise and Fall of a Metropolis*. London: Oswald Wolff, 1984.

Reynolds, David S. *Beneath the American Renaissance: The Subversive Imagination in the Age of Emerson and Melville*. Cambridge: Harvard University Press, 1988.

Reynolds, Larry. "Trash Makes a Splash in Washington." *Management Review* June 1992: 28.

Robbins, Ira A. *The Trouser Press Guide to Nineties Rock*. Ed. Ira A. Robbins. New York: Fireside, 1997.

Robbins, Ira A., et al. *The Trouser Press Record Guide: The Ultimate Guide to Alternative Music*. 4th ed. Ed. Ira A. Robbins. New York: Collier, 1991.

Robinson, Phyllis. *Willa: The Life of Willa Cather*. New York: Holt, 1983.

Roby, Steven. *Black Gold: The Lost Archives of Jimi Hendrix*. New York: Billboard Books, 2002.

"Rock and Roll and Riot." *Scholastic* 4 Oct. 1956: 16–17.

"Rock 'n' Roll." *Time* 23 July 1956: 34.

Rorem, Ned. "The Music of the Beatles." *The Age of Rock: Sounds of the American Cultural Revolution*. Ed. Jonathan Eisen. New York: Random House, 1969. 149–59.

Russo, Greg. *Cosmik Debris: The Collected History and Improvisations of Frank Zappa*. Floral Park, N.Y.: Crossfire, 2001.

Savage, Jon. *England's Dreaming: Anarchy, Sex Pistols, Punk Rock, and Beyond*. New York: St. Martin's, 2001.

Sawyer, Christopher. "Rubber: Billions of Tires." *Automotive Industries* Sept. 1990: 52.

Scapelliti, Christopher. "Like a Rolling Stone." *Guitar World Acoustic* fall 1999: 34, 44.

Scruton, Roger. *The Aesthetics of Music*. Oxford: Clarendon, 1997.

Sharp, Ken. "The Last Hurrah of the Fifth Beatle." *The Goldmine Beatles Digest*. Iola, Wis.: Krause, 2000. 261–71.

Shaw, Greg. "Sic Transit Gloria: The Story of Punk Rock in the Sixties." Liner notes. *Nuggets: Original Artifacts from the First Psychedelic Era, 1965–1968*. Rhino, 1998. 17–22.

Sheff, David. *The Playboy Interviews with John Lennon and Yoko Ono*. Ed. G. Barry Golson. New York: Playboy Press, 1981.

Sheffield, Rob. Rev. of *Version 2.0*, by Garbage. *Rolling Stone* 28 May 1998: 187–88.

Shepherd, John. "A Theoretical Model for the Sociomusicological Analysis of Popular Musics." *Popular Music 2: Theory and Method*. Ed. Richard Middleton and David Horn. Cambridge: Cambridge University Press, 1982. 145–78.

Simels, Steve. Rev. of *Berlin*, by Lou Reed. *Stereo Review* Dec. 1973: 100, 102.

Smith, Bradley. *The Billboard Guide to Progressive Music*. New York: Billboard Books, 1997.

Smith, Patti. "Jag-ahr of the Jungle." *The Rolling Stones: The First Twenty Years*. Ed. David Dalton. New York: Knopf, 1981. 186–87.

Solomon, Debbie. "The Magazine Mountain." *Marketing and Media Decisions* Aug. 1990: 73.

Sorrell, Richard S. " 'My Life Was Saved by Rock and Roll': Personal Reflections on the Age of Rock Music." *Popular Music and Society* 15.1 (1991): 81–89.

Spahr, Wolfgang. "PolyGram Plant Claims Recycling First: German Facility Reprocessing Used, Returned CDs." *Billboard* 24 April 1993: 6.

Spitz, Bob. *Dylan: A Biography*. New York: McGraw-Hill, 1989.

Stax, Mike. "Optical Sound: The Technicolor Tales Behind the Numerous Nuggets." Liner notes. *Nuggets: Original Artifacts from the First Psychedelic Era, 1965–1968*. Rhino, 1998. 30–90.

Sting. Interview by David Fricke. *The Rolling Stone Interviews: The 1980s*. Ed. Sid Holt. New York: St. Martin's, 1989. 295–99.

Stokes, Geoffrey. *Star-Making Machinery: The Odyssey of an Album*. Indianapolis: Bobbs-Merrill, 1976.

Strasser, Susan. *Waste and Want: A Social History of Trash*. New York: Henry Holt, 1999.

Strausbaugh, John. *Rock 'Til You Drop: The Decline from Rebellion to Nostalgia*. London: Verso, 2001.

Strummer, Joe, and Mick Jones. "The Very Angry Clash." Interview by Steve Walsh. *Sniffin' Glue: The Essential Punk Accessory*. Ed. Mark Perry. London: Sanctuary, 2000. n.p.

Summers, Claude J. " 'A Losing Game in the End': Aestheticism and Homosexuality in Cather's 'Paul's Case.' " *Modern Fiction Studies* 36.1 (1990): 103–19.

Swirsky, Brian. "The Slits Original Riot Grrl: An Interview with Ari Up." *Big Takeover* 47.21.2 (2000): 88, 153–56.

Tamarkin, Jeff. Rev. of *Blind Faith* Deluxe Edition, by Blind Faith. *Pulse!* April 2001: 107.

———. Rev. of *Yeah!* by the Alarm Clocks. *Pulse!* April 2001: 108.

Tennyson, Alfred. "Tithonus." *Tennyson: Poems and Plays*. London: Oxford University Press, 1973. 90–91.

Tosches, Nick. "Elvis in Death." *The Nick Tosches Reader*. New York: Da Capo, 2000. 204–10.

———. *Hellfire: The Jerry Lee Lewis Story*. New York: Dell, 1982.

———. *Unsung Heroes of Rock 'n' Roll: The Birth of Rock in the Wild Years Before Elvis*. New York: Da Capo, 1999.

Townsend, Pete. "Meaty, Beaty, Big and Bouncy." *The Penguin Book of Rock and Roll Writing*. Ed. Clinton Heylin. New York: Viking, 1992. 384–94.

Trashmen. Album cover. *Surfin' Bird*. Garrett, 1963.

Unterberger, Richie. "The Beatles." *All Music Guide: The Definitive Guide to Popular Music.* 4th ed. Ed. Vladimir Bogdanov, Chris Woodstra, and Stephen Thomas Erlewine. San Francisco: Backbeat Books, 2001. 28–30.

Valania, Jonathan. "English Settlement: Minders." *Magnet* June/July 2001: 16.

Van Horn, Rick. "Zildjian at 370." *Modern Drummer* Dec. 1993: 30–33, 108–15.

Verna, Paul. "Confusion's the Rule as Jewel Box Begins Reign." *Billboard* 17 April 1993: 86.

———. "Label Puts New Spin on Art of the Deal." *Billboard* 28 May 1994: 1, 80–81.

Verna, Paul, and Melinda Newman. "Artists Driving Trend of Alternative CD Packaging." *Billboard* 16 Nov. 1996: 1, 99.

VH1. "One Hundred Greatest Albums of Rock 'n' Roll." *VH1 on the Web* 23 Jan. 2001 <http://www.vh1.com/insidevh1>.

Viola, Ken. "Incandescence: Memories of the Buffalo Springfield." Liner notes. *Buffalo Springfield Box Set.* WEA/Elektra/Rhino, 2001: 20–21, 27, 51, 77.

Wallis, Roger, and Krister Malm. "Patterns of Change." *On Record: Rock, Pop, and the Written Word.* Ed. Simon Frith and Andrew Goodwin. New York: Pantheon, 1990. 16–80.

Ward, Ed. *Rock of Ages: The Rolling Stone History of Rock and Roll.* Ed. Ed Ward, Geoffrey Stokes, and Ken Tucker. New York: Summit, 1986.

Warhol, Andy. *The Philosophy of Andy Warhol (From A to B and Back Again).* New York: Harvest, 1975.

Wartofsky, Alona. "The Burning Question at Woodstock '99." *Washington Post* 27 July 1999: A1.

Weberman, A. J. "The Art of Garbage Analysis: You Are What You Throw Away." *Esquire* Nov. 1971: 113–17.

———. *My Life in Garbology.* N.p.: Stonehill, 1980.

Wenner, Jann S. Introduction. *Rock of Ages: The Rolling Stone History of Rock and Roll.* Ed. Ed Ward, Geoffrey Stokes, and Ken Tucker. New York: Summit, 1986. 11–14.

West, Red, Sonny West, and Dave Hebler. *Elvis: What Happened?* New York: Ballantine, 1977.

White, Timothy. "Skeleton Key Unlocks 'Fantastic.'" *Billboard* 1 March 1997: 3.

Whitford, Frank. "The Many Faces of George Grosz." *The Berlin of George Grosz: Drawings, Watercolours and Prints 1912–1930.* New Haven: Yale University Press, 1997. 1–20.

Who. *The Kids Are Alright.* Dir. Jeff Stein. Perf. The Who. BMG, 1979.

Wicke, Peter. *Rock Music: Culture, Aesthetics and Sociology.* Trans. Rachel Fogg. Cambridge: Cambridge University Press, 1987.

Wiederhorn, Jon. "Bald Ambition." *Pulse!* July 1998: 36–43, 100–102.

Wildsmith, Steve. Rev. of *Pop Trash,* by Duran Duran. *The Sun News Kicks!* 4 Aug. 2000: 13.

Williams, Paul. "What the Sixties Had That the Eighties Don't Have." *The Penguin Book of Rock and Roll Writing.* Ed. Clinton Heylin. New York: Viking, 1992. 116–23.

Willis, Ellen. "Velvet Underground." *Beginning to See the Light: Sex, Hope, and Rock-and-Roll.* Hanover: Wesleyan University Press, 1992. 110–24.

Winner, Langdon. "The Strange Death of Rock and Roll." *Rock and Roll Will Stand*. Ed. Greil Marcus. Boston: Beacon Press, 1969. 38–55.

Woodress, James. *Willa Cather: A Literary Life*. Lincoln: University of Nebraska Press, 1987.

Wrenn, Michael. *Lou Reed: Between the Lines*. London: Plexus, 1993.

York, Peter. *Style Wars*. London: Sidgwick and Jackson, 1980.

Young, Jean, and Michael Lang. *Woodstock Festival Remembered*. New York: Ballantine, 1969.

Select Discography

Tunes cited in the appendix are not listed here.

Animals. "The Story of Bo Diddley." *The Animals*. MGM, 1964.

Bad Religion. "What Can You Do?" *Suffer*. Epitaph, 1988.

———. "White Trash (Second Generation)." *How Could Hell Be Any Worse?* Epitaph, 1982.

———. "You Give Up." *Into the Unknown*. Epitaph, 1983.

Beatles. "Birthday." *The Beatles*. Apple, 1968.

———. "The End." *Abbey Road*. Apple, 1969.

———. "Helter Skelter." *The Beatles*. Apple, 1968

———. "There's a Place." *Please Please Me*. Parlophone, 1963.

———. "Yer Blues." *The Beatles*. Apple, 1968.

Beck. "Blackhole." *Mellow Gold*. DGC, 1994.

———. "Devil's Haircut." *Odelay*. DGC, 1996.

———. "Minus." *Odelay*. DGC, 1996.

———. "Nobody's Fault But My Own." *Mutations*. Geffen, 1998.

———. "Pay No Mind (Snoozer)." *Mellow Gold*. DGC, 1994.

Birthday Party. "Big Jesus Trash Can." *The Birthday Party: Hits*. 4AD, 1992.

———. "Junkyard." *The Birthday Party: Hits*. 4AD, 1992.

Björk. "Headphones." *Post*. WEA/Elektra, 1995.

Black Flag. "Wasted." *Wasted . . . Again*. SST, 1987.

Blind Faith. "Can't Find My Way Home." *Blind Faith*. Polydor, 1969.

Blur. *Modern Life Is Rubbish*. SBK, 1993.

Byrds. "Fifth Dimension." *Fifth Dimension*. Columbia, 1966.

Chameleons UK. "Time." *Strange Times*. Geffen, 1986.

Coasters. "Yakety Yak." *Billboard Top Rock 'n' Roll Hits—1958*. Rhino, 1988.

Cohen, Leonard. "Democracy." *The Future*. Columbia, 1992.

———. "Suzanne." *Songs of Leonard Cohen*. Columbia, 1968.

Cooper, Alice. "I'm Eighteen." *Love It to Death*. Warner Brothers, 1971.

———. "Trash." *Trash*. Epic, 1989.

Costello, Elvis. "Poisoned Rose." *King of America*. Rykodisc/Demon, 1995.

Cowboy Junkies. "Dreaming My Dreams with You." *The Trinity Session*. RCA, 1988.

———. "Postcard Blues." *The Trinity Session*. RCA, 1988.

————. "To Love Is to Bury." *The Trinity Session.* RCA, 1988.

————. "Two Hundred More Miles." *The Trinity Session.* RCA, 1988.

Cramps. "Garbage Man." *Songs the Lord Taught Us.* IRS, 1980.

Crenshaw, Marshall. "You're My Favorite Waste of Time." *Marshall Crenshaw.* Warner Archives/Rhino, 2000.

Crosby, Stills and Nash. "Wasted on the Way." *Daylight Again.* Atlantic, 1982.

Crucifucks. "Marching for Trash." *Crucifucks.* Alternative Tentacles, 1985.

Doors. "The Wasp (Texas Radio and the Big Beat)." *L.A. Woman.* Elektra, 1971.

Drake, Nick. "Place to Be." *Pink Moon.* Island, 1972.

Dylan, Bob. "Cold Irons Bound." *Time Out of Mind.* Columbia, 1997.

————. "Don't Think Twice, It's Alright." *The Freewheelin' Bob Dylan.* Columbia, 1963.

————. "From a Buick 6." *Highway 61 Revisited.* Columbia, 1965.

————. "Highlands." *Time Out of Mind.* Columbia, 1997.

————. "I Threw It All Away." *Nashville Skyline.* Columbia, 1969.

————. "Love Sick." *Time Out of Mind.* Columbia, 1997.

————. "Million Miles." *Time Out of Mind.* Columbia, 1997.

————. "Not Dark Yet." *Time Out of Mind.* Columbia, 1997.

————. "Tombstone Blues." *Highway 61 Revisited.* Columbia, 1965.

Faithfull, Marianne. "A Waste of Time." *A Perfect Stranger: The Island Anthology.* Island, 1998.

Goldsboro, Bobby. "Honey." *The Best of Tragedy.* DCC Compact Classics, 1995.

Hendrix, Jimi. "Trash Man." *Midnight Lightning.* Polydor, 1975.

Hitchcock, Robyn. "Trash." *Invisible Hitchcock.* Rhino, 1986.

House of Love. "Beatles and the Stones." *The House of Love.* Fontana/Polygram, 1990.

Ian Dury and the Blockheads. "What a Waste." *New Boots and Panties!!* Repertoire, 1996.

John, Elton. "Don't Let the Sun Go Down on Me." *Caribou.* MCA, 1974.

Johnston, Daniel. "Rock 'n' Roll/Ega." *Fun.* Atlantic, 1994.

Joy Division. "Atrocity Exhibition." *Closer.* Factory, 1980.

————. "Colony." *Closer.* Factory, 1980.

————. "Passover." *Closer.* Factory, 1980.

————. "Twenty-four Hours." *Closer.* Factory, 1980.

Legendary Stardust Cowboy. "Standing in a Trashcan (Thinking of You)." *Songs in the Key of Z.* Vol. 1. Gammon, 2000.

Lennon, John. *John Lennon/Plastic Ono Band.* Apple, 1970.

Korn. "Trash." *Issues.* Immortal/Epic, 1999.

Manson, Marilyn. "Disposable Teens." *Holy Wood (In the Shadow of the Valley of Death).* Nothing/Interscope, 2000

————. "White Trash." *Smells Like Children.* Uni/Interscope, 1995.

Mazzy Star. "Wasted." *So Tonight That I Might See.* EMD/Capitol, 1993.

McCartney, Paul. "Junk." *McCartney.* Capitol, 1970.

Metallica. "Disposable Heroes." *Master of Puppets.* Elektra, 1986.

Miller, Steve. "Jet Airliner." *Book of Dreams.* Capitol, 1977.

Move. "California Man." *The Best of the Move.* Repertoire, 1997.

Nailbomb. "Wasting Away." *Point Blank.* Uni/Roadrunner, 1994.

Napalm Death. "Throwaway." *Fear, Emptiness, Despair.* Sony, 1994.

New York Dolls. "Trash." *Rock & Roll.* Mercury, 1994.

NoMeansNo. "Junk." *Small Parts Isolated and Destroyed.* Virus, 1988.

Pavement. "Frontwards." *Watery, Domestic.* Matador, 1992.

———. "Texas Never Whispers." *Watery, Domestic.* Matador, 1992.

Pennywise. "Waste of Time." *About Time.* Epitaph, 1995.

Pere Ubu. "Wasted." *Story of My Life.* Imago, 1993.

Phish. "Waste." *Billy Breathes.* Elektra, 1996.

Presley, Elvis. "Party." *Loving You.* RCA, 1957.

Radiohead. "No Surprises." *OK Computer.* Capitol, 1997.

Reed, Lou. *Berlin.* RCA, 1973.

Replacements. "Sixteen Blue." *Let It Be.* Twin/Tone, 1984.

Rigby, Amy. "The Summer of My Wasted Youth." *Middlescence.* Koch, 1998.

———. "Twenty Questions." *Diary of a Mod Housewife.* Koch, 1996.

Rolling Stones. "Paint It, Black." *Aftermath.* Decca, 1966.

———. "Sympathy for the Devil." *Beggars Banquet.* Decca, 1968;

Sewer Trout. "Garbage In, Garbage Out." *Flawless.* Very Small Records, c. 1989–1992.

Sex Pistols. "God Save the Queen." *Never Mind the Bollocks, Here's the Sex Pistols.* EMI, 1977.

———. "Seventeen." *Never Mind the Bollocks, Here's the Sex Pistols.* EMI, 1977.

Shaggs. "That Little Sports Car." *Philosophy of the World.* RCA, 1999.

Shellac. "House Full of Garbage." *Terraform.* Touch and Go, 1998.

Smith, Patti. "Twenty-fifth Floor." *Easter.* Arista, 1978.

Sonic Youth. "Providence." *Daydream Nation.* DGC, 1988.

———. "Quest for the Cup." *Experimental Jet Set, Trash and No Star.* DGC, 1994.

———. "Total Trash." *Daydream Nation.* DGC, 1988.

———. "Waist." *Experimental Jet Set, Trash and No Star.* DGC, 1994.

Spirit. "Fresh Garbage." *Spirit.* Epic/Legacy, 1968.

Stiff Little Fingers. "Wasted Life." *Inflammable Material.* Enigma, 1979.

Suede. "Trash." *Coming Up.* Nude/Columbia, 1997.

Toshack Highway. "Everyday, Rock'n'Roll Is Saving My Life." *Everyday, Rock'n'Roll Is Saving My Life.* Space Baby, 2001.

Velvet Underground. "Heroin." *The Velvet Underground and Nico.* Verve, 1967.

———. "I Can't Stand It." *VU.* Verve, 1985.

———. "Run Run Run." *The Velvet Underground and Nico.* Verve, 1967.

Who. "Baba O'Riley." *Who's Next.* MCA, 1971.

———. "My Generation." *My Generation.* Virgin, 1965.

———. "Won't Get Fooled Again." *Who's Next.* MCA, 1971.

X-Ray Spex. "Junk Food Junkie." *Conscious Consumer.* Receiver, 1995.

Young, Neil. "Sedan Delivery." *Live Rust.* Reprise, 1979.

Zevon, Warren. "Werewolves of London." *Excitable Boy.* Asylum, 1978.

INDEX

Individual songs mentioned in the text are not listed.

Harvey, P. J., 93, 201; raw sweet sound of, 101; *Stories from the City, Stories from the Sea,* 92

Having Fun with Elvis on Stage, 38, 223 (sec. 9, n. 2)

Hawthorne, Nathaniel, 29

Haynes, Gibby, 146

Headon, Topper, 57

Heart, 11

Heartbreakers, the, 57

Hebb, Bobby, 216

Hebler, Dave, 142

Hell's Angels, 109

Help! (Beatles), 11, 204

Hendrix, Jimi, 10, 86, 216; antiwar song by, 120; and the Beatles, 76; in the classroom, 190; on death, 139; diachronic and synchronic details of, 22, 23; drug use of, 146; explosive career of, 5–6; live at the Singer Bowl, 8–9; party/funeral music by, 169; as secular prophet, 4–7 passim, 213; subgenres played by, 104; in Trash Top Forty, 113. Works: *Are You Experienced?,* 8, 190; *Black Gold,* 113; *First Rays of the New Rising Sun,* 86, 216; *Midnight Lightning,* 113; *South Saturn Delta,* 113

Herman's Hermits, 55

heroin, 87, 121; and Alice in Chains, 178; and first generation punk rock, 56–57; and the New York Dolls, 115; and Pepper, Art, 80; and Pop, Iggy, 227 (n. 11); and Richards, Keith, 227 (n. 12); and "Shattered" (Rolling Stones), 217; and the Velvet Underground, 79–80

Highway 61 Revisited (Dylan), 204

Hill, Raymond, 83

Hitchcock, Robyn, in Trash Top Forty, 120–21

Hitler, Adolph, 160

Holiday, Billie, 164, 165, 231 (sec. 30, n. 2); as artist, 51

Hollies, the, 76

Holly, Buddy, 10, 46; covered by Blind Faith, 114; death of, 135–36, 145, 147; and groove on "Not Fade Away," 111; and origins of rock 'n' roll music, 219 (sec. 1, n. 1); recycling of, by the Rolling Stones, 95

Holy Wood (In the Shadow of the Valley of Death) (Manson), 132

Hombres, the, 45

Home Is Where the Heart Is (Cassidy), 48

Hook, Peter, 176

Hootie and the Blowfish, 100

Hopkin, Mary, 216

Horne, Lena, 231 (sec. 30, n. 2)

Hot Horny and Born Again (Meadmore), 209

House of Love, the, 205

Housman, A. E., 191

Hughes, Langston, 191

Hunter, Meredith, 109

Hüsker Dü, 123, 149

Ibold, Mark, 124

Idlewild, 95

Iggy and the Stooges. *See* Pop, Iggy; Stooges, the

Imperial Teen, 207

Indigo Girls, the, 187

In My Life (Martin), 103

Inside Bert Sommer (Sommer), 38

In Utero (Nirvana), 177; poetic finish of, 158

INXS, 67, 92

Iron Butterfly, 54

Irving Plaza (rock club), 97

Issues (Korn), 131

Is This It? (Strokes), 146

It's a Beautiful Day, 80

Jackson, Michael, 44, 143

Jackson, Wanda, 10, 110, 231 (sec. 30, n. 2); stature of, 64

Jagger, Mick: and effect on Smith, Patti, 204–5; not Lucifer, 123; self-deprecation of, 67, 68; and "Shattered," 217; slurred singing of, 192; in Trash Top Forty, 133. *See also* Rolling Stones, the

Jameson, Fredric, 212, 213

Jefferson, Thomas, 29, 52; on corruption of the Gospels, 5; and place in rock 'n' roll music, 157

Jesus Christ, 213; career of, 4–8 passim

jewel boxes, 31–35 passim; and difficulty opening, 34; fragility of, 35

Jody Grind, the, 67

Joel, Billy, 37, 40, 215; and the melodeon, 126; and poetry, 191; rated worst rock 'n' roller of all time, 36; and romanticism, 157; *The Stranger,* 36

Johansen, David, 115

John, Elton, 79, 208, 209; as artist, 18; Bangs's opinion of, 43, 45; and belief in disposable songs, 77–78; *Don't Shoot Me, I'm Only the Piano Player,* 77; self-deprecation of, 67; in Trash Top Forty, 115–16

Johnson, Robert, 95

Johnston, Daniel, 211

John Wesley Harding (Dylan), 92, 100

Jones, Brian, 105, 120; death of, 121, 203; ; drug trial of, 202; and morbid romanticism, 149

Jones, Etta, 110

Jones, Mick, 58, 61

Jones, Rickie Lee, 92

Jonson, Ben, 191

Joplin, Janis, 76, 225 (n. 22); and morbid romanticism, 149

Journey, 225 (n. 23)

Joyce, James, 160

Joy Division: and morbid-romantic features of *Closer,* 176; and morbid romanticism, 149, 158, 169, 173, 174, 175; premature breakup of, 148

Junkie, 12

Junk Records, 67

Junkyard, 67

Junkyard (Birthday Party), 119

Junkyard Jane, 67

Just Push Play (Aerosmith), 95

Kane, Arthur, 62, 115

Kannberg, Scott, 124

Kazin, Alfred, 29

Keats, John, 233 (n. 37)

Kennedy, John F., 215

Kennedy, William, 29

Kid A (Radiohead), 130

Kids Are Alright, The (film, Who), 228 (n. 11)

Kinda Kinks (Kinks), 204

King, Kim, 86

Kingsmen, the, 30, 46, 117

Kinks, the, 198, 215; and the Beatles, 76; as greatest band ever, 194; influence of, on Blur, 126; and the melodeon, 126, 230 (n. 12); party/funeral music by, 168; resuscitation of rock 'n' roll music by, 145; as seventies dinosaur band, 44. Works: *Kinda Kinks,* 204; *To the Bone,* 126

Kirkpatrick, John, 126

Kiss, 59, 115, 206, 207; comparison of, to Manson, Marilyn, 132

Kitt, Eartha, 231 (sec. 30, n. 2)

Kitts, Tom, 230 (n. 12)

Knack, the, 55; *Serious Fun,* 103

Knocked Out Loaded (Dylan), 54

Knox, Nick, 116

Korn, 102; *Issues,* 131; in Trash Top Forty, 131–32

Kramer, Eddie, 86

Kramer, Wayne, 48

Kurlander, John, 77

Kweller, Ben, 67

La Diva (Aretha Franklin), 55

Lagwagon, 226 (sec. 15, n. 7); *Trashed,* 67

Lamartine, Alphonse de, 175

Lamble, Martin, 147

Landau, Jon, 85

Leaper, Martyn, 99

Leaves, the, 45

Led Zeppelin, 89, 207; as seventies dinosaur band, 44; subgenres played by, 104

Lee, Peggy, 231 (sec. 30, n. 2)

Legendary Stardust Cowboy, the, in Trash Top Forty, 121

Leiber, Jerry, 110, 122

Lennon, Cynthia, 204

Richards, Keith, 105; affected by heroin, 80, 91, 227 (n. 12); recycling of, by the Black Crowes, 95; and rock 'n' roll music as art, 68; saved by rock 'n' roll music, 205. *See also* Rolling Stones, the

Richardson, J. P. (the Big Bopper), 135–36

Richardson, Samuel, 201

Richmond Sluts, the, 12

Rigby, Amy, in Trash Top Forty, 129

Rigoletto (Verdi), 199

Riot Grrl, 150

Rise and Fall of Ziggy Stardust and the Spiders from Mars, The (Bowie), 126

Rising, The (Springsteen), 168

Robinson, Edwin Arlington, 187, 193

Rock, Kid, 146

Rock 'n' Roll High School (film), 191

Rock 'n' Roll Museum Hall of Fame, 67, 188–90

rock 'n' roll music: and anti-rockers, 65; as art form, 18–26, 36, 67, 220 (sec. 4, nn. 1, 12); and classic rock radio, 22; as commodity, 14, 16, 20–22, 221 (sec. 7, n. 2), 222 (nn. 4, 7, 9); death as theme in, 179–83; death of, 38, 43–44, 69, 143, 145–48, 231 (sec. 30, n. 3); and death of bands, 148; and death of musicians, 17, 113, 135–37, 144, 149; decline of, 9; definition of, 10–13, 139, 145–46; as garbage and/or trash, 23, 41, 47–48, 53, 55, 60, 68, 73–74, 79, 97, 225 (nn. 20, 7), 226 (sec. 15, n. 10); —, in criticism, 30, 44; —, and double signification (praise/insult) in criticism, 29, 53, 66, 92–94, 105; —, as insult, 221 (sec. 6, n. 1); —, and trash trope definition, 13–16; great live shows of, 42, 105, 106; and indie (independent) music, 44, 48, 101, 104, 122; invention of, 219 (sec. 1, n. 1); as junk food, 59, 88, 225 (nn. 22, 23); lists and polls of, 17, 37, 60, 63, 102, 103, 109, 203, 226 (sec. 16, n. 9), 231 (sec. 30, n. 2); and lyrics as poetry, 187, 191–92, 234 (n. 5); lyrics of, 14, 18, 68, 17, 110, 133; misogyny in, 123; morbidity of, 14, 17, 137, 149–58 passim, 173, 175,

178–83; and party/funeral dichotomy, 168–69; recording of, 34–35; recycling sounds of, 93–97, 118; as romanticism, 156–59; as salvation, 15–16, 195–96, 203–11; spelling of, 11–12; standardization of, 20–22; subgenres of, 10–12, 104; template of morbid-romantic features of, 179. *See also* disposability

Rogers, Kenny, and the First Edition, 215

Rolling Stone (magazine), 12, 102, 103, 203

Rolling Stone Record Guide, The, 47

Rolling Stones, the, 10, 46, 201, 208, 215, 216, 223 (sec. 9, n. 2); and Altamont, 109; and the Beatles, 76, 71; commemorated by Chadwick, Guy, 205; comparison of, to Coleridge, Samuel Taylor, 156; and effect on Smith, Patti, 204–5; as greatest band ever, 194; great seventies recordings by, 44; and influence on the New York Dolls, 115; and the melodeon, 126; party/funeral music by, 168, 233 (n. 31); peak years of, 101; recycling of, by the Black Crowes, 95; recycling of Berry, Holly, et al., 95; resuscitation of rock 'n' roll music by, 145; and rhythm and blues, 112; and romanticism, 157; as seventies dinosaur band, 44; slovenliness of, 125; subgenres played by, 104; trashiness of, 47, 224 (sec. 12, n. 7); in Trash Top Forty, 133, 230 (n. 15); violence at show of, 105. Works: *Exile on Main Street*, 44, 68, 95, 168, 192; *Out of Our Heads*, 204; *The Rolling Stones, Now!*, 204; "Shattered," 217; *Some Girls*, 44, 47, 217; *Their Satanic Majesties Request*, 38, 95, 223 (sec. 9, n. 2). *See also* Jagger, Mick; Richards, Keith

Rolling Stones, Now!, The (Rolling Stones), 204

Rollins, Sonny, 23, 57

Romeo and Juliet (Shakespeare), 191

Ronstadt, Linda, 44, 47

Ross, Diana, 103

Rothko, Mark, 173